# A MESSAGE
# TO THE CHARNWOOD READER
# FROM THE PUBLISHER

Since the introduction of Ulverscroft Large Print Books, countless readers around the world have confirmed that the larger and clearer print has brought back the pleasure of reading to an ever-widening audience, thus enabling readers to once again enjoy the companionship of books which had previously been denied to them due to their inability to read normal small print.

It is obvious that to cater for this ever-widening audience of readers a new series was necessary. The Charnwood Series embraces the widest possible variety of literature from the traditional classics to the most recently published bestsellers, and includes many authors considered too contemporary both in subject and style to be suitable for the many elderly readers for whom the original Ulverscroft Large Print Books were designed.

The newly developed typeface of the Charnwood Series has been subjected to extensive and exhaustive tests amongst the international family of large print readers, and unanimously acclaimed and preferred as a smoother and easier read. Another benefit of this new typeface is that it allows the publication in one volume of longer novels which previously could only be published in two large print volumes: a constant source of frustration for readers when one volume is not available for one reason or another.

The Charnwood Series is designed to increase the titles available to those readers in this ever-widening audience who are unable to read and enjoy the range of popular titles at present only available in normal small print.

# HOLDING ON

The story of a street in the East End of London and of a family who lived in it. The street in London's docklands was built in the 1880s and the Wheelwright family (originally dockers) lived there until its tragic demolition in the 1960s, when it was replaced by tower blocks. The narrative which rings with the truth, brings the reader right into the life of the Wheelwright family and their neighbours.

# MERVYN JONES

# HOLDING ON

*Complete and Unabridged*

# CHARNWOOD
*Leicester*

First published in Great Britain in 1973

First Charnwood Edition
published May 1988
by arrangement with
Eland Books,
London

British Library CIP Data

Jones, Mervyn, *1922–*
Holding on.—Large print ed.—
Charnwood library series
I. Title
823′.914[F]        PR6060.O56

ISBN 0-7089-8459-2

Published by
F. A. Thorpe (Publishing) Ltd.
Anstey, Leicestershire
Set by Rowland Phototypesetting Ltd.
Bury St. Edmunds, Suffolk
Printed and bound in Great Britain by
T. J. Press (Padstow) Ltd., Padstow, Cornwall

# 1

NUMBER five, Steadman Street was a little larger than any of the other houses. It was built to the same plan, the plan of millions of English houses: a front and a back room downstairs, the same upstairs, a yard and an outhouse behind. But it was wider by two feet, of which six inches had been given to the stairs and eighteen inches to the rooms. It was also higher by two feet—one foot on each ceiling. This raised the roofline and gave the whole street that slight oddity, that appearance of having grown from thought instead of from immediate decision, which often relieves the monotony of great cities.

Steadman, in fact, had built the house to live in himself. Originally a bricklayer, he set himself up in business first by doing repair work, then by building. In 1880 he was able to achieve his ambition: building a street. He bought a patch of waste land on the eastern fringe of London, and here he put his street. One end of it joined the Barking Road; the other petered out among fields, but it was obvious that they would soon be built over, for the great new docks—Royal Victoria Dock and Royal Albert Dock—were directly beyond them.

There were thirty-four houses, seventeen on each side, but the numbering went up to thirty-six. Steadman left the corner sites at the Barking Road end vacant, and after some years of patient waiting he succeeded in selling them, so that number one, Steadman Street, was a general shop and number two was a pub. The brewers named the pub after General Gordon, the hero who had just met his death at Khartoum. Steadman lived in number five and rented the other houses; the tenants, from the start, were mostly dockers. Generally an abstemious man, he sat in the public bar of the General Gordon from seven to eight on Friday evenings, drank a glass of port, and collected the rents. The money from the corner sites had been shrewdly invested. Before the end of his life, Steadman was able to retire from business and meet his expenses out of rents and dividends. He could be seen at a gentlemanly hour of the morning, when there was no one else in the street but mothers and children, going into the shop to buy a twist of tobacco and the *Daily Mail*.

He lived long enough to see the district—Canning Town, it was called, in the borough of West Ham—acquire an identity and lose its feel of newness. He died in the first cold month of the twentieth century; he collapsed in Steadman Street, from shock—so it was said—on reading the news of the defeat at Spion Kop. His son, who had been to grammar school and become an accountant, sold the whole street and went to live in Ilford. Children grew up without knowing that there had been a man called Steadman; the name-plate at the corner, however, perpetuated the name like that of a statesman in France or a saint in Italy. Number five became a rented dwelling. As it was larger, the new landlord charged five and threepence a week for it instead of the usual five shillings.

As soon as these transactions were completed, the Wheelwrights moved in. Finding a permanent home was urgent for them; they had been married for six months and Dora Wheelwright was almost nine months pregnant. They had been living in one room in Poplar. The landlady, who slept badly, had told them that she wouldn't have a baby in the house. Jack Wheelwright was a stevedore, earning better money than the ordinary dockers. Trade was good and there was fairly steady work at the Albert Docks, especially with the munitions cargoes to South Africa. When he found the house in Steadman Street, he decided that he could manage to pay the five and three.

Jack was a tall man, with long arms and legs that took pacing strides. He stood out among the other dock-workers, who as a rule had broad shoulders but short limbs and compact bodies. Holding himself very straight, he had something of the spare, taut look of a soldier. Already, at twenty-two, he wore a heavy black moustache, like General Kitchener.

Girls—the kind of girls who liked soldiers—were swiftly attracted to him. They glanced at him, boldly or shyly, when he passed in the street. It had been enough for him, when in the mood, to seize on: "What you staring at, then? Got nothing better to do, have you?" He had understood, even as a boy, the need and the yielding of girls. Now, a pair of bright eyes could sometimes make him regret being tied. But he took marriage, once it was a fact, as a gain and not as a burden. He liked to pace the broad pavements of shopping streets, more slowly than when he was alone, with Dora's arm in his and the unashamed protrusion of their child carried before them. It was an advance in manhood.

Dora was a big girl, tall enough to look all the better for a certain plumpness. At nineteen, the woman in her was shaping as firmly as the man in Jack. He liked to see her at rest, as he had never seen girls before being married. This state of rest, guaranteed by his hard work, seemed to establish a true balance. She attracted him more, not less, after she swelled. Coming in from the pub at night, undressing quietly without waking her, Jack listened to her deep breathing and felt that what he had told her—easily, as he had told other girls—was now true: he loved her. They agreed that she needed plenty of sleep. It renewed her and manifested her function; it was for her what the proud effort of the stevedoring work was for him. He took to making his own breakfast while she lay in bed, half-waking and dropping off again. He put a cup of hot sweet tea on the window-ledge, handy to the bed. She yawned and stretched, her large mouth a soft pink, her rounded white arms moving slowly. She was softness, yet she was also strength, matching his strength in her own manner; he had seen a lioness at the Zoo yawn and stretch like this. Ready to go out, he bent over her for a kiss. Her blue eyes, which he loved specially, opened slow and wide. Her long hair tickled his cheeks; it was rich golden hair, coiled in a bun during the day, and he enjoyed its morning disorder. Bending lower, he touched the drum where the child was. Sometimes, in the later months, it kicked. "Go on, you've woken him up," Dora said. She always spoke of the child as "he".

At Poplar they paid only one and six rent. Jack's wages went mostly on food. Dora enjoyed eating and he encouraged her, reminding her if she left anything on her plate that she was eating for two. She chewed strongly, opening her mouth so that he observed the disintegration of lumps of beef, pork crackling, jackets of baked potatoes, pie-crust. She was fond of a bottle of stout too, and he knew that this was strengthening for the baby. Also, she liked sweets. She had worked at a sweets-and-tobacco shop, where

5

she had been allowed to finish up the odd quantities within reason. If Jack had any coppers in
his pocket at the end of the day, he brought
home humbugs or toffee squares.

They went to the music-hall, more often than
not, on Saturday nights. The bright lights and
thumping music roused Dora to a rare excitement. She rolled about in her seat, grasping her
belly as if she might drop the child, and
screamed with laughter. Jack welcomed this
laughter as a release; at home, she was content
to smile. He knew already that girls never missed
the double meanings in the jokes; a comedian
could say things to a packed hall that a man
would never say to his wife.

They moved to Steadman Street on a Sunday.
One of Jack's mates helped him to carry the
furniture and the boxes down to the street,
where the hired van was waiting. They had only
a bed, a table, a chest-of-drawers, and two
kitchen chairs. Dora had bought a pair of black
rep armchairs, but the shopkeeper had sent them
round to the new house the day before. So there
was room for her to ride in the van, while Jack
walked.

She enjoyed the ride, though it was a sharp
February day. Crossing the bridge over the Lea
was an entry to a new life; she and Jack had
belonged to Poplar, but now they would belong
to Canning Town. It was still the East End, at
all events.

Suddenly, in the Barking Road, the horse was frightened by the back-firing of a motor-car and bolted. Thrown off balance, Dora grabbed the struts just in time to save being pitched out of the van. She screamed, not from panic but to call Jack. He ran in the roadway, long legs straining to catch up with the racing horse and the swaying van. Before he made up the distance, the driver had got the horse under control and turned into Steadman Street.

Dora clambered out, tottered, and leaned against the door of her new home. All along the street, windows opened or people appeared on doorsteps.

Mrs. Harris, from number three, called: "Had a turn, love?"

"Horse bolted," Dora gasped.

Eyeing her shrewdly, Mrs. Harris asked: "Coming on, is it?"

"Coming out, more like."

"Don't drop it in the street, then. Got your key, have you?"

Dora fumbled in her bag and found the key.

"Come on, dear, I'll see you through. Had five myself and all living. You'll be all right, healthy young thing like you."

There was no time to unload the bed and make it up. Dora stretched out in one of the armchairs and Mrs. Harris pulled down her petticoats.

Jack came running up. Mr. Harris stopped

7

him: "Half a mo, mate. Baby's coming a bit sudden. My missus'll do the needful."

"Will she? Thanks. Might want a doctor, though."

"The missus can send our lad if she needs to. Save your money, otherwise. Your first, is it?"

"That's right."

"Ah, I could see that. Need a steady-up, you do. Come on, the Gordon's just opening."

Jack put down a pint and said: "Good drop of bitter, this is."

"Good house," said Mr. Harris.

"Nice and handy, anyway."

Jack stood at the bar, very straight and unmoving, trying to keep his mind on sizing up the regulars as they came in. The time of waiting seemed long, but it was not.

The Harris boy ran in and announced breathlessly: "It's a boy, Mr. Wheelwright. They're both fine. And Mrs. Wheelwright says, can she have a bottle of stout."

"On the house—right away!" cried the landlord.

Jack looked round the pub as the other men congratulated him and made the customary jokes. It was a welcoming place, with a piano in the corner and a fire already blazing. Over the fireplace, a picture showed a man in uniform, armed only with a revolver, standing calmly at the top of a flight of steps and confronting a horde of savages as they brandished their spears.

A scroll carried the words: "The Death of General Charles George Gordon".

On the following Saturday, the baby was christened with the name of Charles George Wheelwright.

# 2

IT was a street of men, it was a street of women, and it was a street of children.

Jack saw the other men at the beginning of the working day when they took the tram to the docks, and again at the end when they came home. On winter mornings, when it was still dark, he didn't recognise them unless they stood close to him in the queue. They were square, stocky shapes, plodding along the street and then standing motionless on the pavement, silent and purposeful, like animals moving along forest paths. Each had his cloth cap, thick donkey-jacket, corduroy trousers and boots. Each went at the same pace, determined but sparing of energy. The fact of going to work hid the separate identity; it was hard to imagine that each man, lying in bed with his wife half an hour before, had been someone unique and private.

Generally, because he was tall, they recognised Jack before he recognised them. A good-morning was exchanged, more as a familiar sound than in shaped words, and no more was said until the tram came whining and clanking down the road. After they had found places on the slatted wooden seats, it was time for brief utterances, almost entirely about the weather. These men did not speak of the weather as a polite convention, like office clerks or like the upper classes. The weather mattered to them; it governed the working day. If it rained, they would be drenched even through their jackets and the slippery decks would be dangerous. If it was very cold, their hands would freeze as they gripped the iron-bound crates. If there was a fog, incoming ships would anchor in the estuary and there would be no work.

Jack's work singled him out from most of the men in Steadman Street. To begin with, there were men who didn't work in the docks at all: railwaymen, building labourers, coal-heavers at the gasworks, and several who had no trade and took whatever jobs they could find. Since these men used a different tram, he saw them only on Sundays or in the evenings. He travelled to work with the dockers, but he separated from them at the dock-gate because he was a stevedore. His job was to stack loading cargo in the hold—heavy work, but skilled work too, like doing a jigsaw puzzle. Stevedores never unloaded. So a docker did not become a stevedore, any more than a private in the infantry became an artilleryman. London stevedores were the sons of London stevedores, like Jack.

At the shape-up, when men were picked out for work, the dockers jostled and elbowed one another and came to blows if they were desperate. The foreman, pointing his hand, shouted: "You . . . you . . . you." But when it was the stevedores' turn he shouted: "Jones . . . Kelly . . . Wheelwright." Unemployed men or men turned away from other trades could mingle with the dockers and hope for work on busy days. Stevedores worked in regular gangs; if there was work for the gang-leader, there was work for the rest. Jack had been admitted to a gang by men who had known his father at East India Dock. In the natural course of events, he would be the leader in fifteen or twenty years. If there was no work, either at the morning or the afternoon shape-up, the stevedores earned nothing just like the dockers. And their work was just as hard; it could even be dirtier if the hold was awash with water or messy with leaked cargo. But, by a tradition recognised in better rates of pay, stevedores were a cut above dockers.

Some of the men went home on bad days if they lived within walking distance. Others went to the pubs near the docks. Here they talked with sailors who told them what was coming up the river and what was loading at Hamburg, New York, Rio, Bombay. Jack sometimes met sailors he knew. He had shipped as a boy—one couldn't be a stevedore under eighteen, but one could go to sea at any age. He liked to be reminded of his voyaging years: rolling oceans, hard burning sunlight, strange tongues, girls with smooth dark skins.

12

Now he was married and paying rent for a house, he was careful with his money. He sipped a pint slowly, making it pay for time; this was respected in the daytime, though it would have been miserly at night. At cards he was careful too, giving up when he had a clear run of bad luck, recognising a better player when he met one. What he liked best was a silent, thoughtful game of dominoes. In the docks, and also in Steadman Street, he had the name of a quiet man. That was the right name to have; good workers were quiet men, except for a few jokers. A good worker wasn't the kind who rushed about, saving minutes for the bosses' profit. He was the kind who kept up the chosen rhythm of the gang, never imposing effort on others by skimping, tireless, dependable. Like that, Jack was a good worker.

At the end of the working day, the men from Steadman Street met again on the tram going home. Grumbling, muttering, cursing, they talked about the weight of metals, the clumsiness of timber, the stink of hides, the smarting pain of lime or acids on bare hands, the clinging filth of oil; about pulleys that jammed, crates that split, barrels that leaked, the cruel pace when a ship was making a quick turn-round, the wasted unpaid hours when there was a hold-up. But in the grumbling there was a strong heartbeat of satisfaction. The day had been endured, completed—overcome. They owed the world nothing until next morning. With the easy jolting of the tram, in the warm dense air within the steamy windows, they were carried home like warriors to peace.

Sometimes, if the weather was good, Jack walked home. He saved the ha'penny tram fare, and it was good to be in the open after a day in the hold of a ship. He had not the same need as the others to sum up and dismiss the day's work in talk; silence, for him, was the best restorative. What he liked best was to walk home alone, at night, after a long spell of overtime. He went through narrow streets, not by the circuitous tram route. These streets—streets like his own, rows of family houses that drew into themselves at evening—were almost empty. He might meet a few men who had been working overtime too; or a drunk floundering near the door of a pub; or a pair of coppers weightily pacing the pavement. Otherwise, he heard only the resonance of his own stride. His limbs ached at the joints, but he was not really tired. He had never come near the limit of his working strength, and after working all day and evening he could have worked all night. Going home like this, instead of by tram, assured him of his reserves of power.

When he came in late, Dora would be dozing in front of the fire. A bit of sewing, probably, had dropped from her fingers to the floor. She roused herself and made his supper. She managed to tell him about anything curious or funny that had happened during the day, but she couldn't help yawning; so, after he had eaten, he banked the fire and said: "All right—bed."

It was different when Jack was at the docks only for the normal hours. The house was noisy when he came in because the child was still up —the children, as years passed. He imposed, without anger or harshness, the order that derived from authority. Shouting was hushed, rushing from room to room stopped. Supper was eaten as a family meal. Later, as often as not, Jack went over the road to the Gordon. Dora didn't have another meal to make, so she was in bed before he returned. In the silent house, he clumped upstairs drowsily. Beer made him sleepy, as work could not.

Particularly on Fridays and Saturdays, there was hard drinking at the Gordon. Some men— five or six men among the regulars—came there to drink until they lurched to the door, threw up in the gutter, and were helped home. No one thought badly of them; it was their way. There were fights, starting up within seconds at a real or imagined insult. Mostly the landlord was able to stop them, but sometimes they were taken to a finish out in the street. Everyone in the pub got more or less drunk if there was something to celebrate—a birth or a wedding, or someone had done well on the horses. Beer sloshed on the floor as the pint mugs were carried unsteadily about or knocked off the tables. Through the evening, the pub came to smell of beer as a trawler smelt of fish. It was not a place for dominoes or quiet talk—not in the evening. Men seldom spoke of work, though most of them were dockers. The Gordon was their local; it belonged to the street, to release and the close of the day.

Jack Wheelwright, the quiet man, didn't get roaring drunk, nor shout anyone down, nor fight unless provoked—and his strength was known, so no one but a reckless drunk would provoke him. Still, he drank more than in the daytime. The Gordon was a place of release for him too. He liked to feel that it didn't matter if his head was a bit fuzzed and his movements a bit uncertain; there were no swinging hooks or swaying crates here. If there was a singsong, he joined in. Otherwise, he sat at his ease, watching and listening. He enjoyed the loud arguments, the tipsy challenges, and the fights as well. He was a young man still, though no one thought of him as a youngster.

He had no special friends. The men of Steadman Street had a life in common—something like the life of a ship, though more loosely enclosed—that left no need for intimacies. He was naturally linked to a man of about his own age named Bill Whitmarsh; Bill was a stevedore, working in the same gang as Jack, and he also lived in Steadman Street, down the far end at number thirty-one.

And he was linked to Alf Harris, because they were neighbours and from the chance that Alf was the first man he had met in Steadman Street.

Alf was in his late thirties, a docker with the typical stumpy legs and broad shoulders. When he was with Jack, he did most of the talking; aided by his wife, he picked up all the news of the street. Jack was careful not to tell him anything private about his own affairs. Some people said that Alf Harris was not to be trusted; he had blacklegged in the great dock strike, or at least had found work on river craft that were not involved in the strike, which was half-blacklegging. About this, having been a child at the time, Jack suspended judgement. Alf was pleasant enough, and a helpful neighbour in small practical matters.

Jack did not, in general, judge other people. There was not room in Steadman Street to make choices, to avoid anyone—certainly not to have enemies. As Jack saw it, if thirty men in the street had been magically whisked away to be replaced by thirty others, the mixture would be much the same. There would be a few who got roaring drunk and a few who had taken the pledge; a few who treated their wives rough and a few whose wives bossed them. For Jack, his own life was unimaginable without constant adjustment to people—without the street. Yet it was his own life. He existed, unperturbed, at the quiet heart of it.

Deep inside his own life, there was not even Dora. She was his wife; a man needed a wife. He was happy with her. Still, he could have had another kind of wife—small and dark, say, quick-moving, alert and chatty in the evenings. He had known girls like that. When he walked home alone, he thought sometimes of walking home to a different wife, whom he would have loved instead of loving Dora. But essentially he would have been the same man, living the same life.

He shared his life, truly, with only one other human being: Charlie, his son. He came to realise this when the child had a sharp, brief sickness, which looked like diphtheria but wasn't. Diphtheria was a killer, of course. Jack knew that, if Charlie had died, it would have been the death of a part of himself.

Until then, he had not recognised himself in Charlie. But it was just at this time that Charlie, learning to walk and talk and play by himself, began to grow into a boy and, potentially, a man. He was big for his age. He had strength in his hands and, when he was set to put one box inside another, a decisive neatness. He was cut out to be a stevedore.

On Sunday mornings, when Jack had his weekly bath in front of the fire, Charlie was allowed to stay in the kitchen and scrub his father's back. Then Charlie got into the bath in turn, so as not to waste the hot water. Naked, restful in the steamy air, man and boy shared a trusting intimacy, drawing on the same confidence in what they were. Jack never felt this kind of intimacy with the next two children, who were girls.

On Saturdays, Dora went to the butcher's in Barking Road to buy the Sunday joint. When work was short at the docks, she had to skimp on food during the week: fat bacon instead of gammon, neck of mutton instead of chops, marge instead of butter. But she never saved on the Sunday roast. That came first, and then she saw what she had left.

She liked to go to the butcher's with Maggie Harris, who had a faultless eye for a good cut. She would put her head into number three and call: "Going down the shops, Maggie?" If Maggie had already gone, Dora hurried along as fast as she could with the children to catch her up. In theory, it ought to have taken Maggie longer to get out and about, since she had five children to bother with. In practice, the older children looked after the young ones.

It never occurred to Dora, nor to any other woman in Steadman Street, to do the shopping before the housework was completed. Once Jack was off to work, she had to wash up the breakfast dishes; make the bed; wash the children's hands and faces; sweep the floors; clean out the grates and lay the fires; scrub the table; clean

Jack's boots (he had two pairs and wore them alternately); and wash the children's hands and faces again, since they were sure to be dirty when she was ready to go out.

The difficulty was that, even on Saturdays, Dora couldn't force herself to do any of these things at all fast. As a girl, she had been told by her parents and by teachers that she was a dreamer. She had taken this as one of the standard epithets that are thrown at children. Working in the sweetshop, she had managed to arrive all right in the mornings and to go through the business of weighing pounds and ounces and making change without any trouble—stupid, no one had called her. The accusation of "dreamer" had passed from her mind. But now that she had to regulate her day alone, she had to admit that a dreamer was what she was. Halfway through her work, she stopped to talk to Charlie or watch what he was doing, or to gaze through him at a tall and Jack-like Charlie of the future. A quarter or half an hour later, she realised that she had a dustpan in her hand. What was worse, she put off starting the housework at the very beginning. It seemed a good idea to put the children back in their cots after breakfast and have a short sit-down before embarking on the routine. Sadly, the sit-down prolonged itself, getting utterly out of control. The only thing that could rouse her was a child crying; but they were all good children and didn't mind being left alone.

She loved talking to the children, even when they were babies. It never mattered to her whether they understood her actual words or not; they responded, at all events, to her mood. When she had caught herself wasting time, when the family was short of money, when there was news of a street accident or a bad fight—Dora told the children. Had she not had children, she would have talked to a cat or a cage-bird in the same way.

Also, she loved watching the children play and, better still, getting down on her knees to play with them. She loved watching them learn to walk and picking them up—both she and the child half laughing and half crying—when they fell. In fact, she loved simply being with them all day and every day. She didn't think of herself as an authority set above the children—she left that to Jack—but as an equal. Dreaming, she became a child. The empty years of her life had been between the ages of thirteen and eighteen, when she was working; she hadn't really disliked the work, but this, she now saw, was because the shop had often been full of children. Anyway, she had never thought of those years as other than an interlude. Home life was what suited her.

When she got married, she didn't feel in any sense unprepared. From the time when her breasts swelled and she pinned up her hair, young men started making remarks, patting her bottom, and pulling her into quiet corners. She knew what they wanted and didn't in the least blame them for wanting it, but she didn't give it to them because she was waiting for the right one to come along. She met Jack at a wedding party, which seemed to her a nod from fate. He was distantly related to her, though she never worked out exactly how. Both their families had lived in the East End for as far back as they could trace. Indeed, the East End almost seemed to be one big family—or two big families, the Cockneys and the Irish.

Jack was clearly the right one, so she gave him what he wanted. Soon, she found herself pregnant. She hadn't intended this, but she was not worried either. She was sure that Jack would do the proper thing. And she was married before it showed, which was more than some could say.

In Steadman Street, she spent a lot of time talking with other women. About the business of being a woman, they talked with total frankness and with a sardonic humour that sometimes turned grim and bitter, sometimes carried them into storms of laughter. Dora noticed that, in general, they didn't like men very much. They spoke of their husbands as men spoke of their bosses—as members of an alien class whose demands had to be met because there was no other assurance of food and shelter. Dora guessed that this was to some extent a pose. Traditionally, women shared a certain way of talking about men, and men no doubt shared a way of talking about women. Nevertheless, it was not all pose. Maggie, for instance, declared with complete seriousness that she had never enjoyed a fortnight so much as when Alf was in hospital after a loading accident. And the women mostly preferred the daytime life, when the street was theirs, to the hours when their men were at home.

But Dora, although it would have seemed wrong to have Jack about the house all day, did feel a surge of happiness when he came in. Simply, she loved him. She never used the word, because none of the other women did, but it was the truth. She was lucky—she had no doubt of that. She saw that what mattered most in life was to marry the right man, not—like most women, apparently—any man who offered the customary terms.

She supposed that she must be lucky, too, in her body. Nothing seemed to hurt her; she had far less than the average sensibility to pain. The natural processes—natural in the sense that all women, or at least all wives, had to go through them—really were natural for her. Losing your virginity was supposed to hurt, but it hadn't hurt her at all—unless she counted the irritation of a sharp piece of coal under one shoulder-blade, for she had been lying on a sack in the coaling yard of the London, Tilbury and Southend Railway. Having babies didn't hurt her either. To be exact (this applied to both experiences) pain was dissolved in an excitement that was the keenest expression of love: love for her man, love for her child. She felt perfectly well while she was pregnant. When her time came, in Maggie's admiring phrase, she dropped them like a cat.

Regularly, Dora conceived when she stopped breast-feeding. There was a year and a half between each child: Charlie was born in winter, Violet in summer, and Liza in winter again. Dora went through the repeated cycle contentedly—it was natural. Something, some gentle and gradual change, was always happening to her body. It was strange to remember the years when her breasts and her belly had stayed the same size, doing nothing. She was only worried, a little, by the thought that she was getting fat. This was hard to measure; one naturally kept a bit of a roll after a baby was born, and when it was time to revert to normal, she was pregnant again. Anyway, Jack encouraged her to eat hearty meals. "Are you going to mind having a fat wife?" she asked him sometimes. "Always have liked something to get hold of," he replied cheerfully.

Charlie, in an old-fashioned wooden cot picked up for sixpence in the market, slept in the back room from his birth. It seemed peculiar, Jack and Dora both felt, to have an empty room. But when Violet came along, her cot was placed in their bedroom. Dora thought that a little girl was more in need of protection, of her mother's constant presence, than a boy. And as it turned out, little Vi was more fretful than Charlie had been over teething. Dora used to reach out sleepily and lift her into the bed. There she soon calmed, lulled by the warmth of two big bodies. When Liza was born, Dora reluctantly moved Vi to join Charlie.

It was not clear how they would manage with a big family. The Harris' back room was completely filled by two mattresses on the floor, with two boys sleeping on one and two girls on the other. The eldest boy slept on a truckle-bed in the kitchen. Dora was a breeder—her body told her that. As for Jack, it was a strain on him to keep off her when she was far into pregnancy. The way they were going on, they might easily have ten or a dozen children. Like all women who talked with other women, Dora knew how to get rid of a pregnancy; but she didn't believe that she could ever do it. As soon as she knew that she had a fragment of life in her womb, she saw a child sucking at her breast, crawling, learning to walk. Maggie's sixth died as an infant. Whatever Maggie felt, Dora thought that there could be nothing more dreadful than the death of a child. The scare about Charlie came at about the same time. She realised that, if he died, another son would not be Charlie: what is lost can never be regained.

About her man's life, at the docks, she didn't

25

know much. It wasn't the custom for men to talk about work to their wives. She pictured the docks, above all, as a place of regimentation. It was strange that anyone could give orders to Jack, but presumably it happened. Men were directed here and there, they had no right to take a break except at stated times—she could never have coped with this. But it was also a place governed by chance. When Jack left home, he had no idea whether he would be required to work till late at night or whether, on the contrary, he would get no work at all. She couldn't have coped with this either; she liked to count on things, she was put out by surprises.

She understood that the work was hard. Jack was never tired, but some women in the street told her how their men—especially older men— dropped asleep even before they had their supper. Injuries happened at the docks, too; once, Jack came home with two fingers crushed and had to lay off work for a week. So Dora saw each day's work as an adventure into which Jack sallied for her sake and the children's sake. This added to her love for him. A stevedore had to be a real man, and Jack was that if anyone was.

Her own life was limited to Steadman Street and the shops nearby. When she turned the corner into the main road, she was a little daunted by the traffic, the clattering trams, the crowded pavements. Roads like this had always been part of her life, of course; but, now that she wasn't a single girl, she felt that she belonged more truly to her own street. She was done with being whistled at by errand-boys, with trying out strange shops, with the game of going as far as she could on a tram without paying. She was happiest ambling and chatting with the other wives and mothers of Steadman Street, or standing at the door of number five with one eye on the playing children. After a few months, she knew everyone in the street. That is, she knew the women; the men she knew only by appearance and by what the women told her about them.

When she was immersed in what the women called a good chinwag, Dora lost all sense of time. A vastness of developing experience was opened to her, eventful and yet ordered, like a great port full of comings and goings. Best of all, she liked talking with the older women—the grandmothers. They had their worries, certainly; but they had arrived at a state of achievement, formed of the lives they had guided to manhood and womanhood. Dora saw herself moving, with a contented inevitability, toward that achievement. When she got home, she said to the children: "You'll always love your fat old Mum, won't you, dears?"

In Charlie's earliest memories, the most important time in his day was when his father came home. There was, first of all, a noise in the street: male voices, the tramp of boots, doors slammed one after another. Steadman Street became a street of men, and the little boy felt dimly that the change had something to do with him. Then the door of his own house opened and his own Dad came in. His Mum got a kiss —a right smacker, as Charlie learned to say. He was impatient for his Dad's attention; nevertheless, this kiss between his parents had a value for him too, an assurance that home was fully home. Then he was picked up in strong hands, whose grip hurt a little but hurt excitingly, and held close to the manhood that reached him through all his senses—a deep voice, a kiss through the brushing and tickling of a moustache, the smell of tobacco and working clothes. "Have you been a good boy, then?" the deep voice asked. Charlie never knew how to answer; being good was an uncertain concept, and he had almost always been called a naughty boy at some moment of the day. "Have you, then? . . . have you?" the deep voice went on demanding. In the end, his Mum came to his rescue: "Good enough to do, I suppose."

There were days when Jack did not come home until after Charlie had been put to bed. He struggled against sleep, silently and without crying—tears were for minor frustrations, not for a serious disappointment—but with all of a small child's concentrated determination. At last, after an infinity of waiting, he heard the door, the deep voice, and the smacker: all was well. When he was old enough to climb out of his cot and walk, he crept to the top of the stairs. If his parents caught sight of him, Dora shouted: "Naughty boy—get into your cot this minute!" Scurrying back was part of the fun, and he knew they were not really angry. Occasionally, he was awake late enough to hear them coming up to bed, and there was something solemn and strange in the thought that they could fall into helpless sleep just like him—just like the baby, even.

When he was older again, Charlie was allowed to run to the corner of the street and look for Jack coming home. Dora always stayed with the girls, so he felt that he was carrying a responsibility as representative of the home. He gazed at the huge noisy tram as it slowed and halted, then watched the men as they got off and dispersed, some heading for Steadman Street and some for other turnings. When Jack came along, he hoisted Charlie into the air with a thrilling sweep, and then there was the triumph of a ride home piggy-back, high above the doors and windows to which he normally looked up. They came into the house together, as if they had both been away for long hours in that mysterious other world called work. Jack sometimes called: "Here's your two men back!" If Jack didn't appear, Charlie waited for a second tram, even a third. Dora told him to come back after one tram if it was raining or freezing cold, but he never did this and she seldom scolded him. When he had to give up hope, he trailed home slowly and slipped into the house as if he had failed in his task. "Your Dad must be working over," Dora said. "We'll have our supper, then." Charlie could not have explained what "working over" meant, but he grasped that it was an unpleasant necessity confronted by his Dad for the good of the family.

As early in his life as he could understand anything larger than the immediate present, Charlie understood that when he grew up he would go off to work like Dad. It was not exactly a frightening thought, but it was a solemn one. He could see that it was no fun to leave the warm safety of home after a quickly eaten breakfast, every day except Sunday, hot or cold, wet or dry, in the dark in winter. It was no fun even for a big man like his Dad. Sometimes Jack peered out of the window and said: "Don't think I'll go today." When Charlie was small, this gave him a thrill of delight, but he saw the wistful smile on his Mum's face and he soon learned that it was only a pretence. He tried to grasp what it was like, this place called work. The effort of picturing it sometimes gave him the anxious and yet exciting feeling that he was already there. Mostly he felt it as a vast responsibility; it would be a place where he had to know exactly what to do and would be in trouble if he did it wrong. He was daunted, but he reassured himself that, by the time this was required of him, he would be able to meet the demand—like his Dad.

As far back as he could remember, Charlie was aware of being a man. Not of being a boy: that came later, when he spent less time at home and more in the street, with boys of his age. Boyhood was a phase in life, but manhood was his essential self. Both his parents used the word to him constantly. It was "There's a man!" when he reached some achievement; "Men don't cry" when he was upset; "Try like a man" when he attempted something new. He was a little man —they often said that—but a man nevertheless.

In his father, as seen by Charlie, there was grandeur but no mystery. A grown man was himself magnified, completed, freed of all limitations and uncertainties. His mother was more of a puzzle. She was big, she gave him orders, she picked him up and carried him about—she was a grown-up, clearly. But when he sat on her lap, he felt her to be soft, yielding, almost shapeless. It was not at all like the hard, angular shape of his father. His mother moved about the house gently, large but weightless, something like a cloud; his father walked with a firm, emphatic tread. No, she wasn't a man. She was something he needed, and perhaps would always need, but not something he would ever become. She said: "You love your Mum, don't you?" He

31

wasn't sure what this meant, but it was right for her to say it; his father never spoke of love. It seemed to indicate a dependence between them, a give and take. She said: "Always look after me, won't you?" This was more curious; she was looking after him, surely. But he perceived that it had to do with his being a man.

He was clear that he was altogether different from the girls. For one thing, he had been here first. The family had been complete without them, they were additional. He didn't resent them, but that was because he never took them quite seriously. They were very small, and he grasped that they would always be smaller than him. They were weak and helpless; they were not born to responsibilities. When they cried, they were comforted and not reproached. Evidently they were not expected to be ashamed of it, because they couldn't help it. His Dad, Charlie observed, was sometimes amused by them, but on the whole took not much notice of them.

Almost as soon as he could talk, he was taught to remember his name and address: Charlie Wheelwright, Five Steadman Street. He wasn't supposed to go beyond the corner alone, but it was understood that—being a little man—he might somehow find himself out in the wider world, and then it would be up to him to get back again. Steadman Street was safe. There was no question of his not being allowed there; the street was an extension of home, or rather it literally was his home, in a wider dimension. As he came to think of it, he belonged in number five as a matter of innermost security, and he belonged in Steadman Street as a matter of ampler living. Nor was there any formal division between the two. He ran in and out of the house on impulse, without permission. If his Mum wanted him, she came to the door and called him.

The basic game, or the basic pleasure, was simply to run along the street. He often fell down, either because his speed overcame his power of balance or because he tripped on the joins in the pavement. But someone's Mum, walking along the street at the right moment or else seeing him from her open door, was sure to set him upright again with a few words of comfort and return him to his own Mum if he had cut his hands or knees. When he was a little bigger, he learned that this kind of rescue was humiliating and picked himself up quickly— remembering, too, that men don't cry.

Other games were learned by imitating older boys. You could kick a stone along the street, giving yourself a black mark if it struck a door- step or went into the gutter. You could hop without touching a join—this game took a more complex form as hopscotch, the pavement being marked out with chalk. You could dash across the street just in front of a passing cart, feeling the horse's hot breath, dodging its huge trampling feet, and reaching safety to giggle at the carter's threats. You could knock on closed doors and escape before the woman of the house came to see who it was.

As soon as he could play these games, Charlie tagged along with older boys. He began to feel a dual identity. There was always his essential manliness—girls didn't dodge carts—but there was also his definition by age, as a boy, or more precisely as a nipper. Nippers were boys who hadn't started school, and they had the freedom of the street until four o'clock. Then, and also on Saturdays, the big boys took over. They played their own games, making the roadway as well as the pavements into one huge field. In winter they played football, marking out goals with their caps at each end of the street; in summer they played cricket, chalking wickets on the wall of the Gordon. These games lasted until the men returned to the street. On Sundays each home claimed its family and there were no street games.

Nippers could not play football or cricket. They had not learned the rules or the words, and in any case they had no bats and balls. But Charlie longed to play. He always had an urge to press toward growth, to attach himself to boys older than he was. When the big boys started their games he hovered on the pavement, fascinated. "Get out the way, nipper!" they shouted;

but he stayed, or withdrew to his doorstep to return stealthily when they had stopped noticing him. He found that nippers were tolerated—though never thanked—if they ran to fetch the ball when it went out of play. He could throw and kick quite well, for a nipper.

Yet all the time, although the men and the women and the children of the street had their distinctive lives, the street had a life that belonged to everyone. There wasn't space enough to hide anything away. When a fight exploded from the pub to the pavement, everyone was kept awake. When a child screamed in sickness or a woman in childbirth, the neighbours had to hear. When a family was turned out for not paying the rent, everyone yelled abuse at the bailiffs, no matter how often that family had been condemned for being shift-less. When there was a wedding, everyone celebrated. When there was a funeral, everyone stood silent at the door.

Everyone knew when Mr. King at number eleven kicked his wife out. She came staggering and moaning along the street, watched through all the windows. The door of number five opened and then closed. That was fitting; Dora Wheel-wright and Amy King were thick together, they'd known each other as girls. Charlie heard a grown-up woman weeping and was frightened for a while, but then he heard his mother talking in the comforting tone that she used when he really hurt himself. In the morning, he was told to eat his breakfast quickly and run out to play. He caught a glimpse of Mrs. King, asleep in the armchair, with a big blue bruise on her face. He grasped that Mrs. King had done something wrong; he hadn't known that grown-ups could do wrong and be punished. He also grasped that, though she was not to be excused, she was to be pitied. After a time, he saw her go to the corner and get on a tram. "She's gone to her Mum's," Dora told Jack that evening. "Best thing," he said approvingly. A few weeks later, Mrs. King returned to number eleven and everything was as before, except that the Kings' lodger had gone.

So Charlie grew up as a child of Steadman Street, watching, learning, groping to understand the ways of men and women, fitting himself to the shape of his future.

# 3

CHARLIE was four years old when his father was killed in an accident at the docks. As he learned much later, when he understood stevedoring work, the ratchet on a crane slipped and put the mechanism out of control. Jack was standing below a load of heavy crates to steady them as they came slowly down; when they fell, he was crushed. Death was instantaneous, the coroner said.

A man from the company came to number five. Charlie was curious—callers in bowler hats were rare—but he didn't want to break off his game of hopscotch. After the man had gone, his mother came to fetch him home. She didn't call him; she took him by the hand without saying anything, and walked along as if they were going to the shops. But when they went to the shops, she talked. Charlie realised that something was wrong, in a way that it had never been wrong before.

Dora sat down in an armchair with Charlie on one knee and Vi on the other. Liza was in her cot, having her afternoon nap. There must be a right way, she thought, to tell children of a thing like this. She was sorry that the man from the company had gone; he had found the proper words, no doubt from experience. But she knew that what had to be done now was for her alone.

"Your Dad's not coming back," she said. "Not ever. He's dead."

Vi at once started to cry noisily. Dora cuddled and comforted her; after a minute she put Charlie down—he was not crying—to devote herself to Vi. Charlie was sure that Vi didn't really understand what he already knew to be an irrevocable, transforming event. In later years, though Vi denied it, he always maintained that she couldn't remember their father. Liza, of course, never knew anything of Jack but the photograph over the fireplace.

Even before Vi had stopped crying, Maggie Harris appeared.

"Poor little mite! Got something to cry about and no mistake, hasn't she? I'll take her, Dora. No, give her to me—I'll just sit here. Now then, little Vi, you won't do no good by crying, will you? Your Auntie Maggie's going to give you your supper tonight, d'you know that? You be a good girl and you can choose what you want. How about some nice scrambled eggs, all on a lovely hot piece of toast? Like scrambled eggs, do you? There, that's better. How's Charlie taking it, then? Going to look after your Mum, aren't you, Charlie? Only one man in the house now, and that's Charlie Wheelwright."

Dora began to cry, sobbing into a large handkerchief which Maggie produced from somewhere in her baggy sleeves. She cried not because she felt worse but because she felt a little better. At first there had been nothing but the deprivation, the awful solitude, forbidding her to loosen the control on which her life and the lives of the children depended. Now she could grieve, because Vi was on Maggie's lap.

"Mind you," Maggie was saying, "something ought to've been done about them cranes years ago. I gave that man from the company something to think about, I did. It's all very well being sorry now, I said. It's happened before, I said, you know that as well as I do, I said, and what's more it'll happen again. He couldn't deny it. There wasn't a thing he could say. Don't come round here talking about unfortunate accidents, I told him. We all know there's no such thing as an accident without a reason, I said."

Dora was curiously helped by this line of talk. Maggie had never been inside the docks, of course, and what she said might be quite untrue. Yet, now that there was someone to be blamed —blamed by the general opinion of Steadman Street—Jack's death became an event that could be explained, no longer a mysterious blow of fate.

Maggie put a kettle on the range. Dora dried her tears; she had never let anyone else make tea in her own house. She told Charlie to get the cups. He obeyed her silently, carefully, taking on the beginnings of his new responsibility.

39

But after tea they drew nearer to the hardest time: the time when the men would come home from work and Jack would not. Though Maggie kept up her chattering, Dora could not help listening for the sounds of homecoming. She heard them, it seemed to her, with exceptional clarity. She almost believed that she could hear what men were saying to their wives in houses across the street. Charlie, she knew, was listening as keenly as she was. She held him close to herself, uncertain whether it was for his comfort or for her own.

People began to knock at the door. Men who worked in the docks came to tell her how the hooters had sounded and work had stopped on the ship when the accident happened. Bill Whitmarsh had seen it; he described it in graphic detail, and Dora found it less dreadful, because more comprehensible, when she was brought close to it. Women came to ask if there was anything she needed from the shops and if they could help with the children. The front room of number five filled up as never before. Dora said nothing much except "Thank you" and "It's all right" and "I can manage". The neighbours stayed on and talked to one another rather than to her: talked about other accidents they remembered, about cranes and ratchets, about Jack. The waves of talk made a friendly sound, protecting her from the fear of silence. She was not alone, so long as she was in Steadman Street.

While Maggie looked after the girls, Dora cooked supper for herself and Charlie. She had let time run on; it was later than usual. They sat at the table, the two of them, as she sat with Jack when he worked overtime. She had bought sausages, and of course she had more than she needed. But she cooked them all; she felt quite hungry, and she urged Charlie to eat like a big man. It was almost a celebration—a kind of coming of age. Still holding silence at bay, she talked to Charlie about his father. "Never did tell you about how I met your Dad, did I?" And she told about how Jack used to come into the sweetshop to see her for a few minutes; about going out with him, and walking all the way back from Tower Hill because they missed the last District Line train; about how she wondered if he was serious, and found out later that he always had been—he didn't say a lot, but he made his mind up fast. Really, it wasn't the kind of thing to tell a child of four about. It had belonged, in a deep and cherished way, to her and Jack; but she felt now that it was Charlie's inheritance. He understood all about it, that was certain. She went on to tell him about the one room where she and Jack had lived when they got married, and about having to move because the landlady couldn't abide children, and about finding number five, and about getting there in the nick of time for Charlie to be born—"you might have been born in the back of the van,

41

fancy that!" This made him laugh, and Dora laughed too. She laughed helplessly, bursting out again when she thought she had controlled herself, dabbing her eyes, not sure in the end whether she was laughing or crying. She couldn't feel that it was wrong to laugh. The joy of being Jack's wife had to be kept.

When she had put the children to bed, it seemed to her that there was still something she'd meant to do. She remembered that Jack had asked her to darn his socks. He had asked her several days ago, in fact, and it had slipped her mind. She felt guilty—soon he wouldn't have a single pair without holes. This was absurd, of course, but she couldn't convince herself that it no longer mattered. No, it mattered more than ever. She could not end with an obligation unfulfilled. So she sat down by the fire and did the job. Anyway, she told herself, someone would be glad of the socks.

She had just finished when Alf Harris knocked at the door. They had taken a whip-round for her at the Gordon. He had brought the money in his cap—mostly in sixpences and shillings—and he emptied it on to the table so that it made a splendid clatter. A few coins rolled on to the floor; Alf got down on his knees and searched for them, rather clumsily. Dora saw that he was slightly drunk. This amused her, because he was usually a careful man with the liquor. She felt, all the more, that Jack's death had been marked in Steadman Street.

She went to bed slowly, hanging up her dress in the wardrobe, putting things away which she generally left lying about. The bed seemed very big and, though it was a mild night, very cold. She wanted to cry again, but she kept herself from it now that she was alone. It could have brought her to a despair whose dangers were not to be reckoned. After a while, Liza woke up and fretted—she was cutting her first tooth. Dora took her into the big bed, which by degrees became a place of consolation for them both. The child slept again; and Dora too, suddenly exhausted, slept until morning.

Outwardly, the first consequence of the death for Dora was that she found herself dealing with people whom she would not normally have met. These people appeared in hansoms or in their own carriages—once, in a motor-car—causing a gathering of children outside number five from the time they arrived to the time they left. They wore bowlers or Homburg hats, long overcoats, gloves, polished shoes with spats. They had attaché cases from which they produced pieces of paper, and they handled these papers as casually as Dora handled a mop or a brush. They used words she had never heard before; they spoke in accents that gave even ordinary words an unfamiliar sound, so that she was never entirely sure that she had understood them right. What struck her most was that they all expressed profound grief over Jack's death, just as if they had known him intimately, and an equally profound concern for her. Their voices sank to a low register, they sighed lugubriously, and a couple of them pressed her hand and seemed reluctant to let it go. People who had actually known Jack—the people of Steadman Street— didn't behave like this; but then, Dora thought, they would have looked silly, whereas in these strangers it seemed fitting.

First came the doctor. Dora regarded doctors with awe, as controllers of the ultimates of life and death, and had never had much to do with them. Besides, this wasn't the local doctor who had come when Charlie was ill, but a doctor from the hospital near the docks. He was the man, she realised, who would have saved Jack if there had been any chance of that, and she felt that she ought to be grateful to him for having been prepared for the effort. He gave her the death certificate; she put it away with her marriage lines and the children's birth certificates.

Then came the undertaker. He kept saying "Leave it all to me, Mrs. Wheelwright"; but in fact he faced her with all kinds of decisions— about the position of the grave, the wood to be used for the coffin (which he called the casket), the wording of the headstone, and so forth. All these questions seemed to her in one sense tremendously important—at least, she was afraid of getting anything wrong and aware that any error would be irreparable—and yet, on another level of truth, quite unreal. She went through the funeral, everyone said, marvellously. Really, she was preoccupied by sustaining Jack's mother, who moaned and swayed on the verge of collapse, by wondering whether her various decisions had been correct, and by hoping that the children were all right with Maggie Harris, since the funeral took much longer than she had expected. Of all the days of her bereavement, it was on this day that she thought least about Jack.

There appeared also, on the same day as the undertaker, a gentleman who summoned her to the inquest. This, it turned out, was a ritual of the same kind as the funeral, though shorter and less solemn. Sitting at the back of the gloomy, ill-lit courtroom, Dora could neither see properly nor hear much of what was said. But she was not required to play any part, and no one shook hands with her afterwards as the vicar had after the funeral. The inquest, she felt, had the function of reducing Jack's death to the commonplace, to an item in legal routine. It upset her more than the funeral.

Next came a gentleman representing the company—not the man who had first brought the news, but a more imposing person whom she believed (though she was not sure) to be a lawyer. He gave her a paper to sign, whereby she waived all claims. She was intrigued by the term, and pictured herself waving her arms so that a cloud of papers, embodying possible claims, scattered to the winds. She signed without hesitation; she half-believed that the company was to blame, but obviously she could never make them admit it if they didn't want to.

Another lawyer came and asked whether Jack had made a will. This question astonished her; only old people made wills, and then only if they had property. Very well, the lawyer said, Jack had died intestate. That sounded nasty, but he explained that it was all right—everything that had been Jack's was hers. It appeared that this lawyer represented the landlord. He asked whether she wanted to go on living at number five, and she said "yes" at once; she suspected that they'd be delighted to turn her out if she showed any uncertainty. The lawyer asked to see her marriage lines and, on being satisfied that she was Mrs. Wheelwright, entered her name in place of Jack's in the rent-book.

Finally, a man came from the Prudential Insurance. Jack had paid in every week from his twenty-first birthday. Dora never quite grasped what the insurance was for; Jack said it might come in handy if they had bad luck, but she didn't see what form this bad luck might take. However, she knew that steady people with decent jobs paid into the Pru, while casual labourers did not. Now the bad luck was here and the Pru was giving her a lot of money— really a lot, far more than she had ever dreamed of possessing. She was embarrassed by the idea of benefiting from Jack's death, but she reminded herself that she was really benefiting from his foresight. He had known, better than she had, the dangers of dock work.

The man from the Pru came twice: first to explain things to her, and then to give her the money. "I don't know where I'm going to keep this," she said. He saw that she was worried by having so much money in the house, and suggested that the Pru should look after it for her. He could bring her instalments regularly, he said. It would be no trouble—it would be a pleasure. She had only to sign her name, and she was getting used to that by now. For a start, she took ten pounds in new sovereigns. Charlie and Vi were allowed to admire them before she put them in the box where she normally put aside the rent money.

Dora liked the man from the Pru more than any of the other visitors, quite apart from what he brought her. He was a young man, while the others were all middle-aged or even elderly. She could see that he hadn't got used to dealing with the bereaved; when he spoke of his sympathy, he had to search for the right words. He sounded shy and, therefore, completely sincere. She could also see that he wasn't exactly a gentleman, certainly not a toff. He was educated, and like all the rest of them he used words that were strange to her where the business was concerned, but in ordinary conversation he spoke her language and she forgot the difference in his accent. The second time he came, she offered him a cup of tea and they chatted quite easily. It was his last call of the day, he said, and he didn't have far to go to get home. She guessed that he belonged to the East End; he must have got on by scholarships.

Dora was surprised when she realised that a week had gone by since Jack's death, then a fort-night, then a month. She found it hard to reckon time in the ordinary way, either from day to day or within each day. Jack had given her not only a routine shaped by his working hours, but also a discipline to counteract her dreaminess. She never got up now until after the men in the street had gone to work. She usually forgot to go to the shops until the afternoon; sometimes she had to hurry to get there before they closed. She no longer planned the meals. The children thought it was fun to eat whatever she could scrape together after searching the cupboard—toasted cheese, or bread with ham but no butter. If she had nothing else, she went over to the pub for trotters and pickles, and always came back with a bottle of stout for herself. Only the Sunday roast was still an obligation. However, she sometimes forgot to put it in the oven, so it was eaten at tea-time rather than dinner-time.

In the evenings, she was in need of the children's company and let them stay up past their proper bedtime. Sometimes they all dozed off in front of the fire—Dora in one armchair, Charlie and Vi together in the other armchair which had been Jack's. When she had eventually put them to bed, there seemed to be no point in going downstairs again, so she went to bed too. She was more like a big sister, these days, than a mother.

She was deeply unhappy, but unhappiness was not like what she might have expected. It was not a fierce pain nor a distracting grief; it was an emptiness of the heart. "I don't know, nothing seems to matter," she said to Maggie. She played with the children endlessly, but she had no urge to kiss and cuddle them. She wondered if her love for them was somehow blocked, now that her love for Jack was cut off.

The continuance of normal life surprised her, or was not quite real for her, as it could surprise the survivor of an earthquake who had been moved to an undamaged town. When she heard the noise of singing from the pub, or a snatch of talk in the street, or the brisk questions of shop assistants, she was not bitter but wondering—it seemed extraordinary that all this was still the same. She herself felt perfectly well, ate with appetite, and slept soundly; but all this, the functioning of her body, was not quite real either. When she talked with the other women, she was as interested as ever in the news of the street—the eldest Smith girl was engaged, young Tom Kelly had been nicked for pinching oranges, old Mrs. Sutton was in bed with a wicked cough. Yet she was somehow detached, like a ghost watching the living. If she heard something funny, she burst out laughing, and then the echo of her own laughter made her feel not so much guilty as perplexed—had that really been her? She couldn't quite believe that, with Jack dead, she was alive.

What was she, really? She was a widow; but she wasn't ready to be a widow, as she had been ready five years ago to be a wife. She knew plenty of widows, her own mother and Jack's mother among them. Most women became widows. They had a recognised place in the world, a dignity, earned by years of devotion and home-making. She could not assume this place; she had not earned it nor progressed to it, at only twenty-three. But she wasn't a woman of twenty-three either, not properly, for at that age one was a wife. She was nobody. She had dropped out of life.

Dora had never been much good at thinking of the future. Now, she found it impossible; if the present was half unreal, the future was totally so. She had moved naturally from child-hood through girlhood to becoming a wife and mother. With the road broken, she could see no way ahead. Dimly, she could imagine herself in middle age, with Charlie controlling the house and making the decisions, a Jack reborn. But that was so far away that it was no more than a dream. The years between had to be lived first —how, she had no notion.

"You'll get married again, dear," Maggie said. "Nice-looking bit of goods like you. You don't believe it now, that's only natural, but you will."

Dora neither believed it nor wanted it. She had been through the phase of courting, kissing in doorways, falling in love, giving what had been preserved; she couldn't do it again, not in the same whole-hearted way, not without calculating and playing a part. She could not imagine Jack replaced. At night, she tried by way of conjecture to get the feel of having a man in her bed, whispering love, meeting his body with hers. This man was never real—far less real than the man, still featureless, she had longed for in her virgin years. Anyway, it stood to reason that no man would want a woman with three children. A real man fathered his own. The best she could expect was an offer from an older man— widowers existed as well as widows—who wanted a housekeeper. She might be ready for that at forty. At twenty-three, no.

What she had to do, she knew, was to make her life secure in a practical sense. After all, the children must be fed and clothed. For all she knew, she might be pregnant again. Liza was weaned, and Jack had taken her on the last night of his life. However, her period came. That was a relief, to look at it sensibly; but she was secretly disappointed. Being a wife was wholly at an end, when nothing of Jack remained in her.

The grim fact was that she had no earnings. The money from the Pru wouldn't last for ever. The new Education Act, which everyone in Steadman Street considered absurd, laid down that boys as well as girls had to stay at school until they were thirteen. Dora herself could go back to work; the sweet-shop would take her on again, she thought. But she had been paid only eight shillings a week, whereas Jack had brought in thirty or more. At the factories which employed women, she wouldn't do much better. Besides, she would have to pay someone to mind the children. She could take in washing and mending, or do out-work for the clothing trade, but she knew that she worked slowly when she was alone.

The dread that oppressed her was of having to give up the house. It was the one symbol of herself as Dora Wheelwright, of what Jack had given to her and the children. She loathed the idea of bringing them up in the tenements, the real slums. That was poverty. She had lived, as a girl and as a wife, among respectable working people who had their rights and paid their way.

Number five was her home, her place. If she lived at all, she lived here.

Still, she saw no way of meeting a rent of five and threepence. Taking in lodgers would help a bit, she supposed; she and the children could all sleep in one room. About this, all the same, there were difficulties. She was still young, and a single man in the house was bound to try something on, or anyway there would be talk even if he didn't. Single women normally lived with parents or relatives, unless they were loose women, and Dora didn't propose to give house-room to one of those.

These difficulties were never entirely absent from her mind, because they were a part of her unhappiness, an effect of the disaster. But she could not think of them as problems to be solved, certainly not with any urgency. She lived from day to day, washing the children's clothes when they had nothing to put on, finding food when she could have sworn there was none in the house. There was always money. She had no wish to buy anything but the necessities, and Jack was no longer here to drink in the pubs and buy tobacco, so she was actually saving—spending less, at least. Thus, she couldn't bring herself to believe that she would ever be right up against it. The idea was at the same time appalling and shadowy.

What kept her going, both materially and in her mind, was the money from the Pru. The young man came once a month. Since everything in her life had been measured by the week, she never remembered the date and his arrival came as a surprise—a delightful windfall. She went to fetch her box and discovered that there was only one sovereign in it, or that it was empty; she no longer budgeted. This became a joke between them.

"I can leave more if you like," he told her.

"Oh no," she said. "I seem to be managing." But the idea that she could have more money, simply by asking for it, reassured her that she was doing nicely.

Charlie once asked: "What does that man give us money for?"

She hesitated, then said: "It's to make up for your Dad being dead." He said nothing, and she wished that she could explain more clearly. Nothing could make up—Charlie was thinking that, she saw, and of course it was true.

Charlie still played and ran about and shouted in the street, but at home he had become quieter. He took pride in learning to do things for himself, such as making his bed and tying his bootlaces. Sometimes he reminded Dora that she had meant to go to the shops, or offered to bring in more coal from the bin as Jack had done. She had to caution herself not to put too much on him; he was only a nipper, after all. But she saw his pride when she said: "Still got a man in the house, haven't I?"

# 4

EVERY street has a gossip, who may or may not also be a scandalmonger. A gossip spreads what is true, and can be blamed only for making public things that would be better kept private. A scandalmonger spreads what is untrue, if not literally, then through the interpretation placed on the facts. The scandalmonger of Steadman Street was Mrs. Sutton—old Mrs. Sutton, as everyone called her; her face was yellow and wrinkled, her white hair dangled in thin wisps from the cover of a battered old hat, and her back was stooped. She was really not very old, and she scuttled from door to door with energy when she was on her feet. In winter or in wet weather she retired to bed for days at a time with a racking bronchial cough. This affliction didn't help her to look at the world generously. She lived alone. Her husband had left her long ago, merely sending a postcard to announce his arrival in Australia. One daughter, married and living in Rotherhithe, gave her enough money to live on and brought food and cough mixture when she was ill.

When she was not spreading scandal, Mrs. Sutton was collecting the material for it. She went up and down the street on mysterious errands, dawdling to overhear conversations (she was so small that she was sometimes not noticed) or giving children sweets and getting them to talk. Or else she sat by the window of her house, which was usefully placed halfway along the street, peering through the muslin curtains. On Saturdays she was in the local from opening time to closing time, inconspicuous in an alcove as she sipped port and lemon, observing and listening. No one liked old Mrs. Sutton, but what she said was generally believed. "She don't miss much" —that was the grudging tribute.

One fine summer day, when Maggie Harris and Dora were chatting outside their front doors, Maggie said cheerfully: "Well, I did tell you you wouldn't be a widow for long, didn't I?"

Maggie had told her this several times; so had other women. For Dora, it had no more meaning than in the first days after Jack's death. She smiled vaguely. She seldom argued with Maggie.

"Though if I was you," Maggie went on, "I'd make sure of him before long. They don't pop the question, see, without you give them a bit of a push. A man's got it easy so long as he can come and go as he pleases. Trouble is, you can't be sure when he might go and not come back."

These were still general remarks. Dora said inattentively: "Suppose so."

"Besides," Maggie said, "there's talk."

At this, Dora made an effort to concentrate. The phrase was a danger signal.

"How d'you mean, talk?" she asked.

"Well, he's not the Invisible Man, is he?"

"Who isn't?"

Maggie smoothed her apron, a gesture of dignified containment.

"'Course," she said, "it's no business of mine what you do. Putting my old foot in it, I suppose. Sorry I spoke."

Suitably placated, she said a good deal more. Dora listened, astonished at first, then hurt, then indignant. This indignation was the first strong feeling that had touched her for months. It was not altogether unpleasant; she was, at least, involved in life.

Mrs. Sutton's observations were these: A young man, presumably single, came repeatedly to number five. After he had been, Dora shopped without bothering about prices and had sovereigns to change. Each of his visits was longer than the one before. The last time, Charlie and Vi had been sent out to play and the young man stayed for hours.

Dora remembered. In the long summer daylight, without the job of lighting the gas and making up the fire to divide afternoon from evening, she had lost track of time and forgotten to call the children in. Mr. Goodings—the man from the Pru—had mentioned that he lived in lodgings and there was nothing to take him home.

The idea that there was anything between

them, when Dora calmed down and thought about it, rather amused her. He was certainly not the kind who tried things on. He was shy with her, even after all this time—always had to be asked to come in and sit down. Probably, though she hadn't considered it before, he had never had much to do with women. He looked away from her when he talked and withdrew his hand if it touched hers, for instance in giving her the money. Anyway, she could have looked after herself all right if necessary. He was slightly built; she had a notion that there wasn't much strength in his white, slender hands.

And if she ever did feel the need of another man—she would tell Maggie this, she'd like to tell old Mrs. Sutton—then it would not be someone like Mr. Goodings. In girlhood, she had always imagined herself with a big man, a man with thick hair and a moustache, with toughened muscles in taut limbs, swift in his movements and firm in his stride, powerful when he took hold of her. She had found Jack, and a man like Jack was still what she meant by a man. She had been so far from thinking of Mr. Goodings in that way that now she had difficulty in recalling physical facts about him. Well: he had light brown hair, parted in the middle so that a bare pathway reached to the crown of his head. He was clean-shaven, and there was never any stubble on his cheeks. She remembered noticing the delicacy of his hands. No hair on them, of course.

Then an odd thing happened. She found herself thinking about Mr. Goodings at quiet moments in the next week, and also when she lazed in bed, half dozing and half awake, in the mornings. The slander seemed to have made her see him as though it were true, or at least poss-ible. She decided that he was quite good-looking in his way. There was nothing actually wrong with his appearance—no receding chin, say, no beaky nose. His features must be what people called regular; probably that was why she had taken no special note of them. He would do nicely for some girls—not for her, naturally.

The next time he came, she had remembered the date. Indeed, she had spent the day wondering how to behave with him. The prudent thing to do would be to take the money at the door—not to let him in at all. He would be very surprised, though, and probably hurt. Perhaps she could have a short talk with him, explain what was being said, and ask him to send the money in future. The task daunted her; she wouldn't know how to put it, since she was sure that he had no more thought of her "in that way" than she had of him. She couldn't make up her mind. Finally, she took refuge as usual in losing track of time, so his knock was a surprise after all.

"Oh—Mr. Goodings!" she exclaimed. "Come

in, if you don't mind the mess. I don't know, I haven't even tidied up today." Nor had she. She kept on talking, rather too loudly, not listening to anything he said. She put the kettle on and invited him to sit down without any conscious decision.

The room really was untidy. There was even a damp towel, spread out to dry, on the chair where she had asked him to sit—she hadn't noticed, and had to swoop across him to snatch it away. She apologised, and then quite unnecessarily apologised again.

"I think you manage splendidly, with three young children," he said.

This point of view was strange to her. "Three's not much," she remarked.

"Isn't it? I don't know; I was an only child."

"Oh, I wouldn't have liked that. Ever so dull, I should think."

"Well . . . yes, it was dull, sometimes."

The conversation laboured between awkward spurts and halts. This had not happened before; they seemed to be aware of each other in a different way. The change, forced on Dora by Mrs. Sutton, was then forced on him by what he sensed in her. He wondered uneasily whether, simply by staying for tea, he could have implied that he was courting her. But perhaps he really was courting her, or hoping to court her, without having admitted it to himself until now. In quick embarrassed glances, he was aware of her fine blue eyes, the fullness of her lips, and the rich swell of her breasts.

Suddenly, out of a silence, a surge of recklessness took hold of Dora—an innocent rage at Mrs. Sutton. She would give the old cow something to talk about! If they imagined that she, Jack Wheelwright's woman, couldn't trust herself with anything in trousers—all right! So she asked Mr. Goodings to stay to supper.

"Give yourself a treat!" she cried at him breezily. "Can't be too much fun all by yourself in lodgings, can it?"

"If you're quite sure it's no trouble . . ."

"Not a bit! But potluck, mind. Nothing fancy."

He wasn't a big eater, he assured her. She got an extra portion easily enough out of the toad-in-the-hole she was making for herself and the children. Once they came in, she regained confidence. Mr. Goodings became a spectator; there was a family here, in spite of everything. Charlie and Vi washed their hands without being told twice and laid the table properly. Charlie answered politely, but not shyly, when Mr. Goodings asked him how old he was and was he looking forward to starting school. Vi kept staring, but she was only small and Mr. Goodings didn't mind. When she'd gone to bed, he said that she was a pretty little thing. So she was, Dora knew; and it was pleasant to have it said by a man instead of only by other women.

When Dora had settled the children in bed, Mr. Goodings correctly said that he really must go. She saw him to the door, defiantly opening it in full view of the street before shaking hands.

"It's been such a nice evening, Mrs. Wheelwright. An unexpected pleasure."

"Well, same for me, you know. I don't often have company."

He hesitated, fingering his attaché case; then he took a plunge.

"Do you ever get out in the evenings?"

"Not nowadays—no."

An odd excitement touched her, as if she were a girl again. She couldn't help smiling at him; anyway, he needed encouragement.

"If you could manage . . . I mean, somebody could stay with the children . . . would you care to go to a show or something? . . . that is, if you don't mind my asking."

She looked at him, rather dreamily, from closer than ever before. It struck her that she was slightly taller than him.

"Give yourself a treat," he brought out with an effort, capping it by a smile. He didn't often smile; it gave more life to his face.

"Saturday?" she said.

Sitting beside him at the music-hall, she thought of Jack, but not with any trace of guilt. Like the insurance money, this appeared to her as something that Jack would have wanted her to have. She laughed freely and joined in the songs. Mr. Goodings didn't know the words, she noticed. She wondered if he would hold her hand, and she would have liked this, as part of the occasion. But he did not.

The following Sunday, she went to the seaside with him. Of course, the children came. They were excited, almost incredulous, when she told them what was arranged. They had been to the seaside before, but they must have felt—and Dora had felt too—that it was impossible without Jack.

She had to explain the complicated journey to Mr. Goodings: tram to North Woolwich, ferry, train from Woolwich to Chatham, another train to Margate. The trains were crowded. Vi sat contentedly on Mr. Goodings' knee; Dora found room on her lap for Liza, the picnic basket and her handbag. Charlie stood between them, holding on to the window-strap. Mr. Goodings talked to the children, explaining what oasthouses were for and why apple-trees were painted white.

On the beach, sunk in a deck-chair, Dora gazed lazily at the distant sea drawing away to low tide, the little channels gleaming in the sun. Mr. Goodings had bought spades and was helping Charlie and Vi to build a sand-castle. She forgot about them and daydreamed, to the rhythmic sound of the band on the pier, about other days at Margate in her own childhood. When she looked again, after a nap, she couldn't see them and at last discovered them queueing for donkey-rides. She reflected that Mr. Goodings was spending a lot. Still, she had contributed the picnic food and she would ask him to supper when they got home.

There was more room in the train going back. Exhausted, the children all slept. Mr. Goodings asked Dora to come to the music-hall again, not on Saturday but on Wednesday. She would be doing him a favour; Wednesday was his birthday.

"How old will you be?"

He looked embarrassed. Twenty-two, he told her.

"You're younger than me. I thought you were, somehow."

"Does it matter?" he asked.

"No, of course not. But you can't keep going out with me all the time. Haven't you got a young lady?"

"D'you think I'd ask you if there was somebody else?"

This made her laugh. She had always assumed that Jack went out with other girls until there was an understanding between them. And then, looking carefully at Mr. Goodings, she wondered what he thought he was doing, apart from being kind.

When she met him at Stepney Green on the Wednesday, she said directly: "I don't know

64

much about you, do I? Not your Christian name, even."

"It's Herbert."

"Oh. Mine's Dora."

She fished in her bag and said: "I got this for you. Many happy returns, Herbert." It was a tie, the quiet kind that he always wore.

"You know," he said, "this time last year nobody knew it was my birthday."

"What—your twenty-first!" Overcome by pity, she seized his hands. They stood in the street, taking stock of what they now meant to each other.

After the music-hall, sitting on the top front seat of an almost empty bus, he told her more about himself. He found it easier than he expected; it was as if he had been saving it up for someone. His mother had died young, his father had emigrated. He had been brought up by grandparents, then handed on to an aunt. He had no family now and no friends except at his office. Dora understood. He needed her.

A couple of weeks later, Herbert got an afternoon off work and took her to Greenwich, without the children. She was sure that he was going to ask her to marry him. This he did, in his correct way, on a park bench in the great avenue of chestnut trees. She had never been proposed to before, with the option of saying yes or no; it was pleasant, whatever else one thought. But, although she had been expecting it, she hadn't made up her mind what to answer —"just like me!" she couldn't help thinking, trying not to laugh as she looked at his earnest face. She said she would have to think it over.

Maggie, and Steadman Street opinion in general, would certainly say that she ought to jump at her chance. Herbert was sober, respectable, with a steady job, obviously fond of her, fond of the children too; and he was young, which she had no right to expect in a second husband. By customary standards, it was surprising that he should want to take on a widow and step-children. But Dora understood it. He lacked the confidence to create married life; to acquire it ready-made was easier for him. He had found a woman who knew all about the business of living together, making a home, bringing up children. He would not have to guide her through any of that. He would not have to take the lead. Hers was the experience of intimacy and of weathering sorrow; emotionally, hers were the resources.

Did she want him in her life, then? She could not love him—she was clear about that. But he knew what Jack had been to her, and he would neither demand nor aspire to her love. He would not love her, either: well, yes, in a sense, but not in Jack's powerful and possessing way. That —a lifetime of marriage without love—was what she had to decide about. On the one hand, it was a kind of marriage that cost her no pain or guilt. She would have recoiled from displacing Jack, from really loving another man or trying to. On the other hand, she was twenty-three. Love throbbed in her, like the ache of an amputated limb. She found it hard to relinquish it for mere commonsense reasons.

Yet common sense could not be ignored. She had a good friend, and she didn't want to lose him. If only because of Mrs. Sutton, she couldn't go on giving Herbert suppers and going out with him for ever. Then, of course, it was her duty to think of the practical advantages of being Mrs. Goodings. She was no nearer to working out how she and the children could live once the insurance money was spent; in fact, she had put this out of her mind for several weeks.

So she drifted into accepting Herbert—or rather, into not rejecting him. What came uppermost in her mind was that being turned down would be a cruel blow to this vulnerable man. Saying "no" demanded from her a resolute mustering of her will. That became her decision; she felt that she could not do it to him.

When they met, Herbert talked conscientiously of this and that, and touched her only to take her arm as they crossed a street. Only when they said goodbye did he clear his throat and, his eyes avoiding hers, ask: "Have you thought about . . . you know?" To which she replied: "Oh, I really will."

Eventually—they had got off the bus one

night and were at the corner of Steadman Street, deserted because it was raining—her conscience was overwhelmed by what she was making him bear. In a steady voice, as if she were giving the right answer to some official question, she said: "Yes, Herbert, I'll marry you." She felt relief, more than anything else. "That's settled, anyway," she added to herself.

He looked as if he couldn't believe it. She realised how much it had cost him to press the question every time, how he had prepared for rejection.

"Aren't you going to kiss me?" she laughed.

He kissed her for the first time, awkwardly reaching one hand to her shoulder while the other held the umbrella over them.

She led him into the Gordon. She would have embarrassed him by making an announcement; her smiles, and her hand in his, told enough to anyone. No beer-drinker, he had a nip of whisky with water while she drank stout.

Charlie, she found next day, was very surprised. Dora had got used to treating him as a man, or at least as having a man's perceptions. She had somehow assumed that he knew what courting was and why Herbert kept taking her out. But either he didn't know, or more likely he thought that courting was for girls and didn't realise that a woman could get married twice. He stared at her and at last said: "You're not really, are you, Mum?" She recalled—she did have to remind herself of this—that he was only four. She ought to have prepared him, no doubt. Well, it was too late now.

Vi said with decision: "I think Mr. Goodings is nice. So there!" The "so there" was for Charlie; she was getting into a way of taking the opposite side to him on principle. She had grown up rather alarmingly, Dora thought, in the last six months. She was developing a strong will of her own, amounting at times to disobedience. A father's controlling hand, of course, was what she missed. Herbert might supply it, but Dora was not too sure.

# 5

HERBERT was not happy about living in Steadman Street. He had been born in a street like this—indeed in real poverty, his father being a casual labourer. But his mother, who had married beneath herself and regretted it, had brought him up to despise and fear the drunken workmen and their slatternly wives, the street fights, the rough boys who cornered him as he tried to slink home from school. Those were his memories, or nightmares, from before the age of eight. His aunt, in Leytonstone, had lived in another world: bay windows, fearing God and honouring the Queen, a striving for gentility on a tiny income from piano lessons. From this, Herbert had advanced to grammar school and the Pru. The aunt was dead now, but had left him with a clear sense of where he wanted to belong.

Getting back to bay windows, with a wife and three children, was impossible for the present. He did not earn enough to pay more than a Steadman Street rent. Still, he wanted to share his aspirations with Dora, and soon after the wedding he explained to her how their life could change when he got promoted. He was taken aback by her answer. Number five suited her, she said emphatically; she didn't want to move, not ever. She had her friends in the street, the children had their friends, and Herbert admitted that he hadn't kept up with anyone in Leytonstone.

"Don't you ever want to live in better conditions?" he asked.

"Might do the rooms up," she said, looking round vaguely. "Can't say it bothers me, though."

Herbert was unhappy about the outdoor lavatory. He was unhappy about having a bath in the kitchen; he rarely did this, preferring a cubicle at the Public Baths. Most of all, he was unhappy about the lack of a front garden, the sense of being almost in the street. He lay awake in the evening—they always went to bed early—and listened to the ugly, raucous shouting and singing in the pub. When glasses shattered on the pavement and a fight exploded into the street, he lay tense and alert. By his side, Dora slept peacefully.

In the mornings, he left home long after the dockers. He got up early, nevertheless; he took care over shaving, brushing his suit, polishing his boots. While engaged in this routine, he heard the tramping feet pass the door. Sometimes he had a curious impulse to hurry out and join this movement of Steadman Street. But he ate his boiled egg and went at his own time to

71

wait, alone or almost alone, for the bus going west.

He worried a good deal about being accepted in the street. In reality, the worry was hardly necessary, for moving into Steadman Street was not like coming as a stranger to some enclosed, tradition-bound village. People moved in and out of the rented houses, not frequently but from time to time. Kelly at number seven got a notion that there was steadier work at the Surrey Docks and moved to Bermondsey. Butcher at number twenty-five lost his job, which was driving a brewer's dray, through bad time-keeping, fell behind with the rent, and vanished with his family to a room in the Limehouse slums. Young Miller at number twelve, when both his parents died within a year and his sister married, signed on in the Navy. The houses were never empty for long. Dora had become a chronicler of the changes; she would surprise Herbert by telling him that a family whom he had taken to be rooted in Canning Town had come quite lately. She herself, after five years, was regarded as a permanence. Widowhood and a second marriage made people cease to think of her as young. As her husband, Herbert became as much a part of the street as she was.

He had done the right thing by her, too. He could have gone on calling round in the afternoons, getting his bit of lovey-dovey and evading

72

responsibility. But he'd married her—three nippers and all. That was reckoned to his credit.

Still, he worried. Once a week or so he went to the local, lest he should be thought a milksop or a snob. He couldn't detect any lack of friendliness there, though he was on the watch for it. He was stood drinks, and he bought rounds. This obliged him to drink beer, which nauseated him, but he made the effort. Sometimes he was teased about his work. "Kept clean and tidy again today, I hope," a docker would say, or "Lifted any heavy bits of paper lately?" He mumbled some answer, lost in a spreading wave of laughter—no answer was expected, really. The teasing hurt him, but he knew that it was a sign of acceptance.

But he moved every working day between two worlds. At the office, the fashion among the clerks was to assume the airs of young men about town, Burlington Berties. Herbert suspected that some of them had the same background as himself—he never divulged it, and nor did they —though some had fathers working for the Pru and a few were the younger sons of genteel families. They ate penny buns for lunch, but this (according to them) was to save for dinners at Frascati's or tickets at the Empire. The single men talked loudly about the smashing bits of stuff they picked up; the married men talked about the wife turning on the waterworks when they came in after a night on the tiles. A constant subject for humour was the British working man —his idleness, his oafish obstinacy, his crude personal habits, his voracious sexual appetities. There were jokes about packed beds in the East End, about Father pulling out and grumbling "Should have told me you wasn't Mum", to which the daughter replied "Thought you was Brother Bill". Herbert never said anything about his personal life, except to admit that he was married. They would have died laughing at a fellow who got nabbed by a widow with three brats—in the East End, too.

Often he was repelled by them: by their pretences, their frivolity, and a certain hard selfishness under the veneer of charm. He had no doubt that each of them would have slandered or betrayed another for the sake of promotion. There was no sense of a common fate, no code of sticking together, as there was in Steadman Street. Yet this was the class that, through his lean boyhood, he had striven to join. After all, these men had the vital flame of ambition. They were not content to toil at fifty as they toiled at twenty, and for the same wage, like working men. If they made fun of their wives, they also offered them a promise. And they looked out to a wider world; they took pride in the Empire, in England's example to foreigners. In the hour of danger, it was men of this class who went to the recruiting stations.

In the passionate election of 1906, the clerks

spent their evenings booing at Liberal meetings. England was in danger, not from a foreign foe but of falling blindly into the hands of radicals, pro-Boers, and strike agitators. But in Steadman Street everyone wished good luck to the Labour candidate, Will Thorne of the Gas Workers' Union. Herbert, endowed with the vote for the first time in his life, felt that he was being summoned to a personal declaration of allegiance, even of identity.

"They're all voting for this Thorne," he said to Dora.

"Aren't you?" she asked.

"I haven't decided," he hedged. "Don't know much about him."

"Jack voted for him last time," she said unexpectedly. She seldom mentioned Jack—never as a pattern for Herbert. But she was saying, he took it, that a man of Steadman Street should vote for Thorne.

After a long inner struggle, he voted Tory. Despite the privacy of the polling-booth, he had a feeling that Dora would know—a feeling that stayed with him when she didn't ask. He was defending the beliefs that had shaped him; yet, if he helped the Tory to a narrow victory, he saw himself guilty of inflicting a disappointment on Steadman Street and on Dora. As it turned out, he need not have worried. Thorne had a two-to-one majority.

As years passed, Herbert never overcame this

division of himself; he merely got used to it and worried about it less. He was promoted at the office, but not very fast nor very far. It was possible, he thought, that his address and what it implied counted against him. But that could not be helped. Moving toward middle age, he came to believe less in ambition and more in fate. Evidently, life took an ordained shape, against which it was useless to protest.

He was sure that he couldn't have married anyone but Dora. He had always been shy of girls and without confidence for the business of attracting and flirting. Quite easily, he might have settled into a bachelor's life in lodgings. So he never regretted his marriage, nor did he ever consider that he was the one who had done Dora a good turn.

The fact remained that he was at a certain distance from her, as he was from Steadman Street. Perhaps, he reflected, this was for the best. Anyway, it was inevitable. He had no capacity for total intimacy—it would have dragged him out of his depth. As for Dora, he accepted that her desire for total intimacy had been spent once and for all with Jack. He kissed her only in bed, feeling for her lips in the dark. Her body was like a mysterious cave into which he plunged as though dreaming. What happened in bed was a thing apart, neither anticipated at supper nor recalled at breakfast—not linked to the ordinary habit of living together.

He was happiest in the hour before bedtime, especially in winter, in front of the fire. They did not talk much. Over the years, they built up very little in the way of running arguments or regular jokes. Herbert read the evening paper.

Dora sewed, knitted, or more often did nothing. He hardly ever said "Penny for your thoughts". They were her own, and he didn't mind if they had nothing to do with him. All that he required was her presence.

Jack's photograph stayed on the mantelpiece, where Dora had put it the day after his death. She didn't often look at it, and moved it casually when she was dusting. It was a part of the home, like a picture of Jesus in a religious household. The memory of Jack was in the background, not dominating nor even belonging to her present life. But it was not to be challenged. Herbert accepted that willingly.

Dora, at least in the first year, thought a good deal in her ruminative way about the implications of being married to Herbert. About Jack she had never thought; to feel, to love had been enough. She had dropped into life with him as a swimming animal drops, at the right time, into the water. And she had been hurled into widowhood, to make what she could of it. This marriage was different; she had hesitated before it, she had chosen it, she was responsible for it. For the first time in her life, she was in something that had to be managed.

She had given Jack what he wanted simply by being herself. But what she had given him she couldn't give Herbert, who must therefore be given something else. This she saw as caring for him. He needed a clean collar every day; his cuffs had to be turned when they frayed. He was hesitant about asking—Jack, when he did need something done, had demanded it. So she had to look for what was needed and remember to do it in good time, which was against her habits.

She had to plan the housekeeping, too. To her surprise, Herbert was paid rather less than Jack. It was just as well that he didn't smoke and drank very little. The novelty, for Dora, was that he earned exactly the same amount every week. This ought to have given her a sense of security; however, she wasn't used to it and didn't like it. In her first marriage, when she wanted something such as a new hat, she put it out of her mind until Jack had a good week, then went out and got it. Now she had to save. "Everybody saves, except rich people," Herbert said; but this was not so—people in Steadman Street didn't save. Sometimes she wanted to scream because every week was the same. There were no bad times, so there were no high times either. But she never complained about this. Herbert wouldn't have known what she meant.

She had difficulty in taking his work seriously. It had to be done, of course, and she had good reason to know that it was useful. But it was not a struggle, not an adventure—scarcely even an effort. Phrases dropped by the neighbours told her that they considered office work a soft touch, and in her heart Dora agreed with them. Herbert sometimes came home tired, and was prone to headaches. She ordered the children to play quietly or go upstairs, but without conviction. Anyway, she felt that it was for a man to give the order if he wanted quiet.

In the mornings, she made sure that Herbert looked tidy, helped him on with his coat, and waved briefly from the doorstep. A little later, when it was time for Charlie to go to school, she made sure he looked tidy and waved from the doorstep. In marrying Herbert, she seemed to have acquired a grown-up child rather than exactly a man. She shied away from this thought, but it lodged somewhere in her mind.

Gradually, after the first year, she thought less and less about what the marriage meant, until she no longer thought of this at all. They were happy, she supposed. She put it to herself negatively—they didn't have any rows. She had as much as she could have expected; so, she could honestly say, had he. Whatever more she might have had out of life had gone with Jack. Sometimes the longing for Jack struck at her as achingly as in the weeks after his death. But she no longer had the sense of utter emptiness; her life had some kind of purpose. The part of her that missed Jack was distinct from the part of her that cared for Herbert. It never occurred to her to blame Herbert for not being Jack.

Time passed, on the whole, quite quickly. Herbert always remembered her birthday, their wedding day, and the children's birthdays. Assisted by Vi—once Vi was a little older—she remembered Herbert's birthday. The anniversaries always seemed to come sooner than she had expected. Vi started school. Then Liza was ready to start school, and Dora was amazed: where had the years gone? An entire phase of her life—blowing noses, wiping bottoms, toys underfoot all day, a child to talk to at any moment—was over. With Herbert always the same, the growth of the children was the real measurement of time and the centre of her life. That might have been true or partly true, she thought, even if Jack had lived. Ultimately, a woman was there to be a mother.

When she married Herbert she looked forward to having his children. Of all the things she could give him this was clearly the greatest. Anyhow, she liked babies. She was stirred—a bit, at least; it certainly wasn't like with Jack—by a man's body on hers, the thrust, the spurting. She waited for the new growth within herself, the natural cycle interrupted by death.

A year passed. Maggie, who was pregnant again, asked: "Not in the club yourself, are you?"

"No signs," Dora said.

"I should think he'd want one of his own."

"Oh, I daresay he does." It wasn't a thing that Herbert and Dora talked about.

"Gives you your ration, doesn't he?" Maggie inquired.

"Oh yes." Dora reflected and added: "Not all that often, though."

"That must be it, then. Only wish my old bugger would lay off a bit."

Another year passed. Dora came slowly to the conclusion that Herbert wasn't likely to do the trick. She felt some disappointment, more in her body than in her mind. To be practical, there were reasons for relief. The house would never be crowded, and the money would stretch.

She wondered if Herbert minded. There was no use in asking him, and probably hurting him, now that it couldn't be helped. The subject had still not been discussed between them, and never was.

She felt now that there was no real point in having it off. She didn't believe that Herbert enjoyed it much, and she got very little out of it; the pleasure had been mainly in the hope of starting a baby. The marriage existed to meet other needs. She got into the habit of turning on her side, away from him, and falling asleep as soon as she got into bed. Occasionally—once or twice a month—she woke to his panting and fumbling in the middle of the night, and drowsily gave him his release. It was a necessity of his system, like her periods: rather an embarrassment to him, and nothing much to do with her.

Essentially she had never felt Herbert as a man, in the way that she had felt Jack, and in time the possibility of such a feeling vanished entirely. There remained a gentle, comfortable satisfaction in caring for him. Sometimes, when he had one of his headaches, she made him go to bed right after supper. After washing up the plates and banking the fire, she went to bed too and held him in her plump, soft arms until he felt better, as she would have held one of the children.

A time came—she observed it only in retrospect—when she no longer thought of herself as young. More than anything else, it had to do with being the mother of schoolchildren instead of babies or nippers. She was a Mum, in the full sense of the term.

Next door, at number seven, a young couple called Mead had moved in. They had lived in a rented room until the first child arrived; they were at the same stage in life as Jack and Dora when they had moved in at number five. Jane Mead was a pale, wispy little thing who scarcely looked as though she could have carried a child. Responsibility for another life seemed to have come upon her too soon.

"Sorry to bother you, Mrs. Goodings," she appealed to Dora one day, "but could you come and have a look at little Joey? Crying something awful, he is, and going all red in the face. You know, I don't want to have the doctor without I need to."

Dora had a look.

"That's just the colic. Most of them have it, specially boys. He'll get over it. Bit of gripewater from the chemist's, that's what you want to give him."

Straightening up from the cot, Dora caught sight of herself in a mirror. Nowadays, she didn't look at herself in mirrors at all often. She had got definitely fat: fat at the waist, fat in the cheeks, fat round the neck. She gave little Mrs. Mead reassurance, not only by her seniority, not only by her ease and calmness, but also by the mass of her presence. She looked as a Mum ought to look. Herbert and the children, no doubt, felt that too.

When she was thirty, Dora was able to look ahead and imagine a future that, by this time, had a connection with her present self. She rather fancied herself as a grandmother, taking Charlie's children on her lap and explaining about the colic to some grateful daughter-in-law. She would be fatter than now, of course. If you tended that way, as she always had, there was nothing to be done about it. Herbert did not tend that way. Probably, it was now noticeable that he was younger than she was.

He had been promoted again. Money was

easier; they could have paid the rent of a house with a bay window and a small garden. But Herbert no longer talked about wanting to move. Dora believed that he had reached a point of contentment. She was glad; it was what she had set out to give him.

# 6

LONDON was growing, like a giant knocking down walls and uprooting trees as he stretches his arms. It had been going on for more than a century, and it looked as if it would never stop. Farther and farther into Essex, Kent, Middlesex, Surrey, fields and market gardens were buried under new factories, new buildings of every kind, new streets. Already, Steadman Street had an old-established look, as if it had never been anything but a cell in the solid body of the city. The docks handled more trade every year, so there had to be more dockers, just as there were more building labourers and bricklayers, more gas and electricity workers, more drivers for the new motor buses and lorries—and more hopefuls streaming in to compete for work.

Immigrants could be seen spreading away from the docks after a ship from a Baltic port had tied up: wearing odd shawls and headscarves, chattering in strange languages, crossing streets without a glance at the traffic, but usually guided by cousins who had arrived the year before and were already Londoners. When Dora went to the big East End markets, she found herself in a throng of newcomers—mostly

Russian and Polish Jews, but also Italian, Greek, Levantine. The immigrants filled London up, but they did not extend it. They burrowed into the heart of it, as if this made them safer, as if they were determined to be city people and never to see a village or a sea-coast again. So they settled in the tenements of Shoreditch, Bethnal Green, Whitechapel—the districts that had been poor and crowded for generations. Dockland, with the squat rows of family houses, remained English, or at least English and Irish. No foreigners would get work in the docks, anyway.

Londoners had children; people from the countryside, from Ireland, and from foreign parts had even more children. The Board of Education, having decreed that these children should sit at desks from the age of five to thirteen, was building new schools everywhere. Charlie went to a Board School that was younger than he was. Before it existed, children had been taught in a scattering of little schools, mostly run by the Church. The Board School collected children in the mass—seven or eight hundred of them—from all over Canning Town and Plaistow. It was spoken of as "the new school" or "the big school".

To a boy of five, it was enormous. The high-pitched roof, topped by a score of smoking chimneys, rose above the streets like the turrets of a fortress. The asphalt playground seemed limitless; it was daunting to think of playing in a space without corners or turnings. If you threw a ball, it trickled to a standstill instead of hitting a wall and bounding back. If you fell and cut your knee, you were at a limping remoteness from shelter. On foggy days, the surrounding walls disappeared and the playground was the world. Inside the school, the corridors ran on like nightmare roads and you got dizzy gazing up at the vaulted ceiling of the hall. But you were herded into the hall only twice each term, for the Head's opening address and for the prize-giving.

The Head, on these occasions, spoke of the Board as an authority of which he was only the delegate. The Board had created this fine school; the Board could give all the boys and girls a good start in life if they worked hard; but if they broke the rules or damaged school property, the Board would hear about it. The Head himself was a mild, unimpressive man, like an older Herbert Goodings. Charlie imagined the Board as a distant but ever-vigilant power, into whose hands he was delivered for the rest of his childhood.

Getting to school—left at the bottom end of Steadman Street and across two other streets— took five minutes if you ran all the way. It was a point of honour to cut it fine. As the church clock struck nine, the school bell started to ring. You had to be in your classroom before it stopped; if you just missed it, the sudden silence was heavy with doom. If you were late, either you got two cuts with the ruler or you were kept in at the end of the day, according to the teacher's mood. Charlie didn't mind the cuts, but he hated being kept in.

The school had three entrances, each with a stone lintel over which was carved the designation "Boys", "Girls", or "Mixed Infants". Charlie was disgusted to find that being in the Mixed Infants meant being with girls. He was even forced to sit next to a girl. And his form teacher was a young woman who wanted him to like her and sometimes called him "dear". When she used her ruler on him, she was distressed and he was embarrassed.

After two years, he moved up to the Boys and was freed from being with girls. The masters were all men, too. They used canes, which hurt more than rulers, but that was part of being in the Boys. Charlie sat next to Tommy Whitmarsh from number thirty-one, because their surnames came together in the alphabet. Being W's, they had a quiet bench at the back, well away from the master.

The form master was known as Ginger from the colour of his moustache. He had knocked about a bit; he had been a volunteer in the South African War, then an overseer in the diamond mines. He had been obliged to give up real work, he said, after a dose of Yellow Jack—"all I'm fit for now is looking after you brats". He was strong enough when it came to using the cane, though. The boys liked Ginger. When he was in the mood, he forgot the timetable and told long stories about Africa and the peculiar ways of the natives. Sometimes he came in tiddly after dinner; it was rumoured that he had been warned by the Head about drinking. His unvarying attitude, sober or tiddly, was of lordly contempt for his job, the Board, the boys, and the notion of education. He made no pretence of knowing any of the boys by name; he treated them as an audience, occasionally pointing a finger and shouting "You with the snotty nose!" or "You with the pimples!" It was said with respect that Ginger had less trouble keeping order than any other master in the school.

For Charlie, as for all the boys, school was a business of tasks and opportunities. You had to learn your tables up to twelve times twelve, do sums in your notebook, copy out spelling lists, memorise the counties of England and the dates of the kings and queens. Ginger's method was to lead the boys in recitations, bellowing at the top of his voice himself and imposing a rhythm by whacking his cane on his desk. "Let's have it again, louder!" he would yell. "I want those bloody girls to hear you!" It was never suggested that the purpose of this ritual was learning, still less that it might be any use when the boys left school. If the sums were marked wrong, you got the cane or were kept in; if they were right, or if Ginger overlooked any errors, another day was safely past. Yet, to the end of his life, a reflex in Charlie's brain produced "nine nines are eighty-one" or "Henry the Second, eleven fifty-four".

The opportunities were of interrupting the routine. You could get yourself chosen—by shouting "Me, sir" a split second before the others—to take a message, and dawdle with the answer. You could claim that your notebook had been pinched and start a chain of investigations and counter-accusations. If you had the knack you could stage a faint or a shivering fit. The risk was always that Ginger would twig the dodge and lash out with his cane. Up to a point, however, he relished these diversions; a day of solid teaching bored him as much as it bored the boys. Tacitly, master and class agreed that they were matched in an endless tournament—less serious than a war, more tense than a mere game. Charlie was bolder than most, more often in trouble but always coming up with something fresh. After a couple of years, Ginger even recognised him so far as to call him "Bloody Wheelwright or whatever your stupid name is."

Through his eight years at the Board School, Charlie lived in the present. He was more aware of being a boy, subjected to school and pitted against the masters, than of becoming a big boy. He would have been surprised to know that the Head saw him as a fine growing lad, badly behaved at times but worthy of trust. He was in fact surprised when he was made a monitor, charged with keeping order in the playground and the corridors. When he broke up a ring of bullies and rescued a blubbering seven-year-old, he realised that he had traversed an age. The school itself no longer looked huge to him; the hall was a room across which he took short cuts, the corridors were rather meagre. And, for the first time, school was a place where he had serious duties as well as inevitable tasks. He honestly tried to do his best as a monitor. When he was praised by a master he was amused, somewhat embarrassed by what Tommy Whitmarsh and the others would think, yet also gratified. Being a monitor was less fun than skirmishing against Ginger, but he knew it to be more truly satisfying. Intrigued, he savoured the strange taste of authority.

Still, he never confused school with the real world. Playing football on Saturdays in West Ham Park was real. Helping his mother at home was real—he did most of the mucky work, like carrying in the coal and clearing out the gutters, to save his stepfather's good clothes. Earning sixpences by doing odd jobs for invalids and old women was real. Going to the docks and clambering up the wall to watch a big ship tie up was total reality, because it was his future. He was the son of a stevedore; he never forgot that.

Tommy's father had worked with Charlie's, so

Charlie was welcome at number thirty-one any time. The Whitmarshes had three sons, as well as a daughter, but Bill Whitmarsh was fond of boys and wouldn't have minded more of them. He spoke of Jack admiringly: "Oh yes, he was a real man, was your Dad, you ask anybody down the Albert." Charlie listened with deep contentment. He did not set himself the explicit aim of matching up to his father; what he was conscious of was a position to be filled. Whitmarsh was a chunky, quick-moving man, talkative and full of jokes. "Fine woman your mother is, mind you," he told Charlie. "Wanted to marry her myself, but Mrs. Whitmarsh wouldn't have it."

In the family, as the three young Wheelwrights took shape as people, Charlie's role was cast for him. He had grown to be a well-built lad, tall for his age, with his father's thick dark hair and with a strong set to his mouth and jaw that forecast manhood. He was the eldest, and the only boy; he had to be strong and dependable. If his nature had been at odds with that role, he would have been obliged to fit himself to it. But it suited him. He did not feel burdens, nor was he troubled by doubts.

Vi was the pet of the household. She had Dora's golden hair and blue eyes, with Jack's firm features. Somehow she had missed the inheritance of tallness that came from both of them to Charlie; she was always small for her age, light and dainty as a little dancing-girl. In fact, she had a natural gift for dancing and did a solo turn in the school Christmas pantomime every year from the age of seven. It seemed to be her mission in life to amuse and delight the world. She was often cheeky, and if she was told how to behave she answered back smartly. At times she was disobedient and downright naughty; she dodged helping Dora in the home and wouldn't look after her clothes. But she defied authority with a laugh, never with a sulk. So she got away with it most of the time, even at school. At home, Dora and Herbert regularly made up their minds that they would be laying up trouble if they spoiled her; but when it came to the point, Dora seldom found enough resolution to punish her, and Herbert practically never.

Liza, on the other hand, was never any trouble. She was the quiet one—every family has a quiet one. She would sit in a corner for hours, happily absorbed in dressing and undressing an old rag doll, while the family forgot she was there. At school she was timid and, to begin with, rather miserable. Only as she grew older did she establish herself—a girl whom everyone liked because she was without malice or the desire to compete. She was dependable, like Charlie; but she wasn't made a monitor, for she could never have achieved authority. (For quite different reasons, Vi wasn't made a monitor either.) Liza had a round face, a snub nose, light brown hair and big gentle brown eyes. By the age of ten, as she became less pudding-faced, she was not bad-looking. However, she had been a plain, almost ugly child; she must have known it, when everyone who came to the house exclaimed how pretty Vi was. That, Dora thought, had given Liza her quiet, unassuming nature. Secretly, Dora loved her the most. A mother is inclined to love the youngest, the last memory of having babies.

The family paired off, as families often do. Vi was Herbert's darling. She perched on his knee, chattering nineteen to the dozen, when he came in from work. If she wanted permission to stay up late, or twopence for a new hair-ribbon, she could always talk Herbert round in spite of Dora's disapproval. Liza and Dora remained close together, bound by an understanding that needed no words. Charlie stood by himself.

In the first couple of years after his marriage, Herbert made a considerable effort to get on good terms with the children. He came home with surprise presents: marbles for Charlie, glitter-brooches for Vi, liquorice sticks from the corner shop. He organised outings, mugging up his facts in advance and acting as guide. They went to the Tower, the Zoo, Madame Tussaud's, Greenwich Observatory. In summer they picnicked in Epping Forest, rowed on the lake at Victoria Park, and went three or four times to the seaside. He worked hard making a guy for Guy Fawkes Day and decorating a tree for Christmas. He bought a Children's Book of Knowledge—four volumes in red leather—and explained the pictures.

Dora was touched by these efforts, but uneasy about them. It was bad for the children to get used to taking things for granted, when their friends didn't get all these treats. It seemed to her, also, that Herbert was trying to buy the children's affection. He had Vi's anyway, and with the others it wouldn't work. "Just be a Dad like any other Dad," she told him. But that was what he could not manage.

For some time, Charlie went on referring to Herbert as Mr. Goodings, as he had before the marriage. Dora, feeling the awkwardness, simply used the pronoun "he". At last she said to Charlie: "He'd like you to call him Dad, you know."

"He isn't my Dad," Charlie replied firmly.

They settled on Pa. It was a half-comic, dated word, no longer much used in the twentieth century. Still, it was better than nothing.

Herbert never had any authority over Charlie. He scarcely tried to assert it—this at least avoided clashes. Instead of giving orders, he made suggestions to the boy: "I think you ought . . ."; or more often: "Your Mum and I think you ought . . ." Charlie generally did what he was asked, but as a concession that did not infringe his essential freedom. He did not want to humiliate Herbert by defying him and thus embarrass Dora. This seemed absurd, when he was still a small boy and Herbert a grown man; but Dora could not help seeing it.

The outings and presents gradually became less frequent. Partly this was because the money was no longer there when the children—especially Vi—needed more spent on their clothes. Partly it was because they were beginning to lead their own lives. Offered a family picnic, Charlie would answer that he was going out with Tommy.

With his friends, Charlie tried not to talk about his official Pa. He disliked having to admit to the kind of work that Herbert did; he didn't understand what a man did in an insurance office, and didn't care to. He thought of Herbert as a person who had come to live at number five, but who hadn't thereby become one of the family. If his Mum wanted another husband, that was reasonable; but it did not commit him, Charlie. More unchangeable than any hatred was his calm, detached indifference.

When there were conflicts—as there had to be, despite the wariness on both sides—they were left unresolved or ended in compromise. At the age of ten, Charlie got into a fight with a boy from the next street. This boy had stolen a chestnut which Charlie had left in his coat pocket in the school cloakroom. At all events, Tommy reported that the boy had been seen with it; it was a champion conker, unmistakable. Charlie waited near the boy's house through four dark winter afternoons, cornered him at last, and fought him. They were about the same size and both tough and determined. In the end, Charlie got the other boy down and thumped his head on the pavement. Rescued by the lamp-lighter, he was taken to hospital and had to have four stitches.

The boy's mother complained. She was a widow, and this aroused Herbert's sympathy.

"I think you ought to go and tell Mrs. Dixon you're sorry," he said to Charlie.

"He pinched my conker."

"That's not the point. Where would we be if we settled everything by violence? You should have reported the theft to a master."

This notion showed such ignorance that Charlie didn't bother to answer.

"It wouldn't cost you anything to say you're sorry," Herbert almost pleaded.

"I'm not sorry."

After a few more useless efforts, Herbert said: "I intend to go round to Mrs. Dixon's and apologise on your behalf."

"I can't stop you," Charlie said. Each of them could interpret that as he chose.

Two more years brought Charlie within sight of his thirteenth birthday, the time of release from childhood. Despite the satisfactions of being a monitor, school in the final year seemed more pointless than ever. Charlie longed for the day when Mum would take his short trousers to be sold at the jumble sale and he would never see them again.

"I've been thinking, Charlie," Herbert said. "Your Head says you've made a lot of progress. If you worked hard this year, you could get a scholarship and go on to the Central School."

At first, Charlie was too astonished to take this in. He knew that there were boys being coached for scholarships, but they were a tiny group. He and his friends had nothing in common with them.

"What, stay at school?" he asked.

"I want the best for you, Charlie. Everybody ought to make use of an opportunity."

"You can leave when you're thirteen. It's the law."

"You *may* leave," Herbert said, attempting a smile. "You're not obliged to."

"I'm not staying."

"Think it over, please. That's all I ask. It's your whole future that you're deciding about. If you go to the Central School you can do anything —learn a skilled trade." Herbert didn't dare to say that you could qualify for an office job.

"I've got my place in the docks. If your Dad was a stevedore, they keep a place for you. Isn't that right, Mum?"

"Well, I believe they do," Dora said.

"There you are, then."

Herbert did not give up for several weeks. He made Charlie read the Central School prospectus; he gathered facts about local boys who had taken scholarships and assured Charlie that he was as clever as they were. He was defending his values; he felt that it was his supreme chance to leave an impression on the Wheelwright family.

For a time, Dora kept out of it. But one night, as they were undressing for bed, she said suddenly: "Why don't you leave Charlie alone? You know—about staying on at school. He's thought it over, like you said, and he's made his mind up. He's big enough to know what he wants."

"I'm trying to do the best for him, dear. That's only natural, isn't it?"

"What makes you so sure you know what's best? They pick and choose for stevedores, let me tell you. A stevedore's respected—round here, he is. Just because it's not good enough for you, doesn't mean we've all got to think the same."

Herbert was shaken. Dora seldom spoke so indignantly as this. Her Steadman Street accent —not that it had ever changed—was more pronounced than usual. After all these years of peaceful evasion, she was bringing into the open what divided them.

"I'm only giving him the choice," he said. But he knew that he was defeated.

She punched her way, puffing, into her night-dress and dropped her weight on to the bed. Soon she was asleep. He lay awake beside her until the clock had struck twelve, nursing his injury. At last he thought: perhaps Vi would take a scholarship. That gave him some comfort.

# 7

THE war did not take Herbert Goodings by surprise. Those who were surprised, he considered, were people who couldn't see beyond their own personal concerns. Most people in Steadman Street were like that; one had to be fair and blame their limited education.

For years, he had watched the German menace grow. The Germans, under their blustering Kaiser, were challenging British command of the seas, British supremacy in Africa, British trade. When they invaded Belgium, the challenge was direct and he felt it aimed straight at himself. "We can't let them get away with this," he said.

Alf Harris prodded his dirty old pipe with a piece of wire and remarked: "Not asking us, are they?"

"The Belgians are asking for our help."

"Oh, are they?" Alf blew through the stem, shooting a gob of nicotine-juice on to the pavement. "Asking for our help, are they? The Belgians. What I'd like to know is, what have the Belgians ever done for us?"

"That isn't the point . . ."

"Oh, ain't it? What have the Belgians ever done for us? You tell me. Just one thing."

Two days later, Britain was at war. The Harris

family had gone to Southend for the Bank Holiday, coming back on a special excursion train after midnight. Herbert had thought it wiser to stay at home. Anything might happen, he told Dora, even a German landing on the coast.

"Well, we're in it and we've got to see it through," Alf said the next evening. "Warned them, didn't we? Can't have that sort of carry-on, marching into other people's countries."

He had quite forgotten the earlier conversation. Herbert saw in this a sign of the arousal of the English people—late, but not too late. And soon the Territorials were mustering and drilling. The Army was in action in Flanders, and reinforcements marched through the London streets to entrain for Dover. Young men queued at the recruiting stations. At Herbert's office, there were empty chairs within a week.

Resolution grew in him like a breathless hope. He had known something like this as a boy, reaching for scholarships to climb out of poverty, and again when the idea of marrying Dora had come to him. But then it had been a matter of his own ambition or his own happiness. Now he was laying claim to honour. Secretly, awake at night, he wondered whether he was worthy of it.

One Sunday afternoon, when he and Dora were alone in the house, he said to her: "I've got something to tell you. I'm joining up."

"You're what?" The phrase was not yet familiar. Besides, Dora was half asleep after eating a good dinner.

"Enlisting. In the Army."

She opened her eyes wide and examined him as though trying to pin down some extraordinary change.

"You're having me on," she said.

"There's a war. They need men."

"I know. But . . ."

She searched for a way of saying what was in her mind without hurting him. They needed men; they hadn't asked for Herbert.

"It's all right for young men," she tried.

"I'm only thirty-two. This is a big war—not like South Africa. They'll need hundreds of thousands. The children will be all right; they've got a good mother."

"Oh, I'd look after them," she said. He winced at how she took for granted that he was not needed.

"You haven't got the idea I was expecting you to do this, have you?" she asked.

"No. I expect it of myself. I've always said we'd have to fight the Germans."

"Have you?"

He had said it chiefly to other men, he supposed; that kind of talk did not involve women. He was almost sure that he'd said it to Dora too, but she didn't listen to him very hard.

"Why don't you wait and see how it goes?"

she suggested. "Nobody else is going, that I know of."

"Thousands are going, dear. Nobody you know personally, perhaps."

Nobody was going from Steadman Street, she was sure of that. But this was another thing she couldn't say. Men were not leaving the docks, the railways, the factories—the work that had to be carried on in war as in peace. Men were leaving the jobs that didn't matter much or that could be done by women; men who were easily spared.

"It's your own choice, Herbert," she said.

He ached for her to plead with him to stay, to say that she depended on him, even though he knew it could not be true. He told himself that his determination was not yet a reality for her.

But Dora understood more than he imagined. This war offered him, as nothing else in life had, a fulfilment. So he had to go. The contempt, and therefore the cruelty, would have been in holding him back.

Charlie was incredulous. "He don't mean it, Mum. You tell him you don't want him to go, and he'll forget about it."

"He does mean it. He's set on it," she said.

"Well, they won't take him. He'll fail his medical."

"There's nothing wrong with him," she retorted, almost indignantly.

Vi shed a flood of tears and begged Herbert

not to go. Dora grasped that this was all he needed to make his decision absolute. He was a hero now to someone. She did not grudge him that.

He passed the medical and received his instructions. He was to be trained at Aldershot; Dora went to Waterloo to see him off. The train was packed with volunteers, mostly younger than Herbert. Some of them had made it a celebration and were uproariously singing "Tipperary" and the chorus of "Rule Britannia". The platform was crowded with women—a few wives, some mothers, the great majority young lady-friends in their best dresses. Dora felt that she had blundered into a scene that was not meant for her.

Herbert kissed her gently and got into a crowded compartment. Other men elbowed him away from the window, so he was not there when the train moved and the waving began. The young ladies screamed "Bye . . . bye-bye . . . cheerio!" Then they sobbed briefly into their handkerchiefs and went away. Dora stayed for some time on the empty platform, lost in one of her daydreams. She was not sure what she felt, but she knew that it was at odds with the singing and the easy tears. Something here was big and serious. People, especially young people, didn't see that yet.

Twice, on Sundays, she went to see Herbert at Aldershot. She had trouble recognising him among all the soldiers at the station. He looked strange in his peaked cap, khaki tunic and puttees: strange and unlike himself, in the same way as men who dressed up on Sundays for the Salvation Army. As they walked along, he saluted officers and nodded to other soldiers in his unit. But he was not really one of them. He was pursuing an aim of his own, and wearing the necessary disguise.

The first time, Dora took Vi with her. Undoubtedly, Vi was a great help. She chattered gaily all day long, made Herbert explain to her how to tell a sergeant from a quartermaster and a gunner from an infantryman, and turned the day into something like one of their Sunday outings in earlier years. In the teashop where they had a midday meal, people smiled at her lively air and her pretty golden curls. At the end, she hugged Herbert and made him promise to take care of himself and write often, specially to her as well as to Mum. It was a pity she wasn't five years older, Dora thought. She would have been splendid as a young volunteer's sweetheart.

Nevertheless, Dora didn't take Vi the second time. She owed Herbert, ultimately, a leave-taking without pretences, when they would be aware of the course of their marriage: of a compact, an effort, and an achievement at least of respect and gratitude between each other. It was a rainy, blustery autumn day. They sat most of the afternoon, sharing a table with another couple, in a crowded social hall run by the

Garrison Mission. They did not talk much; silences stretched between banal questions and bits of news. Her understanding of why he was here was not a thing to be exposed in words. Yet she believed that, sitting through the dull day, they were closer together than they had ever been. A week later, he went to France.

She had not the least doubt that he was going to be killed. He was a clumsy man with his hands; he would never manage his rifle properly. He was without all the abilities that soldiers needed—the open-air cunning, the speed of reaction, the ruthlessness, the zest to strike first. As she thought of it, war was a drama in which the actors were allotted their parts. There were conquerors, there were survivors, and there were victims.

Herbert was killed in December. At the beginning, people had talked of the boys being home by Christmas, but Dora had never believed it. By now the war marked an epoch, was an altered framework of life; one said, recalling some happening: "That was before the war, of course." The telegrams of death were an established ritual, though this was the first to come to Steadman Street.

Dora was kept busy by Vi's grief. The girl shrieked when she was told, wept most of the next day, sobbed when any family custom or memory gave her the occasion, and collapsed dramatically when they sat down to Christmas dinner. This behaviour absolved the rest of the family from feeling any inadequacy in their own mourning.

Eventually, Charlie said: "Look, young Vi, this is getting on our nerves. You won't bring him back by crying. Why don't you get a grip on yourself and help Mum to carry on?"

"You never cared about Pa!" Vi sobbed.

Charlie didn't trouble to deny this. "You're a big girl now, so behave like it," he said curtly. She rushed upstairs. But after this, apart from significant silences and sighs when opportunity offered, she was her normal self.

It was then evident that the sad thing about this death was that it made so little difference. Herbert had never been the real head of the family. He had made few decisions, and indeed few demands. After his departure, things had gone on much as before; after his death, they went on likewise. Jack's photograph remained on the mantelpiece. Herbert, as a matter of fact, had never been photographed except in a family group.

"Sit in that chair, Charlie," Dora said one evening. "There it is. Somebody's got to use it."

As she looked back, she found it hard to believe that she had been married to Herbert for ten years—twice as long as to Jack. The five years had been an era in her life: her true womanhood, the time when all experience was charged with intense awareness. The ten years were merely a part of the quiet aftermath that was still continuing.

However, these years had changed her. She was far away from youth. She regarded life as an interested observer, concerned with what it would bring to others, not to her. This time, she was entirely ready to be a widow, to compensate for regret with detachment, taking things easy and pleasing herself in small matters. And she was grateful to Herbert for having at least helped to ease the change.

Charlie was now the man of the house. He had been at work for more than two years. When he left school, a letter from the Head describing him as honest and trustworthy secured him a job with the Post Office. In blue serge uniform and pillbox hat, he cruised happily through the streets on a bicycle, delivering telegrams. He didn't see this as real work—only as a pleasant way of spending his time until he was allowed to do a man's job. But it was a stride ahead from school.

To Dora, he seemed quite different from the day he got into long trousers. He had already been responsible; now, he was altogether in control of his life. She no longer had to get him out of the house on time in the mornings. He glanced at his watch (a school-leaving present from Herbert) and went off with the air of a man with serious duties. He came home directly after work or not, as he chose. If Dora asked where he had been, he replied: "With friends". She rarely asked and never objected. He had his free afternoon on a rotating basis, and she got into the habit of doing her big weekly shopping on that afternoon so that he could come with her and carry the heavy packages. By the time he was fourteen, he was taller than she was. She liked walking along the Barking Road with this young man—a new young man, a sort of handsome stranger. Girls gave him the glad eye, she noticed. "Saucy things—grow up too quick nowadays," she grumbled. But really she was pleased.

Charlie knew about girls. At the Board School, you could go to the toilets at the far end of the yard, climb the wall between the boys' and girls' sections, and watch when a girl took her knickers down. If she was the right sort of girl, you could jump down and have a bit of a lark. There was always a protest—"I think you're a horrid beast, Charlie Wheelwright"—but it was a convention. Later, when he was made a monitor, he gave up these games as being beneath his dignity. By then, however, there were girls who would meet him after school and go behind the bushes in the recreation ground. Usually the girl stipulated: "I've got to bring my friend." Charlie went with Tommy Whitmarsh. There was an obligatory phase of joking and giggling before the two girls could be separated. On the way home, the boys

exchanged reports: "She's got real big tits" . . .
"Her hair's ginger down there, I saw it."

When Charlie left school and got into long
trousers, he was able to go to the park with girls
who were older than he was. He found them in
fish-and-chip shops as he went round on his
cycle. Living farther away, they hadn't known
him in schoolboy shorts and, he gathered, didn't
realise he was only thirteen. Even so, they held
back from what he was eager to demand but
hadn't as yet the knack of demanding successfully. "You wait a bit, young Charlie, you've got
the rest of your life ahead of you." Or: "You
just behave!—we're not going steady, not yet we
aren't." One girl—the romantic sort, he decided
—moved his probing hand away gently and said:
"You don't love me, not really, do you?" He
declared that he did, but she wasn't convinced.
He had an inkling of something still beyond him,
something that was more than a game. But the
game, if he could get into it, was what came
next.

One day—it was in the summer of 1914, not
long before the war—he delivered a telegram to
a house that struck him as classy. It was no
larger than number five, but it had a front and
a back garden. The street, which was a dead
end, was as quiet as a churchyard when he
propped his cycle at the kerb and knocked at the
door.

He had to knock twice before a net curtain

111

was drawn aside and, a minute later, the door opened. The woman who appeared was wearing a nightdress and a loose gown, though it was half past ten. Charlie thought for a moment that she might be ill, but she didn't look it.

She ripped the telegram open, read it, and frowned. This didn't surprise him; telegrams, even then, were usually bad news. But she said, crossly rather than sadly: "Damn. He's not coming."

"Any answer?" Charlie asked.

She looked at him for the first time. She had grey-green eyes. She seemed to be questioning him, as if he could make up her mind for her.

"I'm not sure," she said. "Come in a minute."

He stepped into the narrow hallway. She reached out her arm—it passed close to him, bare as the sleeve rode up—and shut the door. Then she went into the front room, this time leaving the door open. He saw her read the wire again, then crumple it and throw it wide of a waste-paper basket.

"Well, he's not coming," she said again. "That leaves me all on my tod. What do I do about that, eh?"

"I don't know, miss," he said.

"What say? Come in here—I can't hear you."

He went in. The room was very nicely done up, with flower-patterned wallpaper.

"You don't have to send an answer," he said.

She laughed, as if this were really funny.

"I don't have to, do I? How right you are. And I don't believe I will. Serve him right, don't you think so?"

"I'll be going then, miss."

She gave him her questioning look again.

"Short visit," she said.

Charlie took off his pillbox hat and fidgeted with it. He couldn't help seeing the white skin above the lace of her nightdress, white and smooth like no skin he had ever seen before.

"I didn't mean to be rude," he said. "I needn't rush, not really."

"That's better. You're quite a bright young spark on your good days, I shouldn't be surprised."

He thought rapidly of stories he had heard, and never altogether believed, from other telegram boys. He might make an awful mistake. She could call the police, she could get him the sack. But if he was guessing right and he missed his chance, she would laugh at him. That would be worse.

He said hoarsely: "Nobody else in the house, is there?"

She smiled, as if he'd said the right thing at last. "Sweet, isn't he?" she said, to an invisible spectator or to herself. He couldn't imagine what to say next. But she went on: "Well, we'd better have a look round, hadn't we? Hold my hand, I'll be scared otherwise."

On the stairs, she was already kissing him.

113

The bedroom was at the back of the house. Sunlight slanted across the rumpled bed. He remembered that anyone could go off with his bike, but it was too late to worry about that now.

"Not with your clothes on, ducky," she said. Amazed, he found himself stark naked with a stark naked woman. Apparently the jokes about lifting the nightie didn't apply here. She pulled him down on to the bed. The sun was hot on his back; he had always imagined this in darkness. Soon they were both panting, dripping with sweat. He let himself go, sorry that it was over, but triumphant.

"What's your name, love?" she asked while he was getting dressed.

"Charlie Wheelwright."

"Not the only thing you do right, is it? My name's Reenie."

"How d'you do?" he said automatically, then had to join in her laughter. "Funny us . . . you know . . . without knowing each other's names, isn't it?"

"Well, first things first," she said. "How old are you, Charlie?"

"Fourteen."

"Go on!"

"Fourteen and a half, nearly."

"Must feed you on raw meat, I suppose."

"How old are you, Reenie?"

"Now, now—a gentleman never asks a lady's age. You are a gentleman, love, aren't you?"

The cycle was still there. Swaying dreamily in Plashet Road, Charlie missed a bus by inches; the driver yelled at him. That evening, it seemed astounding that no one at home could guess what had happened.

Out at work next day, it suddenly struck him that he had made no arrangements to see Reenie again. He mulled over this for a week. The man who had sent the wire didn't live at the house, surely. The best thing would be to go along and hope for the best. If the man was there, he could say that he had a wire to deliver and he'd knocked at the wrong door.

When he went, Reenie was alone; but she didn't take him upstairs again.

"I know what you're after, my lad," she said, kissing him cheerfully. "Nothing doing, though. I'm just about whacked—I'm going to sleep all day long. He's just left, if you want to know."

"Who is he?" Charlie asked.

"Ah, that'd be telling, wouldn't it? Mustn't have our Charlie-boy getting jealous."

"I love you, Reenie," he said on an impulse.

She patted his cheek. "You think you do."

"When can I come again?"

"Let's see. He's going to the races on Saturday. Yes, that'll be nice, Saturday in the afternoon."

Charlie was working on Saturday, but he swapped free afternoons with another boy. He presented himself in his going-out clothes; he disliked being a delivery-boy for Reenie. There was no rush this time, and they had a long talk. She told him that she was on the stage; he couldn't have been prouder if she'd been a duchess. He wanted to go and see her perform, but she was vague about what the show was. He watched and talked to her while she had a bath —the house had a bath with taps—carefully combed her long hair, plastered herself with a strong perfume, and put on a smart velvet dress. By the time she was ready to go out, he felt that he was practically living with her; this feeling, in its way, was as exciting as fucking her. He walked to the station with her, carrying a Gladstone bag which, she said, contained her stage costume.

He went again on his next free afternoon. They were resting in bed when there was a loud knock at the front door. Reenie jumped up.

"Christ! That's him! Thought he was at Newmarket. Get your things on, Charlie, quick!"

She pulled on her nightdress while he dressed. She could hardly keep from laughing; the Box and Cox routine was part of the fun of life for her. He dropped from the window-ledge with his boots still unlaced, and she threw his jacket after him with the collar and tie stuffed in the pockets. Climbing the garden fence, he was laughing too. This was a man's adventure, he thought. He would have loved to tell Tommy the story, but

116

he had made it a rule not to boast to anyone about Reenie.

The war began. Reenie said one day: "You can come whenever you're in the mood from now on, sweetie. He's gone and joined up."

"Has he? That's sudden."

"Must have been drunk, the silly bugger. Men are all the same—never think of anybody but themselves. Anyway, I've got nobody but my Charlie-boy now."

The next few weeks were splendid. Charlie went to the house every day for an hour or so. As a rule, Reenie made him a snack; he wanted to pay her what he saved from his ordinary lunches, but she laughed. All the same, she said once: "Good-hearted Reenie, that's me—dishing it out to a Post Office boy. This won't pay the rent, will it?"

Abruptly, Charlie was transferred to the sorting office. Men were short there because of the war; a troop of boys worked under two supervisors who were too old for the Army. All day, they hurled parcels on to rolling, clanking chutes. It was more like man's work than being a delivery-boy, and the pay was better. But he was kept indoors; by the time he was free, Reenie wasn't. Instead of free afternoons, he had only Sundays off. Then he had to make up an excuse to go out. If he had said that he had a girl, his mother would naturally have wanted to meet her, and he didn't visualise Reenie having tea at number five.

One rainy Sunday afternoon in October, he found the door of the house wide open and the furniture gone. A man in overalls was busy in the downstairs room. He had stripped off the wallpaper and was painting the walls a sombre brown.

"Isn't the lady here?" Charlie asked. He had never known Reenie's surname.

"Don't know about no lady, son. I took the house empty. Moving in as soon as I've done this bit of painting."

"She must have left an address."

"No must about it. Done a flit, if you ask me. The landlord sold off the furniture."

Charlie went home miserably through the rain. Dora was at Aldershot, seeing Herbert. "He'll be going to France soon, he thinks," she said when she came in. They were quiet and thoughtful during supper. Charlie felt that the world had become a harder, colder place.

When Herbert was killed, they had to take stock of the family situation. There was no insurance money—war was a calamity, not a normal risk —but the Pru sent Dora a gratuity with a letter of condolence. Under the Lloyd George scheme, she got a widow's pension. She could have gone to work; munition factories were advertising for women, no skill or experience required. But

118

Charlie wouldn't allow it. She was having a bit of trouble with varicose veins, and the doctor had told her to rest her feet as much as possible.

Vi had been entered for a scholarship. She hadn't been working much at school and stood very little chance in the exam; only Herbert had taken the idea seriously. When Charlie told her that she must contribute to the family earnings, she made a speech about Pa's wishes, then gave in with an air of tragic courage. She left school after Christmas and started at a laundry, ironing shirts. As a concession, part of her wages was used to send her to a dancing school one afternoon a week.

Adding it all up, money was tight but essential expenses could be met. The worry was that prices kept going up. Some people were doing nicely out of the war, no doubt of that.

No one in Steadman Street had money to spare. The docks were frantically busy for short spells when munition cargoes went off to France, but this did not make up for the drop in normal trade. German submarines were sinking a good many ships, so the import lines were using Liverpool and Bristol instead of London. Often the men waited for work all day, as in times of depression. They could no longer pass the time in a pub, because the Government had brought in a law to cut opening hours. The beer was weaker, too, although it cost more. Obviously, somebody was cashing in on this too.

By the time the war was a year old, there were quite a number of missing faces in the street. Some men joined up because they felt it was the right thing to do, some because their ordinary jobs disappeared, some because they got rude remarks from strangers—you couldn't wear a uniform to show that your work was essential. The youngsters generally went when they were eighteen. "We're lucky really," Maggie Harris said. Her Johnny was in France, but he wore glasses and was in a transport unit instead of in the trenches; her Stan had managed to get into the Navy. The rest of the Harris brood were girls, except for the youngest. She assured Dora that the war would be over before Charlie was old enough to join up. "Don't let him go, anyway," she said. "You've given quite enough, goodness knows."

Tommy Whitmarsh's big brother was at the front. He was wounded in a fruitless attack and lay for six hours in No Man's Land; then he was rescued, and the family went to see him at a hospital near Dover. He was nervous and irritable, and refused to talk about life in the trenches. "They won't send him back there, anyhow," his father said. But they did.

Death was no longer something you read about in the newspapers. All the women came to their doors when a telegram boy appeared in the street. When he got off his bicycle and knocked, the women gathered like mourners at a funeral.

Sometimes it was only "wounded". Sometimes it was "missing", and that was the cruellest. Death had the steely comfort of finality. The slow process of recovery could begin.

Little Mrs. Mead was left a widow with two young children. Unexpectedly, she raged at her husband—"He didn't have no right to go!" Mrs. Lawrence at number four, married only a year and childless, bolted her door and didn't go out for a week; neighbours had to force a window and insist on giving her food. The strangest case was that of Mrs. Martin at number nineteen, who couldn't manage to grasp what the telegram said. Her son had emigrated in 1912, and she had no idea that he was in the Army. All the same, he was dead.

Dora, twice a widow, had a kind of seniority among the bereaved. Solid and patient, she sat with them for hours, made endless pots of tea, put children to bed, disposed of dead men's clothes. "Can't afford to go to pieces," other women said. "Look at Mrs. Goodings— wonderful, she is."

The war went on. Vast offensives were launched, and the battles lasted for weeks or months. Terrible stories went round: companies wiped out without a survivor, men drowned in mud, half-trained recruits killed on their first day in the trenches. The front was a raging beast, greedy for more victims. Conscription came in, so there was no escape. Mothers stared at their growing boys, bitter at their good health.

Things were worse at home too. Everything was rationed or in short supply. The Sunday roasts of peacetime were only a memory. Grumbling at harassed shopkeepers, women had to accept lumps of fat and gristle, sausages that tasted of bread, bread that tasted of heaven knows what.

Then came the bombing. You were aware of the Zeppelins, lumbering monsters in the sky; sometimes you could see one through a break in the clouds. Posters advised people to take shelter, but no one in Steadman Street had a basement. Some people slept in their clothes and ran into the street when they heard a crash; others maintained that this was the most dangerous thing to do. The bombs fell at random, often harmlessly—once, to the general amusement, on a cemetery. The target was presumably the docks, but it was the streets like Steadman Street that suffered. A house opposite the Board School was left a mere shell, like the pictures of French houses in the war zone. People went to stare at it, as if they needed convincing that such a thing could happen here in London. The bomb had killed a soldier's wife; eventually, her husband came home from the front safely.

"They could stop the war if they wanted to," Alf Harris said. "But the longer it goes on, the more profits these munitions firms make. That's what they don't tell you."

Probably he was right, Dora thought. But there was nothing to be done about it.

# 8

WHEN Charlie went to the Army, he felt that he had crossed a frontier. Every week he got two letters, one from his mother and one from a girl who was sweet on him. He read them quickly, as a man living abroad might scan a local newspaper from home. When he made the effort to write back, he could think of nothing to say, for any description of how he was living demanded an overwhelming load of interpretation. He wrote that he was keeping well, and left it at that.

Just for a start, being away from London was extraordinary. As he tramped along on route marches, he was astonished by the distances without shops or pubs: the silence, the emptiness, the sheer waste of space. It was winter. Clouds, clinging to sodden hills, brought the sky low. The days were brief between morning and afternoon darkness, a darkness so vast and total that Charlie sometimes stared at it as he might have stared at the sea. He had only a vague idea where he was. It didn't matter much, since he would soon be in France.

The significant fact was that he was in Armyland. It was a country with its own laws, its own customs, its own system of rights and duties, its own classes of the powerful and the powerless, and indeed its own population. In Armyland, everyone was a soldier. The khaki uniform was a general human attribute, like a face and hair. People lacking this attribute, who in London would have been simply people, were assigned here to a special category: civvies. You might not set eyes on a civvy for a week or more. When you saw one, his way of standing and walking looked peculiar; you wondered what he was doing here, as you might wonder about a foreigner. Above all, Armyland was a country of men. In London, Charlie had talked with women and met the eyes of women every day. It was an enjoyable side of life, even exciting sometimes, but it had never seemed extraordinary. In Armyland, like everyone else, he whooped and yelled if a woman was sighted at a hundred yards' distance.

Entering Armyland was beginning again, like leaving school and starting work. The war had lasted so long that, like the motionless front line, it had acquired the stability of an institution. The sergeants and instructors, who had been recruits of Charlie's age when the war began, had rasping voices, sternly set jaws, and faces hardened by incommunicable memories. Armyland had its own kind of security and its own dangers. You could be made to toil to utter weariness, but you couldn't be sacked or underpaid. You could be confined to barracks for failing to salute an officer; you couldn't be evicted for failing to pay the rent. A man's task, in Armyland, was not to make a living. It was to stay alive and to kill. The penalty for failure was not poverty or unemployment, but simply death.

In the outside world, you had a girl. In Armyland, you had a mate; it wasn't the same thing, of course, but it wasn't a pale substitute either. A hard, wary selfishness was the code and creed of Army life. Charlie did not defy this code, but he needed—as most men needed—relief from it, and the relief was in a secure and trusting friendship. You didn't open yourself entirely to your mate, admitting all your weaknesses, any more than you had to a girl. But you were linked to him as you were linked to no one else in the khaki mass.

The camp had a gymnasium with a boxing ring. In London, you belonged to the boxing crowd or you did not; youngsters who took it up were mostly hoping to become professionals. Here, everyone had a go. Charlie, from the start, went into boxing with an intense and driving joy. As he saw it, the gloves were a superb invention. He had been in fights, of course, from childhood on. There was always blood; skin and flesh were sliced away, and the cuts took weeks to heal. If you were fighting someone who would not be a permanent enemy, you had to be careful not to hit too hard. Anyway, a smash on the jaw damaged your own knuckles. But with the gloves you could hit hard, and take blows too, and nothing remained but soft bruises. Besides, the fight had no cause—it was a sport. You struck fiercely, but without anger. The fight led to no resentments; for Charlie, indeed, it led to a friendship.

There was a boxing tournament for each draft of conscripts. The instructor, a retired pro, backed Charlie to win. It had taken only a few lessons for Charlie to pick up this instructor's style: wary circling, swift attack, then a hail of short, savage jabs from the clinch. There was one other strong contender, a man in Charlie's own company. Pete Simmons was taller than Charlie, with arms like sledge-hammers. He relied on his long reach and heavy punch, on measured single blows. Through constant sparring, each man got to know the other's strength and weakness. Sometimes Charlie had Pete bewildered and groping; sometimes Pete had Charlie dizzy from a hammer-blow. Then they watched each other as both fought through the tournament. In the final, they slugged through all the rounds to mutual exhaustion; Charlie won on points.

This was on a Saturday afternoon. They were under orders for the Monday—for the front, no doubt. On Saturday night, the company celebrated the end of training with crates of beer in the barrack-hut. Charlie took off his boots and lounged on his bed. He was bruised and aching; his head—what between Pete's punches and the beer—was a burden that needed pillows for support. Dreamily, but with complete certainty, he was aware of something achieved that mattered far more than winning the tournament. Through the physical striving, the slamming and battering, he and Pete had been drawn together as they could never have been drawn merely by words. A knowledge of the body remained with him: knowledge of Pete's broad chest, the bristling red-brown hairs on Pete's arms, Pete's panting breath, Pete's sweat. This hard, tense, fighting body was not at all like the loving body of a woman; but the knowledge, the intimacy, was of the same order.

On the Sunday, when church parade was over and the weekly spell of freedom began, Charlie said to Pete: "Coming into town?"

There was nothing to do in the dull little town. All the shops were shut, the civvies withdrew to their homes, the girls were one to a thousand soldiers. Damp and shivering, the men wandered about the streets all the long hours until the pubs opened. But they always went. The word "town", the existence of streets and houses, made a negative relief from the barracks. At least you could kick a stone along the pavement, light up a cigarette, push your hands into your pockets—unless you were spotted by a redcap.

"Can't go," Pete said. "I'm on jankers."

Confined to barracks. Charlie whistled at the meanness of it, when they were leaving for France next day.

"Bloody twit," he said, meaning their officer.

Pete said: "Think they're little tin gods, they do."

It never took long for recruits to grasp the basic antagonism of Armyland. The official enemy, the German Army, was an impersonal concept; officers were visible, inflicting stupid orders and vicious punishments, clear targets for hatred. A junior officer deserved, together with hatred, contempt. He might be a year older than Charlie and Pete, but they saw him as a schoolboy, retarded by the cosseting of the upper classes. He hadn't worked, hadn't earned for his family, hadn't grown from child to man in a street like Steadman Street.

"I won't go, then," Charlie said.

"Not go into town? Go on—it's not your fault I'm on jankers."

"No, I don't care. Nothing to do there, anyhow."

They both knew that this was not the point. It was their last free day, their last memory of walking and not marching, going and not being sent. Not to go was a sacrifice, and an affirmation of friendship.

There was no one else in the hut. They found some potatoes at the back door of the cookhouse; taking what you wanted, and scoring a silent triumph over authority, was an Armyland custom. Sliced with a bayonet and laid on the hot lid of the stove, chips sizzled to a rich brown. Mouth and throat were scorched in swallowing —a quick, vivid pleasure. For a long time, they did not talk.

Out of silence—the most precious rarity of Armyland—Pete asked: "You got a girl, Charlie?"

"Yes, I've got a girl," Charlie said. "You?"

"Did have. I packed it in, my last day at home."

"What for?"

"Don't know, quite. Nothing wrong with the girl—nice little bit. I had a feeling . . ." Searching for words to express this feeling, making an unaccustomed use of friendship, Pete stared at the cold white sky beyond the dirty window.

"Pretty grim at the front, must be."

"Expect it is," Charlie agreed.

"Well, then. What I mean is, I had a feeling I might manage better without being tied to nobody. Without nobody to care about. Think that's silly?"

Charlie considered. "No, not silly. Don't know if it's going to help, though. We'll just have to see."

They were silent again. The front, like hell for a devout Christian, was at the same time a reality and a mystery. You couldn't know in advance what it was like to be in continual danger; you couldn't know what it was like to have a bullet in the guts, to be blinded, to be gassed. The only certainty was that, by means of the ordeal, you would discover something about yourself, something that in ordinary life could remain safely unexplored. Meanwhile you could admit to anxiety, as Charlie and Pete admitted to it in the silences of this last English day. That was of value. √

So they came to the trenches. There, things were as bad as they had expected: the constant moaning noise of enemy shells, the horror and confusion of a hit, the lonely peril of patrols at night in No Man's Land. What Charlie had not altogether reckoned with was the nastiness of living in mud. Nothing here was alive and growing—no grass, no flowers, no trees. Nothing, either, was made and firmly shaped as things were—brick walls, doorsteps, paving-stones—in Charlie's world. There was only the oozing mud, always cunningly trying to spread unless it was held back. When a trench wall shuddered and collapsed under a direct hit, Charlie had a wordless insight into the ultimate threat of the war. Worse than destruction, it was to drag the world back into chaos.

Still, in the desolation of the battlefield a trench was a refuge. The sandbags and the barbed wire kept out the reaching claws of death. And the deep trench itself, with its corners and junctions, its hollowed-out storage places, and its steps up to the lookout point, had an air of being established and improved through the four years of war. It was almost a home. Men had lived there before Charlie came, so it seemed reasonable to go on living there.

In this refuge, they waited for the order to attack. The big push was bound to come when the spring rains ended, or when enough young men had reached the age of permissible death, or simply when the generals got bored and restless and forgot their last failure. Charlie's mind, like everyone else's, was dominated by the thought of the big push. He was afraid, certainly; one would have to be an idiot not to be afraid. Yet he also wanted it to begin. When he peeped over the parapet of the trench, a wild urge took hold of him, like the urge to jump when one looks down from a height. He understood how men ran into enemy machine-gun fire, and knew that he would run when the moment came. Since he was here, so far already from normal life, he felt a need to enter totally into this experience called war.

But it was the Germans who attacked. Everything Charlie had expected, everything he had been trained for, happened in reverse. He stood in his trench, loading and firing like a machine, while Germans charged toward him. They dropped into pits of mud, they vanished in shell-bursts; but there were always more of them and they kept coming on. They threw grenades, they jumped into trenches, they stabbed from above with their bayonets. The dash and fury of the attack belonged to them.

The front was broken for the first time since 1914. Every day, the British troops were told that they must hold on at all costs. Every night, they were ordered to withdraw. They marched in pitch darkness, stumbling through mud, plunging into old trenches and fresh shell-holes, dropping flat when the pursuing guns found them. They were loaded with full packs, blankets, ammunition belts, entrenching tools, the whole equipment of front-line life; anything left behind was given to the enemy. As soon as they halted, they had to dig new trenches. In the grey chill of dawn, they stood to attention while a sergeant called the roll. There were always bleak silences; when a name had been called twice and there was no answer, the sergeant moved on. Reinforcements arrived, though never enough to make up for the casualties. The new men were received grudgingly, set apart by their innocence of what had been endured. Some of them died before they had succeeded in making friends.

Step by step, like a boxer forced into his corner, the army retreated. After the first week, the battle was no longer in the muddy desert of war, but in a countryside where ruin was fresh. Farms and villages, set on fire by shells, burned slowly, dirty smoke puffing through rain. Dead cows and horses lay stinking in the fields, their rigid legs upright as stakes. The trees, uprooted and maimed, were still green. Sometimes, by a roadside, the litter of war mingled with things abandoned by refugees: a push-cart with a broken wheel, a cycle, a child's pram. In a chance moment of quiet, a lost dog could be heard howling. The war, like a deadly plague, was spreading its infection across the land.

Fight, march, dig, fight, march, dig, fight, march . . . There was never any rest and never any safety. If they were not in action, then they were under shell-fire. They slept when they could, taking turns, never more than a few hours at a time: slept lying out in the rain, sitting with heads bowed forward, standing and leaning against a trench-wall. They were almost asleep as they marched; now and again one man lurched against another. Utter weariness made danger more acute. As he closed his eyes, a man's last thought was that the enemy was massing for another attack or moving to surround the position. Sometimes men woke, shouting, from nightmares; sometimes they grabbed their rifles and fired without aiming.

No one joked any more. No one sang or whistled on the march. Brief, furious quarrels over small matters flared up, spluttered like damp matches, and faded into the mist of weariness. Each man withdrew into his private effort of survival. For long grim hours, no one even spoke except to assert a grievance.

And everyone had a grievance. One man had done extra sentry duty; another had carried the heavy mortar longer than his fair turn; another had lost his fags and cogitated darkly on who could have stolen them. Such grievances divided the battalion into sour distrustful fragments, but as a unit it had grievances too. If the rations were late, which they usually were, it meant that the Service Corps men were scoffing the food. The ambulance men were too cowardly to come up and help the wounded. The battalion should have been pulled back for a rest and replaced in the battle zone, but it had been forgotten. The officers, of course, didn't know what they were doing.

Once, after marching half the night and digging all morning, Charlie's company was just about to get its rations when the order was given to move again. The digging, as often happened, had been for nothing. The sergeants went along the line, shouting the Armyland phrases that sounded formidable in barracks and hollow in this chilly emptiness: "On your feet! . . . Wakey-wakey! . . . Look lively now!"

"When do we eat, sarge?" someone called.

"When we halt again," the sergeant answered. "Can't eat on the march, can you?"

"What's the rush, anyway?" asked another man.

"Jerry's advancing on our flanks. Want to get cut off, do you?"

It was the usual story. The battalion was always being left in the lurch by its flanking units; this grievance was the bitterest of all. But then, it might not be true. Those who gave the orders had no idea what was going on.

For a few minutes, no one moved. Each man waited for someone else to shoulder his rifle or strap on his pack. And each shared the thought: what if they did not march? What if they insisted on eating and sleeping? Unspoken, this thought was nevertheless as clear as though written on the sky. The sergeants shouted louder, with an edge of fury. The officers stood with assumed detachment, tapping their sticks on their boots —but they knew. In these few minutes, the men regained their earlier selves and escaped from the war. Then some enemy shells whined overhead, and they marched.

Through these terrible days, Charlie thought of home far more often than he had during his Army training or in the trenches. It seemed to him that, in his eighteen years, he had known the best and the worst of life, and that there was a direct link between them; that, if he could endure the worst, he would deserve the best. He thought of his girl, and was glad that she had promised to think of him. She was quite an ordinary girl—simply the girl he'd been going out with when he was called up, and probably of no

136

lasting importance to him—but now she seemed infinitely beautiful and desirable. He thought also of Reenie; he had thought of her from time to time over the last four years, and knew that he would never entirely forget her. Under shellfire, in drenching rain, as he crouched aching on the sodden earth, everything about Reenie came back to him with a feeling of pure delight: the sunlight across the bed, the cleanliness of the white sheets, soap gleaming on her smooth thighs in the bath. All these, now that he understood their value, were more intensely felt in memory than at the time.

Yet, in the end, he was sustained by his responsibilities more than by his desires. Beyond being a soldier, he was a man. It was impossible for number five, as a household, to keep going without a man's earnings. The girls needed him, whether they knew it or not, especially silly little Vi. Above all, his mother needed him. She had lost two men; she must not lose another. It was not even a question of love, but of justice.

Besides, he had an immediate responsibility. Pete was in the depths. Since the beginning of the retreat, he had been obsessed by his grievance. The platoon machine-gunner had been killed, and the officer had ordered Pete to stay with the machine-gun while the rest of the men withdrew to a new position. Since Pete had not been trained to use a machine-gun or to mend it if it jammed, he was put in extreme danger. It was sheer good luck that the Germans, that time, stayed out of touch until the withdrawal was completed. Pete believed that the officer, who had never liked him, had picked on him as a sacrifice. Perhaps so, Charlie thought, perhaps not. The officer had to choose somebody: Simmons, Wheelwright—they were all men whose lives were remote from his. At all events, Pete no longer thought of anything else. He didn't talk even to Charlie, who had been his mate; and Charlie was wary of trying to rouse him with a joke or a probing question, for there was a risk that he would snap back angrily and the friendship would be broken. What worried Charlie most was that Pete didn't sleep, or scarcely slept, in the rare hours when it was possible. His eyes remained fixed and open, not even blinking. Nor, Charlie could guess, did Pete's mind find rest in imagining his home, his girl, the rewards of survival. His detachment was a terrible mistake, after all. What he stared at, endlessly, was the approach of death. This death appeared to him as the outcome of a monstrously unjust conspiracy in which the Germans, the politicians who had made the war, the generals and the platoon officer were joined. And since the conspiracy was directed individually at Pete, and these forces were immensely stronger than he was, death was coming implacably closer and closer.

Charlie knew—one learned fast in war—that

Pete was in a danger beyond the common danger: the danger of destroying himself. To survive, one needed hope. One needed the belief that the means of survival were within one's command. And one needed common sense, which was a close and vigilant contact with reality. If a man yielded to exhaustion or despair, it was this contact with reality that he lost. That was why men shot at shadows, or fired too soon and used up their ammunition, or stood up instead of taking cover. There was no knowing, Charlie thought, what Pete might do soon.

The retreat brought the company, one misty dawn, to a broad open ridge crossed by a cobble-stone road. They dug in at right angles to the road, getting down to a good depth in the soft black soil. But there was, close to the road, an undamaged building which in peacetime had been a toll-booth for the next little town. It was a solid brick structure, about twelve feet high, with windows all round; when the mist cleared, it would make a good observation point. The officer ordered six men to hold it. Charlie and Pete were among them.

After the mist, it was a fine day—the first break in a long spell of rain. Under the high, pale blue sky, the huge fields of France reached to calm horizons. The fresh spring air sharpened the importance of living.

There was no sign of the enemy, no hint of an attack. But, midway through the morning, shelling began. Now the mist had gone, it could be seen that the toll-booth was at the precise top of the ridge. It was a perfect observation point, yes. It was also a perfect aiming-mark.

A shell burst behind the building. Then another burst in front of it, but closer; pebbles spattered the windows.

"They're ranging on us," Charlie said.

As shelling went, it was not intense. Most of the company, entrenched in the field, were as safe as they had been for days. But the brick building, perched on its ridge, was bound to get a direct hit. The only question was whether this would happen before the officer realised it and ordered the men out.

Pete said something. Charlie couldn't hear it, because at that moment another shell exploded and he could only see the silent movement of Pete's lips, as in a film. Then—quietly and with a deliberation that was set apart from reality— Pete put his rifle down on the floor, opened the door of the building, and went out.

Charlie and the other men stared after him. He walked along the road, away from the front line. He walked—he did not run—with his shoulders hunched and both hands in his pockets, as if he was going down a London street after finishing work, as if by going through a door he had gone out of the war. A shell landed near him and he walked on, utterly indifferent.

But he could not go far—Charlie knew that.

Armyland began just down the hill: the battalion headquarters, the guns, the sappers, the redcaps. Men who left the front line had no chance, less chance than by staying there. They were seized, court-martialled, judged and condemned by officers who did not want to understand what they had been through. They were sent to be broken in the glasshouse; now, in the nervous crisis of the retreat, they were likely to be shot.

Charlie went running down the road. He didn't know what to say, so he simply grasped Pete by the arm. Pete wrenched free without even looking round, as if he had been caught in some entanglement. He was out of touch, right out of touch. And Charlie suddenly realised that there was only one way to regain the intimacy through which their friendship had been expressed. He clenched his fists and hit Pete twice, with the boxer's swift rhythm: right to the jaw, left to the ear.

Pete struck back wildly, with no kind of thought or skill. Charlie parried easily. Pete tried to sidestep and press on down the road, but Charlie halted him with a warning, awakening blow. Pete put up his guard, looking with surprise at his own fists, remembering, recognising. By degrees, he got into the boxing stance and so into the reach of reality.

They faced each other on the roadway, moving clumsily in their heavy boots, boxing while the shells burst in the fields. After a minute, Charlie

141

landed a punch hard on Pete's nose. Pete rocked back. As Charlie waited, he touched his nose and stared at the blood on his fingers. Then he said in a low, wondering voice: "Charlie? . . . What's all this, Charlie?"

"Come along now, Pete boy," Charlie said.

The next day, the battalion was relieved and ordered back to a rest area. Before it returned to the front, the German advance had been checked. Grimly, wearily, the war began to heave itself over toward victory.

# 9

AT the age of sixteen, Vi Wheelwright took a dislike to sleeping in the same room as her brother. She slept lightly, and Charlie made a lot of noise. She always woke up when he came in late, though Liza never stirred. If he had been drinking he fell asleep at once, lying on his back, and snored; she was kept awake for hours, disgusted and yet riveted by the ugly noise. What a disaster, she thought, to marry a man who snored and have to listen to it all your life! You couldn't tell beforehand, presumably. She had some confidence that she herself wouldn't marry that kind of man. She would make sure not to marry a man who drank, that was definite. Yet the snoring, together with the creak of the springs when Charlie turned over, signified for her something gross and clumsy about men in general, something that she didn't think she could ever be at ease with.

To Vi, men were mysterious. Of course she knew, as one said, all about it; it was the nature of men that was the mystery. They kept pursuing her, and she knew that this wasn't only because she was pretty. She had a vulnerable quality; it was fun to tease her. She was pursued in the school playground, she was pursued in the streets, and when she went to work at the laundry the van-drivers waited for her every afternoon. She couldn't understand why it was such a triumph for a man to squeeze her bottom or wipe a smudged kiss across her face. She couldn't understand this hungry seizing and grabbing: this need that was so imperious, yet apparently so casual.

Some of the other girls at the laundry, she thought, were terribly coarse. They soon found that they could make her blush with jokes about the men's underwear and the sheets, and they were a worse trial than the van-drivers. They also found out that she slept in the same room as her brother. They had seen Charlie round the neighbourhood; they asked her how big he was, and shrieked wildly when she kept a straight face and said "Five foot ten". This kind of talk made her think about Charlie differently. She could imagine what he'd been doing, apart from drinking, when he came in late. She watched him, peeping from her pillow; he sat on the bed with a contented smile on his face and felt himself under his drawers. Then came the heavy thump as he lay down to sleep, and a minute later the crude, selfish, indifferent snoring. That was what a man was like, Vi thought, after he'd been doing it. And the fact that she was lying close to a man who had been doing it, although he was her brother, made her feel contaminated, endangered. She lay tense, breathless, her hands clenched and her body hot even in winter; she slept worse than ever.

So she asked to sleep in the front room with her mother. "Charlie snores," she explained.

Dora saw that there was more to it than this. Girls got shy at a certain age, she knew, though she couldn't remember going through such a phase herself. Vi had always been a funny sort of girl. But she didn't think it right to give in to all Vi's whims. "Charlie's going into the Army soon," she said.

Guiltily—Charlie would be in danger, after all —Vi could hardly wait for him to go. When the time came, the back room belonged to the girls. And now Vi suddenly wanted to change the look of it. Nothing had ever been done to the house; the wallpaper, the lino and the mats were the same that Jack and Dora had bought eighteen years ago. The lino had been replaced on the stairs and in the kitchen, where it was worn to bits, and that was all. With her own earnings, Vi bought some material with a pretty pattern of roses and made new curtains for the back room. She also bought a mirror and a bedside table; they were second-hand, of course, but they looked very nice with a bit of paint. Dora was astonished by this burst of activity. Liza wasn't much involved; she was still the quiet one, falling in with other people's decisions, though she had left school now and was working in a shop.

"Those curtains do brighten the room up," Dora admitted.

"It needs new wallpaper really," Vi said. "The whole house does. We've never had anything new, have we, Mum?"

"We're not going to, neither, at these wartime prices," Dora told her. "And you'd better mind what you do to this room, anyhow. Charlie's going to come back some time."

Vi tried to put this out of her mind, at least so far as the room was concerned. It was a girls' room, and in her heart of hearts she thought of it as her own. It would be lovely to be quite alone, she felt, to have her private place where no one could intrude. She often went up to the room while Liza, who was fond of cooking, helped to make supper. On winter evenings, she drew her new curtains and put out the lamp, leaving only the warm, friendly and secretive light of the fire. She bolted the door, very quietly because Dora would have laughed at her. Then, slowly, handling everything with care and gentleness, she took off all her clothes. On tiptoe, with one leg extended as she had been taught at the dancing class, she stood in front of the mirror. Motionless, scarcely breathing, she gazed at her firm pointed breasts, her slender waist, her graceful legs. Her body, newly revealed, seemed to her strange—as if she had just acquired it. If it was beautiful, that was her secret. She smiled as she thought of the van-drivers who would never be allowed to see it.

In these early months of 1918, Vi's life changed greatly for the better. Mrs. Finlay, the supervisor at the laundry, was going into business for herself. A small, ladylike person, Mrs. Finlay had been forced out to work by her husband's early death and a bad investment. Vi was not sure what this meant, but understood it to be unfortunate rather than blameworthy. Now, after twenty years as an employee, she was set free by a legacy—not enough to live on, but enough to provide the premises and equipment for a small private laundry. She would need two girls for what she called the fine work, and Vi had always been one of her favourites. Vi was neat, she was conscientious, and she was clearly a cut above the sluts of the laundry, of whom Mrs. Finlay had always been afraid despite her nominal authority. True, Vi lived in Steadman Street and was a stevedore's daughter. But Mrs. Finlay ascertained that her stepfather had worked for the Pru, which accounted for her nice manners. As Mrs. Finlay was a fervent patriot, the fact that this stepfather had died for King and country clinched the matter. The other girl, called Fanny, was not ideal, but Mrs. Finlay was giving her a chance.

The new laundry was in Ilford. It was a quiet district—"quiet" was an emphatic term of praise in Mrs. Finlay's vocabulary—not fashionable, but inhabited by a good class of people. Quite a lot of new streets had been laid out in the prosperous years before the war, and faster expansion was certain once the war was over. Mrs. Finlay had it all worked out; she had been waiting for her legacy for at least ten years, and confidently expecting the end of the war every year since 1914.

The washing and steam-pressing were done on the ground floor of the laundry, which had been a shop. On the first floor, Vi and Fanny worked and Mrs. Finlay had her office. She lived on the top floor. She decided at the outset not to advertise, but to build up custom steadily by leaving cards and then by personal recommendation. Since there was a shortage of laundries in Ilford —another point on which she had informed herself—this policy succeeded.

Vi was paid less than in her old job; Mrs. Finlay explained that they were partners, in a sense, and they had to work toward a balance that would make higher wages possible. However, the atmosphere at work was cosy and informal. Vi and Fanny broke off to eat their sandwiches when it was convenient, not when a hooter sounded, and it was always a pleasant surprise when Mrs. Finlay appeared with tea and biscuits. If there was a rush and they stayed late, Mrs. Finlay gave them supper in her tastefully furnished parlour. Things were more disciplined for the women who did the washing; there was a strict rule that they did not come upstairs. This emphasised for Vi that, at the age of just seventeen, she was out of the anonymous mass of unskilled labour. She told Mrs. Finlay how she had wanted to stay on at school and how, after Herbert's death, it had been impossible. Mrs. Finlay was touched, and assured her that it might all turn out for the best.

She even enjoyed the journey to work. She was going away from the docks and factories, so the bus was never crowded. She sat on top unless it was raining, and enjoyed the fresher air as the bus went gradually uphill. The broader streets, the trees on the pavements, the children in the smart uniforms of private schools—all told her of another London, to which she now belonged through the day. The journey home was less pleasant, for she was leaving that cleaner and calmer London behind. There was also the risk, when she went home late, that a man would sit next to her and make himself a nuisance.

Mrs. Finlay's laundry dealt in quality work. "Special Care with Fine Fabrics," read the cards. There were no bulk orders of shopgirls' smocks or working aprons, such as the big laundry handled. Almost every day, Vi was ironing a lace blouse, a frilly petticoat, or long white gloves. She tried to picture the ladies who wore these things; occasionally they called to collect their parcels, but mostly they sent their servants. On the whole, she enjoyed starching evening-dress shirts most of all. They suggested to her an atmosphere of dinners under great chandeliers, West End clubs, billiard-rooms, cigars—a strange, splendid, dangerous masculine world. She was fascinated to discover that some men wore silk underwear. Once she fell into a daydream, vague and yet alluring, as she gently stroked the soft richness of a pair of silk trunks. Fanny said: "Put a note inside, why don't you? Say: I'm free Saturday night if you are." Vi blushed and quickly folded the trunks.

Even with a brother at the front, she did not often think about the war. It had meant a great deal to her in the early days: glory, heroism, sacrifice. But in those days the men who fought and fell were volunteers; now that good men and bad went without individual choice, the glory had departed. So Vi had come to see the war much as Dora saw it: as a cruel and ugly slaughter, and—so far as women were concerned —a drab business of queues and shortages. In her memory, peacetime was the same as childhood, and she easily blotted out anything that had been unpleasant to recall a delightful world of big family dinners, toys and presents, happiness and freedom. She also remembered that in peacetime young men, or at least the right sort of young men, had dressed nicely. She disliked the baggy shapelessness of soldiers' uniform; anyway, she disliked the sameness. The soldiers whom she saw were on leave and were usually drunk, noisy and rude. They pursued her even more persistently than other men. They seemed to think she was bound to give them what they wanted just because they were soldiers. She suspected that half of them hadn't been at the front at all. Real brave men, real heroes, were courteous and respectful to women.

Mrs. Finlay often went to whist drives, church socials, fetes; it was important to her to show that she belonged to Ilford, and one never knew when one might pick up a customer. Vi was grateful when she was taken along, for the invitation proved that she was worthy of this other London; she noticed that Fanny wasn't asked. She was nervous, of course, but the nervousness itself was delicious. She replied briefly when she was spoken to, for she knew that her accent wasn't what it ought to be in these surroundings. When in doubt, she simply smiled. However, she was confident that she looked all right; the dancing class had taught her to stand and walk nicely. She didn't have the right clothes, but she was able to borrow a frock from the laundry and have it washed again—it was a little secret between Mrs. Finlay and her.

The big event of the season was a charity dance at the Town Hall in aid of blinded soldiers. Mrs. Finlay decided to go. There would be many ladies there, keeping an eye on their daughters but not dancing, and she would have the whole evening to get chatting with them.

Since she herself needed a similar reason to be at the dance, she invited Vi. Vi was breathlessly happy. She loved dancing, but she had been to very few dances—never to a big dance like this.

She wore a real evening dress for the first time in her life. It was white and simply cut; after considerable thought, she decided that it wouldn't be wise to go in for anything fussy. But it was of good, shimmering satin, and not cheap. She would be paying for it out of an advance on her wages for the next eight weeks. She had not hesitated over this; it seemed to her that the great occasion would be flawed if she wore a borrowed dress.

She dressed in Mrs. Finlay's bedroom and they went to the Town Hall in a taxi, another new experience. At the dance, everything was even more splendid than she had imagined: the vast room with its ornate ceiling almost out of sight, the flags and the bunting, the joyous thump or dreamy glide of the music, the booming voice of the MC as he announced the dances. She felt the familiar exciting tremors of nervousness, but she was determined not to be overwhelmed. Some of the other girls glanced at her enviously. They obviously came from posh homes and must have spent far more on their dresses than Vi, but she realised that she had been right to go for simplicity. Gaining confidence, she waited to be approached by a young man. And, though there was a surplus of girls and some of them had to dance with one another, she was never without a partner.

However, she had to admit that the young men were a disappointment. It was the wretched war, of course. Either they were very young— mere boys, younger than herself—or it was sadly obvious that some physical defect had kept them out of uniform. Some had flat feet, some peered at her through squinting eyes, and one poor chap was practically deaf, to judge by his attempts to follow the music. All these men danced badly; she tried to help them along, but it was no fun. So, after a time, she stopped bothering about who her partner was. She danced with half-closed eyes, aware only of the music and of the movement of her own body. Her partner was an ideal, a man of her imagination. She didn't try to visualise him, but contented herself with a vague notion of a firm and skilful guiding hand, of a commanding male figure reassuringly close but not too close. Every dance became a reverie.

She was bewildered, therefore, when the music ceased abruptly in the middle of a foxtrot. She was dazzled, too—literally dazzled, for she was looking into a spotlight. Her partner stopped dancing and moved away from her. She moved too. The spotlight followed her. She was standing in a circle of warm golden light.

The MC boomed: "So, ladies and gentlemen, we've found the Belle of the Ball."

Everyone clapped. They were clapping her.

This was amazing, and yet at the same time it was perfectly natural. She stood quite still, smiling.

"Come up here, please, Belle of the Ball," the MC called. She moved to the platform—not hurrying, aware of her graceful walk—and went up the steps.

"What's your name, my dear?" he asked. He had another voice which did not boom, but was deep and reassuring.

"Violet Wheelwright," she said.

"Violet Wheelwright," he announced. "And a very charming name too. Now I'm going to ask Miss Violet Wheelwright to pick the lucky number out of the bowl."

She did this, and succeeded in reading it out quite audibly. She presented the raffle prize—a silver statuette of a cavalry trooper—to a stout, simpering lady who tripped going up the platform steps. She accepted her own prize, a box of chocolates, and handed it to an attendant. All this she did with complete confidence, as if she were acting in a play for which, without knowing it, she was quite prepared.

"And now," said the MC, "my remaining duty is to save all you young men from being trampled in the rush to dance with the Belle of the Ball. The only way I can do that, obviously, is to dance with her myself. So—on with the dance!"

The band launched into a waltz. And this, at

last, was really dancing. The man, the real and solid man, held her properly and was unfailingly with her at every moment. He was much taller than her; she was looking, most of the time, at his beautifully stiff white shirt or at the carnation in his button-hole. When she glanced up, she saw that he was handsome in a true manly way —the sort of man that any girl would be glad to be seen with. He had blue eyes like her own, fair hair and moustache, and a rich complexion —not a coarse red like some men, but rich. She wasn't sure how old he was, but it was safe to say that he was in the prime of life. This phrase, which she had met in a novel borrowed from Mrs. Finlay, pleased her; it had an assured, mature resonance, like the MC's voice.

However, it didn't matter what the MC was like, since she was never likely to see him again. She was only glad he was handsome because this completed the experience—essentially, the experience of her own beauty and its recognition. All that remained of it tangibly was the box of chocolates. All through a lazy Sunday, she and her mother and Liza ate them until the last one was gone. The story of how Vi had been Belle of the Ball put Dora into a sentimental mood. "Ah, you wouldn't believe how the boys ran after me when I was your age," she told Vi.

Four days later, as Vi was waiting for the bus home after work, a motor-car stopped and the driver got out. She recognised the MC. It was curious to see him in daytime clothes and out of the role that he had so perfectly suited—like seeing a famous actor in the street.

"Miss Wheelwright, surely," he said.

And he offered her a lift in his car. He supplied it, rather, as her right—as if her waiting for the bus must be a joke. Afterwards, Vi suspected that he hadn't come along by pure chance; he could easily have discovered her connection with Mrs. Finlay and the laundry. But even if this was true, it never mattered.

She was only embarrassed about telling him that she lived in Canning Town. This problem melted away, for he suggested that they might go for a spin if she wasn't in a hurry. They drove out beyond the new villas and into open country on the road to Romford. Ultimately, she told him that she would be happy to be dropped where he had picked her up. And, through all the time she was to know him, Vi never let him come near Steadman Street. For that matter, she never knew where he lived either. They came together in an enchanted world, into which she stepped whenever she met him as she had stepped on to the platform as Belle of the Ball.

For inevitably—it seemed inevitable, and she certainly had not a moment's doubt—she agreed to meet him again. And again, and again: once or twice a week, through summer and autumn and winter.

His name was Howard Buckley. After he had

kissed her the first time, he asked her to call him Howard. She did, but for months afterward she slipped sometimes into addressing him as Mr. Buckley. She wanted to look up to him; she was happy to feel that he was, not exactly superior, but in every respect—age, social class, knowledge—senior to her. He called her Violet; no one had ever used her full name before, and it set him apart from all the people who called her Vi. But often, especially when they were holding hands or cuddling, he called her "girlie". She liked this very much.

Howard wasn't inquisitive, but she wanted to tell him all about herself. She explained that her father had died long ago; that she had been brought up by a stepfather, but he had been killed in 1914; and added, while she was about it, that her brother was at the front. Howard pressed her hand with emotion.

"You've given a tremendous lot to England, girlie," he said.

It crossed Vi's mind that she hadn't exactly given either Herbert, who had gone of his own accord, or Charlie, who had been called up. But what Howard said was true in a deeper sense; at all events, it was a beautiful thought. She took out her handkerchief with her free hand and wiped away a tear.

Howard told her that he had tried to get into uniform, but he was classified as essential in his job. He was something important on the railway and spent his days in an office at Liverpool Street. "Some of us have got to keep the wheels turning," he said. Vi became furious when she saw people looking critically at this big healthy man in civilian clothes. She wanted to tell them how it was that Howard was obliged to keep the wheels turning. And, as well as slaving away at his essential job, he gave most of his leisure time to organising war charities. Sometimes, when they were due to spend an evening together, he left a note at the laundry to say that he was needed at a vital committee meeting.

She always looked forward to seeing him, but she wasn't very keen on being seen with him in public. People could be critical, also, about a girl going out with a man in the prime of life. She felt that what they shared was too delicate, too precious, to be exposed to the general view. For Vi, everything gained in value by being a secret, so this was naturally true of her life with Howard. She was glad to find that he felt the same.

Occasionally he took her to see a show or to a dance, but this was always in the West End or some other part of London. It was bad enough revealing themselves to strangers, but risking gossip in Ilford was worse. They met in a quiet side-street, where he waited with the car and she slipped into it when no one was looking. In the long summer evenings, he drove to Epping Forest and they strolled, hand in hand, under the great trees; sometimes Vi could almost believe that she was a child again, clutching Herbert's hand as they walked along the same paths. To finish the evening, they had a drink —he a whisky, she a ginger-beer shandy—at the Robin Hood. Howard disapproved of young ladies going into pubs, but he said that the Robin Hood was a country inn. There was a snug with only one table; they nearly always had it to themselves.

They still drove to Epping Forest when the autumn came. It was even more beautiful, in a sweetly melancholy way, when the leaves fell, and of course it was practically deserted. Vi didn't feel cold with Howard's arm round her shoulders, but on foggy nights he warned her that the damp air was unhealthy, so they got into the car again.

Vi loved the car. She loved the ample depth of the seats, the rich smell of leather, the plaid rugs which she wrapped round her knees if it was chilly, the noble perspective of the long bonnet with its mascot at the end, and the deep throbbing note of the engine. Though she didn't mention this to Howard, it was the only car she had ever been in. She found it remarkable that he could drive and look after the car as well as all the other things he did; it was only during the war that car-owners had begun to drive themselves instead of having chauffeurs. Sitting beside him, she gazed at his serene, watchful profile and admired the deft movements of his strong hands. She could rest in his care, as if they were dancing.

Really, the car was their home—the frame and shelter of their life together. It was in the car that they kissed, that she lay calm and dreamy in his arms, and that her body learned a new, trembling excitement. The first time she got into the back of the car, it was like entering the upstairs rooms of a house where she had known only the parlour. The back of the car was a secret place, just like her bedroom at home. But the secrets of her bedroom had been hers alone; the secrets of this place were hers and Howard's.

She often thought that the things they did there could never have been done—that is, she could never have ventured into them—anywhere else. But this was not for shame. It was because, in this small, dark, enclosed place, nothing had to be declared or decided. She was scarcely aware that his hands had moved before they touched her breasts or her thighs. She felt what happened, but she didn't have to see. Thus, everything seemed gentle, easy and natural. It had nothing to do with the seizing and grabbing —with what other men had wanted with her. So eventually, when the ultimate thing happened, that was natural too.

Sometimes she tried to make herself confront it by using in her mind the words other people used. They were having intercourse, they were fornicating, they were fucking. She knew all the words, but none of them seemed at all connected with what happened between her and Howard. Indeed, it couldn't be expressed in words at all —scarcely even in thoughts. While it was going on, she lay on the rugs in a kind of dazed daydream, aware only of a rhythm that carried her along, just as when she was dancing. Afterwards, she was often genuinely uncertain what had happened—what was desire, what was imagination, what was reality. Whatever had happened, anyway, was completely different from what she had feared and still feared, from what drunken soldiers wanted to do to her. She and Howard had done nothing dirty—nothing nasty. She couldn't have explained this to anyone else, but she felt that he always treated her with perfect respect.

Once, when she tidied her clothes and got out of the back of the car to get into the front, she found Howard standing in the road, deep in thought. She slipped her arm through his; he kissed her very gently on the forehead.

"You'd tell me if you thought I was being . . . unfair to you, wouldn't you, girlie?" he asked.

She said: "I don't know what you mean."

"That's all right, then. I'd cut my right hand off"—Vi trembled, as if he were about to do this—"before I'd cause my girlie an instant's unhappiness. I suppose other people wouldn't understand that."

These solemn words were rare. Most of the time when they were together, she chattered to him gaily, telling him whatever came into her head.

"I had ever such a funny dream last night, I was riding one of those white horses in a circus, I was terrified but I didn't fall off."

"Mrs. Finlay told me a dog bit a postman when he was off duty on Sunday, amazing really, there must be a postman sort of smell."

"I don't like those high hats the Queen wears, I mean to say, her being taller than the King, it's not right, is it?"

She never minded if she sounded ignorant or silly. She hated it when other people laughed at her, but when Howard did, she was glad; she was there to make him laugh, to bring some fun into his serious life. She was his girlie.

When she had been out with him, she told her mother that she had been working late. Dora didn't believe this, and in her heart of hearts Vi knew that she didn't. Tacitly, both accepted a convention which meant that Vi could have a secret.

Still, Dora worried—or at least felt that she ought to worry—over the evident fact that Vi was carrying on with an unknown man. The trouble was this job in Ilford, she decided. A pretty girl might meet all kinds of men up there, men who would make her ashamed of her home, men who wouldn't have any intention of marrying her. And of course there was the war. The man might be a soldier who could disappear at any moment, perhaps a colonial, perhaps even a Yankee now they had joined in the war.

Maggie Harris advised her to take a strong line. "You tell her you want to meet him, dearie. You're her Mum. You've got a right."

Dora reduced this assertion to: "Any time you want to ask somebody in on a Sunday, Vi, you know it's your home."

Vi acknowledged this, but no one appeared. Dora let things drift. In the autumn, she became aware that Vi was not a virgin. She could not have explained how she knew, but she did know. It wasn't the way to behave, of course. A mother was supposed to hope—in theory, to ensure— that her daughter stayed pure until marriage, though anyone who was honest knew that the odds were against it. But Dora couldn't help being glad that Vi had arrived at womanhood— Vi who still seemed so childish for her seventeen years, who had always been so shy with boys and so easily upset. From her own girlhood, she remembered the sheer joy of taking the plunge. She couldn't bring herself to spoil it for the girl by intrusion and questioning. For she also remembered that the secrecy was part of the joy. She hadn't told her own mother about Jack until it was necessary.

On Armistice night, Dora danced until she was

fit to drop. What with her weight, her shortness of breath, and her varicose veins, it was absolutely mad; but there would never be another night like this. Everyone in Steadman Street was in the Gordon, singing with linked arms and dancing until the tables and benches got in the way. Then they surged out to the street and danced as if the November night were in midsummer. Dora kissed all the men—she loved the whole world, she would have kissed the Kaiser if he'd been there. Vi and Liza too danced and let themselves be kissed, Liza with her usual sweet willingness, Vi with a suffering expression. However, Dora didn't spend much time thinking about Vi. What filled her mind was that Charlie was safe, not even wounded, quite safe at this hour of deliverance. She found herself looking at Mrs. Coote from number ten, who had lost her boy only a few weeks ago. Mrs. Coote's eyes were dry, but Dora's filled with tears. It was all very well to dance and get tiddly, she thought; nothing would cancel the suffering or restore the losses of these four terrible years. And she pictured Herbert as she had last seen him, brave and pathetic in his uniform. Then someone brought her a bottle of stout, and she wiped her eyes.

Peace was hard to get used to, like silence after a long-sustained noise. Hardly any time seemed to have passed when Charlie sent a wire to say that he was back in England and had leave for the weekend. All in a rush, his bed had to be made up in the back room, a cake cooked and iced, and the house front decorated with Union Jacks and "Welcome Home, Charlie" placards. Dora didn't see much of him that first weekend; he was in the Gordon from opening time on Saturday, with everyone lining up to buy him pints, and on Sunday he was in demand at the Harris', at the Whitmarshes'—all up and down the street. Of course, he was coming home to Steadman Street and not simply to number five. Each homecoming was an assurance that the street would soon be itself again, a street of men as well as of women and children.

Charlie was among the first to be out of uniform and home for good. Armyland was in chaos; its purpose was gone, discipline could not be enforced, men overstayed their leave cheerfully and spent their time arranging civilian jobs which would qualify them for early release as key men. Charlie's arrangements were made at the docks. He was a grown man now, a returned hero, as well as a stevedore's son. There was no difficulty about his getting a job as a stevedore, and this made him a key man.

So there he was, soon after New Year, tramping home from the tram stop, shovelling down his supper, then moving to the armchair and lighting a pipe.

"Vi's out late," he said.

Dora remembered the tone of voice across the

165

years: the man of the house, resting from work but equal to his responsibilities, demanding to be informed, taking charge.

"I meant to tell you, Charlie."

He listened. Then he asked: "Mean to say she's never told you who he is?"

She shook her head, troubled. It was impossible to explain why she had not insisted on knowing.

"You won't be hard on her, Charlie, will you? She's a funny sort of girl, is Vi."

"Got to find out about this, anyway."

He found out easily enough after a forceful talk with Mrs. Finlay. The next time Vi went to the quiet side-street, there was no sign of Howard's car. She waited, shivering in the winter wind, sure that people were noticing her. It struck her for the first time that she had no means of knowing if Howard were taken ill or involved in an accident. She leaned against a lamp-post, feeling sick, assailed by horrors. But she pulled herself together and took a bus home —there was nothing else to do. On the jolting bus, she felt sick again. With luck, she might be able to get upstairs and lie down without having to talk to anyone.

Charlie was sitting in the armchair with his pipe in his mouth. He had taken up the pipe only recently—the badge of manhood—and tended to let it go out. He held a match to it, filling the room with smoke.

"In case you're wondering," he said, "you won't be seeing Mr. Buckley again."

Vi stared at him, grasping the door-knob, swaying.

"Told you the tale, didn't he? Wife doesn't understand him, I'm sure. Honest, Vi, I thought you'd got a bit of sense."

She ran upstairs and lurched blindly into the back room. She didn't dare to bolt the door; it was no longer her own place. Dora appeared with consoling words and a cup of tea. She wept, miserably, for hours.

In the disaster, there was not even dignity. She really had been a fool; anyone in Steadman Street would say that. It had never crossed her mind that Howard was married. She understood dimly how it was that she had not wanted to know, but no one else would forgive that.

Next day she had a high fever and vomited everything she ate. She stayed at home, hiding from the world. When she went to work, Mrs. Finlay gave her a letter.

"My sweetest Violet,

You will know by now that I have had an unpleasant interview with your brother. I shall not reproach him; others cannot understand that my feelings for you have always been sincere. But I cannot continue to be the cause of discord between you and your family. It is best for us to part. You are young; you will find happiness

167

with another. Weep one little tear, my darling, and forget me for ever.

Your still devoted,<br>Howard."

She put the letter in her secret box. Herbert had given her the box for her tenth birthday; it was lined with mother-of-pearl and had a tiny golden key. As well as a few things from her childhood, it contained her only present from Howard, a brooch in the shape of a violet. She would never wear it again. Carefully, she folded the letter round it.

Later at night, awake while Liza breathed peacefully and Charlie snored, she thought bitterly of cruel, selfish, heartless men. Charlie was hateful; Howard was hateful too. She had yielded herself to be deceived and mocked. She would never do that again. Her body remembered the tender, quivering joy of other nights. Throat dry, fists clenched, she fought it down.

# 10

ON a cold afternoon in December 1921, a man collapsed while shovelling snow in Poplar High Street.

This man, whose name was Arthur Naylor, ought not to have been shovelling snow; he had a weak heart and his proper work, stitching leather, required no exertion. Since the summer, however, he had been unemployed. The factory where he had worked for years had reduced its payroll by a half, partly because of the poor state of trade in general and partly because of the new competition from imitation leather. After fifteen weeks on the dole, he was no longer entitled to benefit; the snowfall brought a chance to earn which he could not possibly refuse. An inquiry into the reasons for his collapse would have established, in addition to his weak heart, that his shoes leaked, his overcoat was in pawn, and his lunch had been a slice of mousetrap cheese. Such facts were not, at that time, remarkable. The unemployment total was almost two million.

He was lifted out of the roadway by a passer-by, a stevedore named Charlie Wheelwright, whose presence in the High Street was also to be explained by the economic situation. He had walked to Poplar to do some bargain shopping. All that week, there had been no loadings at Albert Dock.

"I'll be all right," Naylor said when he came round. "Thanks, mate . . . I'll be all right."

The gang foreman approached and stared at him critically, as one might stare at a dilapidated old lorry which was in no condition to do a day's run. Naylor was under fifty, but he looked like an old man—a little old man, with bent shoulders and a sunken chest. Now, his lips were quivering and his cheeks were bloodless and yellow. He wouldn't look much different, the foreman thought, if he were on the point of death, or for that matter dead.

"Send for an ambulance, shall I?" the foreman suggested.

Naylor protested. "No need for that, no need at all. Don't want to go into hospital. I'll be all right soon, honest."

"Better go home, anyway. Where d'you live? Can you get there?"

"Oh yes—it's just round the corner."

"I'll go with him," Charlie said.

"Don't worry about today, then," said the foreman. "Can't keep your place if you don't turn up tomorrow, though."

"Will your missus be at home?" Charlie asked as they walked along.

"My daughter ought to be there—grown-up daughter. Works on the buses. She was on early turn today. My wife died years ago."

Naylor lived in the basement of an ancient, gloomy tenement building. At the bottom of a flight of worn stone steps, a blocked drain had formed a pool of dirty snow, rubbish from the upstairs gutters, and dogs' droppings. The daughter wasn't in after all.

"Never mind," Naylor said. "I'll be all right now I'm home."

"I'll wait," Charlie told him. "Got nothing else to do. You just have a nice lie-down."

Naylor's bed was in the inner, and even darker, of the two small rooms. It was the kind of tenement in which most working-class people had lived before the Steadmans started building houses. Beds took up most of the space; there was no parlour and no proper kitchen, only a tiny scullery with a cold-water tap.

"Hope she comes in soon," Naylor said from his bed. "Don't want the young ones to come in and find me like this."

"How many you got?"

"There's two at school. Eight and twelve, they are. My eldest, she's nineteen. She's a proper mother to the little ones."

He dozed off. Charlie gazed at him dubiously; the place was bitterly cold. Both the fires had gone out hours ago, or else had not been lit today. The walls were as damp and chilly as paving-stones in the street. Charlie covered the sleeping man with the blankets from the other beds, but they were all cheap and thin and probably didn't do much good. He decided to light a fire and swept out the grate, carefully preserving a few lumps of coal that were charred but still useful. There was some more coal—the cheapest kind, mostly dust and slate—in a bucket in the scullery.

He had just managed to get the fire to burn when someone came in. In the dim light, he thought at first that it was one of the children. No, it was the grown-up daughter in her bus-conductress uniform. She was as small for a woman as her father was for a man.

"What's all this?" she asked.

"Your Dad passed out in the street. I brought him home."

She dashed into the other room.

"He's all right," Charlie called after her. "He soon came round. He's asleep now."

She came back. She had a way of darting to and fro in the little tenement like some small, restless animal in its cage.

"Made yourself at home, haven't you?" she said.

"Have I?"

"We never light the fire till six o'clock. You can see we haven't got much coal."

"I saw that. I felt his hand, too. He was freezing."

"All right. Suppose you meant well."

She took off her uniform cap and sat down.

She had red hair, a flash of bright colour in the gloom.

"I've had no work this week either," Charlie offered.

At this she looked up swiftly, relieved that he was not sympathising from a safe immunity, but still on her guard.

"In the docks, are you?"

"Stevedore. The name's Charlie Wheelwright."

"Mine's Ann Naylor."

She gave her name reluctantly, Charlie thought. He didn't see what to say next, and she showed no intention of saying anything. Standing there, he had a feeling of being too big and clumsy for the room, for Naylor, and for Ann.

"Well, I'll be going," he said.

"Thanks for what you did," she said, dutifully rather than warmly.

"I hope he'll be all right. And if there's anything else I can do . . . you know, to help . . ."

"I'll manage."

Waiting for the bus home, Charlie reflected that he didn't really know if the girl was pretty. The red hair was striking; otherwise, without a proper look in good daylight, one couldn't be sure. He wanted to see her again, decidedly. From her indifference to him, he took up a challenge.

Her father would get better, most likely. It happened that there was a sudden thaw next day, so snow-clearing was at an end. But the weather was grey and depressing. Ships hooted endlessly as they nosed their way up-river in fog. The odds were still against getting work in the docks. Butchers were selling turkeys at knock-down prices and finding few buyers. For working people, for the unemployed especially, it would be a sad Christmas.

In hard times, you had to be proud like Ann Naylor: Charlie understood that. You took help from those whom you knew well, from your family and neighbours. You thought hard before taking help from a stranger. The danger was that you could slip into begging and scrounging—pleading for charity, singing hymns for a bowl of soup, offering your home and your children for inspection. If you came to that, you were broken; you never stood upright again. Naylor might go down to it, Charlie imagined. But the girl wouldn't let him—she would fight. Clearly, she was that kind of girl.

At the weekend, Charlie went round with a sack of coal to make up for what he had used. If they took it, he would have ceased to be a stranger; he would be a friend, someone with the right to help.

The younger children were playing in the dirty asphalt yard of the buildings. So were a couple of dozen other children, but Charlie picked out the Naylor boy by his red hair—not carrots, not chestnut, but a real red like Ann's. A girl who was playing tag with him must be his sister— eight and twelve, the father had said. Her hair was dark. They were both skinny, lightweight, quick-moving—real London children. The light build didn't always mean weakness; kids like these could be as tough and resilient as steel wire. But in time of illness and hunger, there was no nourishing fat to be drawn on and these little bodies were soon in danger.

Ann opened the door when he knocked. She seemed not a bit surprised to see him. It was natural, of course, for him to want to know if the man he'd helped was all right. Also, it was natural to come back if that man had a possibly good-looking daughter of nineteen. If Ann grasped this, it evidently didn't disturb her.

"He's not too bright," she said. "It's on his chest."

Naylor appeared, looking far from bright. The room was cold. It would always have this cold feeling, no doubt, even in summer.

However, Naylor made a brave effort: "Wondered if we might see you again. Didn't say thank-you properly, did I? Come in. Take the weight off your feet."

Charlie sat down; the old wooden chair creaked and wobbled. Ann returned to darning a pullover of her brother's. He was aware of her detachment. It was her father that Charlie had come to see, so far as she was concerned.

Charlie produced the coal, saying that he was just making up what he'd used. Ann was annoyed. She could show that with scarcely a gesture, with a concentrated hunching of her shoulders.

Naylor was dubious. "You oughtn't to be doing that, you oughtn't really." He wanted the coal, of course. Charlie could see that his hands, thrust into the shallow pockets of an old cardigan, were frozen. He also wanted to hold on to some human dignity. He kept glancing at Ann, hoping for a sign from her. But she insisted on his being the father, the head of the household.

"Well, there it is," Charlie said. "Might as well leave it, now I've brought it."

When he left, Ann came up the steps with him. "Listen," she said, "we're paying for that coal."

"'Course you are." He smiled, trying to shrug away the seriousness of the matter; she didn't smile back. "Five Steadman Street, that'll find me. You're paying when he's in work again, right?"

She had to accept this. "Well," she said, "stands to reason, if we could pay for coal now, we'd have bought it."

She was pale; they all had pale complexions. But these pale cheeks made him think pleasantly of yellow roses, gaslight in the mist, winter sunshine. Her eyes looked directly up at him, yet never stopped moving. They were green, gold, almost brown—he wasn't sure. Her lips were thin, very firm, not at all what were called kissing lips, but nevertheless attractive. She was good-looking, sure enough; yet he almost doubted it because she was utterly unlike other good-looking girls. It would help if she smiled, he thought. But he knew that she wouldn't smile, as girls generally did, for no reason except that a man was looking at her.

"Red hair come from your mother's side?" he asked.

"Yes, she was Irish."

"Lovely girls, the Irish."

There was a silence between them: not a significant silence, merely a space created by her, in which he waited and she took her time. Then she said: "You're not buying anything with your coal, you know."

"Forget about the coal. But I'd like to see you again."

"You will. I'm paying you back. I'll remember the address, five Steadman Street."

"You know what I mean. Let's go to the pictures. Meet me next Saturday?"

"I'm on late turn."

"Do a swap, then."

"Oh yes. Anything else I can do for you?"

He took this cheerfully. Already, he accepted

177

that he would take more from her than from other girls.

"I'll be at the fish shop in the High Street at seven," he said.

"I'll be there if I can manage. Don't wait more than five minutes; I'll be on time if I do come."

She turned swiftly and went inside.

Between then and Saturday, he thought of Ann constantly. At work, at home, in bed before he dropped into sleep, her small vigilant face appeared before him—a query, a challenge. Sometimes he was sure that she'd turn up, sometimes he was sure that she wouldn't. He was piqued, almost humiliated, to find that he cared so much. But with other girls, there had never been any doubt of their being where he told them to be on a Saturday night.

There was, at this time, a need in his life: a need for someone to care about. The family, rather strangely, had become a grouping of self-sufficient units. Dora took life very easy. She got up late, made pots of tea at intervals during the day, and spent hours in her armchair, sewing or knitting at her usual leisurely pace. Vi went off punctually to work and returned punctually. She had no adventures now; young men asked her out, were rebuffed, and didn't ask again. She treated Charlie with cold politeness and he knew that she hadn't forgiven him for depriving her of Buckley. Liza, who no longer had a job, did the shopping and practically all the housework. She was willing, even-tempered and undemanding, just as she had always been. Waiting to become a woman—presumably—she allowed life to tick over quietly. So these four people shared the house without colliding, without seeking anything important from one another, indeed without talking much. Had they been in a different class, they would have moved into separate houses or flats; it would not have changed a great deal.

Charlie had no special friends, either. After the war, he had kept up for a while with Pete, but Pete lived miles away in Islington and the friendship became awkward. Charlie suspected, too, that Pete was embarrassed by being reminded, not so much of his breakdown as of the powerful intimacy of wartime. In peace, at home, friendship was more diffused and less intense. Charlie and Tommy Whitmarsh both worked in the gang led by Tommy's father. But, though dockland was an enclosed world, it was not so enclosed as Armyland. Especially, it was not a world in which one drew close to a mate because one lived without women.

So far as women were concerned, Charlie considered—had considered up to now, at least —that he managed very well. He went out with one girl after another: girls of the neighbourhood, sometimes of Steadman Street itself, who attempted no pretences and expected none from him. His style with them was an easy comradeship, a teasing and joking avoidance of depth of feeling. A girl was a cheerful smile, a step clicking beside his stride, a moist hand clutched at the pictures, kisses in a shop doorway. That much made an evening worth while; more was a bonus. The girl knew, of course, that he wanted to get it in. Whether he succeeded was a test of his skill, but also a gamble. Sometimes a girl gave in unexpectedly when he thought the odds were against him; an impulse which he hadn't perceived had been working within her and she gasped out her eagerness, perhaps in case she had second thoughts. Another girl might resist with a stubbornness that surprised him. It was all a delightful game. He wanted the success and the pleasure, but absolute physical need was not involved. If that bothered him, there were certain pubs where you could pick up another type of girl: the type who would open her legs as readily as kiss if she took a fancy to a man, never mind whether she'd seen him before or might see him again.

If a girl resolutely said no, Charlie felt that it was right to go on taking her out. He had contracted for the company and the kisses, after all. Yet he found himself drifting away from her, and she bore him no grudge. It was equally true that the end of the affair was in sight if she said yes. There was no further for them to go, unless into a commitment for which they were not ready—he was not, anyway. One way or the other, a girl lasted between three and six months.

There were moments when he got bored. You said this, the girl said that, you put your hand here, she tried to pull it away—the moves were worked out in advance. Some men said that all women were the same, and Charlie had a fear of reaching a point when he found them so. Sometimes he shut his eyes and lost track of whom he was with—not that he literally didn't know, but it didn't matter, it was aside from reality.

Reality was work; he had always been clear about that. Reality was the strain and effort, the tensed muscles, the thud of the crates, the whining noise of the crane. For two years after he came home, with trade booming after the pinch of war, the stevedores worked hard and regularly, with the bosses always chivvying about sailing times that must be met. Once, Charlie failed to take his hand away from a crate before another came slithering across the hold. Crushed fingers meant an hour's agony before he got to hospital and a fortnight without work or pay. He learned that constant attention was a necessity. In the grip of reality, there was no time for dreaming about girls.

So he was puzzled, even a little alarmed, when the question of whether Ann would turn up on Saturday came into his mind at times beyond his control. Yet he was glad too. This girl was different; she must be, if he felt like this.

Usually, he arrived at a meeting-place a few minutes after the appointed time. Girls were always a bit late, and he liked to have them waiting for him, not he for them. But he had no doubt that Ann would be there—if at all—at seven. Scoring small points would mean nothing to her. As bad luck would have it, he had been loading cement. He had to strip naked, get into the tin bath, and shampoo his hair to get the clinging white dust out of it. After putting on his clean clothes, he wolfed his supper as soon as Liza put it on the table. He ran for a bus and swung aboard riskily after it moved away. So he was at the fish shop at ten to seven. He decided that he would take her at her word, anyway—he wouldn't stay a second beyond five past.

She came round the corner from her home precisely on the hour. His heart jumped. He hadn't felt like this since he was a boy, waiting for Reenie to open her door.

"You managed it, then."

"Yes, I managed it." She smiled at him: a cool, considering smile, but a smile nevertheless.

At the pictures, she watched the screen in the same attentive way, not taking the film too seriously but getting what there was to be got out of it. She never glanced at him, even during the slow bits without any dialogue to read; but he was ready for the exceptional from her. He didn't take her hand nor put his arm round her shoulders. Not the first time—not with Ann.

She wouldn't have an ice-cream in the interval. Either she was reluctant to owe him more than was essential, or she remembered that he wasn't in steady work. But after the film, she agreed to come for a cup of tea.

In the small cafe, the steam from the urn made the air comfortably warm and dense. They faced each other across the table.

"Things better at the docks?" she asked.

"Still slack," he said. "Better than last week. Your Dad found anything?"

"Not yet."

She knew, surely, what the chances were for a man of his age, with broken health written on his face, among two million unemployed. Charlie searched for something to say; this girl did not feed on false comfort.

Abruptly, she said: "We didn't always live in that dump, you know."

"Just since he's been out of work, right?"

"Yes. We had a house, Wapping way. Paid ten bob a week rent. He's in the leather trade, has been all his life."

"Good trade, that is."

"Was," she said tersely.

"Bound to pick up, sooner or later."

"Nothing's bound to pick up."

"You don't think so?"

"I don't think the system's ever going to work again, not really."

Charlie was taken aback. True, "the system"

was now an accepted phrase. At union meetings, from street-corner speakers, in the *Daily Herald*, it was repeated that crisis and unemployment were all part of the capitalist system. Yet it was only a year since the boom had collapsed; with part of your mind, you still thought in the traditional terms of slack trade and good trade. Certainly, you didn't expect such hard, clear thinking from women, and least of all from the girl you'd taken to the pictures.

He said: "You've got a steady job, anyway."

"I hope so." She stared past his shoulder, into an uncertainty which she contemplated without panic. "There's talk of taking the clippies off the buses, with so many men out of work."

"Think they'll do that?"

"Could do. But of course we're cheap—they like that."

He asked her to come out with him again the next Saturday. She didn't answer at once; he had the impression that she wanted to explain something, to state an attitude. Then she said simply: "If you like."

That second time, he took her hand firmly as soon as the lights went down. She made no objection, but went on watching the screen. He went through the routine of cinema courtship: stroked her hair, kissed her neck (girls liked that, everyone knew), and pressed his thigh against hers. She neither resisted nor responded.

But afterwards, she refused the cup of tea. "I'm on early turn," she said.

"I work too."

"Shape-up's at quarter to seven, right? I've got to be at the garage at half past five."

"I'll wake you up."

This didn't amuse her. They walked along in silence; the tighter he clutched her arm, the more he felt her to be estranged. When they reached her buildings, he pulled her into one of the doorways. In the darkness, her eyes gleamed below him like points of light, like clean cold water far down in a well. He dived for it thirstily and splashed a kiss on her lips. While he held her, he was every second more certain that he had made a mistake; with this girl, at this time, the masterful embrace wasn't the right strategy. The trouble was that, with this girl, he was bewilderingly incapable of planning his moves. He had grasped her out of frustration, out of impatience with her independence of him, and above all out of a desire whose strength, even at this moment, astonished him.

When he let her go, she said: "Good thing nobody came along. I've got to live here, you know." Her voice was calm; she denied him even the tribute of indignation.

"We'll go somewhere else another time," he said.

"What other time?"

He had made a mess of things, that was

185

obvious now. But, trying to maintain his confidence, he assumed the direct and casual manner which usually flattened the defences and said: "I fancy you, Ann. I really fancy you."

"You fancy yourself," she retorted.

"What d'you mean?"

"I'm going home. Want to walk with me?"

Sullenly, he took her arm again and they crossed the yard.

"You think I've got to kneel down and worship you," she said. "Well, you've got another think coming."

"Hate being kissed, do you?" he demanded.

"No, I don't hate it. I won't be pushed into it without being asked, that's all."

"What would you have said if I'd asked you, then?"

"I'd have said I've got other things to worry about. I'm running up bus steps eight hours a day, nursing an invalid, keeping two kids out of mischief, buying food out of twenty-eight bob a week, and trying to keep a slum clean and decent. I don't expect anybody to feel sorry for me. There's some worse off. Just don't ask me to go in for the Romeo and Juliet stuff as well. I can't give my mind to it."

They had reached her basement. "Still," she said, releasing her arm, "thanks for taking me to the pictures."

He smiled—the concession was coming. "Same place next Saturday, then?"

"You don't *listen*, do you?" Anger flashed from her like a gunshot in the night. He had not met it before, and it startled him.

"No, not again," she said. "Shouldn't have come this time. It's given you the wrong idea."

"I'll be there next Saturday," he said stubbornly. "You think it over. I'll be there, anyhow."

He went through the week in a mood of resentful self-justification. Sound—surely unanswerable—arguments came to his mind; he found himself muttering them, as if Ann were there to hear him. A man was supposed to kiss a girl, not to ask permission. If she had troubles and responsibilities, she needed a man all the more. Let the Saturday meeting become a regular event, and she could accept his help without shame, be fortified by him. She was lucky to have come across him, anyway; he had no need to be at a loose end, this Saturday or any other. By the end of the week, he had convinced himself that she would show up.

She didn't. He waited until twenty past seven, feeling like an idiot, hoping that nobody he knew and above all no girl had seen him. Then he went home in a black temper. He passed Liza in Barking Road, on the arm of the young chap who had started taking her out. Vi had washed her hair and was kneeling on the hearth-rug, drying it in front of the fire. Charlie grumbled at her—stinking the place out with her fancy shampoo, and keeping the warmth off everybody else too. Maddeningly, she withdrew upstairs instead of accepting battle. He went out again, slamming the door, strode across the street to the Gordon, and drank eight pints by closing time.

Two months went by. He thought of Ann less often, but didn't succeed in forgetting her. He had always forgotten girls before. But then, he had always got what he wanted from them, at least as far as kissing.

One Sunday morning, there was a knock at the door of number five. Dora and the girls were still upstairs; Charlie had come down to get some lime off his boots. He opened the door. It was Ann.

He couldn't say good-morning. He could only shout out her name and stare at her.

She said with precision that she had come to pay for the coal, and tried to hand over the money on the doorstep. But when he urged her to come in, she wasn't reluctant. He realised triumphantly that she had been thinking about him after all. Granted that she saw the payment for the coal as a real obligation, she was also glad of the chance to meet him again on equal terms and to see how he lived. She seemed at ease in number five; no doubt her former home had been very like it. She was at ease with Charlie too, though he was in his braces and hadn't shaved. Being in a room with her, like this, meant something of which they were both sharply aware. It was a strange, brief glimpse of a possible future, which they seemed to be trying out to see if it might work. ✓

Liza came downstairs. Ann was introduced and explained carefully about the coal. Charlie had said nothing at home about the Naylor episode, and Liza evidently didn't quite grasp its complexities. He was grateful that Vi was keeping out of the way.

Liza made tea and started cooking Charlie's formidable breakfast. "I'll have it later," he said on impulse, and to Ann: "Nice spring day. We'll go for a walk." He had never gone out of doors on a mere cup of tea before, but there must be a first time for everything.

Clouds reeled across a pale blue sky, hunted by the wind. Sunshine touched the skin suddenly, like a healing shock. Distantly, they heard the bang and blare of a Salvation Army band, giving the bright morning a tune.

"I missed you," he said.

She looked up at him, thoughtful as usual. "I missed you too. Funny. I didn't expect to."

"Must mean something."

"Must it?" she shot back with her quick defiance. But when he laughed, she conceded: "I suppose it must."

He halted, bringing her to a halt too, and thrust his right hand into the flame of her hair.

"Permission to kiss you, please," he said.

189

"Not here! Oh, you're ridiculous." But she was happy. They kissed recklessly, under the eyes of Steadman Street, making a declaration.

# 11

ANN and Charlie got engaged on a Sunday in June. The day had started cool, so he wore a serge jacket, she a coat and skirt; then, the wind dying, it became swelteringly hot. In crowded West Ham Park, each couple held a patch of territory like a pair of gulls on a cliff. When Charlie held Ann tight, they felt a sweating, itching impatience of the body, the skin tormented by layers of cloth. By joining in an act of will, relief might be achieved. "Say yes, say yes!" he growled into her ear, squeezing her like some innocently rough animal—a bear most likely, she thought. "Yes, yes, yes!" she answered, silencing him by an answer, asserting herself by surrender.

There must be few women, she reflected later, who didn't feel a tug of doubt pulling against the urge to consent. She loved Charlie—she was clear about that. But she experienced love as a need which limited freedom. One would be stronger without this need, she thought, just as one would be stronger if one didn't get hungry or tired. Yet one couldn't deny it; she had learned that in the two months apart from Charlie. She loved the man, so she must face the consequences; she must be his girl, then his wife.

The problem was how to meet the claims of love and retain the firm shape of her own life nevertheless, how to belong to Charlie and still be undiminished Ann. Charlie had great force, great strength; otherwise he could not have compelled her love. She had begun to wrestle with a bear.

It was her own contest and her own love—hers and Charlie's. She would let no one else approve or disapprove. Her sister Marjorie was ready to approve enthusiastically, in just the way that Ann didn't want. Now thirteen, Marjorie was in a phase of eager sexual curiosity. Knowing in one sense, simple in another, she was sure that no one who was old enough thought about anything else. When Ann came in after being with Charlie, Marjorie fired questions: "D'you put your tongue right in his mouth?"—"Does he shoot off in his trousers when he kisses you?" Furious, tightly controlled, Ann hissed: "Shut up, Marj! Shut up this minute!" Young Sidney giggled. He knew all about it too.

Ann's father also approved of the engagement, for reasons that were different but just as infuriating. He thought that Charlie was the right sort to look after Ann. "You haven't had an easy time, I know that. You deserve a man like him." Ann was driven to retort that she had looked after herself, and the family too, perfectly well without Charlie's help. Naylor admitted this—he seldom argued with Ann, or indeed with anyone—but made the same remark a few days later. What Ann dreaded was that, building on Charlie's first appearance, he had come to think of the young man as a benefactor. As soon as she was engaged, she issued clear warnings. To her father: "You ask Charlie for so much as a fag, and I'll walk out of here." To Charlie: "You offer him anything, and I'll break it off that minute." She allowed Charlie into her home as seldom as possible. The way Marjorie stared at him was reason enough.

Charlie, on the other hand, was worried because his mother did not take to Ann. Dora was reluctant to admit this, even to herself. She wanted Charlie to get settled, she was disposed in advance to like a girl whom he fancied, and in general she was more and more inclined these days to sit back and let things happen. Still, she just couldn't manage to get on easy terms with Ann. She was put off by the girl's strong opinions and sharp logic, her closeness to tangible reality. Ann never daydreamed—that was dauntingly evident—never wasted time, never forgot things she had decided to do. Even physically, fat comfortable Dora was disturbed by Ann's lightness, her rapid movements, her perpetual restless alertness: disturbed as an elephant would be, sharing a cage with a mongoose. For after all, they would be sharing the house after the marriage. And she felt, vaguely but emphatically, that Ann was not a woman like herself. Ann loved Charlie, yes, but she would not depend on him. She was not giving herself to him in total trust, as Dora had given herself to Jack. On Charlie's behalf, Dora was hurt by this.

There was something else. Dora was a stevedore's widow (so she thought of herself; her marriage to Herbert became less real every year). She belonged to a proud class—the firmly rooted, essential working-class. Her hope had been that Charlie would marry someone from the same kind of family. Tom Whitmarsh's sister was a very nice girl, for instance. The Naylors, as a family, had no standing that she knew of. "Never heard the name round here, nor yet back in Poplar," she ventured to say to Charlie. In fact, Ann's father had come to London from some Essex village. He'd had a trade, it was claimed, but now he was intermittently out of work or in unskilled work. He lived in a basement. No, it wasn't what she had hoped for.

Charlie could not help being concerned with what his mother thought, and by what Steadman Street thought. When he took Ann to his local, he watched keenly how people reacted to her and considered the worst that they might say of her. With her pale face and fiery hair, she caught the eye but wasn't, in any accepted fashion, pretty. She didn't smile or laugh to appear amiable, didn't speak unless she had something to say, then expressed herself emphatically. She might easily strike people, especially older people to whom she showed no prudent respect, as stuck-up. An odd sort of girl, it might be said.

But then Charlie's pride and obstinacy came to his rescue. Since he knew himself, false modesty aside, to be a man who stood out from the crowd, he would have a wife who stood out too. He certainly wouldn't have a sweet little doll, an imitation film star. Ann had a mind and a will of her own—all right! She would be a handful —so much the better! She might be too much of a handful for some men, but not for him. He came to see this marriage as the final vindication of his manhood.

The trouble was that they could not get married yet. Ann refused absolutely to let him take on responsibility for Marjorie and Sidney. So long as it was necessary—in effect, so long as her father didn't earn reliably—she would provide for them. This meant that she must keep her job; and, with its awkward shifts in the early morning or late evening, it was no job for a wife.

Charlie sometimes argued with her, though without much hope of changing her mind. She said crisply: "You can't afford to get married anyway, can you?" The humiliating truth was that she was perfectly right. Merely to take her to the pictures and buy her an occasional present, he had to count his money and cut down on tobacco. His wages were feeding four people already. Vi managed her finances independently, paying her fares and lunches but contributing nothing; he didn't even know what she earned. She and Liza would both get married some time, but there was no immediate sign of it. If he got married now and Ann gave up her job, how many more mouths would he have to feed? There would be Ann, Marjorie and Sidney, old Naylor in his spells of unemployment, and any babies that might come along. It couldn't be done.

Trade was still slack. A ship would load half its cargo and then wait a couple of weeks for the other half. Foreign sailors shuffled unhappily about the streets, having spent their money. Stevedores worked with meticulous care, placing crates in the hold to the nearest inch, stretching the job to fill the hours. Even so, they seldom worked a full week. While everything in the shops cost more than before the war, Charlie was earning about the same as his father had, twenty years ago.

On Saturday nights, after he had left Ann, he wandered about the streets, too restless to go home and sleep. He knew what he wanted. The kissing and cuddling was becoming as much of a test as a pleasure. He wanted Ann—no one else. In any case, the girls in Canning Town knew that he was engaged, that there was no future in doing Charlie Wheelwright a favour. That left the easy pick-ups; and they, although they had once suited a certain rough and jolly mood, now didn't interest him.

Ann knew what he wanted, no doubt. What would happen, he wondered, if he simply took her? She would resist, but perhaps the act would bring the response, the admission of her own need. It had been like that when he had forced kisses on her at the outset. Possibly, even, she was already waiting for him. She would say no if he asked—any decent girl would—but that was a convention.

In the summer, after they had been engaged for a year, the frustration became intolerable. On warm nights, Ann liked going down to the river. There were wharves on the Isle of Dogs where one could get in by talking nicely to the night-watchman. The waterfront, if no ships or barges were in, was as good as a beach. The sand was gritty, but fairly clean; at high tide, when there was no mud, Ann took off her shoes and stockings and paddled. There were no houses on the opposite shore, so that the wide river, making its majestic bend, had an ocean vastness. Without streetlights, the stars were startlingly bright. The moon, when it was full, made a gleaming splendour of the water. No other place for miles around gave the same sense of spacious freedom; in no other place could they be secure and alone without paying a penny. Lying on Charlie's donkey-jacket, they touched and breathed each other timelessly. Here—because the place was their own, and because she couldn't reasonably say that anyone might come along—Ann allowed Charlie more of herself than anywhere else. A lookout on a passing ship (but no one else) could have seen his hands on her bare breasts, her skirt rucked at the hips.

So, one night, he decided to make a job of it. One hand held her down while the other wrenched at her knickers. He could tell that it would be her first time, and this added to the joy of possessing her. Close above her, he saw her eyes widen at the hot hard touch on her tenderness. He was now at a familiar moment. A girl struggled, of course. But something, if it was only curiosity, made her struggle with a divided will, while his purpose was absolute. Once he had declared that purpose, he must drive it through to conquest.

He expected Ann to struggle more than most girls. He loved her for her spirit, her sharp-edged defiance. A special, rare excitement seized him as he met her strength—strength that no one could have guessed at without knowing that small tense body. Wherever he held her, she jumped like a jack-in-the-box, twisted aside, leaped out of his grip. Her lips were tight-closed, resolute. Her eyes gleamed in the night, angry and entirely fearless.

It was a few minutes before he realised that she meant it. She was resisting him, not for the same reasons as other girls—doubt, self-respect, the shock to the virgin body—but with a determined refusal, on which she must have decided in advance. She hadn't been waiting for him; about that, he had been dead wrong. So it was a real battle. And he gained nothing by being bigger and stronger than her; he wasn't trying to kill her, after all. It was her will that was set against his. There, he thought grimly, they were a good match.

She won, ultimately, because in the heart of the confusion and the frenzy a part of her remained cool and controlled. Choosing her moment, she drew up one leg, released it like a piston, and kicked him accurately in the balls. Her shoes had fallen off; all the same, it hit him hard.

No words seemed possible for a time, as they sat a yard apart, she putting her clothes in order while he buttoned his flies. Then she asked, in a tone that merely requested information: "Did that hurt?"

"Of course it bleeding well hurt!" he roared at her.

"You'll get over it," she said. He caught a note of mockery, perhaps of straightforward humour, that was unusual in her. This might have injured his dignity, but right now he had not much left.

"A man has feelings," he said. "Is that wrong?"

"No," she replied calmly. "Not wrong, it isn't."

She was looking at him as frankly, even as fondly, as ever. She wasn't going to play a scene of outraged virtue, at all events.

"A man has feelings," he repeated. "It's not my fault we can't get married yet. And engaged is sort of married, isn't it? There's plenty treat it like that, in case you didn't know."

"Oh, I know that."

She was silent for a while, putting on her shoes and standing up. The stony sand crunched, loud in the solitude, as it had while they fought.

"I love you, Charlie," she said. "I'm going to be your wife. But it's going to happen properly. What other people do is their business. When I say properly, I mean properly for me."

Suddenly, she knelt down and put her hands on his shoulders. Her voice was throaty now, low with intense feeling—ironically, like the voice of a woman making love.

"This is me, d'you see? You don't do it alone, you do it to me. You do it inside me. That's my womb, in there. That's what it means—being your wife. D'you understand? Do you?"

"Yes, darling. I understand."

She kissed him, clamping her lips hard on his.

"I don't know," she said as she drew away. "I don't think a man ever understands, not altogether."

Yet, unexpectedly, Ann's refusal brought

them closer together. The engagement became a shared ordeal, something like the war, with their future home—all hopes fulfilled, all desires set at rest—as a vision of peace. And he found that he could go through the ordeal in a state of calm. It was Ann's calm that aided him.

They talked more than before. They talked, both of them, more than ever in their lives; neither had, until now, had anyone to whom a certain kind of talk could be entrusted. Often, on the waterfront, they talked when they might have kissed, with no more touch than the relaxed interlacing of hands.

The present—the engagement—was bearable because it was ranged in a long perspective of past and future. The future was secure; their endurance, their investment in it, made it all the more secure. The past had to be gathered in, to be made their joint possession. It was almost uncanny how the same fate had shaped their two lives. The governing experience was sudden death. Fatherless Charlie and motherless Ann had shot swiftly into responsibility, into a central position in a home with two younger children. When they met, beside a helpless man's bed, they had sensed the early-matured strength in each other. Now, as they filled in the facts, it was: "Yes, I know what it's like" and "I know just how you must have felt".

Of her mother's death, Ann spoke with her usual firm exactness.

"She wouldn't have another child. She'd had five—there's three of us now, but two died. She always had a difficult time; no, a terrible time. When she had Sid, me and Marj were shut out of the house so we wouldn't hear her screaming, but of course we did hear.

"She had a way of staring into space when something was wrong as if she'd turned into a statue. Dad's the opposite; worry makes him fidget. So there they'd be, him tying knots in a bit of string or opening and shutting his penknife, and her miles away. I knew there was bad trouble, those last weeks. Even the little ones must have guessed. But I didn't know what. She might have told me, I've often thought, but anyhow she didn't. It's not too easy telling a child you don't want another child.

"So she went to have it got rid of. There's old women everywhere who'll do the job for two or three quid, you probably know that. And it went wrong. It sometimes does. So she was bundled out of the place for fear of the police. At least, that's what I reckon. I don't know how she got home or how far she had to go. Dad was at work, I was at school. When I got in, she was lying on the floor. She was still bleeding and the little ones were staring at her, too scared to move. Marj was six, Sid was two. I found a neighbour and he went to get the ambulance. It took ages to come. It was in the war, so it was an ambulance with horses. I tried to stop the blood with tea-towels and things, but it wasn't any good. She kept saying 'Let me die, I deserve to die and burn in hell'. She hadn't been a proper Catholic, what they call a practising Catholic, for years and years, but it all came back to her then. She started saying prayers in Latin, only she couldn't remember them properly. And she really believed she'd committed a mortal sin, she was being punished for it, and she was going to burn in hell.

"By the time the ambulance came, she'd lost so much blood, anybody would have expected her to die or at least go unconscious. She didn't, though. She died in the hospital, hours later. I couldn't go with her because of Marjorie and Sid. Dad went round, but they didn't let him see her."

Ann concluded: "I've never talked about that. Only to you." Charlie saw that it was a crucial confidence. He also saw what she had meant that night by the river; yes, there were aspects of being a woman that a man did not fully understand. For the first time, it came home to him that, while a man could be crushed by a crate in the docks or shot in the trenches, a woman had to meet dangers inherent in the fact of being a woman. And these dangers arose from the pleasures of manhood, from making love and from making children. Really—the idea was strange to him—a man should be grateful that a woman gave her fate into his hands. So he waited obediently until Ann could be his wife.

They were engaged for almost three years. The time passed somehow or other—afterwards, it hardly seemed possible. Then the obstacles fell away, all within a few weeks.

Ann's father, after various ups and downs, got a steady job. In his worst spells, he had gone— without telling Ann—to a charitable institution where unemployed men could get a free meal for polishing the floors and washing the dishes. To share out the benefit among hundreds of applicants, no one was allowed in more than twice a week. Someone was needed to keep the register: a man of blameless character who was unemployed through no fault of his own. Naylor was given the job. It called for no physical exertion; unless his health broke down completely, he was taken care of for good.

By this time, Marjorie was working. She had started at a local shoe-shop, a branch of a big chain. After a while, she was transferred at a better wage to the Oxford Street branch. She wore lipstick and had her hair bobbed; the management had no idea that she was only sixteen. With her quick, imitative intelligence, she soon picked up West End manners. She had Sid in fits of laughter with her "Can I help you, madam?" in a real lahdidah accent; but at the shop it was no joke—it was an essential of her skill. Only an occasional swift glance of her bright little eyes, a sardonic twist of the mouth, revealed the invader from the East End. She was always first at the shop in the morning and last to leave in the afternoon, so none of the other assistants knew where she lived. The manager had never had an employee who knew the stock so thoroughly, could find anything from brogues to sandals so swiftly, and could guess so intuitively what a customer was going to like. Ann was not quite happy about Marjorie working so far from home. When she was at work herself, Sid ran wild after school; he would never get tea at home after she married Charlie. As for the time it took Marjorie to get back from the West End, that was nobody's business. Still, Ann decided that she couldn't mother them any longer. If her wages were no longer needed to keep them eating and pay the rent, her duty was done.

Then Vi left number five. This was a new Vi, whose emergence could never have been predicted: a serious, efficient career girl. Where was the old Vi, Dora wondered?—flighty, romantic, idle Vi, chatterbox Vi, dancing Vi, Vi who couldn't remember the date or add up two and two. Sunk without trace, in the disaster of the affair with Howard Buckley. Vi even looked different, or rather had made herself look different; she did her hair in a severe, nononsense style with a centre parting. Without a word to her family, she had created a totally new conception of herself and of her future. Now it became a fact: Mrs. Finlay was retiring and Vi was taking over the laundry. Mrs. Finlay would draw a fixed return on her investment, while Vi had a right to whatever the business made beyond it. And Vi would live in the rooms over the laundry, for Mrs. Finlay was buying a bungalow on Canvey Island. Dora, clinging to her image of Vi as a reckless girl, fretted over the risks of her living alone in Ilford. But Vi could do as she pleased—she was of age now, indeed she was twenty-two. In more than five years since Buckley, there had been no men in her life. She wouldn't make a fool of herself again, Dora decided. She would make a sensible marriage when she was ready for it.

But Liza, just twenty-one, was getting married. She had been going steady with a nice young man from the next street. Reluctantly, she became aware that he wasn't the one. She consulted Dora: had she the right to turn down a man who was decent, in regular work, and in love with her—a man she certainly liked—just because she didn't feel that extra bit of . . . "you know what I mean, Mum?" Dora knew, and advised: wait for the real thing. She saw herself in Liza much more than in Vi, and wanted Liza to have a Jack. Suddenly, this happened. Liza had gone to the pictures on a Monday night with the Whitmarsh girl. It was raining when they came out, so they had an ice at an Italian place in the East India Dock Road. There were no other customers; the young man who served the ices leaned on the table and chatted. He was the one. Liza knew because, for the first time in her life, it took her more than an hour to get to sleep.

Tony Varelli didn't look very Italian; his fair hair and brown eyes were Lombard, but could have been English. He had the dual nature of the London Italians. It was more than being bilingual; his gestures and the pace of his speech altered as he assumed his English or his Italian self. Sometimes he whispered to Liza in Italian, and it melted her though she understood not a word. For three generations the family had been planted in the East End, selling ravioli and cassata, counting in pounds, shillings and pence. The children knew no home but London; the old folk retired invariably to the village where, on another plane of reality, they belonged. Tony's father, not so old but rheumatic in damp winters, was staying only until there was a young Mrs. Varelli. The name sounded peculiar in Steadman Street, but Charlie took to Tony and remarked that you'd never take him for a foreigner.

So Liza was married as soon as she could become a Catholic; she understood not much more of this than of the Italian language, but would happily have become a Buddhist if necessary. After the friends and relations had eaten themselves silly in Varelli's Riviera Restaurant, it was the senior Varellis who took the boat train from Charing Cross. Tony and Liza simply put up the "Closed" sign and went upstairs.

Liza had asked her brother: "Couldn't we make it a double wedding?" He knew what this meant: the Varellis would foot the bills. Italians were like Jews in that way, he had noticed— close-fisted when they were making the money, open-handed when they were spending it. But he didn't intend to be indebted to anyone's kindness for his wedding. If the Naylors couldn't pay, which they obviously could not, then the money would be Wheelwright money.

Besides, he was determined to have a Steadman Street wedding. From the church, the bride and groom would come back to number five. The meal would be in the top room of the General Gordon. He was bringing Ann to his home ground.

He would be married in the right way, and he wouldn't be married on the cheap. Certainly it was an expensive business when everything was added up—the hired formal clothes, the hired car, the flowers, the photographs, the four-course meal, the barrel of beer, the drinks in the bar for people who were not actually guests but who belonged to Steadman Street. Charlie had not much saved at the time when getting married became possible; trade had been bad again. But he would rather have put off his wedding for another year than have skimped on it.

They were married, eventually, three months after Liza and Tony. At the Gordon, Liza kissed her brother and said: "Did I tell you? I'm having a baby."

He remembered it later, lying beside Ann after he had poured himself into her. Marriage and motherhood went together, of course—indeed, for many brides the latter began first. But Ann was different. She would want to do this too in her own way. Against his own desire, he hoped that there would be no baby just yet. He ought to be content at present with the joy of Ann's coming to this bed, this room, this house.

# 12

AFTER Mrs. Finlay's retirement, Vi Wheelwright worked harder than before. Fanny had been sacked long ago and had had two successors, neither of them satisfactory. "We've got to face it, Vi dear, there's nobody else like you," Mrs. Finlay used to say. Now that Vi was in charge, and living on the premises, she managed without a helper and did all the fine work herself. She was up late night after night, forgetting the time until the church clock struck the hour. In the morning, she jumped out of bed as soon as the alarm went and was down to open up the laundry before the girls arrived. She never felt tired. It was working for herself, she decided, that made all the difference. It wasn't a matter of money; she put the earnings in the bank every week and paid herself the same as before. The point was that she cared. If the customers got their clothes on time, if the laundry kept its reputation, she was rewarded in the precious coin of contentment.

The girls, of course, didn't care. They worked just hard enough to avoid getting the sack, calculating this to a fine point. They dawdled before starting in the morning, they began to tidy up long before it was necessary in the afternoon, and in between they larked about whenever Vi was busy with customers. She had to keep a sharp eye on them and chivvy them repeatedly. They disliked her; she knew that from the things she found written in the toilets. They disliked her more than they had disliked Mrs. Finlay, she noticed. Presumably, because she was young and had been an ordinary laundry girl like them, they had expected to have an easy time with her. However, she wasn't aiming to make herself popular. She had always set her own standards instead of courting the opinion of others, and she would go on like that.

On the other hand, the customers liked her. Certainly, they got good service and any complaints were looked into without delay. But she felt that they liked her as a person; they understood what she was trying to do in life, and it met with their approval. Some of them were distinctly classy, with large cars and uniformed chauffeurs, but they were always polite and indeed amiable. With the gentlemen, Vi was brisk and business-like, making sure from the start that they didn't get any notions. Naturally, however, she dealt mainly with the ladies, and there were four or five whom she could almost regard as friends. It was remarkable how often their opinions coincided with hers. For instance: films were a bad influence, London was eating up the countryside at a terrible rate, and the modern girl—"not your sort, of course, Miss Wheelwright"—was getting out of hand.

And the working classes were idle. The first time she heard this, Vi flinched. Where did she come from, what was she if she wasn't working-class? It was something one couldn't change, like being English; and to hear these things said was like hearing English faults denounced by a foreigner. But on reflection it seemed to her that she had earned the right to be distinguished from the working classes, just as she was distinguished from "the modern girl". Surely this phrase, the *working* classes, was absurd. Who were the people who worked willingly, not counting the hours, from a sense of obligation? People like her stepfather, Mr. Buckley, Mrs. Finlay. If it was a question of working, she belonged with them.

"I hope *you* won't be going on strike, Miss Wheelwright." This remark, made by one customer after another, made Vi aware that the rumours of a General Strike were serious. She seldom read newspapers. Now she bought the *Daily Mail* and learned that the strike was imminent.

Since leaving Steadman Street, she had gone back there once a week for Sunday dinner; she owed her mother that show of family loyalty. When she arrived this Sunday, Charlie was out at an emergency union meeting. As usual, these days, Liza and her baby were the centre of interest. All the women, because they were women, were expected to fuss over it. Really, Vi was repelled by the baby: a fat, sticky, fleshy creature, an embarrassing reminder of physical processes. And though she thought of all babies as "it", this baby—known as Georgy-Porgy—was unmistakably male, revelling in the admiration of women, just like his father, handsome Tony.

"Pardon? Pardon?" Dora said, as the baby made a loud spluttering noise. Vi, who had lacked the courage to evade taking her turn to hold it, tightened her lips bravely. Dora bent over it, wearing a mock-reproving but really delighted expression: "Georgy-Porgy, I do believe you've done a stinky-pinky!" And she started to laugh, her huge bosom heaving under her black dress, folds appearing and disappearing where her chin and neck merged. Liza laughed too—happily, proudly—and the baby beamed, as if it had brought off some clever trick. The disgusting smell had reached Vi by now, and she would have dropped the creature in another half a minute if Liza hadn't taken it.

To bring them back to adult matters, she said: "This strike's going to be a nuisance, isn't it?"

Liza, mumbling through a safety-pin, said: "Got to go through with it now."

Vi saw that "nuisance"—an obvious comment, she had thought—wasn't how the rest of them looked at it. She tried to retreat to safety: "I'm sure I don't understand what it's all about, really."

"It's quite simple." This was Ann. "The mine-owners want to cut wages, so we've got to stand by the miners."

Ann's statements, delivered in her annoyingly precise manner, often impelled Vi to take the other side of a question. If the miners got lower wages—she wanted to say—that was hard luck, but if everybody went on strike nobody would have any wages at all. She didn't see why Ann and Charlie, for instance, should be obliged to stand by the miners. Vi had an indistinct picture of miners: strange men, grinning at cameras with faces black as niggers. Anyway, she now recalled reading in the *Daily Mail* that the Government had been subsidising the mines with the taxpayers' money, and that British coal could not be sold profitably unless economies were made. But she decided not to argue. If they wanted to stand by the miners, that was their business.

Charlie came in, highly satisfied with his meeting.

"It's all lined up. Pickets on every gate, lookouts all down the main roads, a watch right through the night. They'll never get a blackleg inside nor a cargo shifted, not one."

And the TUC, he had heard, was getting confident messages from every industry. Railwaymen—solid for the strike. Printers—solid. Gasworks and power stations—solid.

"We'll lick old Baldwin!"

Liza, having got a clean nappy on to the baby, began to joggle him on her lap to a chant of: "We'll lick old Baldwin—won't we, love?"

Vi sat quite still. Number five was united, with the rest of Steadman Street, in an excitement that left her cold. This strike was going to be an adventure, something between a war and a holiday, a grand repudiation of the common sense of regular life. Vi couldn't help feeling a little sad that she was not going along with it. She had not admitted to herself how decisively she had ceased to belong to Steadman Street.

Wearing an armband which read "Picket Organiser", Charlie was at the dock gate by six in the morning. As the pickets arrived, he ticked off their names on a typed list. He knew them all. He knew the big drinkers and the abstainers, the Catholics and the chapel members, the betting men and the pigeon-racers and the allotment gardeners. They had been caned at the Board School, they had fumbled with girls behind the bushes, they had jostled for work at the shape-up, they had made terms with a life of bruises and torn muscles. They had no power but in the value of their work; this power was now to be tested.

Across the road, a double line of policemen watched in silence. Most of them were specials, still uncomfortable in their uniforms, hampered

215

by a feeling of playing a part. Yesterday they had been bank clerks or commercial travellers. The East End was strange territory to them; dockers were an alien tribe, rough, untamed, incalculable. An inspector rode up on his glossy chestnut mare and scattered encouraging words. The specials stood stiffly to attention, like soldiers but unlike real policemen. A few of them had been in the war, but most were too young.

Sid Naylor flashed along the road, red hair bright in the slant of sunlight. The strike committee had decided to use boys as messengers, reasoning that the police wouldn't stop them. It was a glorious chance for Sid to ride a bicycle, which he couldn't afford to own.

"They're coming," he reported to Charlie. "Three lorry-loads. Just passed the Custom House."

Charlie gave the word to the pickets. But no messenger had been needed; a swelling roar of anger and scorn charted the movement of the lorries, a roar from dockers massed along the road, hurrying through side-streets, dashing out of their homes. By the time the first lorry came in sight, it had been slowed to walking pace by men filling the road and giving ground only at the last moment. A few stones clattered on the cab, though the union had given orders against them. Charlie could see the pale, set face of the driver, staring fixedly ahead, and the big moustache of the copper—no special—sitting beside him.

In front of the dock gate, the pickets stood shoulder to shoulder. The driver inched forward, as if he could achieve something by revving his engine in bottom gear. Charlie pulled the door open, jumped up, and reached across to put the handbrake on. As the copper drew his truncheon, he dodged and jumped down again. But by now the other door was open and the copper had to defend himself.

The lorry was surrounded in a matter of seconds. A sergeant's whistle sounded from across the road, and the police squad moved to the rescue. A rescue it was, Charlie saw quickly, not an attack. For a few minutes there was a heaving, jostling struggle—a show of force without fury on either side, leaving nothing worse than shins kicked and a few black eyes. A helmet soared through the air like a rugger ball, hailed by cheers. The police got through to the back of the lorry, cleared a path, and protected the blacklegs as they clambered down and got away. "Let 'em go, lads! They won't be back," Charlie shouted. It might almost have been better, he said afterwards to Tom Whitmarsh, to let them in and see what they could do; they wouldn't have cleared a hold in a month. A miserable lot they were—men from the tenements and the dosshouses, men who were always turned away at the shape-up, defeated men who cleaned public lavatories or sold matches at street corners. The bosses could give them work in a strike, Charlie thought, but not at any other time.

The second lorry was dealt with in the same way. The third turned and drove off, amid triumphant jeers, well short of the dock gate.

"What next?" Tom asked.

Charlie stood in the roadway and considered. He had been put forward as picket organiser, presumably, because he was a man equal to responsibilities. But he had been responsible for the Wheelwright family and for paying the rent of number five. That was a man's task, and task enough with a million or more on the dole. This being an organiser was something else. At work, there had always been orders. You didn't decide which ship to load next. There had always been the bosses who managed the docks, the generals who commanded the Army, the landlords who built houses. You distrusted and opposed them, you expected them to make a mess of things; but you didn't imagine yourself taking on their range of responsibility, their life of planning and foresight. Now, with this strike, came a sudden growth, a swift increase of grasp and vision. Charlie felt himself at one with working men all over the country, entering upon this experience.

The docks held firm. The river was still as no one had seen it since the great dock strike which only old men remembered: cranes motionless, barges lashed and drifting, sluices locked. On the third day, a big freighter with a cargo of New Zealand meat steamed out, lonely on the deserted water, to seek another port. The dockers lined the wharves to cheer.

In the East End, anyone who had to go anywhere walked. There were no buses, no trams, no lorries, no delivery vans. Boys, and men too, played football in the streets. Each neighbourhood withdrew into itself, quiet as a village.

In the West End, the streets were full of bustle. Specials hurried about with an important air, guarding this and protecting that. Dispatch riders cut through dignified squares and crescents, roaring their motor-bikes as if they were on a race-track. Department stores and removal firms lent their vans to the Government and got windscreen labels saying "Essential Supplies". Buses, driven by volunteers, maintained an erratic service. In the East End they would have been attacked, but here they were cheered.

Between these two cities—the London that was on strike and the London that fought the strike—Marjorie Naylor travelled every day. She was usually alone on the platform as she waited, anything from ten minutes to an hour, for a District Line train. Some trains didn't stop at Bow Road; the purpose of the service was to carry office workers from the suburbs to the City. Besides, the volunteer drivers enjoyed getting up to speed and breaking one another's record times.

The girls at the shoe-shop talked about the strike as they would have talked about a blizzard or a fog. On the whole, they liked having a good excuse for coming in late. They did not belong to a trade union and the thought that they themselves might go on strike never occurred to them. Marjorie couldn't very well go on strike on her own. It would have done no good, and of course she would have lost her job. So she continued living her double life, now more sharply divided than ever.

In normal times, she changed at Charing Cross to the Bakerloo Line, but in the strike this was too uncertain. She took buses between Charing Cross and Oxford Street if there were any, and walked if there were not. On the third day, she was lucky enough to get a bus both ways, partly because she waited in the afternoon until well after the rush.

"Had the pleasure of meeting you this morning, I think," the conductor said.

He was an undergraduate from Oxford or Cambridge, like most of them. They looked ridiculous, she thought, with their floppy trousers and long scarves.

"Maybe," she said.

"Oh, definitely. I never forget a face if it's anything like yours."

He went off to shout: "Piccadilly Circus!

Statue of Eros!" The first syllable of Eros wasn't pronounced to rhyme with "beer", as Marjorie had supposed; she made a mental note of this.

In the Haymarket, the conductor came to lean over her again.

"I say, I'm finishing after this trip. I suppose I couldn't tempt you to a spot of dinner?"

Curiosity, always a force for Marjorie, rose in her swiftly. However, her native cunning stopped "Yes" in her mouth and changed it to "Well, I don't know". She was intrigued to see the anxious expression that at once appeared on his large pink face. It was extraordinary how easily this could be created.

She kept him pleading, for sheer fun, after they left the bus in Northumberland Avenue.

"I ought to be getting home, honestly. They'll wonder where I am."

"You could give them a tinkle."

"I'm not dressed for going to a restaurant, am I?"

"Well, dash it, look at me. I know a quiet little place, not a bit posh, but jolly good food."

"I really don't know you at all."

"Have to put that right. Peter Medhurst, at your service."

"My name's Antonia Davenport." He seemed to find this entirely plausible. "I'll have to make it a quick meal," she warned him.

"Let's get started, then. We'll get a taxi this minute."

"You'll be lucky."

"No, hang it, you don't say the taxis are on strike too? Still, it's only five minutes' walk."

If the restaurant wasn't posh, she wondered what a posh restaurant was like. There were little lamps on each table and a soft carpet from wall to wall. A waiter pulled out a chair as she was about to do it herself—almost a blunder, she told herself.

The menu was all in French. The technique, Marjorie saw, was to keep quiet while the waiter made recommendations. This he did in English, though with a strong accent; probably he knew that people who had money didn't necessarily talk French.

She ate steadily and purposefully. It was undoubtedly the largest meal of her life. She decided at the outset that, if this man was fool enough to pay for it, she wasn't going to miss anything. She had shrimps, then asparagus soup, then a sole, then a huge sizzling steak with fried potatoes and mushrooms.

"We must have a bottle of bubbly," Peter said, "to celebrate our getting acquainted." Marjorie liked the taste of it at once and cheerfully drank more than half the bottle. She was quite aware that he was filling her glass to get her drunk, and quite confident of keeping her head.

While she ate and drank, he talked. He talked about the fun of being a bus-conductor, about

222

curious passengers he'd met, about a stunning show to which he'd love to take her. Marjorie was a little anxious about what to say in reply to questions; it would be wise, she decided, to be a secretary and not a shop-girl. But he asked no questions about what she did, still less about what she thought. When she made a remark, he didn't listen but only gave her an approving smile, as one might smile at a child who has learned a new word. Her mind still cool and clear despite the champagne, she knew that she was —as they said in the East End—just a cunt with a cotton frock over it.

To the background of his chatter, she tried to imagine what it was like to think of running up and down the steps of a bus—Ann's lifeline for years—as a holiday sport. What it was like to take the years at the Varsity as a right, assuredly followed by a desk in a nice clean office, a heritage of command. What it was like to spend on a dinner (she'd inspected the prices in the menu) more than the dole allowed a family for a week. What it was like to be a man who bought girls like buying pets, with a whistle and a meal and a show of kindness, but ultimately with an assumption of power.

He moved his chair closer to hers and kissed her hand. It was like being licked by a big, clumsy, affection-demanding dog. The waiter, luckily, appeared with the sweet. There was an enormous choice, displayed on a table with wheels; Marjorie had trifle with peaches and strawberries in it.

"Thought we might go round to my place and have a taste of the old port. Nobody there except the servants. My people cut down to the country to sit out the strike."

She examined him with cool contempt. She was now sure that he was really stupid.

"I don't know," she said, broadening the impersonation of innocence. "I don't think I ought to, really."

"It's quite early yet. I've got my car there, so I can drive you home."

"Well . . . just for a little while."

When he called for the bill, she excused herself and went to the lavatory. It was a mean little room at the end of a long corridor, and evidently didn't get cleaned so often as the restaurant. The window was small, but Marjorie had no fat on her bones and she squeezed through neatly. She dropped into a yard, and was in the Strand in two minutes. The only trouble was that she had to avoid buses until the strike was over.

As Ann remarked, Charlie was working a longer day during the strike than he did normally. He was at the docks early every morning and stayed until dark; he reckoned that any further attempts to break the picket-line would be made early or late, when there were no crowds of dockers to back up the pickets. But by the weekend, with excellent reports from all along the water-front, it seemed safe to relax.

"I'll have a lie-in on Saturday as well as Sunday, just like a toff," he told Ann.

But on Saturday, as early as ever, he was woken by a frantic banging on the front door. It was Sid. His sharp, thin face had a scared look, as if he expected to be punished for bringing bad news.

"The docks is working!"

"What d'you mean, Sid?"

"The docks is working, it's the truth. There's hundreds in there. Soldiers too."

Charlie took the bicycle and hurried to the docks. He soon saw what had happened. The lock-gate between the dock and the river was open, and the basin contained a small flotilla of police launches, Navy boats and barges. Charlie felt like a fool; it had simply never occurred to him that blacklegs would be brought by water. But it couldn't have been prevented, anyway. There were hundreds of them, as Sid said, and they were working energetically. From their voices, they were either undergraduates or the same kind of middle-class citizens who joined the specials. Unlike the wretched unemployed men, they really wanted to break the strike.

There was still a picket-line in front of the gate, but it guarded nothing. The gate itself had been opened from the inside. Soldiers with fixed bayonets stood at the warehouse doors and along the quayside. Navy men were working the cranes, skilfully enough. On the surrounding wall, a Navy detachment manned a heavy machine-gun.

An officer was strolling to and fro just inside the gate. He was tapping his boots with his stick; Charlie could remember, from wartime days, the debonair arrogance of the habit.

Deliberately, Charlie went as far as the gate and surveyed the scene inside. The officer halted. They confronted each other across a front line without a No Man's Land.

"Do you want to work, my man?" the officer demanded.

Charlie said: "I'm on strike." It angered him that he had to restrain himself deliberately from adding "sir".

"Keep out of here, then," the officer said curtly.

My father died here, Charlie wanted to say. My grandfather was a stevedore. It is my inheritance to be a stevedore, as it is yours to be an officer. But none of this could be said.

He walked back to the line, or rather straggling group, of pickets. Tom Whitmarsh said defiantly: "They can unload the cargo. They've still got to get it out."

True: they would have to get lorries into the docks. And lorries could be stopped—though not so easily, now the gate was open. For the present, there was nothing to do but wait.

It was still quite early when the lorries came. This time, it was not mere strike-breaking; it was a military operation. First came an armoured car, the turret down, the gun traversing in silent menace. Then three lorries, then another armoured car—and so on. The lorries were driven by soldiers, wearing steel helmets and with wire mesh over their windows.

Against this, the strikers had the traditional resource of working men: their numbers. The news had spread. There was nothing like such a crowd as on the first day, but the convoy was moving against resistance.

"Are we going to try and stop them?"

The question was for Charlie. It was the rough end of leadership, the payment for his new stature.

He looked up at the wall, and at the faces of the sailors with their machine-gun. He knew how life in uniform deadened thought; who could tell whether or not they believed that strikers were traitors, agents of Moscow? The faces were blank and remote, communicating nothing. And then there were the soldiers, invisible in their armoured cars.

For disaster, all that was needed was one finger pressed recklessly on a trigger. The men who waited for Charlie's word had voted to strike; they had not voted to die. In this familiar place, an unknown hatred could start and grow. This bloodshed could take them all out of England, into some strange fierce country.

"Let them through," Charlie said.

Toward midday, when the lorries had been loaded, the convoy returned. Through Canning Town and Poplar and Whitechapel, people stood and watched. Some men spat and cursed, some women screamed taunts, but for the most part there was only a sullen, bitter silence. In the City, past the frontier of Aldgate, the clerks and typists came to their office windows to cheer.

# 13

IN middle age, a man ceases to count the years. With his thirtieth birthday—three big candles on the cake—Charlie was aware of being no longer young. But manhood, not youth, had always been what mattered to him; he could scarcely remember being unready for the serious business of life. After this, on the rare occasions when he had to state his age for some official purpose, he genuinely had to think twice, aided by the date and the convenience of being born in 1900. Thirty-four, thirty-seven—what was the difference? A man is a man. Only when war came did he take note that, with forty coming up in a matter of months, he wouldn't be called up. But the important thing then was that his boys were young enough to be safe, even if one reckoned with a war as long as the last one. Harry was eleven, Ted was eight.

Looking back, Charlie saw the making of the children as the high point of this central span of life. He was grateful that Ann had not yielded to him before marriage. She had never been his bit of fun; bodily as much as in other ways, she was solely his wife. Their love achieved expression in an intimacy that he had not known to be possible, even after running through more women than he could name. He knew now what it was to create desire out of the misty borderland of sleep, to nourish it as if the two of them were shielding a little hopeful flame with their cupped hands. He learned the necessity of mood answering to mood, and the ease of knowing that nothing was lost by waiting, because the rightness was sure to come. He discovered the morning pleasure of the smiling glance that remembered and reminded and sometimes asked for renewal. Not many men, he guessed, knew this complicity—this true marriage.

He had reached Ann's body, it seemed to him, after making a place for it. While he enjoyed it, he was aware of the bed they had chosen together, paid for in twelve monthly instalments; of the sheets she had washed; of the room in which he had grown as baby, boy and man; of this house, his lasting home and Ann's too. All this had value—how much value, the possession of Ann proved and established. He had wanted her with his first snatched kisses. But all the time, even before knowing it, he had wanted her here.

He was making love to her, surely, as a husband makes love to his wife. It was deep and close, and always it reached through time, forward and back. It had a quick hastening rhythm within itself, and a long swaying rhythm outside itself. He felt these two rhythms in their bodies as he felt them in work. He stacked a hold with the sureness gained in other holds, and finished it as a link to other ships yet on the seas or yet unbuilt. And he moved within Ann with growing sureness too; he drew himself out of her with a thought of returning, in years called 1940 and 1950 and others that would be welcomed as they came. A man's life was made in his work and in his woman—what else?

He had to go some distance in this course, he felt, before they made a child. Of course he knew that children were conceived in the swiftest, the most loveless and meaningless, of encounters; but not by Ann, not in this marriage —some deeper than rational belief said that. He had to search for the heart of her, to get to some complete and ultimate meeting with her, before she accepted him in the triumph of creation. After the long engagement, he was now in another phase, more advanced but not yet the highest, in the process of becoming her husband. Meanwhile, he tried. This was the vital differance between making love with a girl—even a girl one could willingly marry—and a wife. Always there had been the French letter, or the pulling out, or the safe time of the month, or if one forgot all these and plunged on impulse and opportunity, then the ironical wish that the full effect of manhood joined with womanhood would not be realised. Now, to realise it was just the aim. He was aware of this from the moment of entering Ann, onward to the outpouring which was not a release for himself but a hopeful gift to her. All of it had a meaning, a richness and a freedom conferred by the purpose.

A little more than two years after they married, Ann became pregnant. It was about the right time; Dora said: "Well, I'd been wondering." Ann herself took up an attitude of commonsense acceptance: "It's nice to know we can do it, I suppose." This didn't fool him; he was sure that she was happy, as he was. Later he became anxious—the baby seemed to be enormous above her narrow hips. He saved up, trade luckily being good, for her to give birth in hospital. All night, he sat on a hard bench in a cavernous hall, jumping up with questions whenever a nurse pattered by. All next day, he dashed to the phone box by the dock gate whenever he got a break. Horrors beat at his mind. They could tear the child to bits, he wanted to shout, to save Ann. But the birth was merely slow, she explained afterwards, not terribly difficult.

The second boy was born at home, three years later. Ann went into labour earlier than expected, while Charlie was at work. When he got home, Dora and Liza were confidently in charge and ordered him to the pub. "What have you been drinking, you great brute?" Ann asked when he kissed her and the infant. More whisky than he could afford in 1931, he had to admit.

One Sunday morning, sitting up in bed and

giving Ted his feed, she said: "I'm not having any more kids, you know."

Life changed like this, suddenly and yet without drama. Charlie folded a page of *Reynolds' News*. He could think of nothing to say except: "Why not?"

"We've got a nice family. It's enough."

"Don't you want a girl?"

"Not all that much."

It seemed curious to him that she didn't want to recreate herself, as he had. But she liked boys; she hadn't wanted Ted to be a daughter.

"What d'you want to do, then?" he asked.

"I'll see to that. I'm going to the clinic."

The birth control clinic had opened not long before in a disused shop. Women dodged into it furtively; Bert Hall at number ten had blacked his wife's eye when he found out she went there; the Irish lads had broken the windows twice. Ann wouldn't care, of course.

Charlie stared at the blue veins in her breast, throbbing as the baby sucked. He wondered how she could decide so calmly that this was to be the last time. But it was her breast, her womb, her body. She had allowed him to reach them, but they remained her own. She would always be firm about that, knowing how her mother had died.

He didn't ask what she got at the clinic; it was her business, and he was sure that she managed it efficiently. He was not happy at losing the vital quality of their love-making, the quality of striving for creation. He understood why Bert Hall had struck his wife. Yet after a time he found that he minded less than he had expected. They had come together, he and Ann, and that remained. They had made a family. They turned to each other now in renewal and in abiding love.

Charlie observed also that the making of children could divide as well as unite. Tom Whitmarsh had married a cousin, or anyway a member of the sprawling Whitmarsh clan. Charlie remembered her as a bright, rather silly girl with a hunger for affection; he had put her on her back several times and she had loved it. He seldom saw her now. They had left Steadman Street and lived in Silvertown. The girl—that is, Tom's wife—seemed never to go out, and Tom seldom asked friends home. When Charlie did see her, she looked tired, dull-eyed, and invariably pregnant. Tom had someone else, a seaman's wife; so Charlie gathered from words overheard in the pub where she worked behind the bar. Tom hadn't discovered and pursued his wife as Charlie had, but had married her because she was, so to speak, handy. What Charlie felt about this, more than anything else, was pity for what his friend had missed.

Charlie was out more evenings than not—sometimes at a union meeting, mostly in the Gordon or meeting friends in some other pub. But he came home with pleasure. He knew that he would find the house clean and tidy, the boys in bed at their proper time, and Ann fresh and alert, quick with a kiss, ready to share whatever he had to tell her. She was like a busy little clock that never ran down. She had the same trim figure, the same firm features and glowing red hair, the same speedy accurate movements as when he had first seen her. She had the same strong will, the same sharp judgments and emphatic opinions. With two nippers on her hands, she found time to listen to talks on the wireless and read books from the public library. Charlie didn't go in for that himself, but it pleased him to have a wife who did.

The alternatives for a woman—the alternative extremes—were manifested in his sisters. Vi, still unmarried, had no life except through her business. Observing this life, Charlie was thankful to have stayed firmly in the working-class. There was no such thing for Vi as coming home from the day's work and forgetting about it; worries from the laundry pursued her even to Sunday dinner at number five. Charlie suspected that she made no more money than a chit of a shorthand-typist got as wages. Her clothes were dowdy, she practically never went to the pictures, she didn't drink—how much of this was economy and how much a sour self-denial, one couldn't be sure. The slump hit the laundry trade as it hit everything, and big firms were crushing small businesses. Old-fashioned little

shops were yielding to chainstores, free houses
to brewers' pubs, owner-driven taxis to company
fleets. Vi cut her prices, but couldn't cut them
enough. She dismissed some of the girls, doing
more work herself, paid the rest less, and saved
every possible penny on fuel and light. And still
she worried. The absurdity, as Charlie and Ann
saw it, was that the less good the capitalist
system did her, the more blindly devoted to it
she became. She railed against the trade unions,
believed that the Socialists were bent on raiding
Post Office savings, considered Ramsay
Macdonald the saviour of the country, and voted
solidly Conservative (she wouldn't call it Tory).
"Conservative!" Ann snapped at her. "A fat lot
you've got to conserve."

Ann frankly disliked her, but Charlie felt sorry
for her, remembering the little charmer that Ann
had never seen. By the mid-thirties, Vi had
entirely lost her looks. Her hair was lustreless,
her face lined—a proper old maid. She and Ann
were of an age, but she looked ten years older.
Indeed, Charlie couldn't imagine that Ann would
ever look like this. The lines on Vi's face were
the lines of anxiety and loneliness. Everyone had
worries these days—everyone but the rich.
However, no woman deserved to take her
worries to a cold narrow bed, without a word
of comfort, without sharing the burden, without
love.

Charlie remembered the girl Vi; Dora still saw

her. "Can't imagine why our Vi doesn't click with some young man," she said repeatedly. "Still pretty, isn't she?" Then she would sigh and add: "Always was a choosy one, though, wasn't she?" With Ann managing number five and Liza settled, Dora's energies—what remained of them—went into weaving plots for Vi to meet young men. Conferences with other Mums would result in invitations to Sunday tea; Vi was dragged along, evidently suffering. These introductions never led to anything, and as the years passed the age gap between Vi and the young men became more glaring. At last, when Vi was turned thirty, Dora brought down disaster by asking: "Seen any more of that Joe Porter, Vi?" Vi's taut lips trembled; her face did, for an astonishing moment, look like a sensitive young girl's. Then she uttered a choked sob and rushed out of the room. Ann spoke firmly to Dora, and there were no more plots.

But Liza was living Dora's life over again, or the life that would have been Dora's if Jack hadn't died. By 1939, she had six children. There was no question of the birth control clinic for her. When one of her children went down with diphtheria, she tried prayer, sceptically at first; the child recovered, and Liza became a real believing Catholic and a regular at confession. Anyway, she didn't mind how many children she had. She found it easier, she told Ann, to manage a brood of them than one or two. In the

Varelli home, daily routines were carried out like school assembly: meals, the afternoon nap (Liza herself always slept), prayers, bathtime. There was a huge tin bath which held two or three children. Those who were in it splashed, while the others kept topping it up from saucepans. Her only regret was that the crowd diminished during the day when the older children had to go to school. However, like the bath, the family was continually replenished.

Liza dressed the children alike, the boys in blue and the girls in pink. All the girls had pigtails with pink ribbons; the knotting was another routine. When they were small, the children were like animated dolls with whom Liza delightedly played. As they grew older, she still cared very little about their manners or their progress in school. Clearly, the idea that they would have to grow up wasn't real to her.

If by some chance Liza had not married, she would have been perfectly placed in charge of an orphanage. She was always glad to look after Harry and Ted for a day, and quite content to have neighbours' children running in and out; all were treated just like her own, and fed if they happened to be there when it was time for a meal. The ice-cream bin was a magnet for the children of several streets. A cornet was a penny, and a lick was free—a lick was an amount varying at random, put on a wooden spoon.

Almost entirely, Liza's life was limited to her

home. She did little shopping, since she fed the family out of supplies delivered in bulk for the restaurant. She enjoyed dispensing hospitality to Charlie and Ann or to her mother, as well as to Varelli relations, but it was too much of a bother to pay visits with her brood. And, what between the effort and the fares, the Varelli family seldom made any excursions. The restaurant was open all day and every day, Sundays included, and closed when the last customer felt like leaving. Really, there was almost no distinction between the home and the restaurant. The children played round the tables, restrained only by an occasional clout from Tony and the danger of being scalded with minestrone if they tripped Liza up. The family ate at a long table in the back of the restaurant, joined by customers if the other tables were full. Tony was in the restaurant practically all the time, playing dominoes or chatting if it wasn't busy. Liza bustled about between the kitchen, the restaurant and the upstairs rooms, cooking, serving, washing up, mopping the lino, making the beds and cots, getting everything done somehow. Only the afternoon nap was sacred, an essential renewal of energy. She had lost her timidity now that she had her own domain, and acquired Dora's kind of contentment. The difference was that she was never lost from her surroundings; Dora's dreaminess had been inherited by no one.

Liza bustled just as much when she was pregnant. She took the pregnancies easily, the births too; she appeared in the restaurant showing off her new baby when it was a day or two old. She actually felt more healthy when she was carrying —"more like myself somehow," she said. Friends assumed her to be expecting unless they knew otherwise, and asked "When's the next one?" as they greeted her. It wasn't easy to tell the difference, for her waistline merely varied from large to larger. Always big-boned and plump—again like Dora—she had cheerfully abandoned any attempt to preserve a figure. While Dora fattened herself on suet puddings and stout, Liza did the same on spaghetti. Her energy was unaffected; like a round, puffing tug-boat, she seemed to gain momentum from weight. But she looked older than her years— almost as much so as Vi, though in the contrary manner. From kitchen steam and a lack of outdoor air, her face became florid and blotchy. She had taken to dressing like an Italian matron in black dress, apron and swinging crucifix. Like this, she could have been any comfortable age, but not young.

Over the years, she became a real Varelli, cockney-English and Italian at the same time. In-laws and cousins were constantly in the restaurant, and to begin with they teased her by making remarks in Italian which she couldn't understand. So she made Tony teach her the language, and after a time found herself using it with the children. It never occurred to her to pronounce it like English, like a pupil learning French at school, so that ultimately visitors from Italy could hardly believe that she had no Italian blood. The Varellis pronounced her name in the Italian way—Leeza—and she preferred this, but she never got the Wheelwrights to adopt it.

It was one way of living, Charlie thought, and it was clearly far better than Vi's; yet it was not what he and Ann had. So far as he could see, Tony and Liza didn't have a real home: a place where they could be themselves and live close to each other. They provided a setting for the customers, the friends and relations, and the swarm of children—but where were they? Charlie had sometimes been there late in the evening, yet he had never seen them talk to each other. Somehow, though Tony and Liza were within earshot of each other all day, they led separate lives as he and Ann did not. So far as Charlie knew, Tony didn't have a woman like Tom Whitmarsh; but he had withdrawn from Liza's pregnancies into a kind of male irresponsibility. "She's having another. It makes her happy," he would say, as if it were an indulgence of hers, like eating sweets—as if he'd had nothing to do with it. He gave little thought to the upbringing of the children or their future; Charlie's efforts to start conversations on this subject got nowhere. Indeed, he took hardly any notice of them. Faced with a childish dispute or an outbreak of tears, he called Liza and went on reading the *Pink 'Un* or playing dominoes. Children were a woman's sphere, Charlie conceded, but surely the father was the chief guide and the final authority. That was part of being a man.

Charlie still liked Tony, but had come to sense in him the lack of something essential, something hard and clear. A man, he felt, had to exert himself under responsibility and discipline, in a world with other men. You needed this manhood —it was a true paradox—in order to come close to a woman, to be of value to her. At its simplest, you had to go out to work in order to come home from work. Hanging about a restaurant all day, doing the same work as your wife but rather less of it, wasn't the same thing at all. Tony was letting himself go, not as despairingly as unemployed men, but in something like the same way. He was getting flabby and pasty-faced; he had a continual smoker's cough from cheap cheroots. Charlie envisaged Italy—the Continent in general—as full of such men.

So Charlie and Ann had two children, and were content. It was a time when a large family was a burden, unless one happened to own a restaurant. Babies were left in church porches or found floating in the river. That had always happened, but in the old days the mothers had been terrified young girls. Now they were the wives of men without work.

At the docks, the shape-up had become something between a charity line-up and a riot. Charlie was one of the crowd nowadays, for the employers had whittled away the distinction between stevedores and dockers. A man had to do whatever work he was given—loading or unloading—and think himself lucky to get it. In the crowd, the non-registered men now outnumbered the real dockers. There were men sacked from every job in the East End, from bricklaying to tailoring; there were seamen without ships; there were Geordie shipbuilders and Lancashire weavers and Welsh miners, bitterly losing the illusions that had brought them to London; there were frightened, weedy men in shiny blue suits who had been bank clerks or car salesmen, or even gentlemen whose investments had gone up in smoke. When the gate was opened, they behaved as if they were trying to get out of a building that had caught fire. The dockers had always elbowed and jostled, but these desperate men, joined by no common feeling, each the enemy of all others, fought like savages. The registered dockers linked arms to keep the strangers back, or used their fists if necessary. One day, when nine-tenths of the crowd was turned away, a man was left on the ground, crushed to death. Charlie stared at the body, humiliated by the beastliness in which he had had a part.

There were three million unemployed in the depth of the great slump. When the figure was brought down to two million, the newspapers claimed a triumph. The dole was cut to starvation point. Old people, when their sons could not maintain them, were forced into the workhouses. Young men drifted aimlessly about the streets and queued for bowls of soup at the missions. After the lost battle of the General Strike, this was a long dispirited retreat for the working-class. And it was a retreat in which many lost heart or deserted. In the catastrophic 1931 election, there were even stevedores who voted Tory.

Yet these were the years in which Charlie felt himself to grow to full stature. In the docks he was a trusted man, as well known for his tireless strength as his father had been. Bill Whitmarsh ruptured himself and had to give up work; by common consent, Charlie became the leader of the gang. The foremen searched for him in the chaos of the shape-up, and he got work if there was any. Though he was sorry for the hundreds who were turned away, he felt no guilt for the pride to which he had a full right. Besides, Tom and the rest of the gang were sustained by him. It was rare in the slump years to work a full week, but Charlie always earned something.

Prices were low and Ann shopped sensibly; they managed.

Beyond each man's struggle for work, there was the struggle of the dockers as a whole to defend what they had painfully gained over two generations. With men clamouring for work on any terms—men who knew nothing of these established claims—the bosses saw their chance. They tried to speed up the work and dodge the safety rules; they faked the reckoning of over-time and dirty-cargo money. The workers resisted grimly, deprived of their traditional weapon—the bosses could laugh at a strike threat. Each conflict had to be argued out by a champion with a thorough knowledge of past agreements, customs and precedents, and an utter determination not to give way. There was nobody to touch Charlie Wheelwright. Once a company official saw the big fellow striding along the quay, he was half ready to give up and save trouble. Charlie was called on by men of his own union, of the other dock-workers' union, and of no union at all. If he wasn't working, there might at any time be a knock on the door of number five. There were risks in the fight; he could be struck off the register on some pretext, he might simply not be called for work. He put the risks out of his mind, and found that he was right.

He had come to think of the Albert Dock as a republic in which he was a leader among equal citizens. Of Steadman Street, his home territory, he thought in the same way. Injustice had to be opposed, the unfortunate had to be helped, the foolish had to be reproved and taught. So long as he knew himself to have the strength, he would do it.

A community needs such a man, and in the hard years Steadman Street was more of a community than ever. If an argument was going on when Charlie entered the bar of the Gordon, someone was sure to say: "Let's see what Charlie thinks". As he walked home, or took a stroll on Sunday, anxious hands touched his arm: "Mind if I just ask you, Charlie . . ." But more often than not, the problems came to him through Ann. She had a capacity for sensing what was wrong before it was put into words. And, though Charlie's decisions were his own, he seldom acted without the aid of her understanding and support.

After Steadman Street ceased to belong to Steadman, it was owned by a company with an office over a bank in Barking Road. A collector came round for the rent on Fridays; the tenants told him about repairs that were needed, or occasionally went to the office. They considered that they had a good landlord, as landlords went. In 1919, each tenant received a letter to say that ownership had been transferred to another company, which had a long pompous name and an office in the City. The rents promptly went up to ten shillings—eleven shillings for number five. Rent control was still in force, but the increase was allowed through some legal wangle or other. However, in that post-war boom year almost everyone was in work and wages were good, so the grumbles subsided. When times became hard, people were at least grateful that the rents didn't go up again. The constant complaint was that this landlord could not be persuaded to do repairs—or only with great reluctance and after long delay. Getting in touch with the company was a problem in itself. The man who came for the rent worked for a collecting agency and said that the management of the property was no concern of his. Alf Harris once went up to the office, to be told by some chit of a girl that individual tenants were not received—what would happen if they all came? —and all requests should be submitted in writing. When anyone wrote, the reply came weeks later and was phrased in a mystifying jargon. No one from the company ever came to look at the houses. They began to need repairs quite seriously; by 1930, they were fifty years old. A deep resentment built up against the company—remote, arrogant, dishonest, and obviously rolling in wealth.

In the panicky summer of 1931, the Bennetts at number seven (little Mrs. Mead had long ago vanished) were served with an eviction notice. Charlie took it as an invasion of protected territory; having the bailiffs next door was almost like having them in his home. George Bennett was a man of forty-odd: a regular soldier before 1914, gassed in the trenches, capable only of light work. He'd had a job as a gardener in the park, but lost it when the Council made a drastic staff cut. He was a stern, reserved man, harsh with his two daughters, bitter about his reduced position. Charlie had never liked him much—all the same, he was a neighbour. Number seven had a smoky flue and a warped door that let in piercing draughts; the landlord had done nothing about them. True, Bennett was behind with the rent. But Mrs. Bennett and the girls went hopping every summer; only a few more weeks, and they could start making up the arrears. And the elder girl, just finishing school, had been promised a job in the Co-op shop. Bennett didn't smoke, drank one pint on Saturdays, didn't bet, never wasted a penny. He would be square with the landlord as soon as it was humanly possible.

"They won't get you out, not if I know it," Charlie told him. Bennett growled that he wasn't asking anyone for help. But Charlie was upholding fair play on behalf of all Steadman Street. When the bailiffs came, neighbours blocked the street and kept them twenty yards from the door of number seven. Charlie, sacrificing a day's work, marshalled the resistance. A reporter scribbled notes, and the local paper headlined "War Hero's Home Menaced"—

248

Bennett had the Military Medal. The British Legion made a loan. The Bennetts stayed. In the end, even the flue and the door were repaired.

Still, some tenants were evicted. Others, unequal to the ten bob rent, found poorer places to live. Old people died. Men got jobs out of London, went to sea, joined the Army. Families dwindled or scattered. The cyclic life of a street in a great city kept up its slow but ceaseless movement. Time strengthened Charlie's authority; it was worthy of note, if not exactly rare, that a man had been born in Steadman Street. Strangers, meanwhile, became neighbours. Through helping and quarrelling, borrowing and lending, making and hoarding memories, the street grew together as it aged.

When he stopped to consider, Charlie was surprised how much he knew of the life that had been lived in these thirty-four houses. Here, a family had moved in and found an infant's skeleton under the floorboards. There, a lad had walked out after being given the strap by his father and worked his passage to Canada—he owned a paper-mill now, it was said. There again, a couple had lived respectably for ten years until the man was suddenly arrested for bigamy. "You could write a book," newcomers told Charlie sometimes.

He loved the street. He loved the look of it. Coming home when it was still daylight on a fine evening, he always paused at the corner. It was peaceful after the noise and traffic of the main road, yet it was always human and alive, with women chatting on the doorsteps and boys kicking a ball about. The houses looked firm and contented with their neat square windows and grey-tiled roofs and puffing chimneys. They took up just what space they needed and eclipsed none of the sky; the sunlight filled a broad path between them. In their two even lines, they gave an impression of leaning back from the roadway and made the street seem wider than it was. Charlie was aware of proportion, of things being right. It was a good place to live in.

It had come through the hard times, this street, and he had come through with it. Gradually, in the later thirties, trade picked up. In the depth of the slump, a dockworker had been better off only than the unemployed, worse off than men with jobs in factories. But as things improved, Charlie was earning as much as anyone he knew. Working steadily through the weekends, he put up new wallpaper in one room after another. Ann got a tea service with a flower pattern to replace the old chipped white cups. They traded in the old wireless for a radiogram and collected half a dozen records—tangoes and waltzes, John McCormack ballads, military marches. In the summer of 1939, they took the boys for a week to a boarding-house at Margate. There would be war, Ann said positively; they must do it while they could.

# 14

WHAT these years were like for Ann, Charlie never altogether knew. Certain things were best not said, even between husband and wife—especially between husband and wife, indeed. She could count on it that Charlie accepted this principle, as all sensible people did. Words were clumsy tools, dangerous when applied to feelings. What could well be lived with, kept to oneself, made grating friction if placed on open record. She did love this man; she was glad to be his wife. It was best to say no more than that. Since no marriage and no life could be perfect—this Ann profoundly believed—nothing was gained by declaring the imperfection.

Charlie would have been honestly bewildered if Ann had told him that she was struggling to keep her end up. He didn't order his wife about, as most men did. He dominated her because dominance was in his nature. She had accepted that in loving him; she couldn't have lived a month with a weak, dependent man. She had no wish to wear the trousers. She had no wish to fight against Charlie. Yet in a way she had to fight, or at least to resist, to defend herself against him—even against his love. So there were two yearnings in her: to share her life with him, and to prevent the loss of herself. She had to draw away from him even while she gave herself. He was seeking to reach her, she knew that. But she was struggling not to be enveloped by him, not to be swallowed up.

She felt these two yearnings, almost pulling her apart, when they made love. There was this great big man all over her, crushing and pounding and squeezing her small body. Big mouth on hers, big hands gripping her, big chest flattening her breasts, big weapon driving through her. She loved it, truly; she'd had no idea how splendid it would be. Some girls, like Marjorie, had sensed it before it came to them, but Ann hadn't. She wanted all of Charlie's weight and strength, all the power of his assault. In bed most of all, she couldn't have done with a mild tentative man. And yet the greater the power, the greater the threat. What gave her joy was just what she had to resist. If she was at one with him, she lost herself. She grasped, after getting the hang of this business, that he wanted her to come when he did. That completed his pleasure, and it completed hers too. She surrendered happily, lovingly, to the flooding power of the man. But sometimes she denied him, at the cost of denying herself. She let him spend himself and relax, and then she came a moment later, triumphing on her own, having the woman's last word. It was a contest, when all was said and done—marriage was a contest, love itself was a contest.

She often wondered if there was something peculiar about herself. Steadman Street—the world, apparently—was full of women who had submitted to the loss of themselves, who were sunk under their men, submerged. There was Liza, breeding away like a rabbit in a hutch. There was Dora . . . Ann was well aware that what Dora could not accept in her was her independence of Charlie, her resistance. That she loved as totally as she resisted, Dora would never see.

On the other hand, there was Marjorie. Marjorie kept changing her job; from the shoe-shop she went to a dress-shop, then she was a waitress, then a hello-girl at the telephone exchange. Then suddenly she was a parlourmaid. This appeared to be a step down, but Marjorie always knew what she was doing. There was a cook, and a kitchen maid, and a char to do the rough, so Marjorie's duties were limited to answering the door and attending to the lady, who was in bad health. Moreover, the lady was often away, especially in the winter. The gentlemen was a Tory MP. Ann saw his picture in the paper: a beefy man with a heavy moustache. It wasn't necessary to ask whether Marjorie went to bed with him; she came to Steadman Street wearing jewellery and smelling of French perfume. After a few years, the lady died and the gentleman remarried. Marjorie got a job with another invalid lady, being recommended ironically because she had looked after the MP's wife so well. She was not a maid now, but a companion. She went with her employer to Monte Carlo, Switzerland, even on a cruise. She had stories to tell of Italian princes and American millionaires; she collected more jewellery, sometimes no doubt by bestowing herself, more often (Ann guessed) by half-promising to. Eventually this lady died too, leaving Marjorie five hundred pounds.

Marjorie had grown into a beauty, very much in the taste of the period. She had long legs, small breasts, a long neck and bold chin, high cheekbones, big mobile eyes, all in the style of Greta Garbo or Marlene Dietrich. She chose clothes well and wore them with assurance. One knew—a woman certainly knew—that men stared at her wherever she went. She presented them with the maddening uncertainty: available if she fancied you, unattainable if she didn't. Charlie treated her as a sort of fictional character. He would make her a low, exaggerated bow and say: "Welcome to our humble home, your lady-ship!" But he was impressed, Ann knew.

The East End remained, essentially, Marjorie's home. She appeared at number five every few weeks except when she was abroad, though always without warning. There, she talked in her childhood accent, gave the children her rings to hold while she did the washing up, and went across to the Gordon at opening time to drink light ale. She brought sweets or toys for Harry and Ted, but always the kind they were used to, the kind she had saved pennies for herself. She was like a spy, relaxing in her homeland after an exciting but testing mission in enemy territory. She spoke of the rich derisively—they were idle, stupid, feeble; they wouldn't know how to polish their shoes if they had to; no wonder they made such a mess of governing. Her opinions remained radical. The only time that Ann saw her angry was when someone in the Gordon declared that England needed a Hitler.

One thing was certain about Marjorie: she didn't give a damn. In theory, she was dependent on her successive employers. In reality, she was ready to walk out on any employer, and any man, at her pleasure. She used them; they didn't use her. It wasn't only, Ann felt, that Marjorie was a spy among the upper classes. She was also a spy for womanhood among men—a spy, or a pirate. "He's like all the rest of them," she would remark at the end of a story about a famous writer or a Harley Street doctor. "Show him a bit of leg and you could tie him up in brown paper." Though she was thirty by the time the war came, she was in no hurry to get married. "Time enough to settle down when my energy gives out," she said.

That was Marjorie, then; she had no need to

struggle for her independence, because she had never conceded it. She had missed something precious that Ann had found—Ann was clear about that. In the truest sense, she was not happy; she had fun, but that wasn't the same. And yet, she was free. She was absolutely herself. When she had left the house—holding herself taut and straight, raking the street with defiant eyes—Ann felt a small, fierce envy of her.

There was some importance, Ann thought, in the seven years' difference in age between herself and her sister. She was nurtured, as Charlie was, in the pre-war years when the family was a complete enclosure: not a cage exactly, but a sort of warm, cosy hutch. But Marjorie had begun her thinking in an uncertain, questioning time. When there was no security, there must be pirates. Women got divorced, or simply didn't get married; it was still exceptional, especially in the working-class, but it was a possible choice, and it wasn't always pitiable as in Vi's case. Women were in the headlines, striding out like men—explorers, air pilots, writers, MPs. You read of a ballerina with an exotic Russian name, and learned that she had been born Jones in Bermondsey or Smith in Manchester. Even the women who lived off men were no longer the old brand of mistress, hidden away in a love nest. They had their open, piratical pride.

As for the family, it kept its apparent strength.

Most people took it for granted. But Ann sensed a dwindling in it, a fear of dissolution, as in most other established institutions. Charlie had no inkling of this; the Wheelwright family and stevedoring, which went together in his mind, reached through his life from past to future. The Naylor family, however, no longer existed. It had never been much of a family at the best of times. Ann's father had been an only child, orphaned early, a man struggling alone. Her mother had cut away from her roots, since her brothers and sisters had stayed in Ireland or returned there. Then she had died, and Ann had kept the family going through her bus-conductress years: but provisionally, only so long as it was necessary. It had been predictable that her father would die—he wasn't made for age—and that she, Marjorie and Sid would go separate ways. Sid, even as a child, had a restless, venturesome air to him, much like Marjorie's.

Naylor died in 1930, quietly and without protest as he had lived. The charity sent Ann a message one day to say he was ill. It was a winter pneumonia, dangerous for a man with his weak heart. He was taken to hospital, the charity paying. Ann went there at visiting time, hating the hushed hopelessness of the ward, the grey old men coughing and spitting in rows of beds. One evening a nurse stopped her: "He's gone, I'm afraid. He just didn't wake up this morning."

257

Marjorie, by this time, no longer lived in the tenement. Sid sold the furniture for a few shillings the same week and moved into a tiny room with his employers; he was then a delivery boy for a butcher's shop. As soon as he was old enough, he became a cabin-boy on a liner. Marjorie arranged this—her employer, or lover, had shipping interests. Soon Sid switched to a Greek merchant line, on a promise of being trained as a wireless operator. The company, however, went bankrupt and he was paid off, or not paid off, in Buenos Aires. This didn't worry him. The weather was marvellous, he wrote; he would stay, for a time anyhow. Most of the businesses seemed to be British-owned and he had already found a job. No more letters came, only Christmas cards with cheerful messages. Ann pictured him without anxiety; like Marjorie, he was a forager in alien country, making his way, still at heart a sharp thrusting Cockney.

Ann felt herself divided by what she had been and what she now was. There was Ann Naylor —stubbornly surviving as simply Ann—and there was Mrs. Wheelwright. Despite the long engagement in which she got used to the idea, despite marriage, she still felt odd twinges of surprise at being Mrs. Wheelwright. It was curious that Dora, who deserved the title far better, was Mrs. Goodings. A part of Ann wanted to be free—to live Marjorie's way, Sid's way. A weightier part of her, normally uppermost, rejoiced in her home, in her satisfied womanhood, in Charlie. You only live once, she told herself. You can't have everything.

Living with Dora was a trial. It was taken for granted in half the homes in Steadman Street, this business of two women sharing a house, being together for more waking hours than man and wife. Ann felt it unnatural; was that because she hadn't had a mother since girlhood, or was she peculiar in this too? By customary standards, she had nothing to complain of. Just as Charlie was a good husband, Dora was as tolerable a mother-in-law as one had a right to expect. She made few demands, she didn't grumble, she never criticised the way Ann managed the house and brought up the boys. If she wasn't really fond of Ann, that was virtually normal. It is a rare mother who thinks any wife good enough for her only son.

To be honest, the old girl was a trial simply because she was there. Ann was never alone with Charlie except in bed (even then, Dora was near) and when they went out. Occasionally, with much preparation and effort, Dora went off to spend a day with Liza and Tony. But these visits, weekly when Ann first came to number five, became fortnightly, then monthly or still rarer. For Dora was now so fat that all movement was the transporting of a mass of shapeless blubber. She had to be heaved up—Charlie was strong enough to do it, Ann wasn't—on to the platform of a bus. She couldn't walk far. Her varicose veins got no worse, but they would never improve.

Ann herself had a horror of being fat; this was one reason why she didn't want a lot of children. She caught herself staring at Dora as a child might stare at a hunchback, knowing that it was decent to look elsewhere but unable to do so. She tried to imagine what it must feel like to carry all that fat about; and, half unconsciously, she touched her belly and her thighs to remind herself that they were still the same shape. To be deft and quick in movement, for her, was integral to being alive. She thought of this ponderous immobility as a resignation from the world. But as a matter of fact, Dora's health was pretty good. Nor was she old. She would be here, Ann supposed, for ever. She ate enormously, still sucked sweets, drank endless cups of tea thick with sugar, and enjoyed her bottle of stout—she was far beyond worrying, she said. It seemed to do her no harm.

Mostly, she sat all day in her armchair, merely waddling across the yard to the toilet or, in fine weather, to the front door to chat with Maggie Harris. But now and then, when Ann was going out to do the shopping, she would say: "I think I'll come with you. Do me good to have a bit of a walk." Ann dreaded this. For one thing, she had to take the children; for another, Dora's tortoise-like pace was a torment to her, especially

260

when it came to crossing the main road. Worst of all, shopping was now like a rare treat for Dora. She lingered by the shelves, she compared different brands of goods, she questioned the assistants about things that were not in stock, she haggled about prices. She had always done this—it was what she understood by shopping—but the years had slowed down an already slow process. Ann had no taste for this part of the housewife's life. She liked to decide quickly, buy what she needed or could afford, and move on in her usual brisk way. "Come along, Mum, do," she would plead. The shopkeepers smiled; they had known Dora a long time.

Otherwise, Dora just sat. She seldom even read the paper, though she liked the wireless. She maintained the same contented expression whether it was broadcasting music or news or a talk or a comedy programme; it was impossible to tell whether she was listening or not. Now that she had no obligations at all, she let hours go by in daydreaming. If Ann mentioned something that had happened during the day, such as a fire-engine rushing along the road or an aeroplane flying low overhead, it was often obvious that Dora had been quite unaware of it. Ann believed that she was hopelessly stupid. The truth was rather that, no longer compelled to thought any more than to action, she had gradually lost the habit of it. She was silent for long stretches, whether anyone else talked or not; but at other times, for no evident reason, she would launch into a long monologue. Increasingly, she recalled the distant past. She told Ann of the doings of people who had lived in the street years ago; as she went on, the lapse of time became unreal to her and she talked as if the incident had happened last week. She told stories about Charlie as a little boy, about Vi as a pert little girl, and about her husband—Jack, of course; she seemed to have forgotten Herbert's existence. The boys loved their Gran. Her stories, being real, were far better than fairy-tales, and when they talked she listened with endless patience. She was on their mental level, Ann considered.

One day—it was in 1935—she decided to come shopping just as Ann was about to leave the house. It was particularly inconvenient, because Ann had to get round the shops in a limited time and go on to the Board School, or elementary school as it was now called. Harry had been misbehaving, and Ann had been asked to see the headmaster. She explained this. Dora said comfortably: "Oh, you've got plenty of time." This was true enough, at Ann's pace; but at Dora's pace, they still hadn't bought apples or Charlie's tobacco when Ann was due at the school. "Don't worry, I'll do it," Dora said. She couldn't go far wrong, Ann decided.

"Mind, it's St. Julien flake."

"Oh, I know. He always has smoked that."

Probably Jack had smoked it, Ann thought. Her mind on the problem of Harry, she hurried off, shopping-bag in one hand and whisking Ted along with the other. She looked round once and saw Dora gazing at the window of a sweet-shop. Irritably, she wondered if the apples or the tobacco would be forgotten.

What happened ten minutes later, according to witnesses at the inquest, was that Dora stepped off the pavement without a glance, straight in front of a car. The driver was not held to blame. "She seemed to be daydreaming," one witness said.

Ann wept at this death, as she had not wept for her own father. It was a shock, of course; Dora had seemed immortal. And, now that she was gone, her virtues stood out in retrospect. She had been kindly, even-tempered, harmless to say the least. She hadn't had an easy life. Ann could have granted her more respect and more comfort—now, it was too late. Ann's tears were not of sorrow but of self-reproach. The accident itself had been her fault, damning proof of her lack of care for Dora. Charlie dismissed this notion, but Ann couldn't free herself from it.

Still, her honesty obliged her to recognise that she had gained. The house seemed larger without Dora's massive presence. Ann and Charlie took over the front bedroom, which was a relief now that the boys were getting bigger. Ann had a new freedom, especially when Ted started school and she had the house to herself most of the day. She could have the wireless on or off as she pleased. She read with concentration, without fear of Dora's rambling monologues. For lunch, she usually had a boiled egg and an apple.

But in this freedom, she realised after a time, there was a catch or at all events an irony. She was now absolutely Mrs. Wheelwright. In Dora's lifetime she had sometimes been spoken of as "young Mrs. Wheelwright"; that was over. She had a solid, rooted position here in Steadman Street. Now that she had come into her full inheritance, nothing more in her life would change. Already there were newcomers to the street—young wives especially—who looked up to her and sought her advice. As time passed, there would be more.

She made the best of it. Ever since she had lived here, she had known a good deal about other people's affairs, partly because Charlie was a Steadman Street man through and through and partly because of her natural shrewdness. But she had stood a little apart, especially from the women's gossip. Now she tried consciously to make firm friendships. There would be no others in her life. She chatted on the doorstep, accepted and offered cups of tea, when she could have used the time better. She even forced herself to spend some time with old Maggie Harris. It was a kind of reparation to Dora, for Dora's death had left a gap in Maggie's life. All the Harris sons and daughters had left home, though two sons worked in the docks. It wasn't much of a life for the old couple, making ends meet on the pension. Alf, though turned seventy, had kept his health; he liked to sit on a park bench when he wasn't in the local, exchanging news and views with other old codgers. Maggie, who had started to get bad rheumatic spells, was alone a lot. Ann shopped for her, called in daily to see how she was, and gave her a bit of what she needed most—company.

Ann's best friend was Mrs. Connolly at number six, just across the street. They had always been on good terms; at about this time, they were brought closer because Harry, who had begun to play street games and wander about the neighbourhood, chummed up with the Connollys' Brian. The door of number six was always open and the kettle always on, and Kate was happy to keep an eye on Harry and little Ted whenever Ann wanted them out of the way.

Kate and her husband Kevin, like thousands of others round the docks, came of families that remained fiercely Irish after three generations in London. "Don't tell me you're not Irish with hair like that," she had said to Ann on first meeting her, and was delighted to be assured that the hair was Irish. Kate was a tall woman, not pretty but with a bold sexual confidence, a couple of years older than Ann. Married very young, she had three children, well spaced out:

Patrick was fifteen, Moira twelve, and Brian seven. Ann was surprised to learn, when they became close friends, that Kate had been using birth control all along—not from the clinic, but from some clandestine network of Irish wives. Kate, for her part, was astonished that Ann told her husband. "It's no business of any man's," she declared. It was no business of the priest's, either. Kate went to mass and was convinced that you had to have a religion; her children, of course, went to Catholic schools. But she confessed only what she wanted to confess. She took a cynical view of the priesthood, from the Pope down. "When they're not after the girls," she said, "they're after the boys." Her conduct was governed less by religion than by a tangle of superstitions, which she obeyed scrupulously. A black cat which lived at number eight complicated life for her considerably—seeing it was lucky on some days and unlucky on others, Ann never quite grasped why.

Both Kate and Kevin were abysmally ignorant of matters that didn't concern them directly. Kate believed that black men were all cannibals, and that no beef or mutton was eaten in Africa. She had never heard that MPs and Ministers had salaries; according to her, they helped themselves out of taxes and raised the taxes when they were a bit short. On this point, Ann couldn't convince her otherwise—indeed, she insisted that Ann had failed to see through the dodge.

266

She read at the speed of a child and was really sure only of the capital letters. But once Ann got to know Kate well, it was clear that she was quick-witted. If Brian was unfairly punished at school, she marched into the headmaster's study and proved his innocence with the keen logic of a lawyer. What Ann liked and respected in her friend, above all, was that Kate was a fighter. She was perpetually in dispute with policemen who stopped children playing, with shops that overcharged, with officials who asked nosey questions. She fought fiercely but without hatred; as she saw it, it was their job to do her down and it was up to her to defeat them. In fact, she enjoyed a fight as if it were a tough, demanding sport.

Ann, if she was in a battle, could match Kate's determination and courage. She could not match Kate's gaiety—Kate's loud, carolling laugh, head thrown back, shoulders heaving. There had been happiness in Ann's life, but up to now there had not been much humour. Planted in Steadman Street, fixed as Mrs. Wheelwright, she needed that.

What Kate did for her, she hoped, Brian was doing for Harry. Harry was a quiet child, rather shy, rather withdrawn. He needed to lark about a bit more, Ann and Charlie both thought. An adventurous, slightly mischievous pal—that was Brian—would be good for him. He was certainly clever; he understood anything that was explained to him, asked intelligent questions, and was on top of his school work. His school reports were not altogether good, though. He was undisciplined—not high-spirited in the ordinary boyish way, but breaking rules for no apparent reason. If he was ticked off or punished, he was sullen and resentful for days afterwards. He disliked school except for the drawing lessons, when he could work by himself; the other lessons bored him. He complained to Ann that he had nothing to do after he finished his sums. No doubt he could have gone ahead faster, and he wouldn't grasp that he must keep to the pace of a class of fifty. Sometimes, as a confused protest, he got all his sums wrong; then the teacher told him angrily that he wasn't trying. Ann herself felt that it was difficult to understand what went on in Harry's mind—or in Harry's feelings, the well-defended heart of him.

At bottom, Ann had not much confidence in her own ability to bring up children. True, she had seen Marjorie and Sid through their motherless years. But she had only kept them safe; she hadn't shaped their lives. She believed now that, if they were able to look out for themselves, it was to their own credit; whereas, if they couldn't manage to settle down, that was probably her fault. Charlie said, and Kate said too, that she worried too much about the boys. You couldn't worry too much, it seemed to her. She read the advice columns in the women's weeklies, and worked her way through books by psychologists from the public library. She was struck by the harm that could be done by a small mishap: an unjust punishment in honest error, or a casual "shut up!" when a child had something to say that was important to him. Dumbly, almost like an animal, the child withdrew into unexplained misery—Harry certainly did. Ted seemed to be happy, a noisy and carefree child like Brian Connolly. This delighted her, for she felt that a happy child was a gift of luck, flourishing in the face of reason and probability like a tree on waste ground.

Charlie, she saw, imagined that children did grow like trees—they had to start small, but if they escaped actual disaster they were bound to become big and strong. The literal size of the boys was important to him. He measured them against a door on their birthdays and cut notches with his penknife. Ted was up to expectations; Charlie was disappointed that Harry wasn't, and Harry—Charlie didn't intend this, but Ann saw it—was made to feel that he had failed. The boys were sure to be all right, Charlie evidently thought, if they had a good home, a good mother (as Ann obviously was) and a good father (as he never doubted himself to be). He took it that a father's duty was to earn money, to exert authority when necessary, to praise and encourage on occasions, and to provide an example of what the

boys must attain—of manhood. All this he did.
Why worry, then?

As for those school reports, Charlie didn't
believe that school mattered greatly. A working-
class lad would have to earn his living with his
hands, and lucky to do it with no end in sight
to mass unemployment. In any case, Charlie was
proud of holding on to his roots. He was among
those who did real work with real tangible
things, the work on which the country depended
—not buying and selling or shuffling bits of
paper. To step out of the working-class, like Vi,
was not an achievement in his eyes but a
narrowing. He told Ann, in pitying rather than
scathing tones, about his stepfather, the clerk at
the Pru—a poor sort of creature, not much of a
man. Charlie wanted his sons to be stevedores,
naturally. And Ted surely would be a stevedore;
he was the one who took after Charlie, in looks
and in the promise of size and strength as well
as in self-confidence. Neither boy took visibly
after Ann, for instance by inheriting the red hair.
But Harry was more her child, that was clear.
What Harry would become—that wasn't clear,
it was hard to tell.

Ann too was proud of belonging to the
working-class. That pride had been the Naylors'
salvation when collapse was near. Yes, she
valued Charlie as he was; no, she didn't want a
son who clerked for the Pru. But if the boy really
had brains? She thought about this when she was

alone. Brains had to be used, surely, as much as bodily strength. Many avenues were closed, of course; the system, and its structure of privilege, saw to that. Still, youngsters from streets like Steadman Street became teachers, and reporters on the papers, and . . . she tried to think of what else. Then she closed the line of thought, afraid of a treachery to Charlie.

By 1939, the questions were no nearer to being answered. Harry was still a quiet boy. He didn't seem to need other people; the friendship with Brian had melted. He was a little frightened of his father, it seemed, but didn't confide in his mother either. Just now, he had a passion for detective stories and took pride in guessing the murderer before he got to the end. The detectives—Sherlock Holmes, Father Brown, Lord Peter Wimsey—were as real and heroic to him as boxers or cricketers were to other boys.

She sat on the beach at Margate, a Mum in a crowd of Mums, getting along toward forty now. She hadn't let herself go, like most of them. Her flesh held firm and her hair still gleamed from regular brushing. At night, she and her man were still eager for each other.

Harry, flat on the sand with chin in hands, was deep in *Murder on the Orient Express*. Charlie and Ted were playing cricket with people they had met at the boarding-house. It wasn't hot; a keen wind blew from the sea. The sun flashed out, then dipped the beach into greyness.

It felt strange to be away from home, to have no shopping to do and no supper to cook. A sense of uncertainty took hold of her. She looked at the *Daily Herald*; Hitler had made another menacing speech.

She thought of the war that was coming. They had talked about it at home, she and Charlie, but never mentioned it during this holiday. It was lucky the boys were still young. But the war would take many of the sons of men who had fought last time—the elder Connolly boy, for instance. "Always have been wars, always will be," old Alf Harris said. Ann's thinking mind protested against this resignation; yet there did seem to be an inevitability about the monstrous toll levied on each generation. The rich were sending their sons to America already, she had heard. Working people would pay once more, the people who had been paying all her life in poverty and unemployment. One had to snatch at a moment of ease and peace—a week at Margate—when one could, and then remember it whatever followed. Harry glanced up unexpectedly; she gave him a happy smile.

# 15

A STRANGE life began in Steadman Street with the coming of war: a life without women. Only a few of the younger men were called up; dockers and railwaymen were classed as essential and left in their jobs. That was normal enough. It had been the same in the other war until the Army suffered heavy casualties. What was new was the evacuation. All children of school age were sent out of London, and most of the women went too.

Some homes were not affected. At number three, there was only the old couple. At number seven, the Bennetts and their fifteen-year-old girl stayed; the elder girl was now married. After a few weeks, the general opinion was that the women who stayed were the lucky ones. There were no air raids after all; indeed, there was no war if one compared it with the battles of 1914. But the evacuees were having a bad time, according to all the rumours that reached London. The Government had made a mess of things as usual. Families arrived where nobody expected them, they had to sleep in barns or derelict cottages, and the country shops wouldn't honour their ration cards. All the letters said that country people—especially the well-off, on whom the evacuees were mostly billeted—were selfish and unfriendly. For Londoners, this enforced migration was an exile among aliens.

Brian Connolly, being over ten, was sent off without his mother. He was billeted on an elderly couple who made him scrub the floors and sent him to bed at seven o'clock. Kate went down to rescue him, gave them a piece of her mind, and brought him home. Officialdom ordered him back again; Kate was defiant. Eventually she went off to Ireland, where she could count on a welcome from cousins, taking both Moira and Brian (Patrick had been called up). Kevin got a transfer to the Liverpool docks so that he could slip over to Ireland periodically. Number six was empty. This was the most extraordinary thing that had yet happened in the war. There had never been an empty house since Steadman Street was built, or not for more than a week. But, since the evacuation, there was actually no housing shortage in London. Charlie used to stare at the blank windows—the Connollys had left the blackout boards up—the smokeless chimney, the doorstep that was never cleaned. It gave him a cold, unhappy feeling. He could not rid himself of the idea that it was a portent—of what, he could not decide.

Ann and the boys went to Devon. Liza went to Gloucestershire with her whole brood; she was allowed to keep only the four youngest under the same roof, with the others elsewhere in the village. So the Wheelwright clan was in fragments. Vi stayed in London, but she had almost given up coming to Steadman Street since Dora's death.

At first, Charlie kept going fairly cheerfully. There was plenty of work at the docks, so he usually came home tired and went to bed early. He was earning good money and spending little of it. He sent Ann a postal order every week and put ten shillings into the savings bank too. He swept and dusted the house scrupulously, cleaned the windows and the doorstep, and kept everything spick and span—Ann could walk in any time, he thought proudly. A soldier's wife at number twelve, left with time on her hands, did his washing for him. He had never done any cooking, but he found that frying sausages or bacon was quite easy. Sunday threatened to be the worst day, what between the quietness and the lack of a real Sunday dinner. He solved the problem by going to Tony's restaurant. Tony was still running it with the help of a niece, though he explained apologetically that the food was nothing like Liza's.

Of course, the hardest thing was doing without Ann at night. London was suddenly a city of deprived, lonely men. They joked about it in work-breaks and at the pub, but the jokes had an uneasy edge. Charlie realised as never before that this thing—sex, love, whatever—was the same for all men and yet unique and secret for

275

each. One could not express exactly what one missed, because it was made out of private intimacies of word and touch. He could have had women, certainly. There were always good-time girls round the docks—more of them since the war. And there were decent women who would have been affectionate and discreet, answering his need with theirs. Betty—the young woman who did his washing—gave him timid, questioning glances. In the blackout, he could have slipped across the street safely enough. But when he thought of taking up with another woman, something about it repelled him: a loss of dignity, a diminution of himself. He wasn't a roving boy now, and couldn't pretend to be. It wasn't only sex that he missed, but the feel of Ann by his side and the secure contented sleep. And yet, staying faithful to her answered no questions. He could establish no habit, no balance in this new way of living; it remained simply a deprivation. As weeks passed, it became worse.

Winter began: an exceptionally hard, freezing winter. He couldn't leave the fire burning all day, and the house was bitterly cold when he came in. By the time he got the range going and the kitchen warm, he was ready to go to bed, so the effort was pointless. He got into the way of cooking his supper on a Primus stove, swallowing it quickly while his hands shivered, and spending the rest of the evening in the pub.

This was practical and it saved coal, but it made the house less of a home than ever. The blackout now began in the middle of the afternoon; the dock work went on by the light of shaded lamps. By the time he got home, he had to grope his way along Steadman Street with one hand on the walls. Some people were good at seeing in the dark—he found that he wasn't. Once, crossing the street to the pub, he walked smack into the lamp-post. At night, when he had taken the blackout boards down, he felt himself in the middle of nowhere. There were no footsteps in the street, scarcely ever the sound of a car or a lorry from Barking Road. There was only the black, empty, icy solitude.

He went to see Ann and the boys for Christmas. The train was packed, mostly with soldiers, and he had to stand in the corridor. After it got dark, he might have been travelling through an uninhabited desert. The train crawled and jolted along, stopping at every station and often between stations. The name-boards of the stations were only dimly lit, and he kept worrying about missing Okehampton. He arrived almost two hours late, to find Ann frozen from sitting in an unheated waiting-room. They had a mile and a half to walk. Charlie had the money for a taxi, but there was only one and it was quickly snapped up by an Air Force officer.

They turned off the silent country road and crunched along the gravel of a drive. By moonlight, he saw the bulk of a mansion. It looked enormous—"This your stately home?" he joked. Ann said it was the home of Sir Arnold and Lady Hawke. She lived over the stables, in what had been the groom's flat. There were two rooms and a little kitchen; it could be made really cosy. Unfortunately, the stable was now a garage, the flat hadn't been lived in for five years, and it was in a bad state. The roof had a number of tiles missing; one window wouldn't shut. It was impossible to keep warm in winter.

According to Ann, Sir Arnold—who was a decent old gent—had objected that the rooms were unfit to live in. But the billeting officer had insisted, and Sir Arnold hadn't wanted to appear unwilling to take in evacuees. He was ready to have the repairs done, at his own expense if there was any trouble about the Government grant. But you had to wait ages to get a builder in wartime.

"I don't know how often I've made up my mind to get in the train and come home," Ann said. But how could she? If she brought the boys back, there would be trouble with the authorities. Besides, the schools in London were closed and Harry was keen on school. Both the boys liked the Okehampton school—that was one bright spot. Nor could Ann leave them. Lady Hawke wouldn't look after them; she complained about having to do for herself and Sir Arnold without servants, as she'd had to since the war began. Ann had gone from door to door in the little town, trying to find a childless couple or a widow who would have the boys. But either they had no room—genuinely or otherwise—or else they had evacuees already.

The next day, Christmas Day, Charlie handed over his presents and did his best to work up the proper atmosphere. But being in a borrowed home, after all, spoiled the whole point of Christmas. They had no decorations; you could buy hardly anything here, Ann said. For dinner they had a joint of beef. The turkeys in the shops were all sold to local people, leaving none for the Londoners.

It was not only number five that they missed; it was Steadman Street. Christmas was the day when everyone was a real neighbour, even people like the Bennetts who normally kept themselves to themselves. Charlie would stroll the length of the street, popping in here and there, sampling someone's mince pies and someone else's ginger snaps. He would be in the Gordon from twelve till dinner-time and again with Ann in the evening. The front doors were closed at the height of the day, while each family ate its dinner and dozed through the afternoon. But even then, one had the warm and cheerful awareness of the celebration in each of the other houses.

Here, there were no neighbours. Ann knew some of the other London Mums, but didn't see them often. The country people didn't make

279

friends. The nearest pub was a long way off, and a harsh sleet was falling. Anyhow, there was no sense in going to a pub where one was a stranger.

Just as Ann was getting supper, Sir Arnold came over and invited them for a drink. His manner was awkward; it could be guessed that he and Lady Hawke had debated whether it was the thing to do.

"I don't think I want to leave the boys, not on Christmas Day," Ann said. "You go, Charlie, why don't you?"

"Bring them along. Big chaps like that—of course," Sir Arnold said heartily. But it hadn't, obviously, been part of the plan.

They crossed the yard and filed into the large drawing-room, where there was a blazing log fire. Sir Arnold introduced his son, Nigel. This was the Air Force officer who had taken the taxi at the station.

Charlie was ushered to an armchair. Ann and the boys sat in a row on a couch; Ted kept scuffling his shoes, despite Ann's whispers. The men drank whisky, while Ann was given a small glass of a colourless liquid, which she later declared to be horrible. There was nothing suitable for children. Lady Hawke, after a long absence—"no trouble at all, I assure you"—produced some raspberry cordial. Charlie took out his pipe without thinking, then decided not to light up. The Hawkes apparently didn't smoke, or perhaps didn't smoke in this room.

Words were sent out hopefully but blindly, like messages in bottles on the sea.

Sir Arnold: "Nice to get out of London for a bit, what? Never could stand much of London myself, I'm afraid."

Lady Hawke: "You must send your husband back with some real Devon cider, Mrs. Wheelwright. The Sampsons over at Tor Farm are famous for it."

Nigel: "In the docks? Really? Jolly good reserved occupation, I should think."

Charlie didn't dislike the old fellow. He had something in his life—the estate, the land—that gave him what the docks and Steadman Street gave Charlie: a sureness, a place in the world. But the son had the hollow arrogance that went with youth, privilege, and an officer's rank.

Charlie had to go back on Boxing Day. There was only one train, early in the morning. He refused to let Ann see him off, and kissed her goodbye in the dark yard, a fierce wind biting the back of his neck. She clung to him fiercely. "I'll come back as soon as I can. I'll find some way to manage it," she told him.

He had a seat in the train, at all events. He stared at the dull earth of the fields, the leafless trees. Somehow, he felt sadder than before he had seen Ann. Time made a difference, after all. They had been drawn apart, and there was a danger in it. Her anxiety to come home, he realised, arose from fear as well as from love.

They hadn't really talked, except to exchange information, in this brief time together. It had been taken up by the boys, the effort at Christmas cheer, and the stupid visit to the Hawkes. At night, they had gone to bed early because of the cold, made love—he, too hungrily and impatiently—and slept. And he knew that he had not reached her, with his body or in any other way. It had not occurred to him that he must begin again to reach her, as at the start of their life together; but he understood it now. A woman—a woman of Ann's age—got used to being without a man, he supposed. What sought an outlet in a man, and had to be restrained, was choked at the source in her. He wondered if it had been wrong to disturb the calm that she had established. Then he wondered if she knew that he understood. It was difficult to speak of these things, and utterly impossible to write.

Ann, feeling restless, decided on a walk in the afternoon. Harry was curled up with a book and Ted was playing with the Meccano set that Charlie had given him, but she dragged them out. It wasn't healthy to stick indoors all day, she told them. They met the Hawkes in the drive, returning in the car from a neighbour's, or what people in this expanse called a neighbour. Lady Hawke rolled down her window and said: "Mr. Wheelwright gone back already? Goodness, that was a short visit." Ann mumbled something and wiped away a tear. Anyone's eyes might water in this cold wind. She could still count the times, since childhood, when she had wept.

In the road, she and the boys had to stand close to the hedge while a herd of cows went by. She had never liked animals. The big, smelly, drooling creatures lurched about, without even the sense to keep themselves pointed in the right direction—stupid! A dog dashed to and fro and barked, but achieved nothing—stupid! The farmer said: "Afternoon." Country people always said good-morning or good-afternoon, whether you knew them or not, but rarely said anything more. He was stupid too, she felt sure. Spending his days with animals, he had no chance to be anything else. And she would be stupid herself, surely, if she stayed for years in this unchanging remoteness. The boys had their school, but she had nothing; it wouldn't be long before she'd read every book in the tiny public library.

Charlie said he was managing all right at home, but she didn't believe it. She pictured him returning tonight to the cold, silent house and opening a tin for his supper. Still, he could drop in on Alf and Maggie; he was sure to go to the Gordon; he would see Tom Whitmarsh and the rest of his mates tomorrow. Instead of worrying about him, she found herself envying him. She reproached herself, but it did no good.

So far, she thought, Charlie hadn't had another woman. There was no mistaking his pent-up hunger, these last two nights. But it seemed to her, in her gloomy and bitter mood, that he was bound to, sooner or later. Perhaps she ought to think nothing of it—a man had that simple physical need. Perhaps she ought even to be glad, if it made him happy. She asked herself whether she would prefer him to have a quick bash from time to time with some little tart, or to find a woman who would look after him. Either seemed intolerable; the former was disgusting, demeaning; the latter threatened her place as his wife. The mere thought of other hands on his body drove her to a shivering fury. And she realised that, whether it happened or not, she would have to live with this thought until she got home.

She could play tit for tat, no doubt. That farmer probably had a prick like a bull—an animal's direct, instinctual power. And when she thought of the plump, heavy country women, she was pretty sure that she had only to give the come-on sign. But it would be crazy. These people were on the watch—stupid but sly— whenever one stepped out of doors. And honestly, she didn't want to. All that part of herself was stilled; only Charlie's brief presence had brought it to a nervous, uncertain half-life. Besides, she could never forgive herself if she did it and he didn't. All the same, he might wonder. He might have the same tormenting suspicion that was making her suffer. This undermining of their trust in each other, she thought, was the grimmest aspect of the separation.

"Can't we go home, Mum? I'm freezing," Harry pleaded.

They went home—if one called it home.

Charlie reckoned on going to Devon again in August, when he was due for his week's holiday. But by then a great deal had happened: the fall of France, Dunkirk, the menace of invasion. Anyway, the docks were working flat out. There was only coastal traffic—the ocean convoys made for Liverpool or the Clyde—but every minute counted in the turn-round. Dozens of the younger men got their call-up papers, and all the gangs were short-handed. So Charlie went to the docks every day, including Sunday. There was always work, even if it was only trans-shipping from barges or clearing space in sheds.

Sunday dinners at Varelli's Restaurant were a thing of the past, for it was locked and shuttered. Tony had never taken up British nationality; so, when Italy came into the war, he found to his astonishment that he was an enemy alien. Being an Italian was not considered so bad as being a German, but Tony had to report regularly to the police and was not allowed to be "absent from his residence". He wouldn't be able to go and see Liza, he told Charlie despairingly, until the end of the war. "You mean you'll never be the

285

father of seven?" Charlie answered. Liza found a solution. She was living near a big Army camp, and the soldiers had nowhere to eat when they were off duty. She discovered an empty shop with a cheap lease and got the necessary permits to open a restaurant. It became clear that there were advantages in being an enemy alien. Excluded from "work of national importance", Tony was allowed to go and join her.

Workmen came and built a brick-and-concrete air raid shelter in the middle of Steadman Street. It was a hideous thing, keeping the sun out of a dozen front rooms. If the children had been at home, it would have made a glorious secret playground. As things were, the good-time girls took their pick-ups to it. This would not last, clearly. Everyone took for granted that London would soon be bombed. Steadman Street, placed between the docks and the railway, was as likely to catch it as any other street.

When Charlie came home in the long, light summer evenings, he often stopped at the corner —the habit of years persisting—and looked at his street with the eyes of memory. Already it was nothing like what it had been. He hated seeing the ugly shelter, the Connollys' empty house, the paint cracking and peeling in the sun all the way along, the deadness of the pavements with few women and no children. Any time now, it might be destroyed: absolutely destroyed, made impossible for human life, like the French villages he had marched through in 1918. He thought about this not with despair but with bitter anger. For what was endangered was this street and the streets like it, not some abstraction called Britain or "the nation". That talk was to be expected from the newspapers and the BBC, and from Churchill with his plummy voice and his fat cigars, but it was still a lie as it always had been. Charlie didn't forget that Churchill had orated about "the nation" before—in the General Strike. He didn't forget the years of poverty, the unemployment, the evictions. The rich had allowed all that to happen. They had been frightfully sorry, but meanwhile they had looked after themselves. Now they had stumbled into war, they would look after themselves just the same. It was here that the bombs would fall, here where the work of London was done. If by chance a bomb did fall on Lord Thingummy's place in Mayfair, then Lord Thingummy would move into his club or a hotel—though he was probably at his country residence already. Working people would have to stick it out, and be praised as usual for their Cockney cheerfulness. They didn't own the docks and the factories, they didn't own their homes; but they would fight the flames there because they must save what they needed to live. They would fight without humbug and without fine speeches, knowing the score, grappling with necessity, as they always had.

Charlie had no idea when he might see Ann again; what the state of affairs would be by Christmas, there was no telling. He missed her as badly as ever. Sometimes, at night or in the stillness of early morning, a spasm of yearning seized him, so fierce that he had to tense his body as if against pain. Yet he had acquired a kind of pride in having sustained himself through almost a year without her. He had kept the house in trim; he hadn't taken to heavy drinking, like some men; above all, he had been faithful.

He had an understanding with Betty. She was more alone than he was; her husband came home on leave in June and was then sent to the Middle East. She broke down and sobbed, her face pressed to Charlie's jacket and his hand patting her shoulder. He could have had her then, easily, but it offended his sense of decency. After that, they talked frankly. They attracted each other— she liked big men, and she had the kind of small neat figure that most tempted him, just like Ann's. The attraction was out in the open now, and words provided a safety-valve. "I'm trusting you, Charlie—I couldn't fight you off," Betty said. He laughed and answered: "Don't know how long I can hold out, mind." Really he didn't know; desire throbbed in him, sharp and strong as ever. He had wet dreams like a boy—about Ann or Betty, he wasn't sure. But Betty's trust, the fact of her vulnerability, made him keep his hands off her.

At the end of August, she told him that she was pregnant. The jokes about embarkation leave, like other jokes, were based on an insight. Charlie felt a responsibility for her, almost as though he were the father.

"You ought to get out of London," he told her. "You've got a right. Go and see the evacuation people."

She stirred her tea—she often made him tea —and pondered.

"I don't know," she said. "There'd be nobody to look after the house. And I've got all my friends here. I'd go potty, I think, without any friends."

The raids began in September. No pilot could have missed the huge Albert Dock, even at night; but the bombers came by day—every day, four or five times. The sky was cruelly blue and cloudless. Ack-ack guns were placed on the quays, and also on the wall where the machine-gun had been mounted in the General Strike. Two or three planes were shot down every day, the gunners and the dockers joining in fierce cheers. But that was not much, for the bombers flew in waves, keeping their formation like arrogant German goose-steppers. You could see the glitter of the cockpit, the iron crosses on the wings, and even the bombs until they gained speed. On the whole, Charlie was surprised that they didn't do more damage. Most of the bombs fell in the water or else outside the wall. Still, one ship was hit and blazed uncontrollably after the oil-tanks caught fire. Three cranes were destroyed; half a warehouse was reduced to ruins. After the first few days, the ships that remained in the dock sailed and no more came. The enemy had put Albert Dock out of action, at least for a time.

The dockers went to work as usual even when there was no more loading to do. They were given tin hats—some of them, for there was a shortage—and fought the fires with long hoses using the dock-water. On the third day, two men were killed and two injured. Charlie didn't see it happen, being on the other side of the dock, but when he heard about it he wondered anxiously if Ann would get to know. It wouldn't be in the papers, he supposed. The next day, a bomb fell close to him and his gang. He heard it whistle, like a shell in the last war, and dropped flat with a remembered quickness. When he got up, Tom Whitmarsh was missing. Charlie felt—again, as in the trenches—that dismayed astonishment: he can't be dead, I was just talking to him. Then someone laughed. Tom had been blown into the water and was swimming to reach a rope.

Whenever they could, the dockers clambered on top of crates and gazed out across London. Bombs were falling all over the East End. There were arguments about whether the Germans couldn't aim, or whether they just got rid of their bombs and cut off home, or whether the deliberate purpose was to spread death and destruction everywhere. There were keener arguments about where each fire was. If a docker believed that his street had been hit, the foreman couldn't stop him from hurrying home.

The East End was being wrecked in front of their eyes. Sometimes a church tower or a factory chimney, a landmark since anyone's childhood, rocked amazingly and disintegrated. Sometimes a cloud of black, ugly smoke covered a whole neighbourhood. Every day, the map was redrawn. A row of shops in Barking Road—including the butcher's where Dora and then Ann had bought thousands of Sunday joints—collapsed into rubble. Charlie had to walk to and from work, because a gaping hole in the road had severed the tram-line.

But, by the end of a week, not many trams and buses were running at all. They stopped when the sirens blew, so it was scarcely possible to keep up a service. Deliveries to the shops were unpredictable. Bakers ran out of bread, pubs ran out of beer, stalls no longer appeared in market streets. In some districts, people had nowhere to buy their rations and were given emergency meals in church halls, like refugees. Nothing could be relied on any more. You turned a tap and got no water; the electricity went off for hours, then on, then off again; the gas supply ceased altogether, which was gloomy for homes that had no electricity. When friends met, they said: "Still all right, then?" in a jocular tone with a grim edge. This was not life, in any decent sense of the word. There was a question in everyone's mind which no one put into words: how long could it last? It wasn't a matter of extermination; the East End still had hundreds of thousands of people and the deaths were here and there, one or two or half a dozen. But a functioning community was becoming a mere mass of people, some homeless, some whose work had gone up in smoke, some wandering about to find relations of whom they had no news.

Abruptly, the raids ceased. The Germans had lost more planes than they could afford, the BBC claimed. The BBC also warned that they were likely to start bombing by night; but for the time being there was a strange, empty-seeming lull. However, by then—on the last day of the daylight raids—Steadman Street had been hit.

Charlie was unaware of it. The late afternoon raid seemed to be a pretty feeble affair, and the all clear sounded as he was about to finish work. As he approached the corner of Steadman Street, he found a bustle: wardens, firemen, the knot of bystanders that always gathered when bombs had fallen. Then he saw it. About the middle of the street, on the opposite side to his house, several houses were wrecked—number fourteen to number twenty-two, he knew later. Some were utter ruins, crushed as though by a giant hammer. The others, gashed and ripped, still had part of a wall or part of a roof. Fragments of the life that had been lived in these houses were starkly, cruelly exposed: half a staircase now leading nowhere, a chair blankly facing a hole in the floor, a row of cups improbably still on their hooks. Bricks, tiles, pieces of wood and countless splinters of glass were scattered in the roadway.

The people who had lived in these houses were safe. The men had been at work; the women and an old age pensioner had got to the shelter. But Betty had been caught in the open. No one knew why; probably she hadn't decided to take shelter until she heard the planes close overhead. Ironically, her own house was intact except for broken windows.

She had died in a flash, the breath knocked out of her by blast. There was no blood on her. The blast had torn off her clothes; Charlie stared at the neat line of her back, the clearly outlined ridge of spine, her small rounded bottom, the flesh he had never touched while it lived. Someone—Mrs. Bennett—came and covered the body with a blanket. Soon, an ambulance arrived and took it away.

In the days that followed, a grim quiet descended on Steadman Street, like the quiet that grasps a company of soldiers after the first casualties. The men talked in the pub in terse phrases, without the usual anecdotes and arguments, or didn't go at all. It seemed indecent to be thankful that the raids had stopped. Betty's death—quiet little thing, nobody had known her well but everybody had liked her—was spoken of with resentment, as if Hitler had picked her out on purpose. It was macabre that her husband was far away, thinking of her, wondering what she was doing, still getting her letters weeks after she was dead. There was a feeling that someone ought to write to him and say that she hadn't suffered, but no one knew what regiment he was in. He would be officially informed, presumably. No one in the street except Charlie knew that she had been carrying a child. He said nothing about it, from an obscure notion that it was a private matter, even now.

When the night raids began, it was understood without question that this was to be a long ordeal. Autumn was here, steadily lengthening the dark hours. A new routine was created. The days were more ordinary, except when a severe raid in the neighbourhood brought a spell of chaos. The docks were working again, after a fashion. But at night everyone took shelter; it was soon agreed that it wasn't sense to wait for the alert, because there was an alert every night. Some people went to Mile End and stayed deep down, on the tube platform. But Mile End was another kind of community, noisier, less disciplined, mostly Jewish. The tube was terribly crowded and strangers were unwelcome. Most Steadman Street people preferred their own shelter. They established regular places, left some belongings there during the day, and gradually built up a second home. When bombs fell on the East End, it was impossible to sleep. They made tea on Primus stoves and played endless games of solo. Then, with the all clear, they went out to make sure that the street was all right. It did, in November, lose two more houses—numbers thirty-four and thirty-six. However, no one was hurt.

The pace of destruction was less savage than in the daylight raids. Sometimes the bombers didn't get beyond the suburbs. Sometimes they hit the north of London, or south of the river, or —to Charlie's surprise—the West End. Terrible things happened, nevertheless. The surface shelters were not proof against a direct hit from a big bomb; one of them was smashed, and everyone in it killed. A hospital was bombed in the early evening, before the patients had been taken to shelter. And what was most appalling was that such a disaster—which would have been remembered for a lifetime, had it ever happened before—was now spoken of for no more than a week. The abnormal was becoming normal. Ultimately, people would have forgotten how to be shocked, how to value life.

Meanwhile, the raids were cutting away at the man-made landscape of the East End. Once, happening to be in Poplar, Charlie noticed the rubble of a house on a corner that seemed familiar. His mother had pointed it out to him; she had lived there as a girl. Again, someone mentioned to him that the school had been bombed—the school he had gone to, and Vi and Liza, and Harry and Ted. It was empty, of course, and no one was hurt. But a part of his life seemed to have been snatched away.

Like everyone else, he was tired most of the time. Two nights a week, he was fire-watching at the docks. In the shelter, it was rare to get a night's sleep. If there had been bombing nearby, he often lent a hand with digging for bodies or survivors in the early morning hours. Then he went off to do his day's work. On Sundays, he planned to see a film or take a walk in the park, to take his mind off things. But he ended up sitting all day in his armchair, smoking his pipe, dozing at intervals. It was all he could do to cook some kind of dinner, wash a few clothes—he had to do that for himself now—and write his weekly letter to Ann.

Once, however, he went to see Vi. She was the same as ever, managing her life competently and asking for no help from anyone. The laundry was still in business, though there was no collection or delivery and her girls were more useless than any she'd ever had—of course, if they were any good at all they'd be earning fancy wages in the war factories. She didn't often go to the shelter, she said. She'd rather take her chance of being killed than be sure of picking up filth and fleas. She asked how Charlie was getting on, and the news of Ann and the boys, but it was clear that the war hadn't made her need her family. Her complaint was that the Americans hadn't entered the war. They would join in at the end and say they'd won it, no doubt, the same as last time. This grievance had not occurred to Charlie. He thought of the war as an English business.

One Sunday afternoon, there was a knock at the door of number five. This was now such a rare event that Charlie, half asleep, thought at first that he had been dreaming. The knock was repeated, firmly and insistently. He peered out of the window and saw a woman in blue Civil Defence uniform, tin hat slung over her shoulder. He was going to be asked some stupid official question, he supposed. Then he recognised her: Marjorie.

She had come round before, she said, but hadn't found him in. This was her first Sunday off duty.

"Just going to have a cuppa," he said, as he would have said in normal times. And a sudden visit from Marjorie did seem normal rather than extraordinary, a revival of life in number five.

"I'll make it. I know where everything is. Give

you a treat, a woman to wait on you for a change."

She bustled about, giving the cups an unnecessary wipe, slicing bread.

"How's Ann?"

"All right. Not much fun for her, out in the wilds."

"Ah, don't I know it? I've been down in the country too. Had a job censoring the troops' letters. A laugh a day—I could tell you some stories. Cushy job, mind. Boy-friend fixed it up for me," she added unnecessarily.

"Then what happened? Chucked the boy-friend?"

"Well, I have, yes. That wasn't it, though. I couldn't keep away from London once the blitz started. Never forgive myself if I missed this little lot." She spoke as if the blitz were some kind of free entertainment.

She was an ambulance driver. Charlie hadn't been aware that she could drive, but it wasn't surprising. She worked at a first-aid and rescue station not far away, and slept there too. Otherwise, for the time being, she had no home.

She went on chatting, telling stories, making him laugh. He knew that she had come deliberately to cheer him up, but that did not make it forced or false; she was enjoying herself too. They had tea at the table, in family fashion. Then they made themselves comfortable in the armchairs. Marjorie stretched one leg over the

298

arm of her chair, like a man. She looked good in trousers. She had taken on the no-nonsense style of the woman in uniform and made something special of it, something her own, as she made of any style.

Quite suddenly, while she was telling him about the letters she had censored, Charlie knew that he would go to bed with her. It wasn't a question of whether, only of when. He looked directly at her, and was certain that she knew it too. She hadn't come with that intention, he thought. With all her sexual readiness, she put value also on friendship with men, and it was natural for her to renew friendship with Charlie. But now their bodies, with the independent will that bodies possess, were demanding to take advantage of having been brought close. The space between them was like a gap across which an electric spark can jump.

He lost track of what she was saying, and lived in expectation. He hardly thought at all of restraining himself. It was not the same as with Betty; Betty had been vulnerable, innocent, likely to fall in love with him. Marjorie could look after herself. She would allow the pleasure to be just that: a pleasure, nothing more. And, because it would be that, he did not believe that it would injure Ann. He couldn't have convinced himself of this with anyone else, but what he recognised in Marjorie made it possible: her honesty, her common sense, her friendship reaching to Ann not less than to himself. In some illogical yet truthful way, he looked to Marjorie to protect Ann.

Still, he didn't intend to grab at her now, today. He was reluctant to let her see the hunger that was in him. And he wanted her to make her own desire quite plain. He was back in the skirmishing of youth, after all. The girls wanted Charlie; Charlie gave the girls what they wanted.

When she had to go, she said: "Come and see me at the station. I do long hours, but a lot of it's waiting time."

"All right, I will."

He did—two or three evenings a week, between work and going to the shelter, instead of being in the Gordon. The station was a friendly place. There was always tea and there was also free whisky, apparently from a bombed pub, though the station officer made sure that nobody on duty had more than one glass. The drivers were men of more than Charlie's age, wearing 1914–18 ribbons. None of them were bashing the girls, he reckoned. There were four girls, but only Marjorie was a driver; the others stayed at the switchboard.

Once, he found that Marjorie was not there. He was pressed to stay—"she'll be back any time." While they waited, the station officer talked about her. All the men, Charlie learned, saw her with dazzled admiration. She was utterly tireless, utterly fearless. She drove where the bombs were falling, through clouds of smoke, through wreckage, through anything. She had changed a punctured tyre by the light of the flames when the rest of them thought she'd taken shelter. Then she would come in, wash the dirt and blood off her hands, and suggest a game of darts. "She's worth any three men," the station officer said.

Listening to this, Charlie wanted her more and more. He wanted her, not as he had wanted Ann, but because of her independence—because they would meet in freedom. But also he wanted her as a prize, as a woman who was splendid in the eyes of other men.

Usually, she walked some distance with him when he left. He put his arm round her waist and she leaned against him, talking or humming a tune as if she didn't quite know what her body was doing, though he was sure she did. When he said goodnight he kissed her on the cheek, like a brother-in-law. But one night she moved her head and the kiss found her lips. They moved into a shop doorway in the old East End way—absurdly, since it was pitch dark in the blackout and the street was deserted—and hugged each other like youngsters. After a couple of minutes, the alert sounded. He heard the clip-clop of her shoes as she ran back to the station.

On the Sunday, a fortnight after the first time, she came to number five again. He wasn't dozing

301

this time; he was impatient for her, but also confident. They had tea, not hurrying. When he moved to his armchair, she sat on the arm and put her hand on his head.

"You're losing your wool a bit, Charlie."

"Can't be helped. I'm forty."

She scrutinised him. "You don't look it, honest."

He put his hand on her thigh, sensing it through the thick serge of the battle-dress. Now that they had arrived, his confidence wavered a little; suppose she was only teasing him? But when he looked at her, he was reassured.

She said: "If you feel like a bit of a romp, you don't have to be ashamed of yourself. It's going to be a long war."

They did romp—chasing each other round the bedroom like kids, wrestling like men, clinching and breaking away, rolling over and over on the bed. Then he pinned her down and took her as he used to take the girls in his young days, concentrating on his own pleasure and knowing that she would find hers.

So this became part of his life—shagging through the blitz as Marjorie called it, chanting the words to the tune of "Coming through the rye". She wasn't living with him; she kept nothing at number five, and never opened the cupboards and drawers which belonged to Ann. She turned up unpredictably, as she always had. Sometimes they went to bed on a Saturday or

Sunday afternoon, sometimes in the evening. Two or three times, being off duty, she stayed all night. This worried him; if a raid started, she would have to go to the shelter with him and the whole street would know. But they took the chance and were lucky. Toward Christmas, the raids became fewer and less heavy. Perhaps the Germans were feeling their losses again.

Charlie couldn't remember when he had last had this kind of enjoyment: without depth, without a pretence of love, yet with satisfying happiness and a keen edge of sheer fun. And also, when they lay side by side after the fun and talked, with a curious lazy contentment, a sense of mind and body at total rest. The whole affair was straightforward, free of complications and misunderstandings, simple and explicit in what they were giving each other—irresponsible in the direct sense of being without responsibility. Suddenly (he was undressing at the time and paused with his shirt over his head) it struck him that he had felt like this in another set of frank and happy meetings, in another war, with Reenie. The comparison was foolish—he had been only a boy. He had always believed that one must march on with life, one couldn't revive the past. Yet he did feel like a boy with Marjorie —a proud, eager, daring, rather clumsy boy, with an experienced woman. A boy even in the fact that she spurred his energy; he never felt tired now, though he was getting less sleep than ever. He could have got dressed and ridden across London on a bicycle, and enjoyed that too.

It all ended in the same simple and easy way. Charlie and Marjorie were having breakfast when the postman brought a letter from Ann.

"What's she say?" Marjorie asked. She was just as fond of Ann as ever; sleeping with Charlie made no difference, to her mind.

Charlie read a few sentences and said: "She's coming back. She's found somebody to look after the boys. Says she'll be here by Christmas."

"Well," Marjorie exclaimed, "isn't that lovely!"

There was no irony in her voice. Charlie saw that she was genuinely glad for him; she knew the depth of this marriage, with the insight of some unmarried women, and she hadn't for a moment sought to be a wife for him. Besides, she would really enjoy seeing her sister. She was content to follow a life without permanence. "No regrets, that's my motto," she sometimes said.

She washed up the breakfast plates and cups while Charlie gave her more details from the letter. Then she ran a comb through her hair, glanced at her watch—"Christ, I must run"— and put on her overcoat and beret.

"One—more—kiss—before we—must part," she sang in the full tone of the old music-halls.

One more kiss; that was that.

# 16

HAD he had a woman, or hadn't he? They said that one could always tell, but when Ann considered this bit of feminine folk-wisdom she saw its absurdity—obviously, some wives were fooled even from day to day, let alone over a year's absence. Charlie made love to her wonderfully on the night of her return. She felt in her body the reality of his love, his happiness with her, his comforting strength. She clung to him, speaking his name like a prayer of thanks: "Charlie . . . Charlie . . ." But she didn't feel—so she realised, waking first in the morning—the tension released, the demanding hunger. Perhaps he had made an effort at gentleness. Perhaps time had quietened the need in him, as it had in her, and it was waking without the hasty surge of last Christmas. But perhaps . . .

She told herself that it was silly to get into a state about it. The past couldn't be altered, and the future was hers. If it had happened, she was confident that it had touched nothing deep in him, that his love had been faithful. Yet the doubt nagged at her. She had always hated not being clear about anything. And she knew that —from time to time, in unexpected twinges, like a tiny piece of glass in the flesh—the doubt would nag at her for the rest of her life.

It was out of the question to ask him, even in the closest moments of intimacy. If it was not true, she was insulting his loyalty. If it was true, she was afraid not so much of his lying to her as of hearing the truth. For then another dishonesty would be created. After the anger to which she had a right, she would have to speak words of forgiveness to ensure that their life together went on; and, deep in her heart, she could not entirely forgive.

Decidedly, she could not stoop to asking anyone else. Hating herself, she went so far as to get into rambling conversations with the few other women who had stayed in Steadman Street; a quickly checked phrase might tell her something. Sharp old Maggie Harris would have noticed anyone coming to number five. But Maggie mentioned no one, except of course Marjorie—Charlie had told about Marjorie's visits in his letters. Still, Ann reflected, it might not have happened here. Even in Devon, she had heard the jokes about fire-watching.

Charlie had written to Ann about seeing Marjorie on the principle that the less you had to conceal, the less likely you were to be caught out. He was apprehensive, all the same, when Marjorie turned up on Christmas Day. Women had a sixth sense about other women, he believed, especially when they were sisters. But

Marjorie did something clever; she came with a new boy-friend. This absorbed all of Ann's curiosity, for they had never seen any of the other men in Marjorie's collection. How she'd picked up this man in the ten days since he'd last seen her, Charlie could only wonder.

The man was a Canadian captain, called Chuck, which apparently was a form of Charlie. He brought a quantity of roast turkey in tins and a bottle of Scotch, so it was a jolly Christmas, even if it was not really Christmas without children. He made friends at once, without any of the distance or the condescension of a British officer. One couldn't tell from his accent or his manners what class he belonged to. It was like that in a new country, Charlie supposed.

Afterwards, Ann said: "D'you think he's married?"

"Couldn't say, love. Don't suppose Marj cares."

"I hope he is. I wouldn't like her to go off to Canada with him after the war. I'd miss our Marj."

Ann was happy to be with Charlie again and happy to be in London, but she felt the incompleteness of this wartime life. Despite his letters, what she had pictured from her exile was the Steadman Street she knew. She was depressed by the ruins across the street, the empty houses, the quiet which was at times as lifeless as that of a country road in winter. She missed the boys, most of all at tea-time when they ought to be coming in and telling her about their day at school. She missed her friends, especially Kate Connolly.

She spring-cleaned the house thoroughly, though Charlie had kept it well. She ranged all over the East End on foot or by bus, learning the new geography of devastation, finding shops that had goods which were becoming hard to obtain. But there wasn't enough to do. After a while, she decided to take a job. She was tempted by the idea of being a bus-conductress again, recapturing a corner of youth. But going into industry was a more direct help to the war effort, a more substantial place for herself in this altered world. There was a place within walking distance, a garage in peacetime, now a workshop for reconditioning the hard-used engines of Army lorries. With a dozen other women or girls, supervised by two engineers over military age, she ground valves and decarbonised cylinder-heads. It was moderately skilled work, calling at least for precision and care.

She shopped in the dinner-hour, eating only a sandwich herself, and got home just in time to make supper. In the evening, if Charlie didn't feel like going to the Gordon, they talked more than they had before the war: making up for the separation, rebuilding their intimacy. Sometimes she sat on his lap and they were like lovers more than a steady married couple, touching and kissing, tender and easy with each other. Then they went to bed, usually early. Air raids still happened, but the regular nightly battering of London was over; people got out of the habit of going to the shelter. Ann and Charlie were ready to take risks, anyway, for the joy of being in their bed together.

One night in May, the alert sounded when they had been in bed for about an hour. They had made love, and it had led—as it sometimes did—to wakefulness instead of sleepiness. He lay on his back, she curled close to him, and they talked. After hearing the sirens they strained to catch the noise of the planes, hesitant before the nuisance of dressing and going to the shelter, clinging to the comfort of bed. Within less than a minute—somehow, they never heard the planes—a fire-bomb crashed through the roof, missing the bed by inches.

Explosions were all around them, cracking, roaring, echoing one joined to the next like a roll of thunder. Then came a wild clattering and crashing as tiles and brickwork pelted into the street. Without respite, there followed a series of shuddering crashes as entire houses collapsed. But Ann and Charlie had to register the disaster only with their senses, as a thing they could think about later. Number five was on fire.

They raced downstairs in pyjamas and night-dress and got busy with the stirrup-pump, pointing its jet upward to the bedrooms. It was hard to see if they were doing any good. Through the windows, the outside world was lit by fires; but in the house it was dark, and a dense rolling smoke was filling the upper floor. Charlie went up a few steps. He could see no flames and couldn't guess where to attack the heart of the fire. But it was gaining—the smoke was getting thicker.

He would have to go up, he realised. He glanced over his shoulder, but couldn't see Ann. It was no use shouting to her in the infernal din. As he reached the top, one of the uprights of the banisters came away in his hand, so that he almost lost his balance and went reeling down again. The wood was hot, the paint sizzling.

The thought came to him, with the speed gathered by thoughts at such a moment, that the odds were too great for common sense. "Don't attempt the impossible", you were told in Civil Defence lectures. If he couldn't beat the fire, he would be trapped. The staircase would burn, the floor would break under him. It was wiser to save the downstairs rooms and wait for the fire engines. But the thought came and went; he didn't so much consider and reject it as simply push it aside. This was his house, his own. He wasn't going to let it burn, not a corner of it, not an inch.

In the bedroom, he coughed raspingly and his eyes streamed. Soon, however, he made out what was burning. The worst of it was the wardrobe.

He saw flames now; they had a dangerous hold on the deal planking and on Ann's dresses. The bed was burning too, though not so fast because the mattress was heavy and the flames got no air —that was where most of the smoke was coming from.

He dropped the pump; it was too slow. With his bare hands, he grabbed the dresses and threw them into the street, smashing the window with his elbow. Then he pulled away the whole blazing door of the wardrobe and hurled that into the street too. The flames scorched his face like a furnace, and bit his hands like the savage teeth of animals.

The blankets were his best weapons, it suddenly struck him. They lay in the safest part of the room—he and Ann had thrown them off in the warm night. He picked one up and used it to stifle the fire on the bed, covering each spurt of flame as one might staunch the bleeding from a man's wounds.

He was winning. He had a moment to wipe his eyes with the sheet. And now he saw that Ann was in the room too. She had fetched the bucket of sand which was kept by the back door —he'd forgotten about it. Somehow, though it was almost too heavy for her to lift, she had clambered up the stairs with it without a steadying hold on the banisters. She went round the room, as methodically as if she were dusting it, and tipped heaps of sand on all the sullen lurking strongholds of the fire. Through the smoke, they exchanged a grim but happy smile: happy with their courage, their comradeship, their love.

They had saved the house—so they always insisted later—before the fire brigade came. Only the back of the wardrobe was still burning, with a glow that must have been visible from the street. A powerful jet of water sped in through the broken window, and Ann just dodged it. Firemen, of course, didn't wait to ask if there was anyone in a house. Charlie went to the window and waved. They ran up a ladder, so he and Ann climbed down. It wasn't the moment to explain that the stairs were still safe.

The raid was at its height—bombs falling, guns firing, searchlights sweeping the sky. In Steadman Street there was a regular traffic jam of fire engines and ambulances. Dazed after his struggle, Charlie couldn't make out what the damage was, but it was clearly bad. The burns on his hands began to hurt piercingly. He was helped into an ambulance, then Ann was lifted in. Right at the end, just before the firemen came, she had run a splinter of wood into the soft pad of one foot and couldn't stand on it. There were two people in the ambulance already. One was a docker, an elderly man who lived at number eleven. He was moaning with pain, his arms and chest covered with ugly burns. The other was a fireman; a beam had fallen on him and cracked a shoulder-blade.

The journey to the hospital seemed terribly slow, with the badly burned man moaning all the way. The ambulance crunched over rubble, swerved to avoid obstacles, bumped in and out of holes in the road. Once it stopped and, after a minute of shouting, reversed and turned— evidently the road was blocked. When they arrived, the casualty room and even the hospital corridors were jammed with injured people, sitting on the floor, lying on stretchers or tables. Nurses worked feverishly at bandaging, medical students went round giving injections, orderlies wheeled trolleys to the operating theatres, women from nearby houses made tea. Ann said she would go home if they'd just pull the splinter out, but she had to wait her turn. A warden told Charlie that half London seemed to be burning —most of the East End and the City. There were whole districts still blazing like forests on fire, where the rescue workers and firemen couldn't get near. It was the heaviest raid since the start of the blitz. Thousands of people had been caught in their homes; the casualties were sure to be frightful.

Bandaged, wearing ill-fitting clothes from the Red Cross, Ann and Charlie went home in the early morning. Charlie's burns would have kept him in hospital for a week in peacetime, but the beds were needed for far worse cases. Columns of smoke could still be seen by the light of a pure, innocent dawn.

Alf and Maggie Harris were sitting on kitchen chairs outside their house. Number three hadn't been hit, but the firemen had hosed it just the same and the ground floor was swamped. Firemen sometimes did more damage than bombs—it couldn't be helped in the general chaos.

Alf was fully informed about what had happened to Steadman Street. Along Charlie's side of the street, from number seven to number nineteen, there was a stretch of destruction. Beyond that, four more houses were uninhabitable but might be repaired. There were not many people about. The bombed-out had gone to a rest centre, the injured were in hospital, the dead had been taken away too. But heavy-rescue men were still digging in the ruins of number seven, which had taken a direct hit. Sometimes digging went on for three days, and miracles had happened in the blitz. However, there was practically no hope for the Bennetts. They'd have done better, Alf remarked, to have been evicted in 1931. Their daughter had been out with her boy-friend, had sheltered in the tube, and had come home a short while ago. She was in the Gordon, being dosed by the landlord's wife with hot tea and the last of the brandy—pretty hysterical, Alf said. From the other bombed houses, two men were dead, three men and a woman injured.

There now began a long siege, in the sense of that word used by doctors. Imagine yourself suffering from a serious illness. You have been weakened by a violent, almost fatal attack. You must obey rules and carry out exercises with unremitting obedience. Often you will feel that you are getting no better; there will be setbacks, even crises. Ultimately you will recover, though you cannot know how long it will take. Thus, Steadman Street went through four more years of war.

The two big gaps in the street, one on each side, were deep fractures in the community. On Charlie's side, the pavement was roped off for a time because there was believed to be an unexploded bomb in the ruins. On both sides, the paving-stones were broken and puddles formed when it rained. People living at the far end tended to use the parallel street to get to the shops in Barking Road. More than anything, an unspoken taboo made everyone avoid walking past the ruins, as a place polluted by evil memory.

Between the destroyed houses, the shelter remained. It was no longer used, because a new and improved shelter was built on the site of the bombed shops in the main road. Anyway, after Hitler attacked Russia there were only a few raids at long intervals. So the shelter ceased to serve as a gathering-place for Steadman Street in time of danger. Sometimes drunks or tramps slept in it. Sometimes, after they drifted home to a safer London, children explored it. But gradually rain and mud seeped in; there was dog-shit, there were rats, there was a mixed and repulsive smell. Deserted, the shelter became a symbol of decay.

Of the two divided parts of Steadman Street, Charlie and Ann found themselves living in the smaller. True, it had the pub, the traditional focus. But the pub was only a shadow of its old self. People at the far end came less often, not liking to pick their way over the broken pavements in the blackout, so it was never full. No one played the piano any more, no one sang. The landlord whom Charlie had known for years retired, and his place was taken by a rather gruff Yorkshireman. As wartime shortages got worse, there was often no whisky for special occasions, no port for the women. At times there was even no beer—or at all events no draught, only bottled ales. And the beer was weaker; it had a flat, second-rate, wartime taste.

In 1943, the shop at the corner—number one —closed down. Because of the shortages, and also because there were fewer customers, it no longer provided a living for the widow who kept it. She accepted an offer to share with her sister, who had a shop in a part of London that had

316

not been bombed. As she had lived over the shop, number one became an empty building.

In 1944, Alf Harris died. He had coughed badly for about a year, but refused to see a doctor. When he was compelled to go into hospital, he lasted only a few weeks. Maggie's arthritis was so bad by now that she could scarcely walk. Ann did her shopping, but she couldn't stand the house without Alf. She went into an Old People's Home; Ann and Charlie never saw her again.

Two houses across the street were empty, the Connollys' and Betty's. Three were lived in. Ann and Charlie kept on close terms with the people in these houses, by now their only neighbours: especially with the Turners at number eight. Stan Turner, a man of about fifty, was a tally-clerk at Victoria Dock; a quiet man, never a leader, but the kind who kept the East End going. The Turners had one son, who was in the Army but hadn't been sent abroad. He married a girl whom he had found near his camp and she came to live at number eight. She was a Welsh girl called Gwen; she found London strange, so Ann helped her to get to know her way about. Charlie liked to see her in the street, a lively young woman with a ready smile and a comical lilting accent.

The gap still divided the two segments of Steadman Street. Even in the old days, neighbourliness had somewhat lessened with distance.

Charlie had never been thick with anyone down at the far end except the Whitmarshes. Old Whitmarsh, now a widower, was still at number thirty-one, and Charlie went along to see him from time to time; but apart from this he no longer had much idea how life was going at the other end of the street. People didn't ask his advice any more, and if they were in trouble there was nothing he could do for them. The old problems no longer existed, and the common peril of the blitz was in the past too. Families had their separate worries: a child going through measles in the evacuation areas, a young man fighting in the Middle East.

Without air raids, the war was more like the other war. The danger, once again, was to the men in uniform. The telegrams came—killed, wounded, prisoner, missing. Life in London was a dreary endurance test. Everything was rationed, even clothes; coal was short in the dark silent winters. You went from shop to shop to get the simplest things: razor-blades, string, shirt buttons, St. Julien flake.

Somehow, the war was harder to bear after victory was certain. Instead of the simple struggle on the Western Front, there were fronts everywhere—the Middle East, then Italy, then Normandy, and the Far East too—and it was hard to make out what was going on. It had ceased to be England's war; the Americans were taking charge after they came in, and the

Russians were doing most of the real fighting. So far as England was concerned, it was obvious that the officers and gentlemen were blundering as usual, and the profiteers were spinning things out while the money rolled in. No one was in a hurry to get it over, except the people from the Steadman Streets. The invasion of Europe was talked about in 1942 and 1943, but it happened in 1944. The war looked like finishing in 1944, but lasted until 1945.

Ann sometimes joked about living in a detached house, like in the posh suburbs. Really, it was depressing to have no one next door. The emptiness in number three, after Alf and Maggie had gone, was like a slow decay growing unchecked. From the other side, where number seven had been, Charlie was sure he could feel cold draughts. One day, a surveyor from the Council came to look round, and then workmen levelled the ruins and put up a huge wooden prop against the wall of number five. It wasn't necessary, Charlie declared. He was insulted, in the depths of his love for his home, by the idea that it needed help to stand up.

Considering what it had endured, the house was in good shape. After the raid—quickly, in case it rained—they nailed hardboard across the hole in the roof. Ann did the job, with Charlie helpless because of his bandaged hands. Later, through a piece of luck, he got hold of some metal sheeting and made a proper repair. If anything, it was better than the old tiles. They slept in the back bedroom for several months; the front room was a real mess, what between the fire and the hosing. Working steadily through the evenings and weekends, they made good the plaster, put up new wallpaper, replaced two charred floorboards, renewed the burnt paint on the bedroom door, and mended the banisters. The broken window held them up longest—the cold weather came before they could get a new pane. It wasn't difficult, however, to get another wardrobe and another mattress; there was plenty of good stuff in bombed and empty houses if you took the trouble to ask.

In these wartime years, everything was short except money. Charlie became a foreman. It was his due; it came to a man at about this age, if he was respected both by the bosses and by the union. For a few weeks he found it strange to give orders, to allocate men at the shape-up instead of being allocated. But it was a natural extension of his responsibility as a gang-leader. He brought home ten pounds a week, sometimes eleven or twelve, and Ann earned another four. This was a tidy sum, even though prices kept going up. The rent, still pegged, was nothing to think about. Charlie saved steadily, watching the figures mount in his Post Office book. One couldn't tell what would happen after the war. The politicians swore that unemployment would never return, but they had made promises in

1918 too. And the boys might have needs that couldn't be foreseen.

Marjorie was no longer in the East End. She stayed in the ambulance service for a while after the blitz, but the days and nights with nothing to do bored her. So she changed her blue battle-dress for a smart green uniform and drove a general about town. She lived in a house in Kensington, where Ann and Charlie went to see her one Sunday. The house was bomb-damaged, but the ground floor was habitable and had more space than two Steadman Street houses put together. The owners were in the country and were delighted to have the place taken care of for a token rent.

Chuck had faded out. "I've got an American now," Marjorie said with a grin. It was a shock when he walked in—he was a black man. He shook hands very politely, handed round drinks, and didn't sit down until Marjorie told him to. Probably he believed that the house belonged to her and she was a high-born lady.

In the tube going home, Charlie said: "D'you think it's right, her carrying on with a nigger?"

"You can't make rules for Marj. She does what she likes," Ann said. Then she lowered her voice and added: "They're supposed to be terrific—you know what I mean."

It was part of Marjorie's frank, open daring, Charlie agreed as he thought about it. She was no snob, at all events—the black man was a sergeant, and she could have picked up any rank in her new job. He was probably better-behaved than the white Yanks, too, from what one heard about them.

Slowly, during these years, London was becoming more like itself. Most of the women came back. Some brought their children, whether the authorities knew about it or not, or else the children reached school-leaving age and had a right to come back. And babies were born —a good many of them, in wedlock and out of it, with fathers who might be English or American or Polish or something else. Gwen Turner had a little girl and gave her a pretty Welsh name, Arianwen. The first time that Ann saw a pram going along Steadman Street, she felt a sudden delight, as if the sun had come out after an age of grey skies. Though it wasn't exactly a pram—they were unobtainable, like so many other things—but a box on wheels which Gwen's husband had put together on his last leave.

Once a year, Ann and Charlie went to Devon to see the boys. He stayed for a week, she for the month of August. Every year, they talked over the possibility of bringing the boys back and finally decided against it. They were quite happy, they were doing well at school, they didn't really miss their home. Besides, Hitler still had bombers and Charlie was wary of a sudden ferocious blow that might take London by surprise, like the raid of May 1941.

The surprise came in the last year of the war, in a stranger way than anyone could have imagined. The Germans started using planes without pilots, which were beamed toward London and timed to crash and explode—flying bombs, they were soon called. There were no sirens, no raids in the normal sense; the things came one at a time at any hour of day or night. You could see and hear them quite plainly, and you learned that the danger time was when the engine stopped. Then you had a minute to rush for shelter. There was something curiously sinister about these devices; they were inhuman, there wasn't a man up there who might dodge the gunfire or turn for home to save his skin, and yet they seemed to have an alien, unfeeling kind of intelligence, like creatures from Mars. People were more nervous, more anxious and short-tempered, in this flying-bomb period than they had ever been in the blitz.

After the flying bombs came the rockets. These were still more inhuman; they descended from the higher zones of space, far above the reach of gunfire or defending aircraft. There was no kind of defence, and not a split second of warning. There was only the explosion, and after it silence—normal life, except where the rocket fell. Clearly, the rockets were in a primitive stage of development and didn't work very well; many failed to explode, many landed in open country or in the sea. It was reasonable to believe that

Germany would be defeated before they did much damage. The chilling aspect of the matter was that the third world war—people made bitter jokes about it, people of Charlie's age who remembered the false hopes of 1918—would be fought with these rockets. Charlie wouldn't live to see it, or would be so old that it wouldn't matter to him. But he feared for his sons, for his London, for the life still growing around him.

The rocket that hit Steadman Street was among the last that came. It demolished the Gordon, totally and with precision, as if it had been designed for that purpose. No one was killed or even injured. It happened at ten o'clock on a fine morning, when the landlord and his wife were out shopping. Ann and Charlie were both at work and knew nothing about it until they came home. Their front windows were smashed by the blast, and they had to live behind blackout boards for the rest of the war.

Charlie was depressed by the loss of the Gordon: not appalled or saddened, as he had been by Betty's death, but depressed as a man might be if his friends all moved away and left him alone. He stared into the fire in the evenings and remembered the crowded bar, the tinkling piano, the round on the house at Christmas, the midnight extension at New Year's Eve. Even the hard drinking and the fights in the old days were good memories now—they belonged to life, anyway. It was life that had been attacked with the Gordon, his own life and Steadman Street's.

Several weeks went by before he could bring himself to go to another pub. Then, with Stan Turner for company, he went to the Prince of Orange. It was out of his territory, the other side of Barking Road; still, to be sensible about it, it was only a short walk. He got used to it, more or less. He had to admit that it was a nice friendly pub, livelier than the Gordon had been for years. But it wasn't the same. He wrote to the brewers to ask if the Gordon would be rebuilt. They replied fulsomely: all their bombed properties would be replaced as soon as conditions permitted, and they thanked him for his interest. However, he wasn't convinced that they would do it if it didn't pay them. And he didn't like the word "replaced"—that didn't exactly mean "rebuilt". It would be a new pub, a different pub. He would never again see the comfortable black leather benches, nor the ornate lettering on the mirror, nor the picture of General Charles George Gordon facing the spears of his murderers.

# 17

MISS HAWKE was a sort of cousin of Sir Arnold's—not exactly a cousin, but a member of the other branch of the family. As often happens in England, one branch had money and social position, while the other simply had the name of Hawke and—in a manner normally expressed only by Christmas cards, yet brought to reality in time of trouble —belonged. Miss Hawke had looked after her mother until she was past thirty, missing her chance to marry; then, for twenty years, she had kept an antique shop in the picturesque old part of Plymouth. The big raid in 1940 wiped out her livelihood and her home (she had lived over the shop). She took refuge in a private hotel owned by a friend, who told her not to think of paying. But she couldn't take advantage of this for ever, and really had no idea what to do.

Sir Arnold came to the rescue by offering her a home in the flat over his stables. It had been in bad condition, he explained in his letter, but recently he had managed to get the repairs done. She would have to look after two boys, evacuees from London, whose mother wanted to go home. She might also give Lady Hawke some help with the house and the garden—"but we'll see how we get on about that".

It did not occur to Miss Hawke to refuse, or even to hesitate. She was to have a small salary and pay no rent, so her material problems were solved. The offer was a kindly one, and it showed what the family bond meant: anyway, Sir Arnold was the head of the senior branch and his wishes carried authority. At the same time, she felt a certain decline in her position—she had never been any kind of a servant, even in this politely disguised form. And she was apprehensive about the boys. They were aged twelve and nine, so it wasn't like coping with babies; still, they were boys and she knew nothing about boys. Moreover, they were from London, probably from the East End, likely to be rough and ill-mannered. She wasn't at all sure that she could manage.

Sir Arnold, too, was keeping his fingers crossed. While his wife was giving Miss Hawke tea, he had a word with Harry.

"I suggested this arrangement," he said, "and I want you to help me make it a success. She . . . my cousin . . ." He hesitated; his wife's idea was that the boys should call Miss Hawke Aunt Agnes, but this sounded absurd from him. He began again: "Someone who hasn't had a family of her own has to get used to looking after lads like you. There'll have to be give and take—yes, give and take. Ted's a bit young to understand this, but I want you to bear in mind that it's up to you to save her from unnecessary worry. In a way, you're looking after her as well as her looking after you."

"Yes, I see," Harry said. Sir Arnold gave him sixpence, hoping that it looked like a sign of trust and not a bribe, and mumbled about having something to attend to. The boy did understand, he thought. A sensible sort of boy, more grown-up than one would think for twelve.

Being called Aunt Agnes—or rather, thinking of herself as Aunt Agnes—did help Miss Hawke. She wasn't a governess; she wasn't here to teach the boys, nor primarily to discipline them. She had to give them hot meals, get them up in time for school, see that they changed their socks when they got their feet wet, and put them to bed with hot water bottles when they had colds. Surprising herself, she rather enjoyed all this. She thought of herself as a substitute mother, not replacing the real one of course, but carrying out a mother's duties—in fact, an aunt. Quite soon, she was genuinely fond of the boys, if only out of relief that her worst fears were groundless.

The boys, on the other hand, found "Aunt Agnes" an embarrassing title. This person was very clearly different from anyone in their family, from Auntie Marj or Auntie Liza, though she looked rather like Auntie Vi. They accepted her services warily. They didn't intend to be guided by her in anything important, nor to go

328

to her in case of trouble. They would rely on themselves, or they would ask to see Sir Arnold, who was a man and a father, or they would write home. But, most of all, they would rely on themselves.

Harry remembered what Sir Arnold had said. Ted also, less consciously, felt that it was unwise to expect too much of Aunt Agnes. If she provided the hot meals and similar essentials, that was quite enough. They avoided intimacy with her, and they avoided conflict, for conflict at close quarters is a form of intimacy. The best way to do this was to make as few demands on her as possible, and to do things for themselves. So they brushed their teeth without being reminded, polished their shoes, made their beds, and kept their room tidy—this in particular, because they disliked her coming into it. A correct and even harmonious relationship was established, which Aunt Agnes imagined to be more friendly than it really was.

One potential conflict was soon resolved. Aunt Agnes fretted because they didn't come straight home from school; their father had sent them money to buy cycles, so they could do the journey quite quickly. But Ted liked playing in the streets with his friends, while Harry enjoyed taking a longer route from the town and cycling about the countryside on his own. He explained to Sir Arnold that their Mum had never bothered where they were so long as they were in for supper. Sir Arnold advised Aunt Agnes to adopt this policy.

They seemed to be alike, the two boys. Both were sensible, independent, and as well-behaved as one could expect East End boys to be. Ted shouted or giggled more often, but of course he was younger. They were not the highly-strung type, either of them, and they showed no sign of missing their parents badly.

But beneath what Agnes saw, they were not really much alike. For one thing, Harry now felt entirely detached from his former life in Steadman Street. He had never, in childhood, been so immersed in it as other boys—had never taken real pleasure in hopscotch and ringing doorbells and travelling on buses without paying. Now, he felt himself to be alone. This didn't make him unhappy; he liked being alone. It was to be alone that he went on long cycle rides, taking right or left turns at random, not caring much where he was. He had little feeling for the countryside; he kept on the roads, was incurious about the looming wilds of Dartmoor, didn't grasp what people did on farms, and was scared of big dogs and bulls. He had few friends at school, either Devon boys or evacuees. Occasionally—more rarely now—he broke a school rule gratuitously, without knowing why, or he burst into fury for a trivial reason, for instance if another boy used his pen without asking. These outbursts were remembered by others long after

Harry forgot them. Both masters and boys kept at a distance from him, puzzled. This suited him. He was quite content without a settled environment. He found it hard to imagine returning to Steadman Street, though presumably he would. That was over, a completed phase. But he had not thought of staying in Devon after the war ended. Where he was, physically, seemed to him unimportant. He would be alone, self-sufficient, anywhere.

He read all the books he could get hold of. He had gone on to adventure stories, but really he didn't like stories so much. The characters—especially boys whom one was meant to admire—struck him as an unnecessary element. He read for information, and preferred travel books and history books. He would like travelling, he thought. On his cycle rides, he moved from one fantasy to another. He would discover the lost cities of the Incas: he would land on a Pacific island where prehistoric animals survived. But the fantasy that he most cherished was not so boyish. Old Mr. Wheelwright—he lived alone in a tiny flat, the neighbours thought him a harmless eccentric, he emerged from time to time to go to the British Museum. Only after his death was it known that he had deciphered the Minoan script.

A girl appeared in these fantasies after Harry was about fourteen. She was very beautiful and passionately in love with him. Dozens of other men longed for her, but she had eyes only for him. She made appointments with him and suffered patiently when he forgot about them; she hammered on his door, he opened it reluctantly. He threw her on the bed and took her impatiently, already back at his work when she sighed "Thank you—thank you!" (this was the ending if Harry was feeling randy); or he told her sternly: "I really haven't any time for you" (this was the ending he preferred). Brief notes informed her that he had gone away and had no idea when he would be back. She was always faithful, he was always independent.

Ted had what Harry lacked: the ability to live completely in the present, where he was. He enjoyed the countryside—it was fun. He fished in the streams with a bent wire, and got Charlie to give him a rod for Christmas when he was older. He stole apples, chased cows and sheep, swam in pools in the summer and tobogganed on the moor in the winter. He was never alone, but always the leading spirit in a gang. He made friends easily, girls as well as boys. The girls were real to him, not creatures of mystery or fantasy. He got behind hedges with them, kissed them, tickled them under their skirts. When he thought about a girl sexually, it was a girl he knew. Ted was a tall, strong lad. Like his father as a boy, and unlike his brother, he looked older than he was.

But he was clear in his mind that he was living

in exile. He belonged to London; he hadn't time to miss it much, but he saw it vividly in the quiet minutes before he fell asleep. It never entered his head that he would not go back there as soon as the war ended, or as soon as he finished school if that happened earlier. Among the boys of Ted's age at the school, there was an unending feud between locals and evacuees—between "louts" and "slummies". Each side captured marbles and conkers from the other side, planned ambushes, launched playground battles. Ted was a determined fighter for the Londoners. It was a struggle waged with ferocity but without hatred; it didn't prevent him from having Devon friends and kissing Devon girls. Still, it kept him constantly aware of what he was.

For the month of August, Aunt Agnes went for a holiday at her friend's hotel in Plymouth. When Charlie and Ann moved in, the flat seemed very small and totally, noisily and cheerfully filled. Charlie treated the trip to Devon as an adventure, claiming that he was lost anywhere beyond Clapham Junction. He teased Ted by pretending not to be able to tell a cow from a bull, or a long-haired sheep from a goat. In the Okehampton shops, he wouldn't utter a word and asked the boys to translate what the natives had said.

He talked a great deal about Steadman Street and the docks, about Tom Whitmarsh and Alf Harris and Stan Turner. It never occurred to him that this London might be less real to the boys than to him—indeed, it was perfectly real to Ted, though not to Harry. About what the boys were doing, he asked few questions; only "Managing all right, are you?" and "Getting on all right at school?" He was content if they kept healthy and reasonably happy until they resumed their proper life.

Ted didn't idolise his father, but he valued him as Charlie wished to be valued. Charlie stood for reality, for the strength and breadth of life, for the manhood that a boy must take on. When Charlie had gone, a door was closed for Ted. But Harry was guiltily aware of a certain relief. Year by year, he found it harder to listen attentively to the Steadman Street news, to laugh at the jokes, to care about the people.

The rest of August was the strangest time of the year. It was a happy time; both the boys sincerely loved their mother. It was a peaceful time, when the three of them talked quietly, went for aimless walks, gazed at glowing sunsets over the hills, were content simply to be together. Yet it had a certain melancholy, for it gave the illusion of a permanence which could not exist—obviously because Ann was going back soon, more subtly because the boys were growing up. In a way, each August recreated the first year of the war, when Ann and the boys had lived close to one another like castaways on an island. But they had been children, and now they were not.

Was Harry growing apart from Ann too? He hated the idea; there was no one in the world he could talk to as he talked to her. She really wanted to know all about his school work and about what he did with his time. She talked about Steadman Street with honesty, not pretending—as Charlie did—that it was much like what it had been. She also talked about Auntie Marjorie's lovers, which made Harry feel very grown-up.

And they kept in touch through the year; Ann wrote the letters, not Charlie. Harry told her what books he read and she commented on them. There was a vogue, in the middle of the war, for reading *War and Peace*. It provided another reality, different but full of meaning; besides, reading it was a kind of tribute to Russia. Ann bought a copy. Charlie said: "One thousand five hundred pages! You'll never finish it." She did finish it, then sent it to Harry for the Christmas of 1943. The next August, they lived through it together, drawn close by favourite scenes and characters.

Yet something divided them. Ann did belong wholly to Steadman Street; she was Charlie's wife all the year, Harry's mother for a month. That month was a short time for renewing threads of feeling. Ann was still brisk, energetic, full of practical sense. She distrusted Harry's tendency to dream, which she noticed although she knew nothing of his fantasies. It came from old Dora, she supposed—it wouldn't do the boy any good.

Going home in the train, she wondered every year whether she had been right to leave the boys to grow up without her. Everything seemed to be going well, everything she could put a finger on. What she didn't know, as time passed, was what kind of men they were becoming.

On a Sunday in 1941, the headmaster of the boys' elementary school had a few words with Aunt Agnes when they came out of church. He said that he could, with fair confidence, enter Harry Wheelwright for a scholarship to the grammar school. If he won it, there would be no fees. Of course, some money would be needed for the uniform and similar expenses.

Before telling Harry, Aunt Agnes spoke to Sir Arnold. He would think it over, he said. And naturally the father would have to be consulted. Some people of that class appreciated education, some did not.

On the following day, Sir Arnold received a telegram from the Air Ministry. His son Nigel, a navigator with Bomber Command, had been shot down over the Dutch coast. The telegram said "missing", but a letter from the squadron-leader told Sir Arnold that there was no hope.

Silence—the silence of final, irreparable grief

—covered the big house. The Hawkes had no other son, not even a daughter; the estate would go to a cousin, a London barrister who would probably sell it. Sir Arnold and his wife were not the kind of people who find comfort in words. She collapsed and stayed in bed under the doctor's care; he tramped about the paddocks and woods, followed by his old retriever, under a low grey sky. He avoided Agnes. She would have tried to console him, and he had no use for anything but endurance. He avoided everyone except the plodding, loyal dog.

But, on the second day of this, he came home up the drive and met Harry returning from school. Conscience smote him—he had forgotten all about that grammar school business. He was not a superstitious man, but he had a sudden sense of the continuity of life, the very thing that seemed to have vanished with Nigel's death. He went straight to the library and wrote to Charlie. Instead of merely reporting the facts, as he had intended, he strongly urged that the opportunity should not be missed. He ended: "I have no knowledge of your financial circumstances, but if that is a problem, I hope that you will allow me to meet the expenses involved. England will need educated men in the years to come, and I should regard this as a contribution to the future of our country."

Charlie read the letter and said: "Ought to do it, I suppose."

Ann knew what he was thinking: Harry would get all kinds of ideas, he would never be a stevedore. She headed this off, saying: "He can't start at the docks till he's eighteen, one way or the other."

"No." Charlie lit his pipe. "He'll have to go right through this grammar school once he starts, won't he?"

"You said yourself you wouldn't have the boys back in London while the war's on."

"That's true, I did say that."

Charlie wrote to give his approval, making it clear that he would meet all the expenses.

Harry won the scholarship easily. The solemn atmosphere of the exam—the silent hall, the bowed heads, the invigilating master in his gown and mortar-board—helped rather than worried him. He had a feeling of confidence as soon as he passed through the arched gate of the grammar school and crossed the paved courtyard. Big boys in uniform, some practically men, walked about talking among themselves and barely glancing at the scholarship candidates in their assorted jackets and shorts. In September, he too would wear a blazer and long trousers. He would have earned it.

Nevertheless, his first year at the grammar school was miserable. There were many rules and ancient customs, which new boys were not told about but were expected to know. One could be punished not only by a master but also by an older boy—this was a shock to him. He had to play rugger, which he hated. The scrum was a horror—the close touch and smell of other boys' bodies, the boots hacking at his shins in a blind confusion. In the summer there was cricket; this he attempted more hopefully, but it defeated him. Seized by panic, he ducked or simply froze when the hard dangerous ball came flying at him. So he couldn't bat, he couldn't take catches, and he was never given a chance to bowl. Games were important at this school, and Harry found himself despised. Worse than lacking in skill, he was also a coward.

Nor did he manage, that first year, to get on top of the work. He was confronted with French, Latin, chemistry, physics. Some boys had started on these at private prep schools, but they were new to Harry. Quantities of homework were set; he couldn't always get through it with Ted in the same room and Aunt Agnes insisting on lights out at a fixed time. It was made very clear that one wasn't simply staying at the grammar school because it was usual between certain ages, as at the elementary school. One was on trial—one could fail. With a painful sense of shame, Harry was afraid that he would fail. Everyone would know: his parents, Ted, Aunt Agnes, Sir Arnold. He had ventured into something beyond his reach. The agonies of this year, despite later achievement, left him with a deep inner uncertainty.

But in the second year he knew that he would not fail. The pace was still hard and the masters exacting, but instead of saying "No, no, you duffer" they now said "Come, come, Wheelwright, you know better than that". He realised that they expected success of him. And he was successful—more so with every year. It was implicitly recognised, and then openly stated as an obvious truth, that he was an exceptionally intelligent boy. He wound up every July appearing even more intelligent than he was, because he performed so well in exam conditions. When he took the School Certificate at the age of sixteen, he got distinctions in English, history, French, Latin and maths. A mere pass in chemistry—science never came alive for him—was the only blemish.

In the school at large, Harry was not popular. He was always bad at games and was classed with the minority of swots. He was still content to be solitary, indifferent to whether he had friends or not. As he grew older, however, he was drawn closer to the other swots. They went for cycle rides on Saturdays and spent the afternoon—in a teashop in winter, lying on warm grass in summer—talking about books, ideas, politics. Harry talked least; general, abstract ideas did not attract him. His best friend (so far as he had one), a boy called Raymond Blythe, was an ardent Socialist. Harry was Labour, of course. But that, Raymond said, wasn't the same thing.

Being an old foundation, the grammar school had a certain social prestige and was attended by boys who might, in a different part of England, have been sent to public schools: the sons of landowners, clergymen, doctors. If the fathers were in uniform, they were officers; indeed, some were regular officers, generally in the Navy. Raymond's father, a solicitor in peacetime, was a lieutenant-commander. Harry was almost the only evacuee at the school, except for boys who had been sent to Devon by private arrangement, not billeted under the Government scheme. It was not considered good form, especially among the swots who recognised only distinctions of intellect, to refer to the fact that Harry's father was a docker in the East End. All the same, he was aware of a background, of certain experiences, which everyone else took for granted. He was invited by Raymond, and sometimes by other boys, to spend a Sunday or a whole weekend. Their houses contained places which were discoveries for him, but were referred to by a casual definite article: the nursery, the dining-room, the guest-room, the lawn, the tennis court. There was also, invariably, the car. Petrol rationing was the wartime hardship most often mentioned. Generally there was a maid, or a housekeeper, or old Nanny who was still helping because of the war.

In the larger houses there were evacuees, who kept out of sight and were spoken of in the same resigned tone as the petrol rationing. Raymond poked fun at class distinctions and said they would disappear under Socialism, but he didn't seem to find it hard to live with them.

Harry acquired a new vocabulary: "wash your hands" instead of "go to the toilet", "listen in" instead of "have the wireless on". He now spoke in what was called standard English, while Ted still talked Cockney with a sprinkling of Devon words. When his parents came, he was conscious of their uneducated speech which no longer seemed natural to him, and sometimes found himself using words that they didn't understand. In August 1944, he was invited to spend a long weekend at Bath with the Blythes. He declined —every day of Ann's visit was sacred—but was guiltily aware that he would rather have gone. The sense of growing away from his family, and of the difficulty of a return, became more worrying as the end of the war and of his schooldays approached. He had hardly anything in common with Ted now, though they got along well enough. Ted accepted, without envy and indeed with some amusement, that Harry was the brainy sort. He himself wouldn't have gone to the grammar school even if he'd had the chance—"all that bloody homework, no thanks!" He stayed cheerfully at the elementary school, doing as little work as he could get away with and waiting for his fourteenth birthday.

In the world of standard English and large houses, there was one puzzling figure: Sir Arnold. Harry was never quite sure where he stood with him. Sir Arnold, really, was not sure where he stood either. Having taken an interest in the boy and directed him toward the grammar school, he felt it right to keep up the interest. He regularly asked Harry how he was getting on, answered the boy's questions when he could, and inquired whether he needed anything—a tennis racquet, perhaps, or a larger-sized bicycle. Sometimes he took Harry for a walk round the estate or a drive in the car; it would have been fair to take Ted too, but Ted was always out with his friends. He knew quite well that he was providing himself with a substitute for Nigel. He found himself able to say "This was always Nigel's favourite view" or "Sambo"—the retriever—"was Nigel's dog more than he was mine, you know." Harry made no particular reply, but none was needed. It eased Sir Arnold to speak of his dead son, even thus briefly; there was no one else to whom he could bring himself to do so.

But Lady Hawke, who was more of a snob than her husband, was resentful. "Are you planning to adopt that boy, by any chance?" she asked once.

"Really, my dear, what an idea. He's got parents. Keep a friendly eye on him, that's all."

In point of fact, Sir Arnold gradually came to see that Harry was not his kind of boy. He didn't care for the countryside, nor for animals—this was evident, though Harry was polite about it—nor for cricket, which had been important in Sir Arnold's life until the war put an end to the local league. He was clever, to be sure, cleverer than Nigel had ever been. But Sir Arnold was not at ease with clever people. So he would draw away from Harry for weeks at a time; then, out of the aching vacancy in his life, draw closer again.

Harry, therefore, was uncertain whether Sir Arnold wanted to keep a distance between them or not. He could enter a world like the Blythes' through common interests (Raymond's mother had taught history before marrying) but in Sir Arnold's world he surely did not belong. He didn't mind the long silences with this inarticulate man; he himself had always been contented in silence. But as he got older, he came to think that Sir Arnold was simply rather dull.

He was anxious not to alienate Sir Arnold, however, because of the library. He discovered the library not through Sir Arnold himself but through Mr. James, who taught English. Mr. James was Harry's favourite master: a youngish man with a real enthusiasm for his subject, who talked to the boys as if they were his own age and was more eager to inspire them to "further reading" than to dwell on the set books. If he could lead a boy to share his enthusiasm, Mr. James liked to walk round the courtyard with him after the class, adding chattily to the teaching.

They had been reading Donne. "This is a rotten selection, you know, Wheelwright," Mr. James said, shoving the anthology scornfully into his briefcase. "You ought to get your nose into a complete Donne."

"Where can I find one, sir?"

"I should think Sir Arnold Hawke must have one." Seeing Harry's surprise, Mr. James added: "He's got about the finest private library in the county. I'd have thought you knew that."

Harry could hardly believe it. Actually, the library had been collected by Sir Arnold's uncle, a bishop of some scholarly attainment. As he had been a bachelor, the books went to the family home after his death.

"Use the library—certainly," Sir Arnold said when Harry asked him. "Not much of a reader myself. I do the accounts in there—that kind of thing. But it's empty most of the time."

Harry began to spend entire Saturdays and Sundays curled up in a huge leather armchair, remembering meal-times with an effort, not knowing whether it was sunny or wet outside. He didn't like to take the books out of the room because the bindings were so beautiful. He was admitted to a treasure-cave; the spell would be

345

broken if he plundered it. Besides, he didn't as a rule read a book from cover to cover. He would spend an hour with poetry, then an hour with Plutarch's *Lives* or Captain Cook's *Voyages*. The bishop's tastes had been varied, or perhaps he had been mainly interested in collecting good editions. There was a complete Donne, certainly, as well as all the poets who had been mentioned at school and some who had not. There was a long row of novels—Scott, Thackeray, Dickens, Trollope. There was a great deal of classical literature, both in Greek or Latin and in translation. There was Clarendon, Green, Acton, and the Cambridge Modern History. Science was not represented, but Harry didn't mind about that.

Also, there were some decidedly peculiar books, which reminded Harry of a remark Mr. James had once made about a section of the British Museum Library to which access was possible only by special permission. Harry didn't understand all the words in these books, but the illustrations were unambiguous. He discovered an engraving, for instance, of a penis—this was part of his new vocabulary—the size of a tree; naked women were clambering up it, kissing or licking it, and one was perched with a smile of triumph on top. At first Harry couldn't believe that these books had belonged to the bishop. But they had the usual name-plate—"Ex Libris: Clarence Hawke"—and some pages were well thumbed. He wondered what Aunt Agnes would have said. This discovery finished his respect, never very deep, for the Church. He read the books warily, with an ear cocked for a step in the corridor, and also with a guilty feeling, as if he'd stumbled on something that it was best not to know about. He never mentioned these peculiar books to any of his friends. Often he wondered about the things that women were described as doing, or submitting to: were these the fantasies of the writers, or did anyone really do them? Ordinary married women like his mother—surely not! Women who had lovers, like Auntie Marjorie—perhaps. But he couldn't imagine ever asking anyone.

He loved simply being in the library, loved the silence and seclusion of the big room. Sometimes for an hour or more he didn't read at all but only handled the books. He loved them as another boy would have loved a shotgun or a well-polished saddle. His eyes lingered on the splendid red and gold of the bindings; he drew a sensuous pleasure from the touch of the leather, the thick costly paper, the glossy smoothness of the colour prints. He couldn't help resenting the fact that these wonderful books belonged to a man who never looked at them. A delicious thought struck him: Sir Arnold had no son, he was bound to leave the books to somebody. Harry felt his heart beating. He tried to put the idea out of his mind, but in vain.

The last year at school was his happiest. Raymond was working for an Oxford scholarship, but Harry accepted sensibly that this kind of thing was not for him. With the School Certificate behind him and no demanding tests ahead, he was allowed to take what sixth-form courses he pleased, mainly English and history. He was treated more or less as a student, working alone a good deal on long essays. Aunt Agnes was simply a housekeeper by now, and had relinquished control over his comings and goings and his bedtime. Ted's fourteenth birthday was early in the year, so he left school at Easter and went to London; the rocket attacks had ended and the war was almost over. One didn't leave a grammar school until the end of the school year, Harry explained to his parents. For three delightful months, he had a room of his own.

Mr. James was also the careers master. He had a talk with Harry in his informal way, strolling round the courtyard.

"Not much cash in the kitty, is there?" Mr. James could be direct and yet easy about this. "Makes a difference in this wicked world. Things like the law are ruled out—you have to pay to be a pupil. There's teaching, but without a degree it's only elementary teaching."

"I can be a docker," Harry said.

Mr. James smiled; they both saw the absurdity of this.

348

"I wonder if you've thought of the library service. Public libraries do a worthwhile job, and I imagine they're headed for expansion after the war. I've looked up the ways and means. You get a job as a junior assistant—no problem about that with your excellent School Cert. You study at evening classes and take the qualifying exams in stages. At the age of twenty-three, as a chartered librarian, you start at three hundred a year. Rather up your street, I'd have thought."

Harry didn't hesitate; it was a promise, a gift, more than a job. Sir Arnold thought it a splendid idea, and Aunt Agnes was awed, but Harry cautiously decided not to tell his parents until he saw them.

He left Devon on a scorching July day. Sir Arnold patted his shoulder on the station platform, mumbling: "Keep in touch—write the odd letter." His suitcase was heavy with books, the beginnings of a library: some Penguins and Everyman classics that he had bought, some presents. These included Macaulay's *Historical Essays* "for all-round distinction" from the school, a Bible from Aunt Agnes, and Tawney's *The Acquisitive Society* from Raymond. Sir Arnold had invited him to choose what he wanted from the library. To keep the memory of the beginning of it all, he took the Donne.

# 18

WHEN Harry got home, the election results had just been declared. Labour had won a landslide victory; the MP for Limehouse was Prime Minister. The old rulers were out in the cold—the company directors, the officers and gentlemen, the knights and baronets and double-barrelled names, the class that had assumed its power to be an unchallenged right and managed the country like a private estate. "They've had their chips," Charlie said with deep satisfaction. They would never get back; that stood to reason, everyone in Steadman Street agreed.

Ravaged and divided though it was, Steadman Street showed clear signs of revival. The Connollys came back, to Ann's delight, before the war ended; Ireland had been terribly dull, Kate admitted. The other empty houses soon filled up, for the first sign of a return to normal was that London again had a housing shortage —a desperate shortage, with so many dwellings in ruins. Families camped in bomb-damaged buildings, sometimes without water or light. People broke locks and invaded empty blocks of flats to which they had no legal title. The police turned them out; the world hadn't completely changed.

Everyone in Steadman Street had a letter from the property company which owned the houses. The company claimed that, with costs at their present level, it could not possibly be responsible for maintenance. Interpreted, this meant that under Labour the rents would stay pegged. The tenants were therefore offered the opportunity to buy the freehold of their homes. If the offer were declined, ownership would be transferred to the Borough Council.

Charlie and Ann disagreed about what to do, and argued for several evenings. Ann thought that being a Council tenant was a good idea. They had always, in principle, believed in doing away with the private landlord and bringing in public ownership. With the Council under Labour control, as of course it always would be, the repairs would be done fairly; if not, one could make a fuss. But her main argument was that the price asked for the freehold—three hundred pounds in the case of number five—was an insult. She worked out that the family had paid nine hundred and ninety pounds in rent since Jack and Dora had arrived in 1900, and hadn't got a fraction of this huge sum back in maintenance.

"You're being taken for a ride, Charlie, can't you see? You're just paying them to get rid of their responsibilities. They ought to give you the house for nothing. Asking you for three hundred quid—it's a bloody nerve."

"It's the price. Any house has got a price," Charlie answered. He resented the idea that the house wasn't worth three hundred pounds. And, he pointed out, it would be worth more and more as the years went by. He and Ann would doubtless stay in it as long as they lived; but when they were dead, the boys would have a nice little windfall if they chose to sell.

"Provided it's still standing up," Ann retorted. "You'll have to pay for all the repairs, mind, if you own it. That's why the landlords want to get rid of it. What about the wall, where number seven was? Held up by faith, it is. What about the roof? We still haven't got proper tiles."

The roof would be repaired, Charlie explained, at the expense of the War Damage Commission. As for the wall, it was perfectly sound. He refused to consider the possibility that the house was not solid, healthy, immortal. It could not betray him, after all the love and loyalty he had invested in it.

He couldn't put into words his deeper reasons for wanting to buy the house. It was true that nobody they knew had ever owned a house; it wasn't in the working-class tradition. But that was just the point. Charlie felt that he was turning his back on the evil in Steadman Street's past: the weekly struggle to meet the rent, the subjection to a remote owner, the fear of eviction. He wasn't buying property. He was acquiring freedom.

Ann resisted stubbornly and didn't pretend to be convinced, and for this he respected her; he was still proud of having married a woman with a will and a mind of her own. But when the decision had to be made, he was the man, the head of the family. He was also the Wheelwright, the inheritor of number five. When the legal formalities were completed and the deeds came, he read through them with lingering pleasure and locked them away with the birth and marriage certificates. Then he went out into the autumn sunshine, crossed the street, and gazed at his home. The house looked bigger than before, somehow—perhaps because of the gap alongside, perhaps simply because its status was unique. No other tenants had bought their houses. He was troubled, in part of his mind, by the possibility that Ann was right. They had never disagreed before on any important matter. But when he looked at the house, he was content. Ultimately, he could only follow his deepest feelings.

He paid by drawing the money out of the Post Office and handing it over to the solicitor named by the company. As the solicitor counted the five-pound notes—rapidly and almost casually, as if they were pennies for a bus fare—Charlie went through a moment of panic. Most of his wartime savings had gone; he hadn't much to fall back on now, if a stroke of bad luck came along. He reminded himself that he had taken that into account. Even if he was ill or out of a job, at least he would have no rent to worry about. And there were no money worries in sight. He had encouraged Ann to give up her wartime job. The boys were working, and each paid five bob a week toward the housekeeping. This wasn't really necessary, but Charlie considered it a sound principle.

The empty houses in Steadman Street were filled, as soon as the Council took possession, by people who had been bombed out. Betty's husband didn't return to number twelve; it went to the family who had lived in number sixteen before the bombing, so they were almost coming home. Charlie's new neighbours, at number three, had lived in the Isle of Dogs. The man, Joe Doherty, was a docker, and Charlie arranged his transfer from the East India Dock to the Albert. The Dohertys had two daughters, leggy girls in their early teens. "About right for Harry and Ted," Charlie remarked to Ann; she smiled, not quite dismissing the notion. At all events, it was good to have neighbours. Old Alf and Maggie would have been glad, Charlie thought, to have the dust and cobwebs swept away and life resumed in number three.

Then Tony and Liza came back to London and reopened their restaurant. They did indeed have seven children by now—or rather, they had five with them. George, the eldest, was in the Army and writing bored letters from India. Clara, just eighteen, was married to an Italian prisoner of war who had been working on a Gloucestershire farm; he was waiting for permission to take her home. Liza still bustled about, but she had aged considerably in the six years since Charlie had seen her. Her hair was grey and her skin was a rough red colour. When she was out with the youngest child, she could have been taken for his grandmother. "We might think about handing over the restaurant if George wants it," she told Charlie.

"What, and do nothing?" he asked.

"We've earned it, haven't we?"

She had earned it, true, even if Tony hadn't. There was no counting the pots she had scoured, the tables she had scrubbed, the quantities of flour she had mixed. Yet for Charlie it was strange to see someone of his own generation—his youngest sister!—thinking of rest and retirement. Life for him was a march, if he ever thought of it through a metaphor; sometimes hard going and sometimes easy, but always steady. There were miles yet to go.

Harry was not surprised when his father said: "Well now, my lad, what are you planning to do?" If anything was surprising, in July 1945, it was that he had been at home three days before being faced with the question; satisfaction over the election result, no doubt had filled Charlie's mind. Life was not complete, in Steadman Street, without work. It wasn't considered normal to sit about. In the months that followed, Harry was to see returning soldiers, home from years of discipline and danger, hang up their demob suits, get out their old donkey-jackets, and go down to the docks on the next Monday morning. Ted had been working since the week after Easter. He was the stores boy at an electrical components factory. When a department needed something, the storeman got the message on the internal phone and Ted went off with it —whistling on his way, swapping jokes with the girls on the assembly-line, finding time for a fag in the toilet. Work was much more fun than school, he told Harry. But the brothers didn't talk much; Harry read when he got into bed, Ted went to sleep quickly. They were set for separate lives—that was understood.

Taking a deep breath, Harry explained about becoming a librarian. He spoke carefully and steadily, having prepared for this. He went into the details of the junior assistant phase, the successive exams, the prospects. Ann's face was calm, interested more than immediately approving. Charlie listened with concentration. His forehead was deeply creased to a certain point, smooth above it. Harry hadn't noticed before that his father was going bald.

A silence, uncertain but not menacing, followed the exposition. Then Charlie said: "Keen on books more than anything else, are you?"

"Yes," Harry answered.

Charlie now looked at his son more directly and asked: "Did you think this up for yourself? Or did one of the teachers put it into your head?"

Harry hesitated, but not long enough for it to be seen. The purpose, by now, was totally his own. Whether Mr. James had suggested it or whether he had found it in a careers pamphlet made no difference to that. True to himself, he felt no guilt in lying to his father.

"I thought of it myself, Dad," he said clearly.

"I see." Charlie was pleased by this. What someone wanted with his whole mind to do, he believed, was likely to be the right thing.

"I'm wondering if there's enough jobs," he said. "There'll be plenty of bright youngsters coming out of the Forces, a few years older than you. You don't want to take all these exams and then find there's no job going."

Harry made another little speech about the expansion of the library service.

"I hope you're right. There's been plans and promises before, I can tell you." Charlie filled his pipe, the signal of relaxation. "Well, you know what you want, anyhow. Me and Mum'll have to have a bit of a think about it."

357

Unexpectedly—Harry, at all events, hadn't expected this—it was Ann rather than Charlie who had doubts. Charlie was resigned to losing touch with his elder son. He had noticed more than Ann thought; he had watched the alien influences—the grammar school, the kind of friendships that went with it, Sir Arnold Hawke's patronage. Only if Harry had presented no ideas of his own would Charlie have said that working in the docks was always possible, and then without much conviction. It was Ted he counted on as the stevedore, the inheritor. One inheritor was enough; even in the old days, not every son had followed his father. As for this librarian idea—well, Charlie couldn't judge what kind of life it promised, but he was relieved to find Harry putting forward something that sounded practical.

Ann, however, wanted to know what being a librarian was really like. A young man must have a good reason, she thought, to take himself away from the life of the working-class—from its honesty, its manifest value, its dignity. A skilled trade, like leather-work, was better in her eyes than mere clerking. She knew more about libraries than Charlie, so she didn't view them with unquestioning respect. She thought of the girls in the local public library. They put date-stamps in the books, they sent out postcards, they collected fines for overdue books and gave change—it was trivial work. The men in charge presumably had real responsibilities, like choosing which books to stock. But she wasn't convinced that Harry could work up to that. Perhaps the top jobs were only for men with university degrees; there were separate avenues, divided by impenetrable screens, in most careers. She didn't want the second-best for Harry. Disappointment might hit him hard.

She went to the library next day—the central library for the borough, not the branch she normally used—and asked to see the head librarian. She was kept waiting, as at the doctor's; this impressed her favourably. Eventually she was admitted to a large quiet room with a desk piled with papers, which impressed her favourably too. She explained in direct terms what she wanted to know. The librarian reassured her—he wasn't a graduate himself, he had come up through the evening classes. His accent, she noted, was more like her own than Harry's was. Moreover, it was true about the projected expansion. The librarian was short of staff at this moment and keenly interested in a boy with a grammar-school education and good School Certificate results. "These girls we have now," he said, "well, they're just killing time till they get married, frankly."

So it was settled. There was no reason why Harry shouldn't start the next Monday, and he did. He could choose his branch, and naturally went to the one within walking distance of home.

Within a week or two, he realised that it was a very poor library. Almost all the books were in a bad state: the covers torn away from the spines, pages loose or missing, scribbles—even obscene scribbles—in the margins. He had known the beauty of books; these gave him a directly physical feeling of disgust. Much of the damage could have been made good with glue or sticky tape, but nobody seemed to care. Harry devoted himself to rubbing out the scribbles, which were mostly in pencil.

There was very little in the library that he would have chosen to read. There were some moral tracts and collections of sermons, and also some memoirs by colonial governors or generals, which had either been donated or bought in large lots at executors' sales. These were never taken out, never even dusted by the staff. The books that were presumably useful had titles like *Woodwork for Everyman* or *Practical Watch and Clock Repairing*. On the fiction shelves, there were uniform editions of the accepted nineteenth-century novelists. These, Harry knew, made the library valuable for his mother. But the "classics" were far outnumbered by romantic love stories by authors he had never heard of. He flipped through them and read sentences at random: "She closed her eyes as his lips brushed hers, knowing that bliss had enveloped her at last." Women in shabby hats and shapeless overcoats took these books out with inexhaustible appetite, hesitating only to make sure that they hadn't read the book before, though often they were vague about that. Whether they were recalling what had long vanished from their lives, or tasting what they had never known, he couldn't guess. Now that he saw more women than ever before, he made the sad discovery that most of them were totally unattractive. They must have known sex if they were married, but surely not love.

He realised that he ought to have looked for a job in a better library; but if he tried to change, it might put a black mark against his name. The first year looked like being the worst, as at school. His boss seemed to dislike him because he had the ambition of entering the profession, and always gave him the most boring jobs. There were two girls, who certainly had no such ambition and no interest in books. If one of them caught his eye, she collapsed in giggles and hurried off for a session of whispering, and more giggling, with the other one. Soon they took to making remarks like "Good-morning, good-looking" or "You've had your hair cut, it looks nice". Harry gazed into the mirror in the men's toilet; it was a fact, he was good-looking.

One day, while the boss was out for lunch, they advanced on him together and the bolder of the two said: "We want to know, definitely. Who d'you fancy, her or me?"

"I hope we can all be friends," Harry replied. They giggled explosively and retreated.

All the afternoon, he was thinking: he had only to go to one of them and say: "I fancy you, of course, Linda. I just didn't want to hurt Pam's feelings" (or the other way round) and the way would be open. He was seventeen, nearer to eighteen; it was absurd that he hadn't even kissed a girl yet. Besides, Linda and Pam thought him a fool—he hated that. But he did nothing. Having missed the chance, he convinced himself that he had been wise; he could do better than kisses with giggles.

The evening classes began in September. The work for the first exam was dull, but easy. Harry expected to make friends—girlfriends or simply friends—among the other students. But the atmosphere was earnest, not at all what he imagined a student atmosphere to be like. As there was only one long lecture each evening, there was no chatting between classes. Afterwards, everyone went briskly out to catch buses or trains. Harry, as it happened, lived in the opposite direction from most of the others.

The girls in the class were mostly plain, heavily bespectacled, and apparently determined —with severely cut hair and scrubbed, unpowdered faces—to make themselves still plainer. They were the serious, intelligent sort; Harry didn't want to give the impression that he wasn't. But one, though also serious and unsmiling, was good-looking and wore long, dangling ear-rings. Harry sat next to her, by luck —it was a matter of alphabetical order—not by design. Necessarily, they exchanged small-talk before the class began.

After several weeks of hesitation, he cleared his throat and attracted her attention as she was collecting her books when the class ended one evening. In carefully casual phrases, hc asked whether she liked films and then whether she would care to see Olivier in *Henry the Fifth* on Saturday.

"This is the difficulty, I'm afraid," she said, holding up her left hand. "This" was an engagement ring. He had never noticed it.

She covered his confusion kindly and from then on became more rather than less communicative. Her fiancé was a librarian, she told Harry, just taking his finals. They intended to work together. It was an excellent basis for a marriage, they both thought.

Harry withdrew into his self-sufficiency. A week could easily go by without his having a conversation of more than ten minutes with anyone. At home, he lived with the rest of the family pretty much as he had lived with Aunt Agnes. He avoided friction, he made his bed and helped with the washing up, he smiled at standing jokes. He could have drawn closer to his mother. But that would have divided the family into the readers and the non-readers:

Harry and Ann on one side, Ted and Charlie on the other. No one wanted this.

During the winter, he had his medical for Army service and was given a deferment until the exam. The prospect of the call-up put a term to the present phase of his life. The Army might not, as they said, "make a man of him"; but he would make a man of himself, by endurance of what he fully expected to be misery.

When the call-up papers came, in the summer of 1946, Charlie gave him a string of old soldier's tips. "Always look busy even if you've got nothing to do. Keep out of sight whenever you can. Never volunteer for anything." Harry listened, without hope that it would do him much good. The basic training was misery, sure enough. He couldn't master the strange customs of Armyland, he saluted sergeants and forgot to salute officers, he dropped his rifle with a fearful clatter in trying to slope arms, he was a rotten shot. He felt himself thrown back to childhood; all his efforts and all his learning since that time were disregarded, valueless.

However, in the "aptitude tests"—which he did easily, as usual—it was decided that he had, of all things, an aptitude for radio transmission, or signalling as the Army called it. He was taken away from the other trainees, all of whom he had feared and loathed, and given a new label: Signalman Wheelwright instead of Private Wheelwright. He was taught the Morse code, radio procedure, the maintenance and repair of radio equipment. Although he never understood much of what he was doing, or how the gadgets really worked, he passed the proficiency tests by sheer memorising.

As a signalman, he spent a year and a half in a flat, bleak part of northern Germany. He lived in a requisitioned house—a wealthy man's house, roomier than Sir Arnold's—in the suburbs of a quite large town. This town had been bombed in a way that made the bombing of London seem like a careful, selective attack. It had been smashed to ruins, and then the ruins had been pulverised again and again, as though it had been essential for some fantastic reason that no two bricks should hold together. It was impossible to make out where the streets had been; there was nothing but a wasteland of rubble, in which bulldozers, during the course of Harry's stay, gradually made new streets, wider and straighter than the old ones. The factories, which were on the edge of the town, were not so badly damaged; but the railway line was broken and there were no raw materials, so they were not working. Most of the people had gone away, because they had lost their homes and because in any case there was no work for them. But several thousands lived in the heart of this ghost town, in huts made out of planks, beaten petrol tins and tarpaulins, on a foundation of roughly levelled ruins.

The Germans, Harry observed, were made miserable by doing nothing. The few who had an occupation toiled for long hours, never thinking to share the work with others. A part of the town that was free of rubble, because it had been a park, was closely sown with beans and potatoes. In 1947, thanks to a change of policy, the British Army began to employ civilians; they worked as if work were a joy, whether they were watched or not. The whole of Germany—of this society interrupted in its busy, devoted work—was like a clock that needed winding, or a car out of petrol. Harry felt that, from the moment when it became possible, everything would function again with unremarkable efficiency, just as a clock that is rewound shows no sign of having stopped. He saw this happen, indeed, before he went home.

He was with a detachment responsible for Army telephone lines. There were two officers and twenty men, all living in the big house. They ate together and there were no sharp distinctions between officers and men; one called the officers "sir", but Harry had used "sir" to the grammar school masters and his boss at the library. He got on fairly well with everyone, without making any real friends. He wasn't very good at maintaining the phone lines, having been trained in radio, but that was typical of the Army and nobody else was very efficient either. After the change of policy most of the work was done by Germans, and done properly.

When Harry arrived, however, the Germans with few exceptions were unemployed, penniless and starving. Shops, or huts serving as shops, opened for half an hour a day to hand out miserable rations. At open markets, people sold their jewellery, fur coats and silver photograph frames —for cigarettes, since the currency was worthless. Army food arrived in a locked van, to prevent the drivers from giving it away or selling it. The man on night guard outside the big house had orders to fire warning shots if civilians approached the dustbins. It was a bitter winter, the coldest for a century. People skulked about wearing old, patched uniforms or wrapped in blankets. Hunger was ugly, Harry found: white faces, scrawny necks, bony hands, infected skin. The soldiers said that the Germans were getting a taste of their own medicine—they hadn't minded gorging themselves while Russians and Poles starved. Or they said that all of Europe was on short rations, including Britain, and the Germans had to come last in the queue. However, most of them set aside bars of chocolate. These were sometimes for children, generally for women.

Almost every soldier had his bit of frat. In the ironic jargon of the time, liberation meant looting and fraternisation meant fucking. You found a woman, like anything else, at the

367

market. You went to her place if it wasn't too crowded, or you brought her back and used the back of a lorry in the unit garage. You paid in chocolates or cigarettes. There were some men who picked up casuals, but the accepted thing was to stick to a bit of frat, to establish a settled habit as a relief from the male, communal Army life. You even had a feeling of merit—you were feeding her friends and relations, maybe her old Mum, maybe her kids.

Harry saw the market in his first week, when he was going somewhere by jeep and the driver stopped to make an appointment with his woman. He soon gathered what the routine was. He would get himself a bit of frat, he decided; it was too easy to miss, he was being unfaithful to nobody, and he was going to be here for a long time. But when he thought it over, he found difficulties. He didn't know what to say to a woman, especially across a language barrier. He might accost a respectable lady—surely there were some—who was merely trading in the market; he might pick on another soldier's bit; he might, in the half-darkness, get involved with a woman who was really unattractive. He recoiled from the thought of scrutinising the woman, rejecting and choosing. For weeks, whenever he made up his mind to go down to the market, he did nothing. It was snowing, or he wanted to finish a book, or he had a cold.

Eventually he went. He strolled about among

the stalls—one said "stalls", though most of the goods were simply laid out on the ground— feeling that the pretence was visibly futile. At the edge of the market, he stopped at what seemed to be a music-stall: a portable gramophone and a pile of records set out on a blanket.

"Have a look," a woman's voice said.

Eyes on the ground, he hadn't seen that it was a woman selling the things. She was about his own height, with the usual pale face of that winter and a scarf over her long, very fair hair. Afterwards, Harry believed that he had found her beautiful at that moment. Actually, he was too unsure of himself to think of this.

He began to go through the records. They were mostly piano or harpsichord music: Bach, Chopin, Liszt. There was a gramophone in the unit; it would be good to have a change from Bing Crosby and Frank Sinatra.

"Five cigarettes each," she said.

"You have no Beethoven?" he asked. He didn't know much about music. At school, he had liked Beethoven best.

"I have all the symphonies at home," she said. "Come and see if you like. The albums were rather heavy to carry."

He went with her, carrying the gramophone. She was obviously a lady.

"You speak very good English," he said as they picked their way over the rubble.

"School English," she replied. "I didn't expect it to be useful like this."

She lived in a cellar, in which her children—a boy of seven and a girl of five—were playing quietly when they arrived. The house, an old house in what had been the picturesque part of the town, had been completely destroyed. She told him later that she and the children had been in the cellar for twenty-four hours before they were dug out. She had lost everything except the emergency beds in the cellar, the gramophone, the records which she had taken down to play after the sirens sounded, and some children's books and toys. "There was also the wine," she said, "but I have sold that." It was Harry who saved her from selling the records. On this first occasion, however, he bought the Fifth Symphony.

The children asked if she had brought them anything to eat. She had intended to buy food with cigarettes after selling some records, but this hadn't happened, so she had to tell them that they would be getting the usual potato soup. They didn't cry, but the boy said gravely: "You promised."

"What was that about?" Harry asked.

She translated. He said at once that he would come the following evening and bring some chocolate. Her thanks embarrassed him; it seemed a simple thing to do.

The next evening—he was on duty until it was

dark—he couldn't find the cellar by the light of a pocket torch. Suddenly he heard her calling: "Here, this way." He had a feeling of coming home, of being rescued from a cold emptiness.

He was shy of asking her name until she asked his. She had trouble in saying "Wheelwright"; it was their first joke together. "I shall call you Harry," she said. She took it for granted that he would come again.

Her name was Eva. Her husband was missing —a prisoner, she hoped—in Russia. He hadn't been a Nazi, but had belonged to an old family for whom loyalty to the nation was a law. Eva was a countess—"which means nothing now," she said. When Harry was questioned by the other soldiers about his bit of frat, these statements were greeted with derision. "There never were any fucking Nazis," they said. Also: "They're all fucking countesses." Harry was sure that Eva was telling the truth.

She was about thirty, he supposed; he could never have asked her age. She had been to London before the war, and talked about Harrods, the Savoy, the National Gallery, Wigmore Hall concerts. This was a London of which Harry knew nothing. He didn't tell her that his father was a docker; she never asked about his family. Her own family, he rather thought, was upper-middle-class rather than aristocratic like her husband's. She had studied as a pianist, and her grand piano was what she grieved for most after the bombing. "Lucky to have kept the records," she said.

From then on, Harry spent all his free time in the cellar. Eva and the children were living off him, of course; it was how most German women lived at that time. He had started to smoke the year before, but now he gave it up and gave Eva all his Army allowance of duty-free cigarettes. This provided her with the equivalent of a decent income. She bought new warm clothes, first for the children, then for herself. At the market, she got a good electric cooker—she had electricity, though she'd lived by candlelight for a period after the bombing—a coffee percolator, plates and cups. There was still an atmosphere of camping out, because furniture was quite unobtainable; they sat on the beds and held the plates on their laps. But the cellar became more like a real home. She managed to get hold of some paint and Harry, working all one weekend, painted the walls a gleaming white. It was amazing what a difference this made.

He never made love to her. He kissed her on the cheek when he arrived and when he left—this was customary in her upbringing, he gathered—and that was all. The men in his unit assumed that she was his bit of frat, and he would have been ashamed to let them know that she wasn't. But how was he to make love to her, in practice? The children were always there. She could have come to the garage with him; but he couldn't imagine her sprawling in the back of a lorry—not Eva.

He realised that he had missed his chance. He should have said to her when he handed over the first carton of cigarettes: "You know what these are for, right?"—meanwhile giving her a slap on the bottom or some such manly gesture. And she would have agreed. She had to eat, after all, and besides she obviously liked him. Yet he wasn't certain that she would have agreed. She never gave the slightest sign, at the beginning or later, that she saw him as a possible lover. She took the cigarettes as a disinterested gift, and in a way he was proud to be considered the kind of man who made such a gift. He simply could not manage the bottom-slapping approach. He was conscious all the time that she was a lady, that she was longing for her husband, and that she was much older than he was. Added together, these obstacles were insuperable. She treated him as a friend, but also to some extent as a kind of adopted son. She sewed on his buttons and chided him when he was careless about his clothes. When she made supper, from a mixture of local fresh vegetables and Army tins, she insisted on his eating a lot. "Look, Karl's finished his plate," she would say.

The longer things went on like this, the more impossible it became to alter them. He was afraid of what might happen if he suddenly tried to bring about the change. Eva might be reproachful: "This isn't what you wanted all along, is it?" She might laugh at him: "Now, Harry, don't be silly." Or she might resign herself, without affection, detached, like a prostitute. He imagined her lying stiffly beneath him, waiting for him to do it and get it over. He would probably make a mess of it. She would be comparing him unfavourably with her husband.

Moreover, he wondered whether he wanted her in that way. Sometimes he thought that he was in love with her—but in love with her beauty, as an image to be contemplated, like a Greek statue, like the Reynolds and Gainsborough portraits of ladies in art books. He found it hard to imagine the touch of her. Maybe, when he did have women, he would find that blonde hair, pale cheeks and slender bodies were not his type. When he had wet dreams and sexual fantasies, he pictured entirely different women: dark, passionate, hot-blooded women. It would be easier with them. They would say: "Come on, give it to me, I can't wait." Or so he hoped.

In the middle of 1947, Germany got back to something like normality. The currency acquired a value, and there was more food in the shops. Eva was given an official allowance as a missing officer's wife. She no longer needed the cigarettes; so, if she felt herself insulted by Harry, she could tell him to stop coming to see her. He could not possibly take the risk.

For he was happy with her, happier and more

at ease than he had ever been in his own home. He sat for hours listening to records, understanding the intricate beauty of music for the first time. She taught him to identify a key, to distinguish the instruments, to pick up the first hint of a theme and follow its development. They talked about books—she was fond of history, too. She had travelled a good deal; she described Paris, Vienna, Rome, the Alps. He felt that he was lucky to be with her, on her terms.

Like lovers—but as true friends—they needed no one but each other. For Harry, the other men in his unit were people with whom he could get along if necessary and whom he forgot when they were out of his sight. Eva had hardly any friends in the town. She had lived quietly even before the bombing, she said, content with her children and her piano. They were quiet children, rather withdrawn after their frightening experiences. They learned some English words from Harry, but regarded him as their mother's friend, not theirs. He was glad of their presence, however; it completed the feeling of home.

Sometimes it occurred to him that he could still pick up a woman, in the accepted sense. But Eva met his real need; sex wasn't so important as it was made out to be, he decided. And, although he wasn't her lover, being unfaithful to her had a meaning. He would feel her steady eyes on him while he scrabbled with some pick-up. In any case, women were less available after the hunger ended. Soldiers who had acquired bits of frat last year still had them, but new arrivals generally had to do without.

In the winter, three months before Harry was due to go home, Eva left the town. Thanks to her husband's former colonel, she was offered a job as book-keeper in a small factory. It was in Bavaria, in an undamaged town, and a flat went with the job. It would have been hard to refuse, even if she had been Harry's mistress—even if she had been in love with him.

They wrote to each other once a week: newsy letters, not very long. After he returned home, they wrote at longer intervals. Two years later, she wrote that her husband was officially presumed dead and she was getting married again.

Driving to Austria in 1960, on holiday with his wife, Harry passed through the town where Eva was living. He still had the address, but he didn't go there. As a matter of fact, he had never mentioned Eva to his wife.

# 19

A FUNNY thing—funny in the sense of peculiar, even fantastic—happened to Ted Wheelwright on the way to manhood. He was rejected at his Army medical. When the jargon was translated, it appeared that he had a weak heart.

He was puzzled rather than shocked or depressed. He wasn't in the habit of looking far ahead, and the fact that came uppermost in his mind was that he had escaped two years in uniform. Yet, when he told his parents, he felt as though he were confessing to a failure: not his fault exactly, but nevertheless shameful, like being a pansy. It was hard to accept the idea of a weakness in his heart, the essential core of his life—the good old ticker, reliably sustaining him awake or asleep. He had always thought of himself as strong. He had run races and played football all through his boyhood. The oddest thing was that Harry, who looked slight and delicate by Wheelwright standards, had gone through Army service. Harry, at this time, was expected home shortly.

Charlie absolutely refused to believe it.

"Must be a mistake. Useless lot, Army doctors —can't make a living as ordinary doctors. Or perhaps some bloody idle clerk's gone and mixed up your file with somebody else's. That'd be just like the Army."

"No sense arguing with them," Ted said. "Don't want to land myself in the Army if I can keep out of it."

"No, but you want to know about your heart. Go and see Dr. Henderson. He won't tell the Army—it's all confidential."

Henderson was the local doctor. Ann had been consulting him about some change of life troubles. A conscientious man, he sent Ted to the hospital for a full examination, staying overnight. Under the new National Health Service, this was free.

Charlie went to have a talk with Henderson when the report came back. If the news was bad, he felt that his duty as head of the family was to get it first.

"Well, there's no mistake," the doctor said. "Your son's heart is a bit of a faulty product. Bound to happen occasionally; the Almighty is engaged in mass production. But it isn't a tragedy. Without an examination, he could have gone on for years and never been aware of it. I daresay he'll live to a ripe old age, provided he takes care of himself."

"What d'you mean, takes care of himself?" Charlie asked.

"Well, no undue strain. Cricket or tennis, certainly—athletics, no."

378

"Will he be able to work in the docks?"

"Oh, that would be most unwise."

Charlie didn't feel like going straight home, so he called in at the Prince of Orange for a pint. He sat down at a table and drank slowly, smoking his pipe. He could not understand the reason for this thing. Doctors never explained causes, only effects. It seemed to him that something had got into Ted, mysteriously, silently— something that had nothing to do with what Ted was really like. He remembered that Ann's father had had a weak heart, but whether it could be inherited he didn't know. It was not a Wheelwright heart, that was certain.

The hard, bitter fact was that there could not be another stevedore in Albert Dock with the name of Wheelwright. Both his sons had fallen away from him: one in his mind or his character, the other because of this strange bodily flaw. He would not be able to set them on their way. He would not see his strength live in them.

He thought, to his own surprise, of Sir Arnold Hawke. One son, killed in the war. Worse things happened to some people. That put it into perspective, but didn't help.

He finished his pint and went home. When he told Ann, she reached her arms round his neck and kissed him. They didn't kiss often nowadays —not in the downstairs rooms in daylight. In her silence, he sensed the understanding that this was a blow to him as much as to Ted.

But the next day, at work, he had an idea and acted on it at once. He asked at the office about an indoor job for Ted. It would be considered, he was told. During the following week, he pulled strings through officials he knew and through the union. The answer was favourable: Ted could start at once as an office-boy and take a six months' commercial course, studying on day release. If he passed, he would have a job.

Ted disliked the prospect, but had no alternatives to suggest. He found the course hard going; he resented being thrown back to the discipline of school, and even at school he had never bothered about passing exams. As it turned out, he failed the course. But the office was short-handed, he was generally liked, and he was allowed to start again. This time, Charlie made him see what it would mean to look for a job with a record of failure, outside the community of dockland. He made a greater effort, and passed.

Harry didn't come back to live at home after his time in the Army. He took a job in St. Pancras, where the library system was said to be exceptionally good, and lived in a furnished room near King's Cross, coming home only on Sundays. At the end of a year, having passed one section of the exams for becoming a chartered librarian, he decided to take all the other sections in the next year. This meant giving up the job and studying full-time at the Regent Street Polytechnic. There was a Council grant, which only just paid for his room and light meals in the cafeteria. However, he preferred not to live at home. He told his parents that he couldn't spare the travelling time out of his studying.

In Steadman Street, no one was astonished that Ted was not in the Army. They had found something odd in the medical, that was all. It couldn't be serious—you had only to look at Ted —but of course the Army didn't need everybody in peacetime. The young men made envious remarks about Ted's good luck and some predictable jokes—"He's got three balls, didn't you know?"—and then the episode was forgotten. As for Ted's working in the dock office instead of on the ships, this was regarded as a clever trick and a reasonable perquisite for a foreman's son.

Only Pat, Ted's girl, knew about the heart weakness. She was inclined to sentimentality and also to worrying, and she pestered him until he told her. He let her have the truth because he couldn't think of a plausible alternative.

Pat was a lost sheep of the war. Her father had been killed in Africa, and her mother had gone off with another man while she was an evacuee. She drifted back to London and found work as a barmaid, living in an attic room above the pub. From the age of fourteen she had surrendered her body to all the men who demanded it with any persistence. She didn't much enjoy this, but she gained reassurance from having someone's full attention, even for a short time. In the wake of the war, there were many girls like Pat.

Ted went to this pub, the Wheatsheaf, rather than to the Prince of Orange. For no particular reason, the Wheatsheaf was favoured by young men who wore narrow trousers and high-buttoned jackets, known as Teddy-boys, or Teds for short. Ted had joined this crowd, drawn by the name as much as anything else, and was soon the leader of those who gathered at the Wheatsheaf. He noticed Pat, threw some remarks across the bar which made her blush, then ignored her for a while. He had the Wheelwright gift of confidence with women.

Someone told him that, if you went up to Pat's room when she was off duty, you might be lucky. The landlord and his wife didn't notice, or probably didn't care. He gave it a try. The door was locked, but Pat opened it out of fright when he refused to go away and rattled the handle noisily. From then on, he went to the attic regularly, pretending to go to the toilet and returning to the bar before closing time. She was a nice little screw, not very enthusiastic or active but full of grateful fondness.

Sometimes he took her out, to the pictures or the dance-hall; this was a sacrifice, since she bored him except in bed, but it established that she was his girl. He let it be known that he would clobber anyone else who touched her. Naturally, he had other girls from time to time.

The weak heart, when Pat heard about it, brought out all her sentimental nature. It was a romantic situation: the strong man with the secret worry, the lovers smiling through the danger.

After they had made love, she had a habit of lying on her back with legs together and hands clasped over her small breasts, like a figure on a tomb. They didn't talk, partly in case anyone came upstairs, chiefly because they had not much to say. Pat was able to float away into a vague dreamland. Really she would have liked to lie all night like this, beside a man who comforted her with his nearness but didn't touch her. She had begun, after some months, to venture on the hope that Ted would ultimately marry her, but she never took the risk of speaking of this.

She was wrenched out of her dreams, one night about ten o'clock, by Ted seizing her hand and pulling it on to his erection. She winced, as though at a mild electric shock; she disliked touching him there.

"Time for another go," he said.

"Oh . . . I don't think we ought to."

"Why not? Bags of time." He was muttering and she was whispering, as usual.

"Mustn't forget your heart," she said desperately. "Mustn't strain it."

This infuriated him. "Bollocks!" he said quite

loudly. He put on a fresh sheath and mounted her at once, pushing her legs apart like a man clearing a path through undergrowth, driving into her fiercely. As soon as he had finished, he dressed and went downstairs.

In spite of having satisfied himself, in spite of the pleasing jokes from his friends in the bar, he was in a glum mood for the rest of the evening. It hadn't occurred to him that he could strain his heart this way. Life wasn't worth living, he felt, if he had to be careful about that. Work bored him, home bored him; he was fully alive only when he was on top of a girl.

He wished he'd never been such a fool as to tell Pat about his heart. She had a nagging, womanish hold on him now: his guardian, almost his nurse. No doubt, as time passed, he would find girls who didn't ask why he hadn't been in the Army, or who assumed that he had been. But he lived in the present.

Still, he didn't consider giving Pat up. Her devotion and her concern for him, once he got used to them, had a flattering aspect. She was reliable, and she was never jealous. He had, altogether, a tendency to take things as they came and make the best of it. Pat was still his girl in 1950, when he was nineteen.

In that year, he was the secretary of a youth club. In general, the Teddy-boys regarded youth clubs as a trap to be avoided—a cunning curb on their freedom, a device to drag them back into their schooldays. But the youngish clergyman who ran this club allowed them to do as they pleased, to play the records they liked, even to bring in beer. Usually he left them alone for most of the evening, returning only to see that they tidied up and to say goodnight. It was like having their own house. The clubroom was large, and well furnished with armchairs and couches.

Self-government was one of the clergyman's principles. There was an elected committee, a secretary, a treasurer, and a set of rules adopted by free vote. The secretary had to arrive first on club nights, open the place up, and close it. Ted immediately saw the advantage of this position —the secretary had the key.

The Teddy-boys—at least, those who had keys to their homes—used to go to the club late at night. They put on only one shaded light and they played no records. They brought girls: girls who had been well filled with gin at the Wheatsheaf, or who knew all about it and were ready for it. Everyone in the neighbourhood knew what went on, except the liberal-minded clergyman.

Among the girls who were present on these occasions, the first to lie back and let down her knickers was generally Lukie. One reason was that her mother waited up for her. She was allowed only one late night out a week, and then she was supposed to be home by midnight.

Ted didn't have much to do with Lukie—didn't even know her full name. (It was Lucasta; her parents had pretensions to refinement.) He was the dominant male in the group and was conceded the right to the prettiest girl. Lukie was heavy and clumsily built, with no figure at all. She had a flat nose, puffy cheeks, and a gold band over prominent teeth. And yet Ted sometimes wanted to get his hands on her big breasts and fat bottom. She wasn't pretty, but in the precise sense of the word she was attractive. The attraction came from her open eagerness, her pleasure in sex. Unlike Pat and most other girls, she was never the passive victim.

One close summer night, things were more than usually confused because they had a bottle of French brandy which had somehow wandered out of the docks. They were lying on the carpet most of the time—three boys and three girls. At any given moment, Ted might be stroking one girl's thigh while another girl had her hand inside his shirt. He luxuriated in an easy, anonymous atmosphere of femininity. He was in no hurry about anything; he was enjoying the brandy. After a time, no one wanted to go on drinking it except Ted and Lukie. After a further time, he became aware that the other girls—one very pretty, one fairly pretty—had been removed to distant couches by the other boys. They had given up waiting for him, no doubt.

Not knowing why, he looked directly at Lukie. Her eyes held his in a sudden quiet. Then she lurched toward him and covered his face with wet sprawling kisses. They rolled over, her hand frantic at his flies. So they went at it, sweating and panting, the room reeling.

They must have both fallen asleep. When she woke him, the others had gone and the light was out. "What time is it?" she demanded. He struck a match; it was half past two.

"Oh, Christ!" she said. "I can't go home now. They'll kill me. I smell of booze, too."

"Well, if you can't go, don't go," he said.

"D'you like being with me?"

"What d'you think?"

They moved to a couch. Much later, they slept a little more.

He was woken by the sound of her sobbing. She was sitting up on the couch, away from him, wearing her bra and panties, dabbing at her eyes with a handkerchief. Her fat shoulder shook like jelly; she was anything but attractive now.

"I told you, it's no use worrying," he said.

"I'm not . . . I just . . ." She threw the handkerchief away and said in a curious hoarse voice: "Take me again, Ted."

"What, now?"

"It's so lovely with you. You've got to."

"See what I can do for you, then."

So he took her, out of pity this time, in broad daylight. People were walking past the club;

387

once he looked up and saw a bus. He had a ferocious headache and his throat was dry in the stale air. He had thought he was about drained, too, but he gave her what she wanted.

She was quite composed as she dressed and combed her hair. She went off without even kissing him again—she had put on lipstick—and he watched her purposeful, waddling walk as far as the next corner. Then he tidied up the room scrupulously. He was the secretary, after all. But he had to work fast to get to his job on time.

The other clerks said that he didn't look well. More than anything else, he was famished; he couldn't recall ever going without breakfast before. He laughed and said: "Rough night. She wouldn't give me a wink of sleep." Everyone roared; of course, Ted had a reputation in the office. He did feel extremely pleased with himself. He had driven the power of sex, the power of his body, to its limit for the first time —and, it now occurred to him, it had done his heart no harm. He decided that he must have more of Lukie. Experienced men said that it wasn't the beauties who gave you the best time, and they were evidently right.

Some time in the afternoon, when no one was talking and his thoughts had strayed from his work as usual, he suddenly realised that he had done it without precautions—not just the first time, but every time. At first he couldn't believe it. He looked in his wallet-pocket; there was the packet of Durex, unopened. He couldn't even remember how many times he had done it—four times at least. You produced literally millions of sperm every time you shot, he had read. He pictured them as in the drawing in the sex book, each one a lively little tadpole, a potential baby. But a woman didn't produce millions of eggs. He was normally careful, but he'd occasionally done it without precautions before and nothing had happened. The odds were on it being all right, surely. Anyhow, he could only hope for the best.

Lukie did not appear at the Wheatsheaf again. His sympathies were directed toward Pat, who was down with hay fever. He didn't have a girl for about a month, which gave him a vague feeling of having done an effective penance. As the time went on, he became convinced that it must be all right.

Then Lukie came to his home on a Sunday afternoon. He had to introduce her to his parents and Harry. She was quiet and polite. After an awkward few minutes, she asked if he would care for a walk.

They went a little way in silence. Then he said heartily: "Haven't seen much of you lately. Been all right?"

Still walking, not looking at him, she said: "I'm in the pudding club."

"Are you sure?"

"Course I'm sure."

"Does anybody know?"

"My parents do. My Mum clocks me. She's got a special calendar with her dates and mine marked on it."

Ted found nothing to say. She went on: "They're wild. They want to kill you. They were wild anyway about me being out all night. I haven't been allowed out again, that's why you haven't seen me. Just today, they had to go and see my Gran. I pretended to feel sick so they'd leave me behind."

"You didn't have to tell them it was me," he said, feeling that this was selfish but unable to keep it down.

"They kept on at me. It's got to be somebody, hasn't it? I couldn't say it was a man from Mars."

"How do I know it was me?" he demanded savagely. "I know how you carry on."

"All right, Mister Perfect Manners, I knew you'd say that. Well, I had my period just before we did it. So there."

They were walking so far apart that a man coming the other way passed between them. The next silence was longer. Then she said: "My Dad's writing to yours."

"Tell him to write to me. I'm not a kid."

"What are you going to do about it, then?"

"I'll see. I've got to think."

"You could have thought at the right time, couldn't you?"

"I could? Who was in such a bloody hurry, then?"

"Blame it all on me, that's right."

It was their first quarrel. And what had there been between them, except a drunken night and a quarrel? Suddenly, he couldn't bear it.

"Cheer up, love," he said, taking her arm. "Not the end of the world, is it? I mean, it's happened to other people."

The next day, a letter arrived for Charlie. He read it carefully, put it back into its envelope and the envelope into his pocket, and finished his breakfast. As he stood up to go out—he left half an hour before Ted—he said: "Don't see you much at the Prince these days. I'll be there about six o'clock."

When Ted arrived, his father had started on a pint. Modestly, he asked for a half.

"Was that the girl—the one who came round yesterday?" Charlie inquired.

Ted admitted this. Charlie's comment on the girl was silent.

They both drank, with a somewhat hollow "Cheers". Then Charlie said: "Never heard of bloody French letters, haven't you?"

"I'd had a few drinks."

"I see. She your girl-friend, really?"

"Not really."

Charlie took out the letter and studied it. "Her father sounds like a right bastard," he said. "You met him?"

"No. She says he's the strict sort."

"Well, I'll have to go along and see him. As if I didn't have enough to worry about."

What Charlie was already worrying about was the disgrace of Tom Whitmarsh. A lorry had been stopped leaving Albert Dock with crates of American-made scientific instruments. When searched, the crates proved to have false bottoms stuffed with nylon stockings. Five years after the war, England was still a country of rationing and shortages. Luxuries and new-style goods were in great demand; for instance, girls would pay anything for nylons. There was continual smuggling through the ports.

Normally, if a docker was caught with a pair of nylons tied round his waist or a watch in the lining of his jacket, the police took no action. The man was suspended from the register for a year and had to find another job. But this was organised and systematic smuggling, linked with a black-market ring. Tom, who had been promoted a few years ago to tally-clerk, had been falsifying the cargo lists. He had been arrested and was on bail. Charlie was in the midst of difficult interviews with company officials, with the police, with lawyers. There was not much doubt that the charges would be pressed; the case would be in all the papers, and Tom would go to prison—for years perhaps, if the judge felt like making an example of him. It was rough on Tom, Charlie's oldest friend. It was rough on

Tom's neglected wife; she had never had much happiness. It was rough on Tom's father, one of the last survivors of the old guard of stevedores. Charlie felt that it was his duty to tell the old man, but he hadn't faced it yet.

As far as smuggling went, Charlie's indignation was directed mainly at the searching procedure and the informers planted in the docks. There had been angry, impetuous strikes when the searches were too insulting, and Charlie was on the side of the strikers. He didn't forget, either, that the rich had their own ways of getting nylons. Yet this kind of dishonesty, this abuse of trust, was alien to the traditions of the docks. Old Whitmarsh would certainly feel that. Charlie felt something else: Tom had been a bloody fool. Too many people had been in the secret, and one of them must have been a copper's nark—Charlie didn't believe that the false bottoms had been discovered by luck. People nowadays, Charlie said to another foreman, didn't know how to look after themselves. The mess that Ted had got into showed this again.

So he was gloomy when he went to see Mr. Pope, Lukie's father. Mr. Pope lived in a semidetached house in Beckton, with a gate, a small front garden, and a bell that played a scrap of a tune. He was just the sort of man that Charlie most disliked: the petty bureaucrat, complete with sparse brilliantined hair and toothbrush moustache. He worked for the housing department of the Council.

Charlie was briefly introduced to Mrs. Pope and to the younger daughter, Corinna. Lukie was not to be seen. Everyone spoke in low voices, as if there had been a death in the house. After some inane exchanges about the weather, Mr. Pope led Charlie to what he called his den, a tiny room with a desk and two uncomfortable chairs.

"This has been a terrible shock," Mr. Pope began. "I've had to have the doctor for Mrs. Pope. However, we'll say no more about that. I don't think you have any daughters, Mr. Wheelwright. It's a considerable responsibility. I've tried to bring my girls up decently. It hasn't been easy, what with the war and all these modern ideas they pick up. Perhaps I should have watched over Lucasta more carefully. There has to be a modicum of trust, I felt—perhaps I was wrong. However, we'll say no more about that."

Despite this recurrent phrase, he said a good deal about all aspects of the matter. What wounded him most, Charlie gathered, was that the vile act had occurred on premises supposedly controlled by the Church. He was a devoted churchgoer, as one might have expected. The clergyman was evidently going to have a difficult time at the next churchwardens' meeting.

Charlie, when he could get a word in, said that

Ted had got mixed up with a certain crowd . . .
"You're a sissy if you don't go along, know what
I mean?" Mr. Pope gave no sign that he did
know. And, Charlie continued, things had
naturally got out of hand when somebody
brought along some hard liquor. But mention of
this was a mistake. Mr. Pope hadn't heard about
the hard liquor; he sat bolt upright, staring as if
he couldn't believe his ears. He made another
long speech, elaborating the view that his
daughter had been lured, all but kidnapped, and
practically raped in a helpless condition. He
referred to her either by the absurd name of
Lucasta or as "our little girl". Charlie wanted to
point out that she was quite a big girl, the same
age as Ted, but decided that this would merely
irritate Mr. Pope.

At long last, Mr. Pope came to the point.

"I don't intend to reproach your son, Mr.
Wheelwright. His own conscience must have said
all that I can say. We have to think of the unborn
child. It . . . he . . . that is, he or she mustn't
be the one to suffer. What we know, that child
need never know. As my son-in-law, the young
man will always find a welcome in this house. I
can't say fairer than that, can I?"

"Well, that's what we've got to talk about,
Mr. Pope," Charlie said cautiously. "I don't
exactly know if Ted wants to get married.
Naturally I don't know if she wants to marry

him, either. There wasn't any understanding between them."

Mr. Pope gave signs of incredulity again. "Mr. Wheelwright," he said, "I've no means of knowing what's considered right in your circles." Here he paused significantly. Charlie saw what was implied: "our little girl" was the victim of lustful, brutal men below her proper sphere— men of the docks, men of Canning Town.

He made no retort. There were other possibilities, he said. Things like this had often happened in the war; adoption societies did an excellent job. As for expenses, they needn't quarrel about that . . .

Mr. Pope interrupted, hand raised in reproof. "I'm not to be bought off, Mr. Wheelwright. I'm sorry, but you force me to say it. And I don't intend to expose my daughter to public shame. A quick wedding—that's customary enough nowadays—and nobody need be any the wiser."

Charlie left, promising to be in touch again shortly.

Now came the worst part of it: a bitter, unhappy battle between Charlie and Ann. Charlie could see no way out of the marriage if the Popes insisted on it.

"They can't force him to marry her," Ann said.

"They can sue him for maintenance of the child. That looks nasty."

"That's what I can't stand!" she cried. "What it looks like—what people will say—that's all you think of."

In a way, this was true. Charlie cared tremendously for reputation, for the standing of the Wheelwrights. He wasn't much disturbed—Ann was, he saw—by what Ted had done with the girl in the first place. He had been quite amused to discover, on looking at Dora's marriage lines after her death, that he had been a love-child himself. But then, Jack had married Dora. It was possible that he hadn't wanted to, more than possible that he hadn't envisaged it when he took her; however, it had turned out all right. There was a code in these matters. It was just as clearly recognised, Charlie thought resentfully, in what Pope called his "circles" as in any other class. You might behave recklessly, but you had to be a man and take the responsibility. If you got a girl pregnant and rejected the solution that she wanted—and of course Lukie could be made to want what her parents ordered—you were guilty of dishonesty, of meanness. Charlie didn't want it said that his son had failed to live up to the code.

Ann swept all this aside. She was furious with Ted, more furious than Charlie dreamed of being. "I never thought you were that hard up," she said to him cuttingly. But she had made Ted admit that the girl had grabbed him. She had also made inquiries at the Wheatsheaf; the girl

397

was a notorious tart, she told Charlie. Mr. Pope should be made to face the fact. It was entirely possible that Ted wasn't the father at all.

"She's not good-looking enough to be a tart," Charlie objected.

"It isn't good looks, it's just willingness," Ann snapped back.

Anyway, what she thought of was the future. Ted wasn't pretending that he loved the girl or that she loved him. A marriage without love, Ann believed, was a sin against the best in man and woman. This marriage would be a disaster —she was immovably certain of that. Ted and Lukie would both come to loathe the trap that was closing on them. The child would suffer far more, in a loveless home, than if it were adopted by people who would welcome it.

"You don't care about human beings!" she accused Charlie. "You don't care about your son, if he's happy or not. It's his whole life we're talking about."

Charlie wouldn't agree that disaster was inevitable. A love marriage was something precious, he thought, but it didn't come the way of everyone. He pointed to example after example of marriages that were harmonious and successful without love, including some that had begun for this reason. Lukie would respect Ted and be grateful to him. They would be drawn together by care for the child.

Ann took no comfort and yielded no ground.

The quarrel—it was a real quarrel, not like the disagreement over buying the house—raged on, with time and the shadow of Pope in the background. It raged in Ted's presence and out of it, in bed at night, and all the next weekend— Harry, fortunately, didn't come home. If Charlie fled to the Prince of Orange, he found Ann refreshed for the fight when he came home.

She never did give up. But Ted, who had said little, grew weary of all the fuss and announced that he was willing to marry Lukie. He had seen her again, this time with her parents' agreement, and felt that he could get to like her; she wasn't a bad sort, she was easy-going when she wasn't rattled. Really, he was taken with the idea of being fully grown-up, with a wife, a child, and if possible a home of his own. Lukie could cook and so forth, presumably, and though she wasn't a good-looker she'd be pretty hot stuff in bed. Then, he was as much concerned as Charlie about the accepted code and about what people would think of him. It seemed to him that his father, rather than his mother, would know what a man ought to do in this situation. And in the end, he was inclined to take things as they came: to get over the immediate problem and hope for the best.

Ann let it be known that she was defeated, not convinced. She took a day off and had lunch at a smart Italian restaurant with Marjorie, who agreed with her attitude, sympathised, and diverted her with stories about love affairs. Then she found her way to the Regent Street Polytechnic, with a vague notion that she might catch sight of Harry. He was taking his final exams. She didn't see him, but being near the Poly soothed her.

Charlie was not proud of his victory. In his heart of hearts, he felt that he and Ann were both right, in different ways. He knew what she thought: he had behaved as a coward, letting others force his will. She would always think that. It hurt him.

At the wedding, Lukie wore white and Ted appeared in a new blue suit. Mr. Pope spared neither ritual nor expense; there was a reception in a local church hall, a meal which seemed to last for ever, champagne, wedding-cake, speeches. It was observed that the groom's mother did not kiss the bride. "I'd made up my mind to do it," Ann said afterwards, "but I just couldn't."

The honeymoon week was spent at Frinton, where the Popes always went for their holidays. As it was August, there was some trouble about getting into a hotel. Ted and Lukie ended up in a crowded boarding-house. Supper was served at half past six; after that, it was impossible to get seats in the tiny lounge, where the new marvel —television—was an attraction. It seemed embarrassing to go straight to bed, so they went to the nearest pub. Lukie drank steadily and became increasingly amorous. The nights were what honeymoon nights should be, but the days were hard to get through. Excluded from the boarding-house, they sat for hours in cafés and went to all the cinemas in the town. They swam in the sea once, but it rained most of the week. They were both glad to get back to London.

Lukie went to her parents' home for a few days to sort through her belongings and decide what she would take to number five. Ted watched a new double bed being installed in the back room—the boys' room, it had been called until now. A man with a little cart took the single beds for ten bob each. There was nowhere now for Harry to sleep, but he had said that he didn't mind. He still had his furnished room. Next year, when he would be twenty-three and allowed to apply for a non-junior librarian's job, he hoped to find a flat.

On his second evening back home, Ted went to the Wheatsheaf. He hadn't been there since getting engaged. The Teddy-boys and the girls greeted him with ribald jokes and bought him pint after pint. Pat was off duty.

About ten o'clock, Ted left the bar to have a pee. This was his real purpose, and he did it; but then, not quite knowing why, he found himself going up to the attic. The door was not locked. There was Pat, the same as usual, sitting up in bed and mending a seam in a cardigan.

They stared at each other for a few seconds. Then he said: "Hello, Pat."

"Hello," she said almost inaudibly.

"Thought I'd see how you're getting on."

"I'm OK. You're married, aren't you? Congratulations."

"Give us a kiss, then."

He intended only to kiss her, for old times' sake. But once he had his arms round her, he was roused by the familiar pressure of her small, hard breasts.

"Don't," she said. "No, Ted. It isn't right."

Yet she clung to him, her body contradicting her words. He pulled down his trousers. She yielded to him passively, dreamily, as she always had. He thought with wonder of the variety of women.

Going down the stairs, he heard Pat crying. He paused, but didn't go back. There was nothing he could do about it.

# 20

THERE seemed to be no prospect of Ted and Lukie having a home of their own. In the old days, rented houses like those in Steadman Street were always falling empty for one reason or another. You simply kept your ears open, at work and in the pub, until you heard of something. But thousands of these houses had been destroyed in the war, or handed over to the Council, or—whenever the landlords could manage it—converted into freeholds. People who had houses at controlled rents, mostly older people, hung on to them tenaciously. The free-hold houses were usually improved with an array of water-heaters, flush toilets, stainless steel sinks and what-not before they were put on the market, and cost a thousand pounds or more. Not yet twenty-one, and still earning a junior wage, Ted had no hope of getting a mortgage. His only chance was to apply for a Council house or flat, and he duly put his name down. But the waiting list was enormous. There were people on it with large families, people with serious health problems, people who could claim gross over-crowding: people living in ancient tenements, in damp basements, in houses officially classified as unfit for human habitation, in furnished rooms. The outlook was poor.

For himself, Ted didn't mind very much. He was fond of his old home and of the neighbourhood, and he got on well with his parents. Anyway, he wasn't in the house a lot. He was in the Wheatsheaf, or knocking about the streets, or tearing along the Barking bypass on a motorbike; he had learned to ride and had a one-third share in the bike. Since his marriage, he lived in more of a male world. He had given up going to Pat's room and chasing the other girls. Lukie knew the whole crowd—she was bound to find out. However, in the later months of her pregnancy, the strain began to tell. He picked up girls several times at roadside cafés when he was out on the bike. It was winter by now and he had nowhere to take them, but there were ways of overcoming this problem; once he had a girl in the waiting-room of a deserted railway station. He felt that Lukie couldn't expect too much of him, considering the reason why he had sacrificed his freedom. He would provide for her and the baby, and come home at night. Beyond that, what she didn't know didn't hurt her.

Lukie, to her own surprise, was looking forward to having the baby. Under the Health Service, one went to a weekly ante-natal clinic. Waiting her turn, she made friends with other young wives and talked about baby clothes, prams and carry-cots. Women who were already mothers told her what to expect in hospital and what the actual birth was like. She was assured by everyone that she would have it easy; her big hips, hitherto a liability, were turning out to be a gift of the gods. She spent Sundays at her old home, sometimes with Ted, more often—and she preferred this—without him. There, she wasn't allowed to touch the washing-up or put coal on the fire. Her parents treated her as a heroine, nobly facing a great adventure. Corinna, fascinated, put her hand on Lukie's vast belly to feel the baby move. There were long discussions about names, with her father suggesting the most recondite possibilities. Aunts and neighbours appeared, full of curiosity and goodwill. So far as Lukie could tell, everyone had forgotten how the baby had been conceived. In her own mind too, the floor of the clubroom and the bottle of brandy seemed infinitely remote.

Ted sometimes offered to take her to the pictures or down to the Wheatsheaf, but she usually said: "No, I'm cosy here. You go if you like." She had lost interest in the crowd, the jokes and the horseplay, the noisy bar. That was still Ted's world, she knew, and she had no wish to keep him away from it. She was a little sorry for him; a girl was ready to start a home and family at nineteen, she thought, but a man wasn't. At night, she felt as if she were sharing a bed with a stranger. Once or twice, groping her way out of sleep on dark mornings, she thought she was touching Corinna, who had come into her bed often during a period of nightmares.

This time at number five was worst for Ann. She made an honest effort to like Lukie; but, as with the kiss at the wedding, she just couldn't manage it. Lukie, she was aware, disliked her in return. They disagreed almost every day about whether the fire was too hot, or whether to have the wireless on, or something of the kind. They invariably disagreed with elaborate politeness, each offering to defer to the other—a politeness that kept dangerous honesty behind a safety curtain. Lukie, who always addressed Ann as "Mother", gave a sustained performance of being sweetly submissive: to Ann, to Charlie and to Ted. Ann wasn't fooled, though. She knew a hard, calculating bitch when she saw one. She was sure that Lukie was biding her time to extend power by degrees and take over the house.

Ann recognised that she lacked the tolerance to share a house easily with another woman. She had friends, such as Kate, but essentially she didn't incline toward the fellow-feeling of womanhood. She had given herself to one man, and that was her only surrender. As she now remembered, she had not enjoyed living with Dora. And this heavy, slow-moving Lukie was another Dora, without Dora's gentleness and intermittent charm. All her life, Ann had been repelled by fat women. When Lukie grew huge, she was still more repelled. She had always seen a pregnant body, including her own, as gross and ugly.

Lukie didn't do much to help in the house. Ann didn't want to share the work with her, and in fact often said "No, no, I'll see to that"; yet she thought Lukie lazy, all the same. She herself had refused to alter her active habits while carrying Harry and Ted. In particular, Lukie hardly ever went shopping. She asked Ann to buy things for her, including cigarettes—Ann had a prejudice against women who smoked, especially when they went about with the cigarette stuck to a lip, as Lukie did.

And Lukie let it be known, cunningly but clearly, that she had not been brought up in a house like number five. If it was cold or raining, she said "Well, I'll brave it" before going to the outhouse. Ann explained that there was no bathroom, and offered to fill up the tin bath any time that Lukie wanted it. But a bath in front of the fire was not for Lucasta (the name irritated Ann, too). Either she had a bath at the Popes' on Sundays, or else she stayed disgustingly dirty— Ann wasn't sure. Her fingernails were seldom clean, at all events. Her implicit attitude was that she had been dragged down by her connection with Ted. But you couldn't drag down a tart, Ann thought.

But Lukie's gravest fault was that, while being

sly, she was stupid. As used by Ann, this word covered a number of meanings: ignorant, superficial, mentally lazy, incurious. Lukie, in her submissive role, seldom offered an opinion on any subject that came up. If asked, she said "Oh, I don't know" or "I've never really thought about it"—implying that the effort of thought was somehow abnormal, not what she was used to. She never looked at a book, scarcely at a newspaper. The Popes were Tories, as one might expect, but Lukie offered no opposition to Wheelwright political attitudes. At the most, she might say: "Much of a muchness, all these governments, aren't they?"

So it was a bad time for Ann. Her health was troubling her, too. In addition to the change of life nuisance, she had something the matter with her kidneys. She looked her age or more, for the first time in her life. Her splendid hair turned white, swiftly, almost as if Lukie had done it. Charlie still loved her, she trusted in that; but they rarely made love nowadays. It seemed public, with Ted and Lukie in the next room.

She found that she needed more rest, and resented the failing of her energy. Occasionally, to her shame, she even dozed in her chair—for all the world like old Dora. She could only hope that the baby would not be too noisy.

The baby was a boy. It was decided that he should be called Alexander, after the poet Pope. Ted didn't mind; he shortened it to Alec, which sounded all right. Lukie proved to be a competent mother, doing everything that had to be done, feeding the infant from breasts bulging with milk. However, Alec really was extremely noisy. He got colic at four months and screamed relentlessly for spells of anything up to two hours. Ann, feeling guilty, escaped from the house for a chat with Kate.

Suddenly, deliverance came: Ted was given a Council flat. Charlie and Ann saw clearly that it was a fiddle on Mr. Pope's part; there were thousands of people in greater need. But only a saint would have raised that question.

The flat was miles away, right outside London. It was in a vast housing estate, still in its early stages, called Harold Hill. From the fifth floor of a red brick block, the windows looked over woods, fields, busy roads and half-finished houses. Charlie thought that the journey would be terrible. It seemed natural to him that, if you worked in the docks, you lived near the docks. In his young days, the penny tram-ride had been considered a drawback; most dockers walked to work. But all that had changed since the blitz, and dockers were suburbanites nowadays. Ted could manage quite well, catching the train at Romford. He was buying a motor-bike of his own and intended to ride to work in summer.

Charlie and Ann were alone in number five again, as they had been during the war. But this time, it was for ever. The boys were not coming back.

1952 was a mixed year. The Tories were back in power; certain gains, such as full employment and the Health Service, seemed to be secure, but it was plain that England's masters were her masters still. Rationing was abolished, and people were naturally glad about that. Yet the feeling of fair shares went with it, and prices were shocking nowadays. If you were drawing good money—for instance, as a foreman—you were all right. Charlie bought a television set. He knew people who were buying cars on hire purchase; working-class people would never have dreamed of such a thing before the war. But the poor—the underpaid workers who had no unions to fight for them, the pensioners, the war widows —had to count every penny, the same as ever.

He didn't feel old, but all kinds of things reminded him that the years were piling up. He was a grandfather. He was bald, he was developing a paunch, Ann had white hair and poor health. He found himself losing track of things and reacting with surprise to changes in the lives of others. Workmates went on the pension, youngsters looked middle-aged, school-boys appeared at work, infants worried about the eleven-plus exam. Old Whitmarsh died, bitter and lonely, with Tom in prison.

Liza and Tony went off to Italy. They would

have a house and a patch of land in the ancestral Varelli village, and make their own wine. "You'll come and stay with us after you've retired," Liza said. Charlie felt that it wasn't the most tactful remark. He had no urge to travel, anyway; he and Ann still went to Margate every August. The atmosphere at the restaurant changed when young George took over. It became a hangout for illegal bookies, wide boys and good-time girls, so Charlie stopped going to it.

Steadman Street was livelier and less of a ruin. Where the gaps had been, asphalt was laid and prefabs were put up: curious box-like houses, not built but made in factories. Charlie was glad to see them, of course—homes were desperately needed. On the other hand, the prefabs put off the day when there would be real rebuilding, when the street would look something like its old self. He wondered if he would ever see that day.

The prefabs were allocated by the London County Council, not by the borough, so the people in them came from all parts of London. Naturally, they were mostly young couples with small children. They made friends with one another, not with the old Steadman Street families. Few of the men were dockers. The newcomers passed the time of day with Charlie, and some of the wives asked Ann about the shops, but that was all. Charlie's days as chief citizen of Steadman Street were gone, never to return. Indeed, the street was not a community in the old style. With the television, people stayed at home and kept to themselves. The Council evicted one family for being behind with the rent—nobody knew about it until afterwards.

The General Gordon was rebuilt. Charlie was delighted with the new sign, copied from the old *Illustrated London News* drawing of Gordon's death. But the building itself, in bilious yellow brick, was more like a suburban café than what he understood by a pub. There were radiators instead of a fire, flimsy tables topped with Formica, and beer served in tall glasses instead of proper mugs. In place of a piano, there was a gadget which played deafening records when someone put a coin in the slot. It was his local, of course; he had at least one drink there most evenings, trying to feel at home. But it wasn't the old Gordon.

1952 was, above all, the year when Marjorie got married. Incredibly, she was forty-three. "Last chance to get aboard the Skylark," she said. The lucky man—and the phrase meant something, Charlie thought—was called Hymie Herzberg. Charlie was distinctly put out when he heard the name, but he told himself that there were good and bad in all races. Hymie turned out to be very Jewish indeed: he flashed five-pound notes in pubs, tried to teach Charlie Yiddish words, and told long Jewish stories—which, to Charlie's bewilderment, were much the same as anti-Jewish stories. It was all very much in Marjorie's style, Charlie reflected. If she went for a nigger he'd be black as your hat, and if she went for a Yid he'd be a real Yid.

Hymie owned six tailors' shops, but it was easy to see that Marjorie wasn't marrying him for his money. She was crazy about him, and he was crazy about her, as he declared at the top of his voice. He explained that he'd been married young: "So I was wet behind the ears, so I thought any woman who'd have me must be a goddess." The marriage was a failure, but he'd felt it right to keep a home going until the children were on their own. Charlie approved of this. The divorce—"the friendly sort," Hymie said—had just gone through. One could understand how a woman would find him attractive, if she didn't mind Jews. He was as tall as Charlie, square-shouldered, with thick hair on his hands: a real man, decidedly.

On the Sunday before the wedding, Hymie called in his car to take Charlie and Ann to the house he had bought. It was a huge Victorian mansion, built for some shipping magnate. The main room was big enough for a public meeting. Hymie kept saying: "You've got to imagine it the way it's going to be", and indeed the house looked pretty dilapidated, with mildew spots on the walls and pieces broken off the ceiling mouldings. Hymie explained with gusto how he had knocked down the price by getting a surveyor to list all the defects in a report the size of a book. Also, Hackney wasn't a smart district. But neither Hymie nor Marjorie wanted to live anywhere but in the East End.

The wedding was supposed to be for close relatives only, but Hymie evidently had about thirty of them. Charlie and Ann were the only goys, as Hymie called them. The synagogue was more like a church than they'd expected. A convoy of cars went to a West End hotel for the reception, which was on a scale that made the Popes' effort look like a snack in a sandwich bar. Charlie ate until he felt like bursting, losing all count of the courses. One waiter was kept busy doing nothing but carry out empty champagne bottles. The speeches were full of blue jokes, as funny as an old-fashioned music-hall. Then the tables were removed and a band played. There were so many people that you couldn't see an inch of floor when dancing started. Charlie and Ann didn't know the modern dances, but they had a gallant try. Hymie danced twice with Ann, and Charlie danced with Marjorie, who looked lovely in a close-fitting silver-grey dress. "Waist hasn't changed, has it?" she asked him. It had not. Harry danced with a Jewish girl with enormous dark eyes, Hymie's daughter. Ted and Lukie hadn't been able to come.

Ann and Charlie were thinking of going home when Marjorie told them: "You've got to come to the airport." They found themselves squeezed

414

with Herzberg relatives into a vast Daimler with a chauffeur in uniform. Amid shouting and kissing, the happy couple disappeared to board the plane for Nice. The Daimler then drove all over London—South Kensington, Golders Green, Stepney—emptying in stages and ending up in Steadman Street. Next day, when Charlie was at work, it all seemed like a wild dream.

Ann had a new interest: furnishing Harry's flat. His first fully-qualified job was in Clapham, and he had the second floor of a converted house near the Common. There were two good-sized rooms. He hadn't much idea what to put in them, so Ann prowled round the shops, keenly comparing prices and hire-purchase terms. Harry begged her not to tire herself, but doing this made her feel young and strong again.

One Saturday afternoon, when she went to tell Harry about a sheepskin rug that she'd discovered, he was having tea with a girl. Ann was overjoyed; she had been waiting for this for years. She tried not to look as if she were inspecting the girl, who was shy and spoke very little, in an almost inaudible voice. What Ann saw, she liked. The girl—introduced as Susan Dean—had long fair hair and delicate features. She looked rather fragile, but obviously the strapping type was wrong for Harry. She wore a simple black dress which suited her admirably, and she had taken off her shoes; nervously, she shuffled into them after Ann arrived.

Harry had met Susan through Raymond Blythe. After Oxford and Army service, Raymond was in London with a job in publishing. He had not changed much, except that he now considered himself a liberal with a small "l". He had lost touch with Harry, and tracked him down through the Library Association. Harry was grateful; he still had hardly any friends, and Raymond proved to have dozens. Soon, Harry was going to parties full of "interesting" people; he inserted the quotation marks in his mind, since some were genuinely interesting while others were hollow talkers. He himself was a listener, stating his opinions only when they were requested, but then not caring whether they conformed to the general view or not. (In Raymond's class, the general view at that time was that Socialism was an outdated dogma and the trade unions were the curse of the country.) Thus he gained a reputation for thoughtfulness—"there's more to him than you might imagine." He was aware of Susan for the first time when he was under fire and she said, making a visible effort: "I think Harry is quite right." He met her at three other parties before he dared to ask her for a date. He was sure she must be someone's girl, but she wasn't.

Nor did she have many friends, he discovered. It was her shyness, indeed her unhappiness, that made him fond of her as he got to know her. She came from Lancashire and hated her parents, who belonged to the prosperous but boorish middle-class. She was in London against their wishes and they had insisted on her living with an uncle and aunt, whom she hated too. She was a typist—"so-called editorial assistant, but typist really"—in the same firm as Raymond.

Harry found that Susan put no value on herself. She was convinced that she was asked to parties out of pity, or to make up the numbers. She didn't enjoy the parties, but they were better than going back to her uncle's house. She preferred concerts, so Harry took her to concerts and gazed at her while she listened, absorbed in the music, eyes closed, happy for the time. When he asked her to come to his flat for tea, he expected her to refuse. She said simply: "Oh, can I?"

He kissed her as they stood under a tree, sheltering from the rain during a walk on Clapham Common. "Thank you—that was nice," she said very quietly. When autumn came, the kissing was in his room. They embraced on the divan-bed, fully dressed except for shoes, listening to records. When he told her that she was beautiful, she said quickly: "You needn't say that, you know." And she declared that she was awful—skinny, unhealthy-looking, awful. She hated seeing herself in the mirror. Harry might have thought this a flirtatious pretence, but that was impossible for Susan.

On the occasion of Ann's visit, she left first, inventing an appointment. He rang her up and asked her to come to tea the next Sunday.

"Will your mother be there?"

"No, she just happened to drop in. But she never comes on Sundays."

On the Sunday, Susan said: "I felt terrible. I mean, she could have thought all kinds of things."

"She doesn't condemn people," Harry said. "In fact she's a very good sort of mother. You'd like her." He began to tell Susan about his family. He was frank about their class position, but left out the story of Ted's marriage.

They moved to the divan and she kissed him more passionately than usual. Aroused, he slid his hand along her thigh and then began to open her dress, which buttoned in front.

She sat up suddenly and, gazing seriously at him, asked: "Do you want to make love to me?"

"Yes," he said.

"I want to, too," she whispered. "Only not now. Please don't . . . do those things now."

She explained that it would be her first time. Harry assumed the role of the reassuring male, determined not to let her guess that it would be his first time too. She said that she would get herself fitted with a diaphragm; a girl in the office knew all about it.

They made a careful plan. She told her aunt that she had been invited to the Blythes', in

Devon, for the weekend. Raymond promised to cover for her if there was a phone call, which was quite possible. Curiously, she didn't mind Raymond knowing that she was sleeping with Harry. Once committed, she showed a kind of quiet pride.

When he undid a button—it was the same dress—she said: "Turn the light out, please." He did this. It was dark for a moment; then he drew the curtains back, admitting the yellow beam of the street-light.

"No, don't do that."

"We're on the second floor."

"Please, darling. I know I'm silly, but . . ."

He could see a little by the gas-fire, after all. But he never quite saw her; she stepped out of her panties and dived into bed in the same moment. Her body was smooth and delicious, but cold despite the fire and trembling. She gasped when he kissed her breasts, again when he touched the inside of her thighs. "Now!" she whispered.

However, she was dry and tight. He had to struggle, feeling that he was brutalising her, to force his way in. He came to his climax quickly, then left her lying like a corpse. He knew that he had given her nothing but pain.

It was a bad beginning. But Susan now showed an unexpected determination, and applied herself to sex as if she were learning the piano. She talked to the girls at the office; she studied books. Apparently, she told Harry, she needed a lot of foreplay.

Harry also read books. They were both conscious of being adult, sensible, not like their parents' generation. By degrees, things improved. They were able to assure each other, truly, that they were achieving pleasure.

But Susan said unhappily: "I ought to be having orgasms."

"It says that women vary a lot about that."

"I know. Still, I wish I could."

And she did, sometimes; but she could by no means count on it. Failure made her wretched. She sat up in bed, saying: "I did think I was coming that time. I'm so awfully sorry."

Nevertheless, they were in love. They had avoided the word for some time, but eventually they agreed that they were certain about it. Harry could not have said honestly that he thought of her all the time; he enjoyed his work and, during the day, it excluded everything else. But he longed for her when he was alone, and thirsted for her body when he was in bed without her. They met, at least for a meal, almost every evening.

He wondered if he should ask her to live with him. But it wasn't practical—her parents would come storming down from Lancashire; there might even be trouble with the landlord. Should he marry her, then? Without being at all clear why, he felt that this wasn't right, at least at the present stage of what they called their relationship. And yet, why not? They were in love; he couldn't imagine wanting anyone else; they were old enough to make a serious commitment.

So he proposed to her, on a bright day in early spring, under the tree where he had first kissed her. In a new red coat with a scarf over her head, she looked particularly beautiful.

She said: "Bless you, darling. I could see that was coming—you were keying yourself up."

"Will you, then?"

"Oh . . ." She looked in every direction, desperately. "I don't . . . I mean, I love you . . . I don't see myself, married. I don't think I'm up to it."

"Of course you are, sweetheart."

"I like it like this. I just want to be your girl." An idea struck her. "We can say we're engaged —how about that?"

They said they were engaged, and even gave a party at the flat. The new status simplified the matter of sleeping together, which had always caused problems. Susan told her aunt that she was spending the night with Harry's parents, who were not on the phone, so there could be no check. She declined to go to Steadman Street in reality, saying that she was sure Harry's parents were splendid, but the mere idea of parents flustered her. Harry, however, had to meet the uncle and aunt, and then Susan's parents when they came to London to scrutinise him. They were indeed appalling, but they approved of him. They also approved of long engagements.

Harry didn't tell his parents that he was engaged. There would have been no point. But Ann, once when he was at number five for Sunday dinner, said with careful casualness: "You still seeing that nice girl I met, Harry?"

"Yes, I'm still seeing her."

"Any chance of wedding bells?" asked Charlie heartily.

Harry answered with a violence that came from he didn't know where: "I'm not going to be forced to get married like Ted, if that's what you think."

Looking back afterwards, Harry could trace step by step how things began to go wrong between him and Susan. Summer ought to have been a time of happiness, as well as of greater convenience for a London love affair. Somehow, it was neither. Susan often wanted to make expeditions at the weekends—to Ken Wood, to Richmond Park, to the country—while he preferred to stay at the flat. Though they had first kissed under a tree, she showed a dislike of being fondled in the outdoors, even of walking with his arm round her waist. She didn't think of love as a continuous activity, but as a state of . . . what? perhaps of the emotions; perhaps, he sometimes thought, merely a state of mind.

One afternoon, lying on the grass in Hyde

Park, he drew her down beside him and embraced her. As soon as she could, she freed herself.

"Don't let's do that, Harry."

"Why ever not?"

"It's so . . . common."

Statistically, it certainly was. Couples all round them were doing it.

Harry said angrily: "It's what you'd expect of a chap from the East End, I suppose."

Her eyes filled with tears. "I never meant . . . Oh, how could you say that?" For Susan, to be accused of class prejudice or race prejudice was far worse than to be accused of immorality.

He begged her to forget it—it had "slipped out". Nevertheless, it had been said. Nothing said between them could be forgotten.

They found themselves arguing more often: about where to go together, about their friends —they seldom liked the same people—and about the flat. Susan wanted him to get a flat in a modern block, with a lift. She was embarrassed by meeting other tenants on the stairs, especially when she left in the mornings. He told her that he couldn't afford anything else.

"You really hate this flat, don't you?" he challenged her.

"I hate some of the things in it. I mean, look at this." She indicated a cut-glass vase, in which he had put white roses.

"My mother gave me that vase."

"Oh, I'm sorry." Her tone, for the first time, was ironic.

"You're ridiculous about my family," he declared. "Just because you can't get on with your own parents, you needn't take it out on mine."

"I was talking about the vase. There's good taste and bad taste, isn't there?"

"I don't mind it. After all, you're not living here."

"What am I, then? Just one of the girls you bring here?"

"What the hell do you mean—one of? Don't you know me at all?"

She stumbled to the divan, sobbing. This time, she had said the unforgivable. Harry, to his own surprise, was able to contemplate her for a long minute without pity, with mere irritation. He detested tears; they froze his feelings. He went to her and tried to comfort her, but as a duty.

She didn't stay the night. This had never happened before, after they had planned it. It was no good if the mood was wrong, she said. And he didn't see her for over a week. Her friend at the publishing firm phoned the library to say that Susan had a cold. It was a lie, he was sure.

There was a great reconciliation: mutual apologies, frank discussion, good resolutions, kisses, bed. And yet, after all this, things were not as before. They both knew that the reconciliation had been too elaborate, consciously shaped to supply reassurance. They were now working to preserve a love affair that had lost what it had always been short of: spontaneity. Susan had no more orgasms. They tried new sexual positions, an embarrassing business. She condemned herself—she was frigid, useless to a man, awful. She talked of getting some therapy, maybe psycho-analysis (not that she had the money). Harry was alarmed at the idea of their intimacies being described to other ears.

And she became unwell. She had a succession of colds, real ones and indeed quite bad ones. She loathed herself with a running nose and watering eyes, and avoided seeing Harry. He admitted to himself that he didn't enjoy seeing her in this state. When they did meet, they didn't go to bed, and he no longer felt close to her without possessing her in this sense. She also had difficult periods and attacks of nausea. During a restaurant meal, she would dash to the lavatory and be sick, returning white-faced and quivering. It was all psychosomatic, they agreed. But this understanding provided no cure.

Raymond, who was having an enjoyable affair with a woman novelist—divorced and experienced—invaded Harry's flat for a frank talk.

"Look, old boy, it just isn't working out. That happens, you know. You're simply making her miserable—she isn't a strong character. You ought to split up before things get any worse. I mean, you're both civilised people."

"Go away," Harry said.

"Now look, Harry . . ."

"Just go away."

As Raymond went downstairs, Harry took hold of the cut-glass vase and smashed it against the wall.

When he saw Susan, he asked her icily how she had dared to discuss their relationship with Raymond. She denied it, quite truthfully. The fact was that she had broken down and talked to her girl friend, who had discovered her in the lavatory, sick and weeping. The girl must have talked to Raymond. But Susan could not bring herself to explain.

"Are you saying I'm lying to you, Harry?"

"Draw your own conclusions."

Very quietly: "You want to get rid of me, don't you?"

He said nothing. She crept out of the flat, like a child sent out of the grown-ups' room. Later, he heard from Raymond that she had changed her job. He never saw her again.

Raymond, when he and Harry were once more on friendly terms, said that it would never have worked out—certainly not as a marriage. Harry and Susan were too much alike; they were people who found it hard to give themselves completely, to let things happen without worrying. But now that they realised this, said Raymond, each of them would find it easier the next time.

Scarred, defeated, Harry was far from convinced of this.

# 21

"TIME, like an ever-rolling stream . . ." The line from the hymn he had sung at the Board School sometimes turned up in Charlie's mind. Time was indeed like a river, irresistible, powerful beyond man's control. But, like a real river, it did not run evenly. There were rapids and crashing waterfalls; there were pools in which the movement was invisible; and only in the later years of life, when memories made the stream broad and deep, did time pass steadily like the Thames below the bridges.

Charlie was now in this great calm flow. He was fifty, he was fifty-five, he was moving toward sixty. What lay ahead—the pension, old age, taking it easy—no longer seemed strange. He was prepared for the space without landmarks, the sea.

But, thank goodness, he was not travelling alone. More and more in these years, he depended on Ann. Unexpectedly, rewardingly, they meant more to each other than ever, now that there was no more passion and—without the eyes of memory—no more beauty. Twenty and thirty years ago, he had believed honestly that his life centred on her. Yet there had been so much more: the boys to bring up, his mother to care for, the affairs of the street, the docks, the union. It had taken him a lifetime to find out that love was essential to the old, not to the young. It seemed to him that this—the last stage of the voyage—was what love and marriage were really for.

It was good that Marjorie had caught on to this in time. He saw her quite often. She appeared unexpectedly, as she always had, driving a small, fast sports car which drew admiring attention from the youngsters in the street. It was her own; she said that Hymie was a lousy driver and wouldn't let him touch it. From time to time, Charlie and Ann were asked to dinner at what they called the Herzberg residence. It was always a slap-up feed, with white wine, red wine, brandy and cigars afterwards.

One summer—it was in 1956—young Sidney turned up. He was still young Sidney to his sisters, though his red hair was grey at the temples. There was a reunion dinner at the Herzbergs', even more lavish than usual. Sidney had made money, in ways that Hymie understood though Charlie didn't. His wife, Anita, spoke English with an amusing accent; she was a good-looker but running to fat, as Dago women often did, Charlie had heard. "Remember doing the messages in the General Strike?" Charlie asked. "Doesn't seem like thirty years ago." Sidney changed the subject. Clearly he wasn't Labour now, or whatever it might be called in the Argentine. Over the brandy, he told them that England was finished. He was glad he'd cleared out, and he'd advise any youngster nowadays to do the same. Charlie was about to contradict, but Marjorie got in first and gave Sidney a good lecture, which he took with a complacent smile. He was staying only a week in London; Anita wanted to see Spain, Italy, Greece.

Harry and Ted were both getting on in the world. After three years in Clapham, Harry got a job at Bracknell New Town. Charlie and Ann went out there and were driven along wide concrete streets, past hundreds of new or half-finished houses. It wouldn't have suited them, but it was nice in its way. Harry explained that his job was a fascinating opportunity. He was building up the library service from scratch and introducing all the new ideas: a record library, a picture loan service, films and film-strips for use in schools, tape-recordings, microfilm. He was decently paid, apparently, though he didn't consider this important. He had a flat in the still incomplete town centre, he had a car, and he was collecting a carefully chosen library of his own.

Harry now wore spectacles, which took a bit of getting used to but really suited him. He was handsome in a more mature way, like the reliable young husband and father in an advertisement for new houses. But there was no sign of his getting married. The fair-haired girl in London had faded out—Charlie and Ann didn't know why—and since then nobody else had appeared.

"There can't be just nobody," Charlie said. "You don't think he's carrying on with a married woman, do you?"

Ann said: "I don't think so. How am I to know? He doesn't like being asked questions." She pondered for a minute, the lines deep in her forehead, and said suddenly: "Oh, I wish he'd find somebody, Charlie. I don't believe he's happy."

Ted looked older too. In his early twenties, he was already putting on weight. Charlie suspected that he drank a lot of beer and took no exercise; he would have looked better if he was doing the physical work that suited his size and build. Within a few years, he changed his job twice. First, he took an office job with a food-processing firm near Romford. Charlie was sad to see the breaking of the last link between the Wheelwrights and the docks. But the new job paid better, as well as saving fares. Not much later, Ted became a commercial traveller—or a representative, as it was called nowadays—in the same business, though for another firm.

So he had a car; he had always wanted that. It was the firm's car, strictly speaking, but he kept it at home and was allowed to use it at the weekends if he paid for the petrol. Occasionally he appeared in Steadman Street, though his work didn't really take him into London. Obviously, he was happy. He loved the variety of the salesman's life: driving from town to town, chatting with a score of people every day, stopping in cafés and pubs. Ann was doubtful about the strain of driving, with his heart condition; but he explained that he never drove for long at a stretch. He covered only Essex and Suffolk, and if he was still on the road by evening he could stay the night at a hotel and charge it to expenses.

There were more and more cars about, even in the East End. The Dohertys had one, the Connollys had one—there were several in Steadman Street. Charlie rather disliked seeing them there; he couldn't exactly say why, but it didn't seem right. The parked cars broke the line of the roadway and pavement, the only clear line that was left since the bombing and the arrival of the prefabs. He disliked being hooted at while he was walking across to the Gordon, taking his time. He disliked finding a car, belonging to a visitor at another house, outside his door. He missed the sight of children running about freely and kicking a ball in the street. Once, a child was knocked down as a driver reversed without looking. The child wasn't badly hurt, but it showed what could happen.

Charlie did not buy a car. Secretly, he wasn't sure that he could pass the driving test; his reactions were not so quick as they had been.

Besides, he didn't fancy taking lessons from some young smart-alec. There was also the financial aspect of the matter. He was putting his money into improving the house, which was much better value to his thinking. And he wanted to keep some savings to supplement the pension. He had no intention of being supported by his sons.

While Ted drove about, Lukie stayed at Harold Hill. After seven years of marriage, there were three children: Alec, Joan, and little Charlie (Ted had rebelled against fancy names). Harold Hill—like Bracknell New Town, probably—was a good place for families, and Ted had succeeded in moving from the flat to a house. Lukie's parents wanted him to get a house in a private development, but he was quite satisfied. The Council house had a nice garden and a modern kitchen, and the rent was much less of a burden than a mortgage. Within five minutes' walk and without crossing a main road, they had a row of shops, a pub, a children's playground and a primary school. Neither Ted nor Lukie ever did walk for more than five minutes. On Sunday afternoon, if the weather was good, they packed the children in the car and went to the seaside. Ted cursed at the traffic, but Lukie derived a placid enjoyment from moving steadily along in a procession of cars like theirs, containing families like theirs, going where they were going. Sometimes they had tea with her parents, or with Corinna—who was married and living at Chigwell—but not often with Ted's parents. "I know where I'm not welcome," Lukie said. The year at number five, though it seemed long ago and she seldom thought about it, was still an unpleasant memory.

Charlie was sorry to see so little of the children. They were his living continuance; they were Wheelwrights, and he was gratified when the second boy was given his name. But he had no real idea what they were like, except that they were plump and healthy. When he did see them, he tried to get on to some kind of terms with Alec. The boy remained expressionless, giving dutiful and grudging replies to questions. Charlie saw himself through a child's eyes: a big old man with a bald head, puffing smoke from a pipe. He couldn't expect Alec to understand that he had once been a young Dad, and before that a boy.

In general, Charlie couldn't quite work out what he thought about this new generation of children. He did not, in the traditional grandfather's way, find them noisy and undisciplined. From what he could see, Ted and Lukie were too strict as parents—always telling the kids to sit still, stop sniffing and wipe their noses, or something like that. Too strict, or else too careful. Children nowadays seemed to live in a world that was safe, guarded and predictable. Charlie's feelings on the subject were mixed up with his feelings about the England of the 1950s. He had fought all his life against poverty; it must be good that people had cars, washing-machines, television sets. Yet he missed the singsongs in the crowded bar of the old Gordon. It must be good that children had good teeth and rosy cheeks; that they wore new, warm clothes, had elaborate mechanical toys, and watched children's programmes on the telly. But they no longer dashed across the road in front of horses —it was too dangerous with cars—or knocked at doors and ran away, or cheeked the coppers. That kind of thing was called "juvenile delinquency" nowadays. Did they feel that to grow up without risk, without daring, was to grow up without fun? Or was that an old man's nonsense? Charlie didn't know the answers.

At all events, he was keeping up with the 1950s by improving the house. This idea came to him when he saw how much pleasure Ann got from fitting up Harry's first flat. "All right— now we'll do something about old number five," he declared. It would give Ann still more pleasure, and a reward for all her housekeeping labours; and it would give him a purpose in this phase of life, a plan and an aim. It was a delayed retort, too, to Lukie's implied criticisms. Above all, it was an affirmation of his faith in the house: the house he had saved from fire, the house he had made fully his own.

He did one thing at a time, paying out of his

wages as far as possible and dipping into savings only after careful calculations. First he put up new wallpaper in all the rooms. He did the job himself, stripping down to the plaster and making good a number of cracks which he discovered, caused either by natural ageing or by the shock of bombs exploding nearby. Then he had good glass put in the windows instead of the cheap glass you couldn't see through properly, which was all that had been available in the austerity years. The roof had been repaired at the cost of the War Damage Commission, but now Charlie had it re-tiled all over. In the kitchen, he got rid of the old range and presented Ann with a gleaming electric cooker. Then all the open fires were replaced—downstairs by coke-burning stoves which could be regulated by turning a knob, upstairs by electric heaters. He was rather sad to see the last of the old coal fires, but it was a fact that they spread dirt and caused unnecessary work. Anyway, the borough had been declared a smokeless zone and it was now against the law to burn coal.

Alternating with these improvements, purchases were made: new armchairs, a new table—small for the two of them, with an extension on a gate-leg for company—new carpets, new curtains, new lamp-shades. Ann had to be persuaded every time: "Go on, we don't need that," she would say. Her attitude was of sceptical amusement at this passion for change. But he always said confidently: "You'll be glad when you've got it." She did the choosing, going from shop to shop as she had for Harry. Charlie trusted her to get the best value for money.

The big decision was the building of a bathroom. At first Charlie thought only of a toilet joined on to the back of the house; then he resolved to make it a bathroom while he was about it. It would cost a fair amount, but it added to the value of the house. He got estimates from three different builders, held lengthy discussions, and examined a variety of baths and toilets. He settled for a cheap, quite old-fashioned toilet, rejecting the types that flushed with levers or press-buttons. It seemed to him unnatural not to have a chain to pull. On the other hand, he was captivated by the latest thing in baths, a delicate green in colour, with hot and cold water coming through the same tap. When he had his first bath in it, he lay there for over an hour, topping up with warm water from time to time and gazing at the gently revolving ventilator in the wall.

All through these years, Ann was more or less unwell. There was a period when she was distinctly better and stopped seeing the doctor, which led Charlie to believe that it was all over with—it had been a bad patch, connected with the change of life. In reality, the symptoms continued: weariness, lack of appetite, and internal pains which she now accepted as part of her being. There was no point in talking about it, because there was nothing new to say. The subject bored her—she'd always despised people who went on and on about their cherished illnesses—and she didn't want to worry Charlie. However, she knew that she ought to be sensible. She decided to see Dr. Henderson again if the pains got any worse. Eventually, they did; Henderson said that she should have come to him before. This was in 1957. She was fifty-five.

She had to go into hospital for tests. This was a fussy business: being fetched by an ambulance with the neighbours staring, being carried up to the ward on a stretcher, staying in bed for a week. Ann felt that she was being fitted into rules that had been made for really ill people, not for her. She came home with a regular chemist's shop of pills and tonics, which all had to be remembered at various times of the day.

Having been in hospital made the illness public. Gwen Turner knocked on the door, sympathy in her lilting Welsh voice, and asked what she could do to help. A little too sharply, Ann said she didn't need any help, thank you. Kate Connolly declared that doctors made too much fuss and there were more profits made out of pills than armaments. A Guinness a day was worth all the pills in the world, in Kate's opinion. Ann laughed, but didn't take this advice. It was old Dora who had lived on stout.

Marjorie was deeply concerned. She regarded

illness with the mystified awe of a woman who was always in perfect health. She insisted on Ann's seeing a top Harley Street specialist who was a cousin of Hymie's. Ann considered this absurd, though it was an experience to be ushered into the quiet consulting-room—ushered in the moment she arrived, instead of waiting for hours as one did at the local surgery. Dr. Herzberg said that she was getting just the right treatment already and he had nothing to suggest. It would have been a waste of money, but Dr. Herzberg didn't send a bill.

She got no better. She wasn't expecting to get better; Dr. Henderson had explained that certain illnesses could only be stabilised, kept at the same level. But in the winter, she realised that this was not being achieved; she was getting worse. She was sent into hospital again, this time for a course of treatment that lasted a month. It did no real good.

Now she had to live the life of an invalid. Henderson called in regularly, telling her not to come to the surgery. She sat in her armchair most of the day. She was bad at this; her arms and legs twitched, reminding her of her old brisk energy. She jumped up when she caught sight of a rucked carpet-edge or dust on the window-sill. The cruellest thing was that her eyes were failing. She could see perfectly well—it wasn't a question of needing glasses—but the eyes got tired and throbbed painfully when she used them much. An hour's reading, or even watching the television, gave her a headache. Whether this was connected with the basic illness, Henderson was not sure. Perhaps it was part of the general decline of her body.

For she was an old woman now. Her cheeks were yellow and sunken, her breasts were withered. Her weight was down to seven stone; when she was really tired, Charlie carried her upstairs like a child. Her only consolation was that it was better to be thin than fat.

Though she resented the necessity bitterly, she was compelled to let people help her. And there was plenty of help; the old neighbourliness of Steadman Street was still alive, at least in the group of houses between Barking Road and the prefabs. Kate Connolly and Mary Doherty took turns to do Ann's shopping. Arianwen Turner— the war baby, fourteen years old now—came in and read to her every day after school. Marjorie came often with grapes or chocolates or Swiss cherry jam.

Still, Ann had stretches of time alone, time when she had nothing to do but think. During the early months of 1958, she realised—not in a flash, but with a certainty whose gradualness made it absolute—that she was going to die. It might be weeks or months or perhaps even years, but it was coming; it was upon her. The Naylors had never made old bones.

She didn't ask the doctor about this, for she

knew that it was a question that doctors always evaded. She said nothing to Charlie. It was clear that he was not allowing the possibility to enter his mind; he had simply adjusted himself to a new factor in their life together, to Ann's being unable to get about. She was fairly certain that Kate understood, and probably Marjorie. Hymie must have been told by his cousin that the disease had a certain course. No one spoke of it, however, and Ann did not speak of it either. She had no use for comfort, and she would not drive anyone to utter false reassurances.

Her first impulse was to fight. There was such a thing as the will to live, she knew, which made an effective difference. And she had never been the kind to give in, to lose her grip on the shaping of events. But, turning it over in her mind, she came to think that there was a greater pride, a higher courage, than the pride and courage of fighting. She would conclude her life in the recognition of truth, calm instead of frantically struggling, eyes open in the face of death.

Just at this time, a great happiness came to her. She was neither religious nor superstitious, yet she could not help feeling that it had been granted to her to ease the ending of her life. Harry had a girl at last. It was about time—he was thirty. And when Ann saw the girl, even though nothing was said about marriage, she was sure that the link was firm. Otherwise, the girl would not have been brought to see a sick, ugly old woman.

The girl had the surprising name of Jojo Fox. She was Josephine on her birth certificate, she explained, but no one had ever called her anything but Jojo. Or, in her childhood, Joujou —her mother was French. Emphatically, she was a catch for Harry. Her father had been in the Diplomatic Service, but had retired early and now, as Jojo put it, "sort of pottered about"— a bit of business, a bit of amateur farming. The Foxes lived near Bracknell, in a beautiful Georgian house of which Jojo produced photographs. But she loved the house, clearly, because it was beautiful and not because it was what estate agents call "desirable". You saw, at a first meeting, that she was quite free from snobbery. Charlie found this remarkable, but Ann pointed out that the worst snobs were always the people who hadn't much to be snobbish about, like the Popes.

However, Jojo was a catch mainly because she was young and extremely pretty. She had a round, cheerful face, sparkling dark eyes, and black hair which was cut short and done in curls —the gamine cut. You wanted to smile the moment you looked at her, especially as she was smiling most of the time herself. She looked even younger than she was, partly because of her round face and partly because of the clothes she wore: sweaters, tartan skirts, bare knees, woollen stockings like boys' socks, and on her head a white tam o' shanter with a red pompom. In fact, she was twenty. Her parents had wanted her to go to a university, but she had failed the exams—"Actually, I'm rather dim," she said, smiling. She had had various temporary jobs: once demonstrating gadgets at Harrods, once giving children rides at the Zoo. At present she was living at home, also pottering about.

Jojo enjoyed coming to number five. Indeed, she sometimes came on a weekday, without Harry. She learned where things were kept, made tea, and even made lunch twice: nothing fancy—"I'm a rotten cook, you know"—but sausages and chips the first time, fried eggs and tomatoes the other time. She had a hearty appetite and finished by mopping up with a piece of bread, which Ann had not thought of as Embassy manners. Meanwhile, she talked nineteen to the dozen, mostly about Harry, who worked too hard and didn't eat enough, in her opinion. Midway through a monologue, she would stop suddenly: "I say, am I tiring you, Mrs. Wheelwright?" But really she couldn't take Ann's illness seriously. "You'll soon get over it —you're looking lots better today," she would say with her brightest smile. Ann forgave her easily; she was young, she'd had an easy life, thoughts of death and unhappiness were far from her. She came into the house, in the old phrase, like a ray of sunshine. A ray of sunshine does not understand or reflect; it does good by its existence.

Charlie was as pleased as Punch with her. Ann, while she liked Jojo very much, thought that she would have to be a bit less school-girlish to make a go of it with Harry. She would have to read a few books, share his interests, and occasionally stop talking. Charlie disagreed; Harry wanted shaking up a bit, he said—a girl like this was exactly what he needed. They discussed Jojo enjoyably, proudly. It was very different from bringing themselves to accept Lukie.

The fact was that Charlie could still get pleasure from being with a pretty girl. He remembered having a girl with dark curly hair once, not long after the war—the first war. He couldn't recall her name—he was bad with names nowadays—but the feel of her full, moist lips came back to him. Jojo used to give him an affectionate kiss on the cheek if she was in the house when he came in from work. Once he said: "I'll have you up those stairs if you're not careful, young lady." She was delighted: "Oh, Mr. Wheelwright, I do believe you're a dirty old man!"

In July, Ann had to go into hospital again. "She'll always be in and out, I daresay," Charlie said at the Gordon. But Ann knew that she would not come out again. What was human diminished and what was animal—the mere body—remained, she thought; one knew, as a dog knows when he goes to the vet to be put down. She remembered her father, fading out of life in this same hospital. It was not hard, after all.

Once she was in the hospital, she was entirely sure. The doctors scarcely paused at her bed when they made their rounds. The nurses, however, were exceptionally kind and attentive. She was not here for medical attention, but to be made comfortable.

She asked Charlie not to come every evening at visiting time. She didn't like a circle round her bed; one person at a time was enough. Sometimes it was Marjorie, sometimes Harry, sometimes Ted.

She said to Marjorie: "I don't know how Charlie's going to manage without me. That's all I'm worried about."

Pretending not to understand, Marjorie said: "He's managing pretty well, same as he did when you were away in the war."

"No . . . without me. You know."

Marjorie took her dry, skinny hand, but said nothing.

After a minute, Ann said: "Men need us, Marj, don't they? Men aren't strong, not really. I'd have liked to live, for him."

The next evening, Charlie came. She asked: "Are Harry and Jojo getting married?"

"He hasn't said anything. I'll try and find out."

"I'd like to see it."

Charlie missed the meaning of this, but he spoke to Harry. Yes, Harry said, it was understood. Jojo was against engagements, announcements, and that kind of thing; but it was understood.

"Your Mum wanted to know."

"I see."

Harry understood; she was dying, then. He had to find a way of suggesting a quick marriage to Jojo without giving this as a reason; she could not divide herself between solemnity and happiness. But Jojo didn't need a reason. "Fine," she said, "let's go."

She didn't want a fuss. Her mother could only just persuade her to put on her best dress. The wedding was in the registry office, in the presence of Mr. and Mrs. Fox, Charlie, and Harry's assistants. Charlie, taking the day off, had lunch at the Foxes' and took the train back to London in time to be at the hospital and tell Ann about it. Harry and Jojo started on their honeymoon by car. They had borrowed a cottage in Wales, just for a week.

Ann was under heavy sedation by now. She was drowsy even at visiting time; she had to make an effort to follow what people said, and still more to speak. In the early mornings, before she got her first drugs of the day, she was in severe pain. But the sky was blue, and she could see a London plane tree in full leaf, close to the window by her bed. She could hear birds chattering, early buses in the road, sometimes a ship hooting as it came up river to the docks. She was grateful to be dying in summer.

One evening, by a misunderstanding, both Harry and Ted came. She looked from one to the other, achieving a smile.

"Remember when we were together, just us?" she said. "Wasn't too bad, at least in the summer. Lovely . . . that big hill . . ."

She reached out her hands. Harry held one, Ted the other.

"You were good boys," she said. "You were always good boys. I've been lucky."

Before falling asleep, she thought: Charlie was coming the next evening, she would be able to say goodbye to him.

But when he arrived at the hospital, he was directed to the house-surgeon.

"I'm afraid she's sinking, Mr. Wheelwright."

Charlie stared. "How d'you mean, sinking?"

The doctor stared back. "Surely you've been able to see that your wife's dying."

Charlie hurried up to the ward. There were screens round Ann's bed. She opened her eyes; she could see him, but she could not speak. He sat on the edge of the bed with his arms round her. When visiting time ended, no one disturbed him. She died as the long summer day merged into a clear night.

# 22

HARRY and Jojo were drawn together, it was reasonably clear, by the attraction of opposites. She hadn't been in the habit of going around with this kind of man, nor he with this kind of girl. When they met, each felt the satisfaction of a need, the acquisition of what had been lacking in life so far. She gave him gaiety, charm, laughter, the delight of quick impulses and unexpected fun. And she had needed reliability, someone to hold her steady— an older man, in fact. The formula had produced many successful marriages; Mr. Fox cited the example of Asquith and Margot.

The Foxes were glad to get Jojo settled. She might have done something crazy, after all. Her two brothers were ten and twelve years older than she was. They had moved ahead on predictable lines—one had followed his father's career, while the other was at the Bar—and made correct marriages. It was all a little too easy, Mr. and Mrs. Fox felt. One didn't get through life without problems, and Jojo had always been a bit of a problem child.

She was conceived in a moment of passion when the Fox marriage was going through a tricky phase. She was born in Teheran, which she couldn't remember; however, it seemed to Harry the right sort of place for Jojo to be born in. In her early childhood her parents were separated, though only because of the chances of diplomatic life. Mr. Fox was sent to wartime Russia, clearly no place for a woman and a small child. Friends lent Mrs. Fox a house in Scotland, where Jojo grew up healthy but rather wild, without suitable companions—*une petite sauvage*, Mrs. Fox said. Then she was taught by governesses in Ankara and Lima. When Mr. Fox became Ambassador in Pnom-Penh—these outlandish appointments were just beginning to appear on the diplomatic scene—she was put in a boarding-school in Sussex, which she hated. It was mainly for Jojo's sake that he retired early.

Unlike most of his neighbours in the Berkshire big houses, Mr. Fox did not deplore the proximity of the New Town. He was pleased by having been able to buy his house at less than the normal price for such a property because it was within the New Town area—pleased both by the saving (he wasn't rich) and by his defiance of stupid snobbery. It was high time for working-class people to have a decent environment, Mr. Fox considered. At the same time, he didn't actually know anyone in the New Town.

After leaving school, Jojo developed a habit of sharing flats in London with other girls, then abandoning them and coming home. Her jobs were amusing, but always temporary. Obviously, she had no idea what she wanted. And her friendships puzzled Mr. and Mrs. Fox. It wasn't exactly that they disapproved, but they could detect no pattern. At one time it seemed to be all the smart set, friends of friends of Princess Margaret, fashionable dances, weekends on yachts. At another time it was all poets, guitar-players, bottle parties, weekends at experimental communities. She mentioned a great many young men, often not knowing their surnames, but wasn't in the least serious about any of them. Harry, after two years of this, could only be a relief.

Mrs. Fox said uncertainly: "Do you know, his father works in the docks."

Mr. Fox replied: "My dear, there's nobody more respectable than the British working classes. And besides, look what he's made of himself."

Harry met Jojo entirely by chance—romantically, one could well say in view of the beauty of the setting. He had reverted to his boyhood habit of long, solitary, aimless rambles. Thus, he was walking in the woods on a fine Sunday afternoon in late April when he came upon Jojo picking bluebells. Not looking where he was going, as usual, he almost bumped into her. She had been watching him: watching this strange, thoughtful man. That was his first sight of her, holding bluebells and smiling.

"I'm so sorry," he said. "Is it private land here?"

"It is actually," she answered. "I'm trespassing too. Do you care?"

So he helped her to pick bluebells, then walked home with her. Her parents were out. They sat on the lawn, drinking gin and tonic, and talked easily.

"I must go," he said at six o'clock. "I've got some work to finish. I hope we can meet again."

"Let's fix something, then."

They met often. She was off London, she said; the country was so marvellous in spring. He kissed her within a week, astonishing himself. She said: "Oh, that's super. Do it again."

A few days later, she rang the bell of his flat at eleven at night. She had been at a village pub with friends, then on an impulse she hadn't felt like going home. She advanced into the room, looking round inquisitively.

"This is where you live, then."

"I was working," he explained.

"I thought you might be. I've come to disturb you."

It was like his boyhood fantasies, but he had no desire to send her away.

She came close to him. While they kissed, she took off his spectacles. Then she drew back a little and said: "You look quite different without them."

"Improvement, or not?"

"Oh, I like you both ways. It just means there's more of you. I say, can't you see me without glasses?"

"Certainly I can. I don't need them at all badly."

"Well then, I'll tell you when to wear them and when not."

She undressed without drawing the curtains, indeed standing by the window which overlooked the town centre square. He hadn't expected her to be a virgin, but was astonished by her ease and sureness in love-making. Orgasms were no problem. Yet all the time, there was something in her of the playful, romping child. She talked continually, which was a new experience for him. It was a kind of running commentary: "Jojo loves that . . . Jojo wants it quicker, gallop, gallop! . . . Jojo's coming, hold tight, here she comes!"

Cuddled against him while they rested, she said: "Jojo's ever so happy. That's all Jojo wanted to be sure about."

"Harry loves Jojo ever so much," he said with an effort.

"Jojo loves Harry a million billion times . . . I say, let's go away! Let's go away at once."

"I get my holiday in August. I work, darling."

"Oh well, it's ever so nice here."

In the morning, she refused to get up. He was to find that she was capable of having lunch in bed. Going off to the library, he saw her father's stately old Rolls—well known in the neighbour-hood—parked opulently three feet out from the kerb.

After he had slept with her three or four times, he asked: "Don't your parents wonder where you are?"

"Oh, that reminds me. You're coming to dinner on Saturday. I'll collect you."

In the car, she said: "I've told Daddy and Mummy I want to marry you. That's OK, isn't it?"

"Jojo, you're fantastic."

"We ought to get champers, you see."

After a minute she added: "We needn't actu-ally get married any particular time. It's all a formality, obviously. It just tells Daddy and Mummy how things are. I've found the man in my life, in case you weren't sure."

There was champagne. Mrs. Fox was welcoming, but Harry could see that she was still stunned. After a time, she removed Jojo "to talk about some new clothes". Mr. Fox and Harry discussed the Suez adventure, agreeing that it was lunacy.

Jojo herself suggested getting to know Harry's parents, and this was an immediate success. Harry, however, didn't tell them he was engaged. The Foxes evidently grasped the prin-ciple of not getting married at any particular time; the Wheelwrights were likely to think that, if there were no money or housing problems, an engagement naturally led with no great delay to a wedding. Harry was not in a hurry. He was getting the enjoyment of a delightful affair together with the assurance of permanence—the best of both worlds. More seriously, he had a feeling that Jojo needed to adjust gradually to the idea of being a wife, an idea that could not have entered her head a month ago, an idea that she had picked up like a new craze. He hoped that she wouldn't feel let down, reduced to routine, when it became a reality. Decidedly, she wasn't much like a wife yet. He was not even eager to have her living in the flat, perhaps because he was sure of her as he had not been sure of Susan. He got pleasure from awaiting her and from her smile as she came in (she now had a key). Anyway, there were no difficulties. She stayed the night whenever she liked. Sometimes she went to London for a few days, staying with friends, but probably she would go on doing that after they were married.

But in August they got married after all, in quite a rush, because Ann was dying. Harry had a certain feeling of guilt about this. It was not the best of reasons, and it could be said that he had deceived Jojo. However, in her eyes it was all a formality.

On the way to Wales, she said suddenly: "Truth or dare."

"Truth," he replied. She was quite capable of daring him to overtake on a blind corner.

"Did you want to say no?"

Keeping his eyes on the road, Harry asked: "No to what?"

"To will-you-take-Josephine. Because, you know, I did. Just for a second, I thought: now you're in for it, Jojo, are you crazy, you'll never be able to get out of this."

"I did have that reaction," Harry said slowly. "Quite possibly everybody does. It's just nerves."

She put her hand on his leg and said: "We'll always tell each other the truth, won't we, lover-man?"

"Of course we will."

"OK. It's your turn now."

"Truth or dare," he said. It was one of her favourite games. She chose truth, and he asked her how old she had been when she lost her virginity. Seventeen, she said. He didn't want to know who the man had been.

In Wales, she wore him out: not sexually—he could satisfy her, with an effort—but by wanting to run races, climb rocky cliffs, and swim naked in icy tarns. The only relief was that they stayed in bed all morning. He was rather glad to get home.

She moved into the flat in a haphazard way, leaving some of her clothes and possessions at her parents' home. This was sensible, he thought; there was not much cupboard space in the flat, and it was only ten minutes' drive.

Once, when he was working and she went over to the house without him, it came on to rain heavily and she rang up to say that she would sleep in her old room. On the whole, he was glad that there had been no need for a sharp break.

When he went to the hospital, she visited friends in London or saw a film. She wanted to come with him, but he would not allow it. "She gets tired," he said. "You talk too damn much, darling." He was smiling, but it was the truth.

Ann's death appalled her. She and Charlie were the only two in the family who had refused to contemplate it. She insisted on coming to the funeral, and sobbed helplessly while Lukie stood by with a controlled, expressionless face. Afterwards, she asked how old Ann had been.

"Fifty-six," Harry said.

"How ghastly! It's not old to die, is it? I mean, Daddy's more than that. But actually I thought she was older."

"She looked older, but only since her illness. She used to be very attractive. I'll find you some photos. Do you know, she had gorgeous red hair."

"They must have been very much in love."

"They were. For thirty-five years."

Charlie had postponed his holiday; dockers now got a fortnight. He couldn't think of going to Margate without Ann. Indeed, he didn't want to take the holiday at all. "It's only having to go to work that keeps me going," he told Harry frankly. But when Jojo urged him to come to Bracknell, he was grateful. The evenings in the empty house were hard to bear; he was afraid of taking to drink.

As there was only one bed in the flat, it was arranged that he would stay at the Foxes' house. He was ill at ease, constantly worried about breaking one of the thin porcelain cups or the slender glasses. If he was asked about his tastes or preferences, he said: "I'm not fussy. I don't want to be a bother to you." Mrs. Fox assured him truthfully that no guest could possibly have been less trouble. She was touched by the sight of the big, lost, helpless man. She had not much experience of grief.

Most of the time, Charlie was scarcely aware of his surroundings. He woke every morning wondering where he was. Then he remembered that he must stay in bed until nine o'clock, when his hosts had breakfast. He read the newspaper carefully, killing half the morning, though he wasn't used to *The Times*. Often his mind wandered into the past. He jerked upright, startled, if Mr. or Mrs. Fox came into the room. In the afternoons Jojo usually came; he felt easier with her. In the evenings he watched some television and went to bed early. One day succeeded another; the achievement was to get through them.

He was unable yet to imagine life without Ann. Other men had got over the deaths of their

458

wives, he supposed—but they hadn't had wives like her. Only now was it clear to him how totally she had sustained him. He had not told her what she meant to him, how deeply he loved her. Of course he had told her when he was courting, and sometimes later, in bed; but not often enough, not within miles of it. He found himself remembering their unhappy times; the happiness, somehow, was harder to recall. Tormentingly, he went over all the times when he had spoken to her roughly, or ignored her feelings, or forced decisions on her. Outsiders might say that he had been a good husband, but he knew that she had deserved infinitely more. And he had been unfaithful to her. He convinced himself that she must have known—she saw right through him, always had. But, being Ann, she had said nothing.

So his thoughts went on, a reality far stronger than the room he was in and the voices around him. He took in something of Jojo's chattering, but not much. He spoke very little. Mrs. Fox thought that he was best left in silence; Mr. Fox considered that an effort should be made to stop him brooding.

One evening, Mr. Fox said: "I wonder if you could explain to me—of course I'm quite ignorant on the subject, I only know what I read in the papers—why it is that the dockers keep going on strike on what appear to be trivial pretexts."

"Ah." Charlie stirred. "You don't want to believe the papers, Mr. Fox. It's like this, you see . . ." And for about an hour he was away from Ann. Mr. Fox's profession had made him a good listener, supplying the right mixture of questions and mild objections to keep the talk going. But afterwards, Charlie was as depressed as ever. He realised that Mr. Fox didn't care about the docks; he had been trying to start a conversation. And Charlie resolved to talk to them more—he was staying in their house, it wasn't a hotel. Yet he wasn't up to it. He was up to working out his time as a foreman, and that was all. As a man, he was finished.

The fortnight came to an end. "You must come again—maybe for Christmas," Mrs. Fox said kindly.

"I appreciate that," he said. "But I've got to learn to manage for myself, Christmas and all."

Winter came. He had a superstitious feeling that he ought not to leave number five again. He was surviving—if he got through the winter, always the hard time, he'd be all right. He had his Christmas dinner at the Herzbergs'; Jews or not, they made a big do out of it. Spring came, then summer. After all, summer was the hardest time. A year ago, she left home; a year ago, he was doing the visiting routine; a year ago, she died. In 1959, he didn't take his holiday. He was surviving, for what that was worth.

Harry was learning to live with Jojo. He felt

strong enough in his love to see her faults clearly; and as she was perfectly frank about them, it was all a great joke. For instance, she really was a rotten cook. The simplest dishes turned out half-raw or burnt black, because she had no idea of timing. He boiled his breakfast eggs himself —he was always up first, anyway. If the dinner was hopelessly ruined (she always called it dinner, though it was seldom more than a supper) she would say: "Oh, fuck it, let's go out." They were almost expected at the New Town Grill across the square. The cheerful, elderly waitress would greet them with: "Made a mess of it again, dear?" Sometimes they drove to her parents' and took pot-luck. Harry disliked doing this, but Jojo wasn't at all embarrassed. It was still, in a real sense, her home.

She was by far the untidiest person he had ever known. The flat was littered with used Kleenex tissues, clothes she'd worn the day before and dumped on chairs, unposted letters, open newspapers, and—worst of all in Harry's eyes—books left face downward. While she was apologetic about her cooking, she was not a bit ashamed of being untidy; it was how she lived, that was all. "I suppose you've always had someone to clear up after you," he said. She replied, smiling: "That's right, and now I've got you." Indeed, she made a counter-accusation out of his tidiness. "Don't bloody well fold up your

trousers when you're going to make love to me!"
she shouted.

Her talkativeness was a fault that charmed
him. They would never be like those couples
who have run out of things to say to each other,
he reflected. Besides, her opinions were worth
hearing; she had a quick if unsystematic intelligence and she had met many people with ideas.
Though she didn't read much, she was interested
in politics, the theatre, music.

But he couldn't do any work in the evenings.
It was almost more disturbing to know that she
was silencing herself with an effort, to hear an
occasional "I say, darling . . . no, never mind,
it'll keep" than to let her talk. When she let
herself go, he listened for ten minutes and then
said: "Right, love, you've had your ration." If
she began again, he crumpled a piece of paper
and hurled it at her. This was all in fun, of
course. Yet he felt a release in the
mock-violence.

The only thing that worried him at all
seriously was her extravagance. They were living
at a normal middle-class standard, with wine
once or twice a week, a West End theatre about
once a month, and plans for a holiday abroad.
But Jojo was incapable of looking ahead.
Luckily, she didn't care about clothes; however,
if she liked the look of a majolica plate or a
home-weave cushion-cover, she went straight
into the shop and bought it. Harry received his

462

cheque on the first of the month. From the twentieth, he woke up every day wondering if Jojo was out of money yet; it was never later than the twenty-fifth. He tried to impress on her that they were living on a salary. She promised to reform, but simply couldn't. On her twenty-first birthday, she came into a legacy. This, if anything, made matters worse: to any reproaches, she answered: "Look, we've got Aunt Alice's money now." But the interest on Aunt Alice's money was only a hundred and fifty pounds a year.

Even with the increments and promotions he could look forward to, Harry couldn't see how they would manage when they had children and when they moved from the flat to a house. Luckily, there was no immediate need to worry about these contingencies. She was perfectly content with the flat—naturally enough, since she had her parents' house as an extension. As for children, they discussed this and decided to wait. Jojo, at first, was in favour of starting at once. Harry saw that it was a new enthusiasm; she hadn't begun to reckon with the readjustments, the limitations on life, the sheer work. The notion of being a mother, like the notion of being a wife not long ago, had caught her imagination. He put a reasoned point of view: they were just starting out on marriage, the first phase had to be enjoyed for itself, they could well afford a few years of coming and going without ties, dropping in on friends and being dropped in upon, holidays wandering about instead of advance bookings at seaside resorts. Jojo was convinced. She hadn't thought of it that way, she admitted.

Their life really was fun. They were asked out far more often than Harry had been as a single man, partly because everyone loved Jojo, partly because they took their place in the visiting round of married couples. They had more invitations from London than they wanted to accept, considering the long drive after work and the cost of petrol; still, getting the invitations was pleasant. In and around Bracknell, they belonged to two distinct, though occasionally intersecting, circles. There were the people, living mostly in picturesque villages, who knew the Foxes: some with private incomes, some commuters to London, all living on a wealthier standard than Harry and Jojo but not showy—Jojo hated show-offs. Then there were the New Town people: teachers, doctors, the architects and other staff of the Development Corporation. In both circles, you were assumed to be progressive; the general middle-class view of life had changed under the impact of Suez, the Aldermaston marches, John Osborne's plays. Life was based on the car and the telephone. Given a chance to go out, Jojo seldom refused, though Harry sometimes said: "You go without me, darling."

As if this were not enough, Jojo had

464

completely adopted Harry's family. She hadn't much of her own; she was very close to her parents, but she had little in common with her brothers and was bored by their wives. The Wheelwrights—working-class people, "real people" as she liked to say—opened a new world to her, as unknown and intriguing as Turkey and Peru in her childhood. She was able to dominate an argument about housing conditions or the so-called elimination of poverty by announcing: "Well, my father-in-law says . . ." No one else had a father-in-law in the East End. There was an element of inverted snobbery and even of exploitation in this that made Harry uneasy, but he knew that there was genuine respect as well. Above all, there was affection. Jojo was as fond of Charlie as of her own father.

Every second or third Sunday, they drove to London and spent the day with him. Jojo enjoyed these days enormously, and Harry saw that what she enjoyed as much as anything else was being in a house that was a real home, where two generations of children had grown up. Considering how she had grown up herself, this was a revelation to her. She was even capable of keeping quiet while Charlie told stories of Steadman Street. "Old Maggie Harris next door, she helped when I was born, my Mum and Dad hadn't even got the bed in" . . . "The Bennetts lived at number seven then, they were nearly evicted but we stopped it" . . . "Bert Hall at number ten, he was the old-fashioned kind, he blacked his wife's eye when she did anything he didn't like."

Systematically, with Harry as reluctant guide, Jojo made the acquaintance of the whole family. They started with a visit to Ted and Lukie. "It won't be much fun," Harry said, but Jojo was keen. She was at her best on these occasions; quite out of her element, she won through by sheer friendliness and honest curiosity. She had the children chattering to her and got on good terms with Ted, who took her for a drive round Harold Hill and made her scream with laughter at commercial travellers' jokes. It was only with Lukie that she couldn't break the ice. A Kleenex on the carpet ruined what chance there was, and Lukie remained stolid and forbidding.

Another time, they went to the Varelli restaurant. Harry had not seen his cousin George since they were both children, and had to introduce himself. Jojo made herself at home here too, and had a marvellous idea: why not go to Italy for their first real holiday and look up Aunt Liza? This was a great success. They slept in a tent by the stream that ran past the Varellis' house, ate enormous meals, and helped to pick the grapes. Liza and Tony were like real Italian peasants now, and it was curious to hear them talk Cockney, occasionally forgetting an English word. Jojo spoke some Italian, though she tended to get it mixed up with Spanish. Her

French, naturally, was perfect. Harry had been to the Continent twice on package holidays, but going with Jojo was completely different.

Her greatest ice-breaking triumph was with Aunt Vi. Even Jojo quailed at first, confronted with a precise, tight-lipped old lady who reminded her of her house-mistress at boarding school. There seemed to be no common ground at all. Jojo tried talking about a play she had seen, and Vi said that she never went to the theatre. "Never ever?" Jojo asked, and boldly invited her to come to a matinée. To Harry's amazement, Vi accepted.

Working at the library—it was a Thursday matinée—Harry wondered how it had gone off. Jojo didn't come back until one in the morning. She was silent and thoughtful for once as she undressed. Then she suddenly wanted to make love, which she did with great passion and an unusual tenderness. The following evening, she said: "Aunt Vi told me about her tragedy."

She had driven Vi home after the play and been asked to stay for supper—"very simple, I'm afraid", Vi had said. With her usual directness, Jojo had questioned her about her life. At first, the answers were brief and reticent. Then, as though in a session of hypnosis, it all poured out. "I can't think why I'm telling you this," Vi said repeatedly. "I've never told anybody, never, never." But it did all pour out: the story of forty years ago, how Vi had been the Belle of the Ball

—"I was really pretty then, believe it or not"—
and the nights with her lover, to whom she
referred throughout, Jojo reported incredulously,
as Mr. Buckley. And she had said (Jojo couldn't
help laughing when she told Harry this): "I
never took all my clothes off, mind."

When Vi finished the story, Jojo asked:
"Didn't you ever see him again?"

"No, never."

"And you didn't have any other lovers after
that?"

"No, I just felt I couldn't."

At this, Jojo started to cry. Vi said: "Now,
now, dear . . ."; then she crumpled up and cried
too. Jojo put her arms round her and they both
wept for minutes on end. Eventually Vi
controlled herself and said in her usual dry,
precise tone: "So you see, that's how my brother
ruined my life."

This was the worst part of it for Jojo. She had
never imagined Charlie as capable of cruelty,
even unintentional cruelty. A dent had been
made in her vision of working-class life: open,
frank, kindly, cheerfully sexual, she had taken it
to be.

Harry didn't know what to say. The story was
as new to him as to Jojo. He pointed out that
Charlie had acted according to his inherited
morality. They concluded that such things
couldn't happen in 1959.

The only complete failure was dinner with the

Herzbergs. On the surface, there was plenty of common ground; Marjorie and Hymie bought majolica plates, went to the theatre, and travelled abroad. But on the way home, Jojo declared that they were show-offs. "Just what one might expect, I suppose," she added. Harry was surprised to discover that she was tepidly, but ineradicably, anti-Semitic.

Time passed, amusingly and delightfully. Jojo did not change, but Harry did not want her to change. He forgot their second wedding anniversary, and she thought it a huge joke: "That's really being married, isn't it?" In 1960 they went to Austria, and in 1961 they went to the Dordogne.

Then she said one morning: "I didn't have my diaphragm in last night."

"What, you forgot?"

"No, I want to have a baby. We've done the waiting, don't you think so?"

If he had said "no" he would have made her unhappy, and he couldn't bear that. The baby was born less than a year later. It was a boy, called after the two grandfathers, Ronald Charles.

# 23

ANN had predicted that the marriage of Ted and Lukie would be a disaster; but they were not the kind of people who allow disasters to reach fulfilment. Since they were married, they went on being married. In 1960, on their tenth anniversary, he took her to the London Palladium, followed by a slap-up late supper. It cost him a packet. However, it was once in a long while; though they had neighbours who were willing to keep an eye on the children, Lukie didn't care about going out. She enjoyed this occasion less for its own sake than because it was the proper thing—it was her due. She made a home for Ted, she looked after the children; this was now formally recognised.

They seldom thought, and never spoke, about the circumstances of their marriage. That was all water over the dam. Ted sometimes thought that, given a free choice, he could have walked off with some smashing piece. But the smashing piece would have demanded expensive clothes, she might not have been a good mother, and he'd have had to worry about whether she was behaving herself when he was away. So he was better off with old Lukie.

As for Lukie—a realistic woman—she was

aware that, without what had happened, she'd have stood a fair chance of not getting married at all. She had a husband with a good job, she lived in a decent house, she had three children growing up nicely. You couldn't ask for much more. Admittedly, she was a step down in the social scale by her parents' standards, and also by comparison with Corinna and her husband. She lived on a Council estate; the children's speech and manners, like Ted's, were what might be called common. But this didn't worry her. As she thought of it, England was inhabited by an overwhelming mass of "ordinary people" with only thin slices of rich people at one extreme and slummies at the other.

Even so, she didn't want much to do with the Wheelwright family. She saw Charlie as a left-over, a remnant of a departed world which turned up in "All Our Yesterdays" TV programmes: smoke-blackened little houses, outdoor toilets, cloth caps. She had lived for a year in that world, and it was enough. On the rare occasions when she saw Charlie, though he didn't inspire her with active dislike, she was thoroughly bored. She did dislike Harry, because he was trying to pretend to be what he wasn't. And that wife of his, with her "Actually" and "I say" and "You must come and see us at Brack-nell"! That was one thing that Lukie had no intention of doing.

According to a TV programme—Lukie got

most of her information through this medium—
people like her were living in the nuclear family,
whereas people in some countries went in for the
extended family. This evidently meant having
your in-laws and cousins and their kids walking
into your home six times a day. It was supposed
to be better, according to Professor somebody
who summed up the programme. But Lukie was
clear in her mind that it wouldn't suit her.

She didn't need more than she had. Every day
was pretty much the same, barring the weather,
and that was what she liked. She had a busy time
to start with, cooking breakfast—Ted ate a lot,
being never quite sure what he'd get for dinner
—getting Alec and Joan off to school, then
seeing Ted off. Then she put her feet up for half
an hour and listened to the wireless. Housework
took up the rest of the morning, and one of the
other wives in the street usually popped in for a
cup of tea. In the afternoon she put little Charlie
in the push-chair and went shopping. She took
her time, debating purchases in her mind, chatting to women she knew, occasionally taking a
bus to get something that wasn't in the local
shops. If the weather was good, she sat on a
bench for an hour while Charlie enjoyed himself
in the playground; it had a merry-go-round,
swings and a sandpit. Then Alec and Joan were
due home, so she had to make tea, with plenty
of bread and jam to make up for the slenderness
of the school dinners.

Ted was not expected home at any particular time. He came in at six or seven if it was an easy day; sometimes he was much later; about once a week he stayed at a hotel. The children were disappointed if they had to go to bed without seeing him—they were fond of their Dad—but they grew up accustomed to the uncertainty. For herself, Lukie didn't mind. She went to bed after "News at Ten" whether he was in or not. He had suggested having a phone so that he could ring if he was kept away from home, but she never worried, so she said it wasn't worth the expense. If he came in after she was in bed, she seldom heard him moving about downstairs. He was quiet on his feet, as big men often are. Sometimes she was dimly aware of him getting into bed, of added warmth and a smell of beer. But often she didn't wake up; she was a very sound sleeper.

The woman next door once asked her—women got on to that subject at times—how often she and Ted had sex. About once a fortnight, she said. "Quiet life", commented the woman next door—whether enviously or the reverse, Lukie neither knew nor cared. The truth was that Ted wanted it more often, but she said she was sleepy or she had a headache or it was her period. She couldn't always get out of it; she was his wife, after all. Being pregnant was a good time, she thought, because the man had to leave you alone for months. She was hoping

473

for a fourth child, but no sign yet. If she could have this fourth child only at the cost of having sex more often, it wasn't worth it.

Once, not long after Alec was born, Ted said to her: "You used to be dead keen on it—what's the matter with you now?"

"That was before we were married," she replied promptly. He laughed, but she couldn't see what was funny about it. It was different for a man; they went on wanting it till they were too old to manage it, she realised that. But a woman got satisfaction out of watching the kids grow up. She tried to recall the sensation of sexual excitement, but it was gone. One might as well try to recall a pain.

Indeed, to Lukie's mind there was something indecent about a married woman feeling like a girl. That Jojo! she thought. You could see she'd given Harry a good sample before they were married, even if there was no baby to show for it. And from the way she looked at him, and sat on the couch with her leg touching his—as if they couldn't wait to get out of Lukie's house—you could also see that they were hard at it every night, probably doing all kinds of dirty things. But a couple of years later, there was still no baby. Jojo didn't want to lose her figure, no doubt. It wasn't much of a marriage without a family, Lukie was sure of that.

Ted saw this, too. After first meeting Jojo, he said: "I bet she gives old Harry plenty of work.

They're the sexiest of the lot, these lahdidah young ladies. Strip off in Oxford Street, they would." It was remarkable, Lukie thought, how often she and Ted thought along the same lines. You grew together through being married.

She didn't know whether Ted had other women. The idea was unpleasant, but she refused to let it worry her. He was attractive to women—she noticed glances when they went swimming in summer—and his desires were strong. So it was quite possible. Sometimes she thought it was a certainty: why kid herself, honestly? But what was she to do about it? She couldn't follow him about, with three children on her hands.

There were two consolations, both of considerable importance to Lukie. In the first place, he was discreet. He never came home reeking of perfume, or with lipstick on his shirt collar, or anything like that. There were no compromising traces in the car, which the children might notice on Sundays. She was sure, too, that he wouldn't carry on with a woman in Harold Hill. She might be deceived, but she would not be humiliated.

Secondly, it was out of the question that Ted would ever go off with another woman altogether or want a divorce. She knew him better than to be afraid of that. He had his feet on the ground; he wasn't the romantic type. Above all, he knew where he was well off—here, in the home she made for him.

Ted did have women, a great many women. If there was a source of pride in his life, this was it. He had a vague feeling that every man had a right to some achievement. He wasn't a stevedore, he wasn't a librarian—he had women. Most of them were one-night stands; he seldom involved himself in anything that could have been called an affair. But the map of Essex and Suffolk was dotted with places where he had been with women: houses, hotel rooms, beach huts, and simply quiet roads where he had stopped the car.

He had certain principles. He didn't force himself on women; he availed himself of them when the opportunity arose. With experience, it was easy to tell when a woman was interested. A glance, a smile, a certain kind of walk when she knew he was looking at her—that was enough. If he finished a trip without striking any luck, then it was like making no sales, or like a dull day when the sun didn't come out. He didn't worry about it; he simply went home to Lukie and the children.

Another principle was that he didn't spend much money on women. He was earning a fair amount—what with salary, commission and padding the expenses—but it was all needed. First and foremost, it was the family's money. If he had promised to buy a new Lego set for Alec or a doll for Joan, he put the necessary couple of pound notes in his hip pocket, and there they stayed until he got to the shop. All that a woman got out of him, when he made the contact, was a few drinks and perhaps a dinner at a Chinese restaurant. When he met her for repeat performances, she got flowers or a box of Black Magic chocolates. After all, as he saw the situation, she wouldn't be doing it if she didn't enjoy it as much as he did.

Sometimes, though not often, he made a mistake. There were women who thought it was fun to raise false expectations, and there were prick-teasers who didn't intend to go all the way. Ted was blunt with this type. "You know what we're here for, love," he said. "I shan't ask you again." There was always a chance that she would give in at this point; she might be the kind who wanted to tell herself afterwards that she'd had no option. If she said "All right then, don't" he immediately took his hands off her and said: "OK, I'll drive you home." He wasn't going to let anyone imagine that he was hard up. There were plenty more fish in the sea, as he usually remarked as he started up the car.

When he was about twenty-five, he more or less gave up trying anything with young girls. They had been a delight, these girls—the smooth unlined skin, the little breasts going hard under his hand, and best of all the whispers: "Oh, I never had any idea it could be like this." But as the years went by, they were less available. There was a new style in young men: hair over

the ears and fancy shirts. Ted had no intention
of looking like that. He disliked having to adjust
to the fact that he was no longer young himself
—at least, not so young as he had been—but it
couldn't be helped. From now on, his experiences were with women, generally rather older
than he was. Mostly they were married: sometimes separated from their husbands, sometimes
not. He found advantages. They were grateful;
sometimes they cost no money at all, sometimes
they even gave him presents. He got into bed
more often, which was clearly better than some
uncomfortable hide-out or the back of the car.
He could do things with them that he could
never have suggested to Lukie. And he was made
to feel young again—"Go on, you're not twenty-
seven, are you?" they would say.

Certain men, Ted was aware, went with pros-
titutes. He considered this both pitiable and
disgusting. If a woman whom he guessed to be
a tart gave him the come-hither in a bar, he
looked the other way. He thought of the women
he went with as respectable, and so they clearly
were from what he gathered of their lives. They
behaved sensibly in public, they kept their
homes clean and tidy, they were fond of their
children if they had children. It wasn't their fault
if they were highly sexed, or if they had
husbands who gave them as little fun as Lukie
gave him. Almost invariably, they were in his
own social bracket. He liked that; he felt at ease

in houses of a certain size, houses that were built to much the same plan whether they were on Council or owner-occupied estates. He could find the lavatory without asking, or go down to the kitchen and make tea—most women appreciated this; a good fuck made your throat dry. Drinking the tea, they talked about the telly programmes they had both enjoyed.

Very rarely, he found himself off his home ground. Once, having dinner in a hotel which was above his usual standard—he was in an old-fashioned country town—he noticed a woman at the next table, also alone. He was struck by the way she ordered the waiters about. She didn't seem to be aware of his existence until coffee; then she suddenly stared at him. She was tall, slim to the verge of leanness, really beautiful. He got the message and followed her out to the car park. She got into a long, rather old Alvis and leaned across to open the passenger door. They drove for miles, very fast, along winding roads. Finally they reached a Tudor cottage, smaller than his house at Harold Hill but probably worth thousands. She led the way up narrow stairs and pulled him down on the bed, which hadn't been made up. There was a mirror in the ceiling; he had heard of such a thing, but had never seen one before. She came before he did, going off like a bomb. After the first time, she said in a clipped aristocratic voice: "You're rather good." They did it three times, in different positions.

She had a necklace—or the word would be a collar—which she didn't take off; the diamonds were real.

She didn't ask him to stay all night, so he phoned for a taxi and went back to the hotel. The taxi-driver seemed to be savouring a private joke, and Ted had an idea that it was at his expense. It occurred to him that the woman hadn't either asked his name nor given her own; in fact, they had scarcely spoken. It was certainly an experienee. It bore out what he had always suspected about women of her class; very likely he could have had dozens, if he knew where to meet them. Yet he didn't have the usual relaxed, cheerful sense of achievement. It was almost as though he, the man, had been used as a prostitute.

This happened in 1963. Not long afterwards, Ted was invited for a weekend by Harry and Jojo. The brothers had very little to say to each other nowadays, but they kept up the custom of meeting about twice a year. Lukie was hardly ever present; Jojo was, and it was thanks to her that the conversation kept going. Usually, what was arranged was a Saturday lunch in London. But Jojo, since she had Ronnie, was now less mobile.

Harry and Jojo had moved from the flat to a big house. Not quite knowing what to do with Ted, they gave a party, and from his point of view this was absolutely right. By half past nine, the room was full of attractive women, mostly married and about thirty, just what he liked. Jojo herself still looked as pretty as a picture. Strictly speaking, the top of the bill was the French girl who lived in the house and looked after Ronnie. But she was only a girl; he was past that kind of thing.

Ted drank a good deal. After a time, he suspected that it was having an effect; he wasn't used to wine and there had been no proper supper, only snacks laid out on a sideboard. However, all the guests were letting themselves go a bit, so he assumed that no one minded. He told a couple of his favourite stories. Jojo was amused, but some of the others—the men rather than the women, curiously—didn't crack a smile. Probably they missed the point, he decided. Just when he was wondering if he'd gone too far, a doctor's wife told the one about the man who could screw his head off. Ted knew it, of course, but he roared with laughter because it put him at his ease. Still, he had never heard a woman tell that kind of story.

Jojo kept on smiling at him. He could scarcely believe that this meant what he would assume if he were in a pub or a hotel lounge, and yet it looked emphatically like that kind of smile. He smiled back; she smiled more broadly, eyes twinkling. Then she got up and walked out of the room. Ted hesitated. They were brought up to do as they pleased, women like Jojo, and it was a fair bet that she didn't get all she wanted from Harry. He decided that he would be a fool if he didn't see whether there was anything doing.

She went upstairs and into the spare room— Ted's room. That was it, then. He didn't know that Jojo had suddenly remembered leaving a book there which she wanted to finish.

When Jojo grasped what Ted was saying, she exclaimed incredulously: "Oh, no!" Then she burst out laughing. But seeing his expression, she kissed him on the cheek and said: "So sorry I can't oblige."

He sat down on the bed when she left him. Suddenly he hated her, the house, everyone in it. No woman had ever laughed at him before.

Harry was irritated when Jojo told him. "That's the last time we have him here," he said.

"Oh, don't be silly. He's sweet. Everybody thought he was lovely."

"Including you?"

"How d'you mean—bed-wise? He was rather a gorgeous brute five years ago, actually. He's going off, though. You look younger than he does."

If Ted had heard this, he would have been hurt but not altogether surprised. When he looked in the mirror after a bath, he was no longer flattered by what he saw. He was putting on far too much weight. He could feel the soft fat on his arms, his legs, his jaw. And he was losing his hair. That was in the family; Charlie had gone bald in his forties, Harry was showing signs. But Ted was only thirty-two.

He was out of condition. He had been making plans for years to get more exercise—swim all the year round, go for long walks, play tennis. A man in his street put on a track suit and jogged round the estate before breakfast; Ted had thought it ridiculous, but was changing his mind. But he never got around to putting these resolutions into practice.

He thought sometimes of how he would have looked if he had become a stevedore: hard muscles, flat stomach, sinewy hands with a powerful grip. In childhood, he had gazed at his father in the tin bath with admiration—and gazed happily, confident of being like that when he became a man. It was not his fault, the way things had turned out.

But he stopped worrying about this after he got into bed with Mavis. She was ideal; he couldn't remember a better stroke of luck. She was the wife of another rep, an acquaintance rather than a friend. Ted and this man were at a pub one evening when Mavis came to join her husband. The talk turned on the subject of how women spend their day. The men maintained that the busy housewife—the woman whose work is never done—was really a myth.

"Well," Mavis said, "I do get bored in the

afternoons, I admit that." With this, she caught a look from Ted and lowered her eyes.

He knew where she lived. As soon as he could manage it, he turned up in the afternoon and rang the bell.

"I was in the neighbourhood," he told her. "I thought of you, getting bored. Come to cheer you up."

She looked at him, faintly smiling. They understood each other. They went through the formality of a cup of tea and a chat, then went upstairs. It became an arrangement, once or twice a week. Very conveniently, her street, on the edge of a new estate, backed on to a wood. Ted left the car some distance away and took a path through the wood; if he met anyone, he was out for a stroll. He was in at the back door in a flash, unseen by neighbours. Mavis's husband made long-distance trips, and the children were at school until four.

To look at, dressed, Mavis wasn't much. On the dumpy side, with short legs, she was the kind of woman one doesn't notice in a crowded room. What was remarkable was the transformation that came over her in bed: she threshed about, she gasped and moaned, she seemed to liberate another creature whose existence couldn't be guessed at before or after. This capacity that women had for being two different people was, Ted had always thought, the fascinating thing about them.

"D'you carry on like this with your husband?" he asked.

"When I'm lucky," she said. "It doesn't happen often enough."

Roused by her, he made extra efforts. When he was with her, he too was something more than himself: more than a man moving into middle age, overweight, short-winded. He was young Ted again, the boy who gave a girl the bashing of her life and roared off on his motor-bike.

Mavis was in this state of ecstasy one afternoon while heavy rain slashed at the bedroom windows, when she was suddenly aware that something ghastly was happening. At first, it came to her as something utterly mysterious. She had never seen a man seized by a heart attack.

It took her a few minutes to escape from under his body, which had become an inert weight. Then she stared at him, horrified, not knowing what to do, trying to become the other Mavis. She had an urge to scream—no, the neighbours would come. She found her watch. She hadn't very much time before the children came home.

She dressed, took an umbrella, and ran to the phone kiosk. There was someone in it, and she had to wait a minute. When she got home, she wondered what she could say to the ambulance men. They might think that Ted was her husband, but the neighbours would know. Just possibly, she could pretend that he was a friend who was staying. A naked man? Making a tremendous effort, she went upstairs and got Ted into his shirt and trousers. His limbs were like lead.

The ambulance was prompt, but the hospital was five miles away. The doctors tried heart massage. It was too late.

At the crematorium, Lukie sat without listening to the service, going over what had happened in a mind that worked more slowly than usual. Ted had been having tea with friends, she gathered. He had never mentioned doing that before; it might be true, and again it might not. It made no difference now, she decided. She wondered if Ted had been as surprised as she was. She'd had no idea, until Charlie told her today, that Ted had always had a weak heart. It had never occurred to her to ask why he hadn't been in the Army. She knew that the life insurance premiums were quite an amount, but had no idea what they were for other men. The company was paying out handsomely, at all events.

She sat with one arm round Joan. Little Charlie was mystified; Alec, thirteen now, was being very controlled and grown-up. Lukie's mother sat next to her on the other side, then her father. The Wheelwrights were on the other side of the aisle. Already, Lukie had rejoined the Pope family.

# 24

TED'S death was a bad knock for Charlie: not so desolating as Ann's and yet, in a way, more cruel. The death of a young man—a son, above all—is hard for an old man to accept. Charlie felt that he had no right to be a survivor with a sound heart. Things were happening in the wrong order, upsetting nature.

He was sorry for Lukie. Ted hadn't been altogether a good husband, Charlie suspected, but he had built up a home. Now she was on her own, with three children. He spoke kindly to her at the crematorium, and a couple of weeks later he wrote to her, inviting her to bring the children on a Sunday. She didn't answer. He wrote again before Christmas and still got no answer, not even a card. He didn't imagine that she was laid low by hopeless grief, but he pictured her stolidly resigned to a narrow, monotonous existence. Evidently she wanted nothing more to do with him—with the Wheelwright side of Ted. He admitted that he was hurt.

He had never seen much of his grandchildren, and he had to reconcile himself to their forgetting him. He wouldn't forget them. Alec was a quiet, serious-looking boy, maybe with possibilities; Joan was surprisingly pretty; the youngest was only a nipper, but there was no forgetting his namesake. It would be hard never to see them again, not even to know what became of them. True, he had another grandson. But Ronnie was a baby—Charlie might be dead before he became a boy with a discernible future. Besides, he was born into another class, another kind of world. He might well become more of a Fox than a Wheelwright.

As other people saw it—the few who cared—Charlie had adjusted himself to living without Ann. He managed in practical matters somewhat better than he had in 1939. He was alone for good and all now, so he had to grapple with it. Certain modern conveniences, such as the laundromat, helped. He developed quite an interest in cooking, taking advice cheerfully from Mary Doherty next door, and always made himself a good Sunday dinner. He was a regular at the Gordon, sometimes dropping in for a look round and half a pint, sometimes staying all the evening. His interest in other people's affairs was undiminished, or rather restored; he wasn't wrapped up in himself, he cared about who was off sick after an accident at work and who was trying to find a new job. A fine old chap, they thought at the Gordon—splendid, the way he kept going.

He had to keep going. It was his last pride, and his last duty to Ann. Shock and mourning were forgivable in the dreadful months after her death, but then he had to pull himself together. He was ashamed of having felt that he was finished; no, he was still a man, still what Ann had known him to be. He imagined her quick frown when he let things slide—omitting to shave on a Sunday, for instance—and her approving smile when he upheld the framework of life. But the sorrow endured, the dull aching pain, the loneliness. These endured year after year, and he knew that they would be with him until he died. There was survival, and there was a stubborn satisfaction in holding himself upright, but there was no more happiness.

Alone in the house, at night after he had switched off the telly, he sometimes talked to himself. He didn't ramble. He simply uttered a familiar phrase aloud: "Might as well turn in" or "Going to be a frost tonight." When he first became aware of this, he was alarmed; it was a senile habit, surely. But he decided that it was all right. He wasn't talking to himself—he was talking to Ann.

Since 1960, he had been taking his holidays. The first time, he wondered if he could get through a fortnight without Ann and without work, but it was another test that must be passed, and he was certainly in need of a rest. He didn't go to the seaside; that was for younger people, he decided. After careful thought, he followed the advice of another foreman who was a keen fisherman. This man knew just the right river—the Test, down in Hampshire—and just the right simple pub which had four bedrooms to let and offered a reasonable weekly rate. Charlie's last experience of fishing had been as a boy, dangling a bent wire in the Lea for minnows. He spent money on a proper rod and got all the advice he could. If a thing was worth doing, he had always believed, it was worth doing well.

The fortnight was a success. For a man of his age, there was a dignity, a sense of the fitting, about this activity. It was a real activity; you had to keep your eyes open and your fingers at the ready; it wasn't an excuse for day-dreaming, as people sometimes said. But you didn't dash about and pretend to be young, like some old fools who insisted on playing football. Satisfyingly, he was able to enter a friendly and knowledgeable world, fishing in the daytime and talking about fishing in the evening. The next year, however, he went only for a week and spent the other week at home, doing odd jobs in the house. Retirement was in sight; it was wise to get an idea of what it would be like.

After he was sixty, Charlie thought off and on about giving up work. The usual retiring age was sixty-five, but he could rely on being allowed to stay until sixty-eight or so. Beyond that, there would be questions, hints, and eventually dismissal. When he first considered the matter, it seemed to him that the obvious thing was to keep going as long as possible. There was nothing to look forward to but idleness and solitude, the enduring of empty days. The less of that, the better.

But, through 1963 and 1964, he came gradually to see arguments on the other side. The men he worked with, especially the gang-leaders, knew his age. If they didn't know, they asked with assumed casualness. Each of them was in line for a foreman's job; they were men in their forties or fifties with family responsibilities. It would be unpleasant, Charlie felt, to be a dog in the manger. And it would be undignified to carry on until he was forced to go.

Besides, the docks were changing. Newspaper articles made out that the London docks were old-fashioned and inefficient, that new methods were overdue. Charlie regarded this line of talk with suspicion; new methods were always a code for harder work by fewer men. Still, it was a fact that trade was no longer what it had been. The big export cargoes were loaded, increasingly, at Tilbury; the ships with transfer cargoes were deserting British ports for Antwerp and Rotterdam, where the turn-round was said to be faster. There was often an ominous quiet at Albert Dock. Understandably, men strung out the work; it was Charlie's reluctant duty to crack the whip. With the new guaranteed weekly wage, some men took the day off for the slightest reasons. The bosses wouldn't put up with this for ever, Charlie knew. Modernisation was bound to come—container traffic and all the rest of it. It would mean new rules, new techniques, and a farewell to old skills. Charlie didn't want to see it. It was better left to new foremen who would pick up the way of it.

Then there was his state of health. Nothing serious was wrong, but all kinds of minor irritations presented warning signs. When he bent his back, it ached; the doctor sent him to the hospital for X-rays. There was some wear and tear, to put it simply, in his spine. Also, he was going slightly deaf. It was a docker's knack to catch shouted words through the noise of cranes, and Charlie was losing this knack. And, now and again, a dizzy spell forced him to sit down for a few minutes. He could live with all of this, and work too, but he couldn't count on doing so at sixty-eight. It would be stupid to work himself into real illness and retire as an invalid, with no one at home to look after him.

He had to think of the money aspect. He was earning forty pounds a week, so a drop to the old age pension—four pounds ten for a single man—would mean coming down with a bump. Still, he wasn't in the position of having to work till he was a dodderer from fear of poverty, like so many in the old days. He had started to save again after paying for the improvements to the house, and had nearly four hundred in the Post

Office, not counting a hundred which was a foreman's retirement bonus. He owned the house; he owned the television set and everything else he needed. Probably he would have to dip into his savings for holidays and a few other expenses, but that was what savings were for. The money would last his time. He neither expected nor wanted to live very long—probably up to seventy, seventy-five at the outside. Widows lasted into extreme old age, but he had noticed that widowers seldom did.

In October 1964, a new Labour Government came in and raised the pension. It was still only enough for necessities, but one could live on it. Charlie made up his mind, except for fixing the exact date for giving up. His sixty-fifth birthday was in February; he didn't like the idea of dark winter days at the outset of the new stay-at-home life. He worked until May. He would take it easy for a few weeks, he decided, and then go fishing before the peak holiday season.

When the time came, giving up was less painful than he had expected. On the final Friday, some of the older men had a session at a pub opposite the dock gate. Charlie wasn't allowed to pay for a round. They talked quietly, recalling the chances and changes they had lived through. Charlie was lucky to be going, the others said, before the horrors of modernisation.

The weekend was like any other weekend, except for Joe Doherty buying him drinks on

Saturday night. Full realisation came on Monday morning. Charlie woke up at his usual time and wondered whether he would go on doing this or not. He tried to enjoy staying in bed, but it was no great pleasure, so he got up and made breakfast. Then he walked a longish way along Barking Road, taking note of shops which he would now have time to try out for the sake of variety.

Collecting his pension was an odd feeling. There was a short queue at the Post Office: mostly women, a few old men, a couple of younger men drawing sickness benefit. Several of them greeted one another; they made it a social occasion, evidently. The pension seemed like mere pocket-money after Charlie's normal pay-packet. With prices as they were, he could have spent most of it the same day on food for the weekend, tobacco and beer. But he was going to cut down all round and live on the pension except for special occasions. He ate and drank and smoked more than was good for him. With any luck, he could take a bit off his waistline before long.

He stopped buying a newspaper. Of course he didn't need to save fourpence a day, but he was pleased with himself for having thought of the small economy—it all mounted up. If it was raining, he made do with the news on the wireless. Otherwise, he walked to the public library and read the papers there. He had to wait his turn, but that didn't matter. He read the *Sun* or the *Express*, the *Mirror* for a bit of a laugh, and sometimes *The Times* if he was in a serious mood. He also sampled all kinds of magazines, from the *Angling News* to the *New Statesman*. The reading-room too was a meeting-place for pensioners. One could spend all morning there quite easily.

On fine days, he went for walks. He spent little on fares—nothing at all, usually—but from time to time he bought a Rover ticket, which entitled him to travel on buses all day. Rover tickets appealed mainly to children, but he didn't see why he shouldn't make use of them. That summer, he got to know London better than ever before in his life. The city was changing fast; there were huge office buildings everywhere, new hotels, vast comprehensive schools, all kinds of glass and concrete structures. He couldn't honestly say he liked them. But he didn't want to be an old fogey, grumbling at everything unfamiliar.

People had changed too. There were immigrants all over the place: blacks, Indians, Pakistanis, anything you could think of. The bus-conductor was usually a black, taking the fares with his odd singsong accent—Charlie missed the old Cockney "Any more for any more?" Parts of the East End were like darkest Africa; the immigrants had taken over. Some people hated them, and Charlie felt that they shouldn't have been allowed to come; they didn't belong, England wasn't English any more. But he felt sorry for them more than resentful. They looked lost, out of place in the treeless streets, cold and unhappy in the sharp winds.

But even English people, the younger ones at least, looked different. There were men with beards, men with side-whiskers, men with hair over their shoulders; and these weren't always students or what people called beatniks—a long-haired youth might be driving a van or delivering the post. In the streets, Charlie sometimes couldn't tell a boy from a girl—though, he reflected, he was getting past it if he could only go by the hair. The young men wore blue jeans with patches that didn't seem to be anything to be ashamed of, and T-shirts with words written across them. The girls, and even middle-aged women, wore tiny skirts that showed practically everything as they came up the steps of a bus. It was as if a new race had appeared in England: people like grown-up children, fond of vivid colours and loud music, passionate for novelty, concealing nothing of themselves, curiously happy and carefree. Charlie couldn't dislike them or disapprove of them, but it was too late for him to understand them.

Well, it was all something to think about. Even being alone wasn't so bad. Sometimes, as he cleared away after his supper and settled down in front of the telly, he realised that he hadn't spoken to anyone all day, or not beyond "Nice day" and "Keeping all right?" He was getting used to it. When he did talk to people it was a real pleasure, no longer taken for granted.

Apart from the neighbours and the regulars in the Gordon, he saw Marjorie more often than anyone else. She still appeared unexpectedly in her little car, though there were so many cars nowadays that she sometimes had to park down the street. She was looking older at last; she was not so far from sixty, after all. There were crows' feet round her eyes and she admitted that her hair was dyed. But she kept her trim figure, her brisk walk, and her liveliness—as Ann would have, if her health had held up. Charlie enjoyed just looking at her. It occurred to him that, if Ann had died earlier than Marjorie's marriage to Hymie, he and Marjorie could have got married. Things had turned out otherwise, so it was no use thinking about it. But Marjorie wouldn't have minded, he believed.

Once she said suddenly: "We had a good time, didn't we? You know, in the blitz."

"Bloody marvellous," he said.

"You know, Charlie, they all thought I was never frightened, driving that ambulance. But I had to force myself to face it, every time. Having you—making love—was what I needed to keep going."

"I needed you, too," Charlie said.

"Yes, I knew that."

She reached a hand to him, and he felt its warmth.

"Do you think Ann knew, ever?" he asked.

"I don't think so. When you love somebody, you think they know everything you do. But it isn't so, really."

"I always loved her, Marj."

"Yes, of course you did. I didn't make any difference to that. I just borrowed you and returned you in good condition."

Harry came once a month or so, and Jojo twice during the summer. She was rather tied down by Ronnie, she explained. However, she wanted Charlie to come and visit them. Charlie felt that this invitation was rather less enthusiastic than it would have been years ago; it came out, somehow, as if it were an obligation. He told himself he was imagining this—he mustn't get touchy, another risk of old age. So he accepted. But he didn't go in the summer, because he had been away fishing in June and it was wise to string out these treats. He went in October, before digging in for the winter.

He couldn't come to terms with the big house. It wasn't cosy, like number five, nor was it comfortable in the upper-class style like the Foxes' house. It was merely sprawling and awkward. He had the impression that Harry and Jojo hadn't come to terms with it themselves. They seemed to be camping out, putting up with difficulties which they hadn't expected, like people landed by a travel agent in the wrong sort of hotel.

Also, living in this house seemed to get on their nerves; they had rows, or quarrels, or incidents. Charlie wasn't sure what word to use, because they said things—Jojo especially—which they clearly didn't mean and which had no apparent consequences. What would have counted as a real quarrel, between him and Ann, was evidently no more than letting off steam. Jojo was all smiles two minutes afterwards.

"Did you post my letters?" Harry would ask —this was a typical incident.

Jojo looked at him as if he'd been talking Chinese; then she said dramatically: "Oh, I've had so much to think about, it just never ends."

"Can't I rely on you for the smallest things?"

"They weren't my bloody letters, were they? I'm fed up with running errands for you, truly I am."

"Darling, you were going out and I wasn't. You yourself offered to take the letters." Harry's tone of calm logic, Charlie could see, infuriated Jojo more than anything else. She was the kind of person who feels most injured when she is undeniably in the wrong.

"Well, I remembered to offer and I didn't remember to take them. Obviously I'm hopeless, so you'd better do your own remembering in future."

On such occasions, Charlie didn't know

whether he ought to tell them both authoritatively to stop being silly, or merely make some pacifying remark, or pretend to be deaf. He left after ten days. The visit had been indefinite, and that seemed about right. He wasn't sure about coming again next year, but rather wanted to because Ronnie would soon be old enough to remember him.

Winter, like everything else, was not so bad as he had feared. Financially it was difficult to manage, because of the cost of fuel; he felt justified in drawing on savings for this purpose. But his routine was much the same. He still walked, so long as the weather was dry. Rather to his surprise, he felt that he was in better health. The old bones, the spine especially, must have benefited from a rest.

Yet there were bad days: days when he felt the shadow of that hopeless, heavy depression from which old people living alone were said to suffer. These were the days when it rained or snowed, when the dark sky pressed down on London. There was no sense in going out, and inside the house it was dark and gloomy; he needed the light on to see properly, but the expense seemed wasteful. The street was even more silent than usual. He couldn't settle to reading—he had never been much of a one for books—and all the radio programmes struck him as silly or as irritatingly, painfully bright. Time passed with leaden slowness; sitting in his chair, he tried not to look at the clock and then found that only ten minutes had gone. It was on these bad days that being alone, being without Ann, living without a future, became close to unbearable.

He spoke of this to someone he saw from time to time: Arianwen Turner. It was somehow easier to reveal himself to a person who was only on the fringe of his life. Arianwen was now a student at one of the new universities and was living—in sin, though nobody used that expression nowadays—with a young man. Her parents were aware of it and she mentioned it to Charlie as if it were perfectly normal; so it was in 1965, he supposed. When she spent the weekend at home, she usually dropped in to see how Charlie was getting on. She was a kind-hearted girl, he'd always known that. Loneliness was as remote for her as starvation in some far-off country, but she tried to understand it. Naturally, with the optimism of youth, she reacted by thinking of a practical remedy. "You ought to get a dog," she said.

Charlie smiled; did she imagine that a dog would change his world? Yet, thinking it over later, he decided that it was really a good idea. A dog had to be fed and exercised; he would have some routine for the day, some obligations to a creature more helpless than himself. And the house would not be utterly silent. He would not be utterly alone.

He decided to get a small dog, because it was a long way from Steadman Street to the park, so he would have to carry it on buses. Besides, a small dog would eat less and therefore cost less. Obviously, he couldn't afford a pedigree dog; anyway, people always said that mongrels were more intelligent. The best place to go was the Battersea Dogs' Home. He was pleased with the idea of appearing as a rescuer to a dog that nobody cared about.

When he got there, he was almost over-whelmed by the sight of so many dogs leaping up to greet him, scrabbling at their cages, barking or whining, gazing at him with their appealing eyes. Those who didn't find buyers were put down, he knew. He'd have liked to buy the lot; he even thought seriously, for a few minutes, that he would enjoy having two or three dogs, a kind of family. But no, it was impossible.

He settled on a puppy with a comical black patch above one eye. It was more a fox-terrier than anything else, but with long ears like a beagle. A silly-looking dog, a joke of a dog, a dog with hardly any chance in the lottery. It had come in half-starved, Charlie was told, and it was still only a scrap of a thing. He decided to call it Scrap. All the way across London, it wriggled ecstatically on his lap and kept licking his hand, as if it simply couldn't believe its luck and wanted to commend itself in case he changed his mind.

For the next few weeks, Charlie's main occupation was training Scrap to know his name, to come when he was called, to be clean, and to stop barking at the word "Quiet!" Scrap was intelligent, sure enough. It was fascinating to watch him acquiring a shape to his life, like a baby moving toward becoming a child. For instance, to begin with he rushed to the door and demanded a walk whenever he felt the urge; but he learned that walks happened after breakfast and after lunch, and he ceased to expect them unless he saw Charlie putting on his coat. To begin with he was always desperate for food, and once he nosed a cupboard open and dragged down a piece of bacon; but he got to know his supper-time and to rely on his tins of Pal and his biscuits.

It had certainly been a good idea. Charlie had bought the dog to counter the loneliness in the house, but he found another, quite unexpected advantage. When he was out with Scrap, people smiled at him. Sometimes they stopped and patted Scrap or asked how old he was. It made a difference, for Charlie, if they simply looked. The curious fact was that a man with a dog was a person, whereas a man alone was a component of the crowd in Barking Road.

Yet the smiles and the good-mornings, more often than not, were from strangers—from people who recognised him as an old man with a nice little dog, but didn't know him as Charlie Wheelwright.

He was losing neighbours. In 1966, half of Steadman Street was taken away from him. First, the prefabs on the opposite side of the street were demolished. This was a complete surprise to Charlie; he hadn't walked past them for a few weeks and hadn't noticed that the windows no longer had curtains, the tenants had gone. Workmen came and took the houses to pieces, as if they were the building sets that children play with, and carted the fragments away in lorries. It was all done in a day. They were not proper houses, of course, but they had been homes, and it was a shock to see them vanish in this breathtaking manner, like the tents and booths of a fair after a Bank Holiday.

Charlie hoped that real houses would be built, fitting into the gap between the old houses that had survived the bombing and making a real street again. But for some weeks nothing happened. Then the tenants in the old houses got letters from the Council: their homes were to be demolished too. They had to go—the Turners and the others. Charlie realised that he wouldn't see Arianwen again; it was too much to expect her to come to Steadman Street just for his sake. As the houses belonged to the Council, the tenants were rehoused in various places. Some were glad to move into modern flats, some were regretful, some had mixed feelings. They had no option, anyway. Only the Connollys declined the offer of rehousing, and decided to end their days with their kin in Ireland.

For months, the houses stood empty with sheets of corrugated tin over the doors and windows. No one in the neighbourhood had any idea what was going to happen or when. Then the demolition men arrived and the houses were smashed to bits, not quite in a single day but faster than Charlie would have thought possible. There was nothing left on that side of the street except the pub. Again, there was a mysterious pause lasting for months. The Council put up a fence and sternly worded "Keep Out" notices, as if anyone would want to trespass on an empty space. There were not even ruins of the kind that had attracted youngsters after the bombing; the demolition work had been brutal but neat.

Eventually, machines appeared and started working away behind the fence. So far as could be seen, all they were doing was digging a colossal hole. Charlie knew that a building must have foundations, of course, but this was a hole deep enough to put houses inside. The clanking and screeching were continuous; one couldn't listen to the wireless all day. At weekends, the silence seemed uncanny.

Then, at long last, the new building began to go up. Evidently it was to be a block of flats; most people on the waiting list wanted houses, but rarely got them nowadays. So Steadman

Street would never be a street again, as Charlie understood the word. This was redevelopment—like modernisation, applied to family life.

Once it was going up, the building went higher and higher. A huge yellow and black sign-board appeared: "Ham Point. 88 New Homes." Charlie realised that it was to be what people used to call a skycraper—a high rise in the new jargon. He had seen a number of them on his bus rides. Ham Point went up and up and up, until it had twenty-two floors.

In the mornings, and until past noon, an enormous shadow covered number five. When Charlie opened the bedroom window, he had to lean out and crane his neck-to see whether the sky was clear or dull. All that faced him was this great slab of glass and concrete. He moved his bed into the back room, the boys' room as he still called it in his mind.

Tenants moved into Ham Point. Charlie was pleased every time he saw a furniture van, but when the building was filled he had a curious impression: there still seemed to be no one there. This was ridiculous, because there were eighty-eight families where seventeen had lived in the old days. Yet where were they all? The main doorway seemed to be used only at the time for going to work and returning. During the day, there was hardly any sign of what Charlie had known as street life: children playing, women chatting on the pavement. One reason, it struck him, was that the wives had to work so that the rent could be paid. With rates and central heating, a flat cost six pounds a week—more than his pension, a quarter or a third of a man's wages. The children either were not allowed to venture out or didn't think it worth while; taking a lift all that way down, for a nipper, was like a train journey. But the whole strange situation could be explained quite simply: you couldn't expect street life where there was no street.

For Scrap, Charlie noticed, Ham Point did not exist. He never wanted to cross the street; there were no interesting smells over there, presumably. The people in the flats were forbidden to have dogs or any kind of pets. And the building was too big to have a meaning for Scrap; it was out of any scale that he could cope with. It was out of Charlie's scale, too. It diminished him; he didn't feel his right size until he got inside number five again. He had adjusted himself to many changes in Steadman Street, but this was something that he did not hope ever to get used to.

# 25

A CHANGE came over Harry's life after Ronnie was born and after he moved to a house. This was natural, and it was also natural to believe that the change was for the better. Everyone assumed this: his father, Jojo's parents, Jojo herself, and all their friends. One had a family, one had a real home. It was a fulfilment.

Yet Harry could not feel this. Instead, he had a baffling, irritating sensation of being pinned down against his will: or perhaps of being entangled in a network of fine but unbreakable threads. He could not admit this to anyone, certainly not to Jojo who was herself the principal thread. That it was his own fault, he had no doubt. He had nothing to complain of—he was simply living like other men. Something was missing in his character: the ability to yield himself, to come to terms with others. He felt free only when he went for a long walk, alone. He had counted on leaving this side of his nature behind after getting married, but he had failed.

There were four problems, none of which showed signs of being dissolved by time: the house, money, the child, and his relations with Jojo.

The house was simply too big for him. He had always been happy in small places: number five, the flat over the stables, a furnished room, the flat in Clapham, the flat in Bracknell. They had bought this place not because either he or Jojo really wanted a big house, but because she wanted an old house. The Georgian mansions, which at least were sensibly planned, were beyond their means; therefore they had settled for a former vicarage, a Victorian monstrosity with vast useless halls and landings. Jojo had taken it on with a mixture of enthusiasm and amusement, turning all the inconveniences into jokes. Living in it, to begin with, was a new game. Later, she was sometimes as ill at ease in it as Harry; but they were never frank with each other about this.

Her untidiness was now a serious matter. In the flat, if something was not in its proper place, at least it couldn't be far. In the house, he had to search room after room. Jojo was quite capable of putting a book or a letter down in a room which, she swore, she hadn't entered for weeks, such as the scullery beyond the kitchen, the guest room, or a loft to which they referred —because the wind came in and made strange noises—as the ghost room. Some objects vanished without trace, as they do in large houses. Harry established a smallish room as his study, announcing a strict rule that nothing in it was to be moved. But Jojo did move things when she dusted; she also brought things into the study which had no business there, almost as bad an offence in Harry's eyes. More and more, his office at the library was the only place where he felt really at home.

Her buying mania, which had eased off when there was simply no more room in the flat, took on a new lease of life with the house. She bought bigger things: glass-fronted cabinets, full-length mirrors, a grandfather clock. She found these things at auctions, when houses like their own were being sold up. They were all bargains. Or rather they would have been bargains if they had been needed; he could never get her to see this.

The house and money were closely related subjects. Naturally, they had to buy more furniture; it was stupid to have empty rooms. Naturally too, they had to put up new wallpaper in place of the vicar's gloomy lincrusta, buy curtains, buy carpets, buy a few pictures. After one shivering winter under the high ceilings, it was obvious that they couldn't live in the house —especially with a child—unless they had central heating. But half the value of the central heating was lost without draught-proofing. Harry could object to none of this; nevertheless, the cost of each item appalled him. In addition, there was always something that needed repair. If it wasn't the banisters, it was a gutter; if it wasn't a gutter, it was the glass roof of the conservatory. Whenever possible, Harry did these jobs himself to save paying piratical builders' bills. He did them slowly and badly, hating the task and grudging the time lost from his real work or from reading. Jojo helped when she was in the mood, but she was even less practical than he was and merely got in the way. Much of the time went in wrangles about the right way to do things.

There were other necessities—at least, they were necessities for Jojo. They had a succession of au pair girls. Jojo wanted a housekeeper, like her parents; Harry vetoed this, but agreed to a cleaning woman. They had to ask friends to dinner, invite London friends for weekends, and give occasional parties—one mustn't vegetate, Harry admitted. They had to have holidays. Once they went no farther than Cornwall, but Jojo made it clear that this was a sacrifice. A real holiday meant going abroad.

Generally, it was Jojo who drew the money out of their joint bank account. Harry was repeatedly sure that they were heading for disaster; but when the statements came in, they were never so bad as he had feared. He discovered that Jojo was being given money by her father. This shamed him, and he declared that he wouldn't let it go on. Jojo swore that she never asked; Daddy had been in a generous mood, and after all he didn't need all of his ambassadorial pension and his director's fees. Then Harry found a credit entry in a statement: S. G. Fox, one hundred pounds. She had

511

borrowed from her brother. Confronted with this, she said it was a short-term loan till the next cheque from Daddy. So they depended on Daddy, after all; and, humiliating though it was, Harry knew that he would accept this dependence.

Little Ronnie was involved, or would be involved within a few years, in the money problem. Jojo wanted to send him to a private school; she had a friend who taught at one, very enlightened and progressive. Harry pointed out that the state schools in Bracknell were enlightened too. The teachers were young and enthusiastic, the buildings were new, and it would be free—"if you don't mind my mentioning that little detail, darling." At his birth, Ronnie had been put down for Winchester. It was understood that this was merely taking an option; they could decide later whether he actually went there. But Winchester had launched Jojo's brothers successfully, and a boy's grandfather could pay the fees through some tax concession. The trouble was that Ronnie would not pass the Winchester entrance exam unless he followed the private prep-school avenue from the start. As Harry saw it, one couldn't with decency stand up for comprehensive schools—a major point of controversy at this time—and buy privilege for one's own child. As Jojo saw it, the child's future was what mattered and Harry was only thinking about money, as usual.

512

She implied, when the argument came up, that she was devoted to Ronnie and Harry was not. There was enough truth in this charge for it to be wounding. Ronnie was bursting with health, restless and noisy. He was the only one who gloried in the big house; he was constantly running along the corridors, slamming doors, clambering up and down the stairs, yelling for help when he tripped over or got into difficulties. The study was no refuge for Harry; Ronnie loved to open the door and shout "Boo! I'm here!" Harry tried locking the door, but then Ronnie stood outside and cried.

There had to be some discipline in a child's life, Harry believed. But if he made rules, Jojo forgot about them and Ronnie was free to ignore them. Inheriting all his mother's charm, Ronnie had practically everyone on his side. Jojo couldn't say no to him, his grandparents adored him, au pair girls and visitors were captivated by him. Sometimes Harry snapped: "For God's sake take him up to his room and let's have some peace." Jojo gathered the child in her arms: "Dad doesn't want us, Ronnikins." Bewildered, and sensing that his parents were at odds, the child sobbed pathetically.

"Now I hope you're satisfied!" Jojo shouted.

"Darling, he's got to learn he can't do exactly as he likes."

"I can't bear it when you make him so

unhappy. He's only two." Or three, or four; Jojo was reluctant to think of him growing up.

"But if he doesn't learn now, it'll be harder for him later."

"I see, it's all for his own good. Well, you're not kidding anybody. You're just getting him out of the way to suit yourself."

Well, yes: Harry did feel a sense of relief when Ronnie was out of the way. In his gloomier moments, he was afraid that he wasn't cut out to be a father. He lacked the patience, and especially he lacked the ability to enter a child's world, to get real enjoyment out of childish talk and childish games. He had never been very good at this even in his own childhood. Jojo was effortlessly superb at it; so far as being a good parent consists of being a companion to a child, she was perfect.

So it was all tangled up together, and ultimately it all led back to the terrible question: could he go on being married to Jojo? He loved her—he was honestly certain of that. In bed, they still achieved a delight that eclipsed all the problems. Lying contented as she dropped into sleep in his arms, he could say to himself: they had this, nothing else mattered. Yet another part of him knew that it was not true. The rest of it did matter. He did not like living with Jojo. He recalled the happiness of having an affair with her: her voice on the phone, waiting for her to come to the flat, kissing her before she took her beret off—and being alone when she had gone. Now she was his wife. It was six years, then seven, then eight; but they had not grown closer together.

Perhaps it was marriage that he wasn't cut out for. Or perhaps, to be honest, the mistake had been marrying Jojo. He could not have foreseen how little her character would develop. At the time, he hadn't even considered this; now, it had become crucial. She was still a girl—charming, playful, self-centred, unreflective, irresponsible. Her little ways were no longer so amusing; her untidiness, her extravagance and her cooking had ceased to be jokes years ago. So far as he could tell, she would be the same at forty. But then her prettiness would have gone—it was prettiness, not beauty—and she would be a bore to other people, even a grotesque. And so, love would go too.

Strangely, the thought sometimes came to him that he ought to have married Susan after all. Poor Susan, earnest, neurotic, self-deprecating Susan—well, she had been more his own type. They would have gone through agonies, but they might have fought their way out. At least they would have struggled together.

He and Jojo merely struggled against each other. For a long time, they had taken it that quarrels were part of a loving marriage, or simply part of a frank modern marriage. Indeed, the quarrels ended with kisses. But by now they were having quarrels of a different kind: less stormy, colder, in which the blows were planned. These quarrels did not end with kisses. They ended something like this:

"If you can't listen, there's no sense in my talking."

"Not if you say the same thing over and over again."

"Perhaps you'd better think it over when you're in a calmer mood."

"I'm perfectly calm, I'm just bored. I'm going to bed. Are you coming?"

"No, I think I'll read."

Then they did not speak, or spoke only on practical matters with careful politeness, for the next few days.

At last, after almost eight years of marriage, what they had both been hiding showed itself horribly. The cause of the quarrel was suitably symbolic—a book. It was one of the few valuable books that Harry personally owned, a folio *Arabia Deserta*. He found it on the kitchen floor when he went for a glass of milk; he almost trod on it.

Jojo was slicing oranges (hot orange with burnt sugar was on the short list of fashionable dishes she could manage). Harry pointed to the book accusingly.

"May I ask what this is doing here?"

"Oh, I think Ronnie was looking at it. It's got pictures of horses, he's keen on that."

"If he's taking books out of my study, it's the last straw."

"Oh Christ, even if he's interested in the same things as you are, you stop him. I suppose you're afraid he's competing with you."

She picked up the book. Harry shouted: "You've got sticky fingers!"

"Yes, I'm working for you."

"Let me have the book."

"It's all right, I'll put it back."

"You'll give it to Ronnie again. Anyway, you don't know where it's kept."

"I'll put it back, I tell you."

"Jojo, give it to me."

She moved away from him with a teasing little dance. He pursued her clumsily and grabbed her arm.

"Harry, you're hurting!"

"Give me the book, then."

He took hold of it, but she wouldn't let go. He squeezed the soft flesh of her arm until she had to give up and he was victoriously in possession of the book.

"Look, Harry." And there was a large bruise, already blue—she bruised easily.

He said nothing. The necessary apology would not come.

In a low, intense voice that he had never heard before, she said: "You bastard."

He went to put the book away, first wiping it carefully. Then he sat at his desk for a long time, staring at the wall. He knew what had happened. He had enjoyed the merciless pressure of his fingers—had enjoyed hurting her. For those extraordinary seconds, he had hated his wife and she had hated him.

Curiously, there was not the usual sequel of icy hostility. By good luck, friends came round in the evening; Jojo was charming, her lively girlish self, wearing a long-sleeved dress. When she and Harry were alone, she kissed him and said: "We friends again?" He achieved the right answer. They made love, passionate in their relief.

But they had merely recoiled from disaster. When the next quarrel came—quite soon, of course—they knew that the violence stood between them.

These days, Jojo was often away in London. For a time, when Ronnie was a baby and they had just moved, she had lived contentedly in a narrow radius: their own house, her parents' house, the homes of nearby friends. But then she felt the need to be "in touch" again. It was essential for her to see a play or a film or an exhibition that was being talked about. Sometimes she dashed off on the spur of the moment and Harry found a note when he got home. She took up again with the girls—women now, but she always called them girls—whom she had known before her marriage. Finding that she was in circulation once more, they asked her to parties. Harry was invited too, but seldom went.

Her absences usually caused some inconvenience. She omitted to do the shopping before she left, or took the car when Harry needed it, or forgot about a Bracknell invitation so that he had to find an excuse. However, he had no wish to prevent her from going. As things now were between them, the tension was lowered when they were not constantly together. While she was away, Ronnie and the au pair generally stayed with the Foxes. Harry enjoyed the peace of a brief return to bachelorhood.

It occurred to him—it was bound to be a possibility—that she was having an affair. But he thought not. Sometimes she drove home in the small hours, when she could quite well have stayed the night in London without his objecting. When she did stay, it was with a girl and the girl's husband. She left the phone number: Harry rang up on one occasion because Ronnie ran a sudden fever, and she was there. He supposed that she flirted with young men at parties, probably let them kiss her, probably assumed a romantic wistfulness and got pleasure from saying "No, please, we mustn't." The thought that this might lead to her sleeping with one of the men, even if it was without emotional involvement, sometimes caused Harry a spasm of fury, sometimes plunged him—alone late at night, trying to read—into misery. His knowledge of her body was the last stronghold of past happiness; if it was given to another man, there was not much left. But it would be fatal to question her. She would start being unfaithful to punish him.

Jojo's enthusiasm for sex had taken a rather theoretical or voyeurist turn. She read pornographic novels, borrowed from someone in London. She made remarks about their friends like "I'm sure he's a masochist, what d'you think?" And she had long intimate talks with the au pair—a girl called Yvette, from an aristocratic French family but of advanced opinions, politically a Maoist. Yvette, who also made frequent trips to London, was having an affair with an Arab student, apparently a lover of great virility and sophistication. In the evenings, Jojo and Yvette washed up together in the kitchen, made coffee, and chattered in rapid French. From the sitting-room, Harry could hear them but couldn't follow much. Once, however, he caught: "*Ab, il est sensass comme ça, il est spécialiste de la bouche.*"

Jojo's voice: "*Tu aimes ça, toi?*"

Yvette's voice again: "*Mais il faut tout essayer, non?*" And they both laughed.

In June 1967, Jojo suddenly said: "I want to go away for a holiday."

"Now, you mean? I suppose I could try to switch my dates."

"No, I meant just me. I could do with a complete break."

This seemed to Harry not unreasonable, a mere extension of the way they were now living. But he explained that the problem, inevitably, was money. He hadn't expected to pay for a holiday for Jojo and their usual holiday in August. To this, she said that she had been asked to stay with a group of friends at a rented villa in Spain. It could cost scarcely more than the fare, and her father would pay.

It might even be an economy, Harry saw. Perhaps she wouldn't want the August holiday. He would give it a miss, or go away without her for a week's walking.

So off she went. Ronnie and Yvette stayed with the Foxes, but had to come home after a week because Mr. Fox had 'flu. Yvette strolled about the house in skimpy dresses or a bikini; the weather, as it happened, was almost as hot in England as in Spain. He had the impression that she thought he was a poor fish not to take advantage of his wife's absence. But she would be sure to tell Jojo. They would discuss him— the idea was appalling.

Jojo sent postcards, once even wrote a letter, and returned relaxed and happy. She had stayed several days longer than planned, but Harry didn't resent that. The break had clearly been a success. The summer passed with only a few quarrels; in August, he went walking in the

Cotswolds. In September, she agreed peaceably to Ronnie's starting at the local school.

On a rainy night in October, just as they were going to bed, the telephone rang. Jojo always answered it, as she had nine-tenths of the social life. She spoke very quietly, saying "I see . . . Yes, I see." When she rang off, she covered her face with her hands.

"What's happened, darling?"

"I've got to go to London."

"Whatever d'you mean?"

She stared at him for a long minute. Then she said: "It's Giles. He's been hurt in a car crash."

"Who's Giles?"

"My lover, damn it. Don't look so bloody surprised."

And of course the holiday had been with Giles. Defiantly, Jojo behaved as if Harry ought to have guessed this too—"what did you think, honestly?" She said that she had gone in the hope of getting Giles out of her system, but it hadn't worked out. Harry wasn't sure whether to believe this bit. She was in love with Giles now, at all events.

As for the situation, their future—that kind of thing would have to wait. Harry saw that she would never forgive him if he tried to stop her from going to London. Giles might even be dead; she hadn't been able to get things very clear, and perhaps they were keeping the truth from her.

Harry went out to the car with her.

"Mind how you drive on these wet roads, Jojo."

"Oh, stop nagging, I can't stand it."

She drove off, crashing the gears. She always crashed gears and it always annoyed him.

To his surprise, she was back the next afternoon. Giles was not badly injured; he had been unconscious, but it had turned out to be concussion and not a fractured skull.

"What's going to happen now?" Harry asked.

"I don't know. I hadn't faced it, I suppose."

"You mean you'd have gone on having this affair, if the accident hadn't happened? Deceiving me, if I may use an old-fashioned phrase."

"I hadn't faced it, I tell you. I don't want to leave you, Harry. One can love two men, or d'you think that's impossible?"

"I think it's not much fun for the men."

She made a sudden decision. "I'm going to try and beat it. Really try. I won't see Giles. I just won't go out of this house." She smiled, almost happily. It was another new role.

Harry learned that Giles was a novelist, also the author of two plays which had been given Sunday night productions at the Royal Court. A few critics considered him brilliant. Harry found the novel—there was only one—in the library and read fifty pages; it had no plot and not many grammatical sentences, and he couldn't make head or tail of it. The author glared from the dust-jacket photograph: a burly young man, evidently, with a bushy beard. He was twenty-three, six years younger than Jojo. Sixteen years younger than Harry—that was more relevant.

For six weeks, Jojo didn't leave Bracknell. She looked after the house, shopped carefully, and was more like a satisfactory wife than she had ever been. Yvette appeared mystified. Jojo even started a campaign; the headmaster of Ronnie's school was reluctant to have a parent-teacher association, so she canvassed other mothers and got Harry to write to the county education officer.

Giles was not mentioned. Jojo had to beat this herself, Harry decided; he could offer nothing but security and understanding.

Then she disappeared. He found her gone when he came in from work; there was no note. She had gone by train, because he had taken the car to the library. She had been rung up and had been on the phone for half an hour, Yvette said.

He felt that it was useless to speculate. Perhaps she would never return, perhaps she was making another try at getting Giles out of her system, perhaps she would resume the affair as before—he didn't think he could bear this, now that he knew about it. The most likely explanation was that she herself didn't know what she was going to do. She had packed only enough for one of her short trips.

He rang up the girl whom Jojo stayed with. A brief hesitation, then: "She's staying here, but she isn't in right now. I'll get her to ring you back, shall I?" Jojo did not ring back. Harry wondered if he ought to go to London; presumably he could get Giles's address from the publisher. He thought suddenly of his father. If he didn't fight for his wife, old Charlie would find it incomprehensible. But Charlie was a man of another kind.

After three days, Jojo wrote:

"My dear Harry,

I know now I've just got to live with Giles all the rest of my life. I have honestly tried but it's no good. I am truly sorry, I've caused you a lot of unhappiness I'm afraid. But we were happy at the beginning, you must remember that and I won't forget it. You will hear from a sollisitor (Jojo couldn't spell, needless to say) about getting divorced, I trust we can do that without fuss. Let me know what you think about Ronnie. Giles and I can make a home for him, of course. Sorry again, no more to say, is there?

Yours, not faithfully I'm afraid, Jojo."

Harry did his normal day's work. Afterwards, he drove to see Jojo's parents, and was relieved to find that he had no news to break to them; they had received a letter too.

"I blame myself," Mr. Fox said. "She didn't grow up in the right way to become a mature person. You've done a great deal for her, Harry,

525

I hope you know that. Don't be in a hurry to agree to a divorce, will you? She might very well get over this fellow after a bit of actually living with him."

Harry wanted to shout: how much more must I go through? He said goodbye quickly and went home. Instead of having dinner with Yvette, he took a tray of food to his study.

Later, he decided that he needed a drink. He hardly ever drank alone, but there was a bottle of cognac for guests. Without in the least intending to, he finished it. He had seldom been drunk in his life, and he was astonished when he needed to clutch the banisters to go upstairs.

Yvette's door was slightly open and her light was on. Harry walked in without hesitation, feeling that he was moving in a dream. She was sitting on her bed varnishing her toenails, completely naked. As in a dream, she didn't look at all surprised.

"Your wife has really gone, then," she said.

"Yes, she's gone."

"Well, come into bed."

He undressed and lay on her, but he couldn't get an erection. This too seemed to be within Yvette's experience. She said: "You drank a lot and you are unhappy—it's normal."

But he hid his face in the pillow, shaking, sobbing, ashamed and helpless.

In the morning, Yvette took Ronnie to the Foxes'. Harry moved in with a bachelor friend, a young teacher who had a flat in the town centre, designed and furnished like his old flat. He did nothing about the house except to lock the door. Later, it turned out that Giles had always wanted to live in that kind of house.

Harry conceded everything in the divorce, including custody of Ronnie. However, Jojo didn't ask for alimony. From this time on, Harry went into an emotional deep freeze, deliberately refusing to examine his feelings. To friends, he said simply: "I don't think I want to talk about it." Some of them had the impression that he was relieved. He was resigned, certainly; he knew himself at last; he would never again seek for more in life than he could cope with.

Long before the divorce reached the courts, he had a new job. He would never have been able to make a move while married to Jojo, but the time had come when he had a right to a more senior position. The only one being advertised at the moment was in Northumberland. Harry was wryly amused—one couldn't get much farther away. He hesitated only because of his father. But he would be living well within his salary in future, so he could easily afford a monthly trip to London.

The local authority offered him a loan on easy terms to buy a house, but he preferred a flat.

# 26

"I DON'T know why—things haven't come out the way I expected," Charlie said. Scrap looked up sympathetically. Charlie often talked to Scrap; it wasn't ridiculous, he was addressing someone. But he tried not to grumble too much. A dog, though he couldn't understand the words, was sensitive to an unhappy tone.

In his prime, when he gave advice and grappled with problems for the whole street, Charlie had been proud of his ability to look ahead and guess right about how things would turn out. This was what he had lost. Perhaps it was because Ann was no longer here to help him, perhaps because he was old and out of touch, perhaps because the world was unpredictable in a new way.

He had never imagined that Harry and Jojo were heading for a break-up. When it was a fact, Harry said that the marriage had been a failure. Such things hadn't happened in the old days; at least, Charlie hadn't been involved in them. They had happened in another class, the class into which Harry had insecurely moved. Charlie didn't exactly disapprove of divorce, but he felt uncomfortable in a world in which divorce was commonplace, marriages were said to fail like shops or small businesses, men let their wives slip through their fingers. It was a failure of tenacity, he couldn't help thinking—a failure of effort. He and Ann, at the start, hadn't expected complete harmony to come automatically. It had been necessary for them to build a marriage. But they had ruled out the possibility of failure, chiefly through the force of love, partly no doubt through pride. And through effort, the pride had been justified and the love had been strengthened.

Another thing that hadn't happened in the old days was that people who had become part of a family walked out of it, like Lukie and now Jojo. Charlie missed Jojo. After a year or so, he felt that he was missing her more than Harry was. Harry had his work, and was resolutely absorbed in it; Charlie had very little by now. And he would never see Ronnie again, since Harry had waived even visiting rights. Children changed fast and forgot fast. A child in a car, perhaps being taken to see the Tower of London, might be Ronnie. One of these young men with long hair—perhaps driving a car, waiting impatiently as Charlie crossed the road—might be Alec. There could be no recognition. It was hard, surely, for a man to lose all his grandchildren. Charlie knew that age was a time of narrowing, a time of deprivation, but he hadn't reckoned on its being as bad as this.

Even the older generation of the Wheelwright

family was in fragments. In 1968, his Christmas card to Vi was returned, marked "Not known". He inquired at the laundry. It was under new management; Vi was believed to have bought a country cottage, but no one knew where. Charlie hadn't seen her for years. They had both sensed, no doubt, that keeping up a pretence of caring for each other was no longer worth while at their age. Still, he was hurt that she hadn't even sent him word of her retirement and the new address.

He had drifted apart from Liza, too. They had exchanged letters ever since she had gone to Italy, and she had reminded him that he was welcome to come for a long visit now he had time on his hands. But he had decided not to go; his spine wouldn't stand a long jolting train journey, flying was expensive, and he was reluctant to leave Scrap in kennels. After this, the letters had dwindled to Christmas and birthday cards.

Landmarks in the year matter to the old as they matter to children. When Charlie was sixty-nine, he got a pair of gloves from Harry and a card from Liza; Marjorie probably didn't know the date of his birthday. As it happened, he had bought new gloves not long before. After opening the parcel and looking at the card, he said: "Well, that's my lot, Scrap." The rest of the day would be like any other.

He decided that he must let Marjorie know when seventy was coming up. She and Hymie would ask him to dinner. Of course, he might not reach seventy—you couldn't know. He was no longer equal to long walks and the doctor was warning him about high blood-pressure. He didn't care much, so long as he didn't have to undergo a long illness.

As you got older, he reflected, one year was much like another. He no longer read the paper or watched the news with any real interest; sometimes he simply gave it a miss. There was a Labour Government, but it didn't feel the same as in 1945: no sense of achievement, no expectation of change. What did happen was nothing to be glad about. Trade was terrible, there was unemployment again, the Government was even trying to pass a law against strikes. Joe Doherty declared that he wouldn't vote Labour again. Charlie himself was most affected by the constantly rising prices. For a man with his span of memory, some of them were almost incredible: three and six for a pint, a shilling for a bus to the park, practically his week's pension for a pair of shoes. He had given up trying to live on the pension. He was damned if he would ask his son for money, and he was damned if he would apply for national assistance and have officials prying into his affairs. So he drew on his savings, at first only for purchases such as clothes, later as a regular necessity. There was no sense in leaving money behind him, surely.

An odd thing had happened shortly before he

was sixty-nine. He had answered a knock at the door to find himself confronted by two men he didn't know.

"Mr. Charles Wheelwright? We've come to measure the house."

"Measure it? How d'you mean?"

"Size of rooms," the man said tersely.

"What for?"

"We're from the Council. Want to see our identification?" The tone implied that he was being obstructive, they hadn't time to waste talking.

"This isn't a Council house, you know. I own it."

"Still got to be measured," the other man said. This man was more breezy, as if it was a bit of a joke.

"If that's all you're going to do, I don't mind," Charlie conceded. He picked up Scrap, who had been trained to be suspicious of strangers. The men went all over the house with their steel measure, calling out figures to each other in loud voices and completely ignoring Charlie.

"What's the point of this?" he asked when they had finished.

"You'll be informed in due course."

He was left with an uneasy, baffled feeling. Could he be required to take in lodgers, he wondered, as under the wartime billeting system? He couldn't believe it, but no other explanation occurred to him. However, nothing happened. Months passed, which surely amounted to "due course", and he was not informed of anything. Apparently it had been pointless after all. Nowadays, he reminded himself, he was living in a world of surveys, statistics, facts accumulated for their own sake; officials had to justify their existence. So he forgot all about it.

Then, in July 1969, he returned from his week's fishing to find a letter from the Council —the Borough of Newham, as it was now called, though there was no such place as Newham. It was the kind of letter that one had to puzzle over to get the meaning out of the jargon. But he gathered that "it was proposed" to acquire his house. He was invited to "treat"—presumably, to come to terms about selling it.

He sat down at once and wrote to say that he had no intention of selling. However, he was very disturbed. It wasn't in the nature of bureaucracy, he knew, to take no for an answer. In the evening he met Joe Doherty in the Gordon and mentioned the letter. Joe and all the remaining Council tenants in Steadman Street had received notice to quit. More redevelopment was coming—perhaps another high rise, though nobody knew.

Within a few weeks, they were all gone. The Dohertys went back to the Isle of Dogs, where they had lived before the blitz. They took a flat on the fifteenth floor of a high rise—"if you can't beat 'em, join 'em," Joe remarked. The other tenants dispersed, in the usual way. The prefabs were demolished, and the grim sheets of tin went up over the doors and windows of number three and of the surviving houses down the far end. As in the war, Charlie had no neighbours. But now, number five was the only inhabited house in Steadman Street.

He was in trouble, he knew that. Normally, there were two people he could talk to: Harry and Marjorie. But Harry was going to miss his trip to London this month; he was going on holiday for all of August, taking a boat journey along the Norwegian coast. And Marjorie was in worse trouble than Charlie, for Hymie was suddenly and dangerously ill.

Charlie went to see her. It was all a mystery, she said. Hymie had never had a day's illness in his life; now he had been attacked by a rare virus. Naturally he was being cared for by good doctors—"Dozens of them, all arguing," Marjorie said, trying to joke about it. Every drug they gave was a shot in the dark. The patient might turn the corner at any moment, or he might die. Marjorie looked like an old and frightened woman; Charlie hadn't the heart to inflict his own difficulties on her.

So August passed, without any further threat. Charlie began to feel hopeful. The high-rise slabs were huge, but didn't cover much ground; they could quite well leave a small house standing, as they had left the pub across the street. He was a freehold owner, after all. He knew that they could drive him out if they were determined, but it might be too much bother for them. They might have decided so—of course, he would get no reprieve; he would simply hear no more. But then, they might merely be having their holidays. He could only wait.

The blow fell in early September. He received a notice of compulsory purchase. At the end, he was informed of the compensation that would be paid. He could hardly believe his eyes; they were giving him only four hundred pounds.

Obviously it was no good writing letters now. If he wanted to save his house, or even to get decent compensation, he must plead his case in person. He took a bus to the Town Hall. But here he could find only the Health Department; the other offices were somewhere else, now that West Ham and East Ham were merged in Newham. He took another bus, paying another shilling. (Soon there would be no more shillings; they were even doing away with English money, he'd heard.)

He asked to see the Town Clerk, whose signature appeared on the compulsory purchase notice. From the smile that the young lady at the reception desk gave him, he gathered that it was like asking to see the Prime Minister. He explained what it was about, and she said: "You want the Legal Department." He made his way there, puffing as he climbed two flights of stairs. After explaining his business again, he was told to sit down in the outer office. He waited for an hour and a quarter, thinking of Scrap, who wasn't used to being shut in the house all this time.

At last he was summoned to see an official, or possibly a lawyer. This man listened—or didn't listen, Charlie rather thought—and then hunted through a large file.

"Ah yes, five Steadman Street. The compensation is at the normal rate for site value. It's only the site that's involved, you see."

"But what about the house?"

"It appears to be a decayed property, badly affected by bomb damage, with one retaining wall supported by a prop. I see from the District Valuer's note that it could reasonably have been condemned as unfit for habitation, even apart from the proposed redevelopment. In those circumstances, only site value is payable."

"I'm the one to judge if it's unfit," Charlie said stoutly. "I'm living in it. It's sound and dry, I can tell you. And all the bomb damage was repaired—that wall could stand till kingdom come."

"Our report shows otherwise, I'm afraid."

"Well, it stands to reason you know more about a house if you live in it than if you just look at it."

536

"I can't discuss that point." The official looked very stern; then he reflected for a moment and said in a slightly more human manner: "Let's face facts, Mr. Wheelwright. The house was built in 1880. Houses of that type have a limited length of life. It isn't Blenheim Palace, you know."

"It's my home. I've spent more than four hundred pounds on it, one way and another, on top of buying it—and that was on top of paying rent all my life. I added a bathroom, I had new tiles put on the roof, I did all the repairs the minute they were needed."

"Ah, if you wish to claim increased compensation on grounds of good maintenance, you can do so. You'll have to furnish us with complete details of all work carried out. I can't make any promises, but it may be worth your while to claim."

"Right, I'll see about it. Why are you pulling everything down, anyway? Nobody'll get a patch of sunlight in their windows if you put two of those big blocks that close together."

"I can't give you any information on the proposed redevelopment. If you're interested, you should see the Planning Department."

Charlie did this the next day, first looking in the telephone book to find out where it was. After an even longer wait, he was received by an official who produced a plan the size of a table-cloth.

"As you see, Mr. Wheelwright, there's to be a parade of shops along part of the street, with maisonette accommodation. The area has been short of shopping facilities ever since the war. On this remaining section, there will be garages."

"That's where my house is."

"Oh? Only two houses in that section, I see."

Charlie took a deep breath and asked: "D'you think it's right, with thousands of people needing homes, to pull down houses and make room for garages?"

"I don't decide these matters, Mr. Wheelwright. You'll appreciate that there's a certain ratio of garage space to housing. Most people have cars nowadays, don't they?"

"Nobody in the street was ever asked about this, you know."

"Come now, Mr. Wheelwright. All these plans are approved by your elected representatives on the Council."

"I'd have had something to say to them if I'd known about this."

"But the plan has been available for inspection by any member of the public who chose to call in here."

"Why should I call in, when I didn't know this was going to happen?"

"I suppose that's one of the problems of democracy. Deep waters, Mr. Wheelwright."

In the evening, Charlie took a sheet of paper

538

and tried to list all the improvements he had made to the house. They were clear in his mind —his memory was sound, except for names— but he despaired of making the statement out in the acceptable formal language. He read through the purchase notice again and saw that he was entitled to make submissions through a solicitor. Indeed, the Council would pay the solicitor's fees.

He knew no solicitors. Hymie could have helped; there must certainly be a sharp lawyer in the Herzberg family. But Hymie was dead. Charlie hadn't heard for some days from Marjorie; now he got a letter from her, posted in Paris. "I've run away," she wrote frankly. She had taken the first plane after the funeral. She felt the need of a complete change of scene; she would be back—"London's my home, always will be"—but she couldn't say when. Probably she would spend the winter with Sidney in Buenos Aires. Hymie's house was to be put on the market.

Charlie found a solicitor simply by walking along Barking Road. The man listened sympathetically and made notes on a pad.

"Well, we'll do our best. Councils aren't in a generous mood, in the present financial climate. This work that's been carried out—I suppose you've got the receipted bills?"

"No, I never kept them. It was years ago. I

never imagined anything like this was going to happen."

"That's a pity. More than a pity, I'm afraid. But we'll do what we can."

After about a month, the solicitor came round to see Charlie. The compensation was to be increased to five hundred and fifty pounds. With what remained of his savings, he would have not quite eight hundred.

"When do I have to get out?" he asked.

"By the first of January, 1970."

It was late October now: damp misty weather, cold for the time of year. Charlie wandered about Canning Town and Plaistow, aimlessly, like a tramp seeking shelter. Scrap got tired, whined, and had to be carried. There seemed to be no houses for sale; most of the older houses were still rented, either from landlords or from the Council, and the greater part of the district had been redeveloped. At last, he found a house with a "For Sale" board. It was less attractive than number five, being identical with the others in the street, and it needed fresh paint, perhaps repair work too. However, it was a house. Charlie copied down the agent's address, walked there, and asked the price.

"Three thousand five hundred."

He almost laughed. Possibly he had the down payment for a mortgage, but nobody gave mortgages to pensioners.

"Have you anything cheaper?"

"Slightly cheaper. That's about the range."

"What about houses to rent, or flats?"

"Well, houses to rent hardly ever come on the market any more. They're put on sale when a tenancy is determined. The flats we have are all furnished. The cheapest at the moment is eight pounds a week, or single furnished rooms are available from five pounds. Rooms are normally rented to people with jobs who are out all day, you'll appreciate."

Charlie worked out that if anyone was willing to let him have a furnished room, and if he bought his food with his pension, he would have a roof over his head for not quite two years. Probably he would have to cook on a gas ring. He would have to give up his armchair and almost all his familiar chattels. There wasn't much chance of being allowed to keep Scrap. The idea of ending his days in the home of strangers, tolerated if he conformed to their rules and habits, filled him with gloom.

Harry came to stay the next weekend. He didn't express any regret for the doom of his old home, but he was concerned about Charlie.

"You can always come and live with me, Dad. I've got a three-room flat. It's really rather nice."

"In Northumberland, eh?"

Harry looked uneasy. "Well, you see, I've only had this job for two years. It would look peculiar if I applied for a move. I could probably

541

find a position in London, but it would be a step down."

"I wouldn't want you to do that, son."

"Well, do consider it, Dad. Why don't you come up for Christmas and see how you like it?" Harry paused for a moment, then added: "I'll pay your fare."

"I've not come to that yet, thanks all the same," Charlie replied.

It would be strange living with Harry, he thought. Long ago, as a boy, Harry had drawn away from the Wheelwright world and everything it stood for. Yet they had never quarrelled; they had retained a distant, uncomprehending respect for each other.

All the same, Charlie didn't want to go. His pride was not extinct; he would stand on his own feet as long as he could. "We'll stick to old London, won't we?" he said to Scrap. So he made up his mind; he would take a flat at eight pounds a week and stay in it as long as he could pay. Ultimately, he would have to take refuge with Harry; but perhaps he would be dead before that.

He would go north for Christmas, however. The only alternative was to be alone; he had spent every Christmas since Ann's death at the Herzbergs'. And he would stay for a few weeks, maybe a couple of months. It would be worth while to save some rent and heating costs during the winter. It would ease the transition, too. He didn't want to be anywhere near at the time when number five was knocked down.

For he had to realise that, when he left the house before Christmas, he would be leaving it for the last time. He went through all his possessions, trying to decide what to keep. To save paying for taxis and porters, he would take only one suitcase to Harry's. He could pack all his other things into a wooden box, which he managed to buy for ten shillings; the landlord of the Gordon agreed to look after the box and the television set. Nevertheless, some things that he cherished would have to be thrown away. It was astonishing what one accumulated in a lifetime. A man who came round with a horse and cart—they still survived—was willing to buy the armchairs and the beds at knockdown prices. The rest of the furniture would have to be left in the house.

When Charlie went out, he noticed that people glanced at him curiously. Doubtless they were surprised that he was still here. He thought of the days when everyone in the street, the women especially, had mustered to fight against an eviction: Ann sturdy and resolute, Kate shouting scornfully at the bailiffs. Now the destruction of a home was nobody's business. It was just something that happened, like the death of an old music-hall comedian whose name was vaguely familiar.

At the Gordon, a few of the men with whom

he was on nodding terms said: "Soon be leaving us, then?" He answered: "Yes—staying with my son for a bit, then I'll be taking a flat." But he couldn't bear to talk about it. If someone said "Seen a lot of changes round here, I suppose", he made a brief reply and let the subject drop. Anyway, he went to the Gordon no more than once a week. It was humiliating to sit there, making half a pint last.

Coming home, after he had been to the shops or for a walk with Scrap, he paused at the corner and gazed along the line—the imaginary line, the line of memory—of what had been Steadman Street. Soon there would be nothing left. It wouldn't be written up by historians, like deserted villages discovered in strange parts of the world. Probably there were no photographs of the street as it had been at its peak of life; no one had thought then of placing on record what was natural, part of the scenery. Nothing would remain but memories in scattered minds: Liza's in Italy, Kate's in Ireland, his own somewhere or other. When these minds ceased to exist, that would be the end. For Steadman Street, as the man at the Town Hall had said, was no palace. It had been only a place where men and women had been born, loved, got married, brought up children, struggled to keep going, been happy or unhappy, died or gone away. It was foolish now to be sentimental about it. He would have liked to die here, but that couldn't be helped.

Still, he thought it was fitting that number five was the last house to survive: the last in which a meal would be cooked and a bed slept in. It had been the best house. Because number three was still standing, you could see that number five had been a bit bigger than the others. It was the only house where the same family had lived for seventy years. Seventy years less two months, at all events.

On a dark morning in December, Charlie woke to find that he could not move. He was panting for breath, as if he had a tight iron band round his throat. He was in pain and yet not in pain; a dull wearisome ache was spreading through his whole body. When he tested his limbs, he could raise his left arm and leg, but not his right.

He wasn't mystified. It was a stroke; old men had strokes, he knew. The doctor had once asked: "Any neighbours got the key to your house? Just in case, you know." He had intended to make some arrangement, but it had slipped his mind. Now, of course, he had no neighbours. There were eighty-eight families across the street, but no neighbours.

After a time, Scrap came upstairs. He didn't see Charlie at first; he wasn't used to Charlie lying in bed. He barked impatiently, then became anxious and whined. Charlie tried to talk to him, but he took no notice. Thus, Charlie realised that he had lost the power of speech.

He couldn't control his lips or his tongue; they quivered and flapped about, useless blobs of flesh.

So he was going to die in number five, after all. He hoped it wouldn't take long. It could have been a peaceful end, except for Scrap. It might be days before anyone broke in. But Scrap was well fed—he wouldn't starve for quite a while.

But, as it happened, the postman came with a registered letter from the Town Hall. Charlie was supposed to sign for it. The postman could get no answer when he knocked, but could hear the dog barking. He knew that the old man lived alone. He found a policeman, and the policeman used the radio net to call an ambulance.

Scrap was furious when the door was broken down, and still more furious when Charlie was carried downstairs. Charlie wanted to tell him that it was all right, but could only wave his left arm.

"What'll happen to the dog?" one of the ambulance men asked.

"Leave him here for now," the other man said. "Phone the Council later on. They've got some kind of a service."

# 27

## The Last Thoughts of Charlie Wheelwright

I WANTED to die in old number five. But supposing I had, the old house would have stayed empty afterwards, getting full of dust and cobwebs. Maybe it's better like this; we're dying at the same time, number five and me. I expect it's gone now. I'll ask Harry to have a look. It was a bad knock when they told me they were going to pull it down, but now I'd rather think of it gone than standing empty and lonely. Lonely—it was the last house in the street. Like being the last man left alive on an island. What's the sense of being number five without being number five Steadman Street? It's the street that's gone, and all the people. People make a street, not bricks and mortar, after all.

It's more like a street in here. People move in —new chap in the bed by the door just yesterday —and they go. You get to know them, like neighbours. Some talk a lot, some crack jokes, some grouse, some just keep themselves to themselves. Never thought I'd get to know new people right at the end of my life. They'll talk about me a bit after I'm gone, same as if I'd died in Steadman Street when it really was Steadman Street.

Geriatric ward, they call it. Don't think I'll ever get my tongue round that. It's like being a kid, I can't manage long words. It was terrible those first few days when I couldn't talk at all. The doctor said to me: "Don't worry about your speech, it'll come back." Some doctors think a bit and tell you things like that. Others don't tell you anything, they just work on you like a garage mechanic works on a car. I can say more or less what I want to now. The words come out funny, though. Some of the nurses can understand me perfectly well, some can't. They're the ones who can't be bothered. Nurses vary, same as doctors.

I know what it means all right, geriatric ward. It's for old people. Old men in here, of course —the old women are over in the other wing. You get separated out when you're a kid, then you get separated out again when you're old. You spend most of your life trying to get together with women, then you're separated from them when you're past doing anything with them. I think it's worse for the women. They don't see anybody but other women. But in here, we're all men but the nurses are women. Girls mostly, student nurses. It's good seeing them.

We're not all ill in here. We're all old, though. Of course, nobody's going to get any healthier, any more than they're going to get younger. We're here to be looked after till we die. But some won't die for years. This is going to be their home.

Amazing what it must cost to keep one old man in here. Food, clean sheets every day, doctors' salaries, paying the nurses and orderlies, keeping up the hospital. Average it all out, I daresay I'm costing three or four times my pension. Suppose I was outside, if I asked for three times my pension they'd laugh at me. Nothing's too good to keep us alive. Drugs, injections, operations, whatever you need. Only one thing they'd refuse—that's if you were to ask to die. You're not even supposed to talk about it, the nurses call it getting morbid. But when you do die, they won't break their hearts. Why should they? You're old, geriatric, your time's run out. I've seen three die since I came in. Screens round the bed, clergyman comes, nobody in the ward talks. Then the bed's wheeled out. And then it's wheeled in again with clean sheets. Room for another old geezer. Another name the nurses have got to learn.

I might not die for quite a while. Have to have another stroke, I suppose. I'll get to know these nurses pretty well, might even see some of them get married and leave. Nurse Mayhew, she's engaged. Going to marry a computer programmer. Good job, I suppose it is. She says she'll go on nursing, but she's bound to start a family before long. Good hips she's got, real mother's hips. Lovely piece for a man, too. They never guess you think about that kind of thing when you're old. But you're still a man. I'm still a man, Nurse Mayhew.

Well, I'm seventy. Three score and ten, the Bible says; anything more than that's a bonus. I never reckoned to break any records. Old Churchill, he was ninety. Amazing for a fat man —you've got to be thin to last, as a rule. That writer, philosopher, can't remember his name— he was nearly a hundred, ninety-seven I think. Thin as a rake, he was. Of course, they had easy lives. No stacking cargoes for them. I don't think I'd like it, living to be ninety. You're old at seventy, even if you've got your health. I wouldn't want to be old for twenty years.

Not too bad, my birthday. Had a present from Liza—beautiful picture book, views of Italy. Made me wish I'd gone there. Just as well, though. Imagine having a stroke out there, lying in a hospital not understanding a word anybody said. Don't suppose their hospitals are much good. All the nurses would be nuns. Never could understand that, a girl wanting to be a nun. None today, none tomorrow, ain't never going to have none. Thousands do, all the same.

Yes, a present from Liza. Harry must have given her the name of the hospital. Nothing from Marjorie. Don't know how I'll get in touch with her when she comes home, now she's sold that house. I don't want to die without seeing Marj again. Hope for the best, that's all I can do.

Harry came at visiting time. Brought a cake with seven big candles. I couldn't blow them all out, he had to help. Nurse Dickinson squealed: "Oh, you funny boy, you never said it was your birthday." She's got that awful squeaky voice, goes right through you. Well, we ate the cake— a slice each round the ward, and had to give one to Nurse bloody Dickinson. Like being ten years old, it was.

The worst thing in here is being treated like a kid. Nurse Dickinson talks like that all the time: good boy, funny boy, naughty boy, eat it all up now, time for bye-byes. Of course, it had to be her on duty the time I wet my bed. Some of the really ill ones do it all the time, shit too, can't help it. I hope I never come to that. I'm all right usually; just that time, don't know how it happened, I was half asleep really. "Oh, I thought you were a big boy!" she squealed. I had to have a plastic sheet for two days— horrible cold feeling. It isn't because they expect you to do it again, it's just a punishment. Makes you feel helpless. Well, helpless is what we are.

I'm still a man. Can't remember being a child —really a child, wetting the bed and that kind of thing. Children don't grow up nowadays so fast as we did. We had to. You brought in wages at thirteen, it was a matter of course. But becoming a man was a secret thing, a private thing at least. It was when you had your first girl. You didn't talk about it, the way the lads do nowadays. I was fourteen. Stroke of luck—wouldn't have happened if I hadn't been a telegram boy. She wouldn't believe I was fourteen, thought I was years older. She was older herself. Not a girl really, a woman. Lovely body. Shut my eyes, I can still see it. She went off to sleep once and I just stared at her. Lying there—still see her, could have been yesterday—with one arm over her face. Because of the sunshine, that was. She never drew the curtains. There was a window above the bed, garden outside, no other buildings. The sun streamed in. We were covered in sweat sometimes. Smell her, I can, never mind about see her.

What was her name? Can't have forgotten—my first woman. I have, though. I'll forget my own name next. No, I won't: Charles George Wheelwright. I wouldn't have had a middle name if it wasn't for the picture in the pub, Charles George Gordon. Those black men killed him with their spears. He stood on the steps, knowing they were going to do it. There's a real man for you. A quick death, though. Better than fading away in hospital. My Dad died sudden, my Mum too. Never knew what hit them, either of them. It's the best way.

Ann died slowly. She died in here—in the other wing, that is. I had my arms round her. She couldn't talk, but she knew I was with her. I hadn't been to see her the day before. I wondered afterwards if there was anything she'd wanted to say to me. Goodbye isn't much. It's everything, and yet it isn't much. I wish I was religious, so I'd believe in seeing her again. That must be a big comfort. But if you can't believe it, you can't.

Oh, I loved her. Strange to think some men go through life and never know what love is. Doesn't matter how much fun you have with women, it's not the same without love. I'd look at Ann when we were in bed, I didn't think nice bit of stuff I've got here, I just thought: Ann. Ann, my own, my precious, my girl, my woman, my wife. Ann, my life. Suppose she'd died when I was thirty, I don't think I'd have married again. Well, perhaps. But not loved again, the way I loved her.

Little body she had, firm but light. I could carry her about like a child. I've always liked them small, big men generally do. There was that one who used to do my washing. Lucy— no, Betty, it was Betty. My type, she was. Could have had her, but I never did. She was dead when I saw her naked. It didn't seem true, her lying there in the street, stark narked, stone dead. I'd have cried if I'd been alone. I could cry now, thinking of her.

But Ann was strong. Strong all through. I had to fight for her, I had to win her. Anything she didn't want to do, she wouldn't do it. She kicked me in the balls. It hurt, she meant it to. Any other woman, I'd have slapped her face and held her down and shoved it in. But I was going to marry Ann. I loved her and I respected her. Men respected women in those days.

The truth is, it wasn't so easy to respect yourself. When you couldn't pay the rent, when you stood by the dock gate and didn't get called. I had more chance, being a stevedore. The dockers had it rough. The nons and the unemployed, it was hell for them. A man felt he was —I don't know what, a thing, useless, not a man. Then he had to go home and say: I couldn't manage, I've failed again. Men of England! England didn't want men. I'll never forget that.

A man is only a man, when all's said and done. Strong arms, steady legs, straight back, clear head: there's not much more to it. When all that's gone, it's time to die. I can still sit up even if my back hurts, hold a spoon, feed myself, if I can't do much more.

Ann knew I was a man. That's how I could win her and hold her, strong as she was. I'd have thought Harry could hold that little Jojo—well, he couldn't. They never had a marriage like mine, either of the boys. There's something wrong if a married man's chasing skirts all the time, like Ted. When you're married the way I was married to Ann, you don't need anything else. That business with Marj, that was just because of the war. I think my nerves were bad. I might never have done it, but for seeing that little Betty dead. Is that honest? I don't know. I enjoyed it with Marj, I've got to say that. Maybe some women are made to give men what Marj did: not exactly love, sort of fondness, sort of a sexy friendship, and bags of fun. That's what Reenie could give. Knew I'd get her name in the end. Reenie, Reenie. Thank you, Reenie; thank you, Marjorie. You were there at the right time.

Well, women are different. Look at these nurses. Look at them—got nothing else to do, have I? They lean over you, their hair comes loose and touches your face, they show their legs; I'm still a man. Nurse Mayhew, she'll be a good wife. Those strong hips, those strong shoulders, strong face, sweet and calm. That little Nurse Shepherd, the one who's always smiling, she's more the kind for a quick bit of what you fancy. All the doctors have been through her, you can tell. Good luck to them. I'd have given her something to smile about when I was young.

I ought to be ashamed of myself, an old man like me, last few months of my life. But I'm not ashamed. A man has a right to his thoughts. A man has a right to be a man. I wish they knew what a man I used to be, these nurses.

I suppose it's silly to say men aren't what they were. There'll always be men and there'll always be women, while there's a world. But I've never seen a man like my Dad. I was only four when he died, but I remember. The strength of his hands when he picked me up: the strength, but the gentleness too. He used to let me watch when he had his bath. I never saw my Mum having her bath, that wouldn't have been proper. But my Dad: he was as tall as I am, not so heavy though, darker than me, a line of dark hair down his back, I remember that. What a man for a woman! I think I understood that somehow, even when I was a nipper. A real man; they all said that, old Bill Whitmarsh said it often. He died sudden, never weakening, never ill. He died young. The dead stay young they say.

But I'm old. I've lived my life. I've done my best, you can't do any more: for my wife, for my sons, for my mates and my neighbours. It all ends here, in the geriatric ward. I've nothing now; this bed doesn't belong to me, nor these pyjamas, nor this plate and spoon. You might say: what's it all been for? But I don't feel like that. Life's worth living, just because it's life.

My Mum said once there's nothing in the world so sad as a child dying. Losing life when it's still ahead of you, that's the cruellest thing. What does a child feel, dying? Can't bear to imagine it. Children died in the blitz, screaming, burning. Marj saw one, all its face burnt away. What have they got to say about that, these clergymen?

It shouldn't happen. A lot shouldn't happen —war and hunger and poverty—but it does. It shouldn't happen to a dog, as Hymie used to say. I suppose Scrap's dead. The Council's got a service—you can imagine what that is. They might have taken him back to Battersea, but who'd buy him? Poor little Scrap. He depended on me, when nobody else did. Could have saved him, perhaps, if I'd been able to talk. Too late now.

I saved the house, once. Ann and me, we saved it. It could have burnt to cinders before the fire engines came. I couldn't save it the second time. When you're up against authority, it's worse than bombs. Ann said I shouldn't have bought it. I daresay she was right. If I'd been a Council tenant, I could have been rehoused. In one of those skyscrapers? Thanks very much. No, I'm not sorry I bought it. It was mine while it lasted, old number five.

It's gone now. I wanted to hand something on, but that's one thing I couldn't do. I've made my will. There's some money; I shan't die a pauper. It'll come in handy for Harry. All the same, it's only money, it's not like a house.

No, I think I do hand something on. I hand on my life. When you get down to it, the world isn't houses nor even palaces, nor docks and factories, nor books and pictures. The world is men and women, same as a street is, or a town. Every life adds to that. What have I done, come to add it up? I've been a stevedore, I've been a foreman in the Albert Docks, I've been a son and a husband and a father. That's quite enough to say.

I don't know if I'll see the screens go up. Ann saw them. Ann always knew what was going to happen, and she was never afraid. If I have another stroke, if I'm unconscious, I won't see them. That doesn't matter. When they take the screens away, it won't be just skin and bones lying here. Up to the end, it will be a man.

## THE END

*Other titles in the*
*Charnwood Library Series:*

## PAY ANY PRICE
### by Ted Allbeury

After the Kennedy killings the heat was on—on the Mafia, the KGB, the Cubans, and the FBI. . .

## MY SWEET AUDRINA
### by Virginia Andrews

She wanted to be loved as much as the first Audrina, the sister who was perfect and beautiful—and dead.

## PRIDE AND PREJUDICE
### by Jane Austen

Mr. Bennet's five eligible daughters will never inherit their father's money. The family fortunes are destined to pass to a cousin. Should one of the daughters marry him?

## CHINESE ALICE
### by Pat Barr

The story of Alice Greenwood gives a complete picture of late 19th century China.

## UNCUT JADE
### by Pat Barr

In this sequel to CHINESE ALICE, Alice Greenwood finds herself widowed and alone in a turbulent China.

### THE GRAND BABYLON HOTEL
#### by Arnold Bennett
A romantic thriller set in an exclusive London Hotel at the turn of the century.

### A HERITAGE OF SHADOWS
#### by Madeleine Brent
This romantic novel, set in the 1890's, follows the fortunes of eighteen-year-old Hannah McLeod.

### BARRINGTON'S WOMEN
#### by Steven Cade
In order to prevent Norway's gold reserves falling into German hands in 1940, Charles Barrington was forced to hide them in Borgas, a remote mountain village.

### THE PLAGUE
#### by Albert Camus
The plague in question afflicted Oran in the 1940's.

### THE RIDDLE OF THE SANDS
#### by Erskine Childers
First published in 1903 this thriller, deals with the discovery of a threatened invasion of England by a Continental power.

## WHERE ARE THE CHILDREN?
### by Mary Higgins Clark
A novel of suspense set in peaceful Cape Cod.

## KING RAT
### by James Clavell
Set in Changi, the most notorious Japanese POW camp in Asia.

## THE BLACK VELVET GOWN
### by Catherine Cookson
There would be times when Riah Millican would regret that her late miner husband had learned to read and then shared his knowledge with his family.

## THE WHIP
### by Catherine Cookson
Emma Molinero's dying father, a circus performer, sends her to live with an unknown English grandmother on a farm in Victorian Durham and to a life of misery.

## SHANNON'S WAY
### by A. J. Cronin
Robert Shannon, a devoted scientist had no time for anything outside his laboratory. But Jean Law had other plans for him.

## THE JADE ALLIANCE
### by Elizabeth Darrell

The story opens in 1905 in St. Petersburg with the Brusilov family swept up in the chaos of revolution.

## BERLIN GAME
### by Len Deighton

Bernard Samson had been behind a desk in Whitehall for five years when his bosses decided that he was the right man to slip into East Berlin.

## HARD TIMES
### by Charles Dickens

Conveys with realism the repulsive aspect of a Lancashire manufacturing town during the 1850s.

## THE RICE DRAGON
### by Emma Drummond

The story of Rupert Torrington and his bride Harriet, against a background of Hong Kong and Canton during the 1850s.

## THE GLASS BLOWERS
### by Daphne Du Maurier

A novel about the author's forebears, the Bussons, which gives an unusual glimpse of the events that led up to the French Revolution, and of the Revolution itself.

## THE DOGS OF WAR
### by Frederic Forsyth

The discovery of the existence of a mountain of platinum in a remote African republic causes Sir James Manson to hire an army of trained mercenaries to topple the government of Zangaro.

## THE DAYS OF WINTER
### by Cynthia Freeman

The story of a family caught between two world wars—a saga of pride and regret, of tears and joy.

## REGENESIS
### by Alexander Fullerton

It's 1990. The crew of the US submarine ARKANSAS appear to be the only survivors of a nuclear holocaust.

## THE TORCHBEARERS
### by Alexander Fullerton

1942: Captain Nicholas Everard has to escort a big, slow convoy . . . a sacrificial convoy. . .

## DAUGHTER OF THE HOUSE
### by Catherine Gaskin

An account of the destroying impact of love which is set among the tidal creeks and scattered cottages of the Essex Marshes.

## FAMILY AFFAIRS
### by Catherine Gaskin
Born in Ireland in the Great Depression, the illegitimate daughter of a servant, Kelly Anderson's birthright was poverty and shame.

## THE SUMMER OF THE SPANISH WOMAN
### by Catherine Gaskin
Clonmara—the wild, beautiful Irish estate in County Wicklow is a fitting home for the handsome, reckless Blodmore family.

## THE TILSIT INHERITANCE
### by Catherine Gaskin
Ginny Tilsit had been raised on an island paradise in the Caribbean. She knew nothing of her family's bitter inheritance half the world away.

## THE FINAL DIAGNOSIS
### by Arthur Hailey
Set in a busy American hospital, the story of a young pathologist and his efforts to restore the standards of a hospital controlled by an ageing, once brilliant doctor.

## IN HIGH PLACES
### by Arthur Hailey

The theme of this novel is a projected Act of Union between Canada and the United States in order that both should survive the effect of a possible nuclear war.

## RED DRAGON
### by Thomas Harris

A ritual murderer is on the loose. Only one man can get inside that twisted mind—forensic expert, Will Graham.

## CATCH–22
### by Joseph Heller

Anti-war novels are legion; this is a war novel that is anti-death, a comic savage tribute to those who aren't interested in dying.

## THE SURVIVOR
### by James Herbert

David is the only survivor from an accident whose aftermath leaves a lingering sense of evil and menace in the quiet countryside.

## LOST HORIZON
### by James Hilton

A small plane carrying four passengers crash-lands in the unexplored Tibetan wilderness.

## THE TIME OF THE HUNTER'S MOON
### by Victoria Holt

When Cordelia Grant accepts an appointment to a girls' school in Devon, she does not anticipate anyone from her past re-emerging in her new life.

## THE FOUNDER OF THE HOUSE
### by Naomi Jacob

The first volume of a family saga which begins in Vienna, and introduces Emmanuel Gollantz.

## "THAT WILD LIE . . ."
### by Naomi Jacob

The second volume in the Gollantz saga begun with THE FOUNDER OF THE HOUSE.

## IN A FAR COUNTRY
### by Adam Kennedy

Christine Wheatley knows she is going to marry Fred Deets, that is until she meets Roy Lavidge.

## AUTUMN ALLEY
### by Lena Kennedy

Against the background of London's East End from the turn of the Century to the 1830's a saga of three generations of ordinary, yet extraordinary people.

## LADY PENELOPE
### by Lena Kennedy
Lady Penelope Devereux, forced to make a marriage of convenience, pours all the affection of her generous nature into her children . . . and her lovers.

## LIZZIE
### by Lena Kennedy
Tiny, warm-hearted but cruelly scarred for life, Lizzie seems to live only for, and through, her burly, wayward husband Bobby.

## ACT OF DARKNESS
### by Francis King
What happens inside a family when an act of brutal violence suddenly erupts without warning or explanation?

## THE LITTLE DRUMMER GIRL
### by John Le Carré
The secret pursuit by Israeli intelligence agents of a lethally dangerous and elusive Palestinian terrorist leader.

## THE SHAPIRO DIAMOND
### by Michael Legat
Set in the late 19th century, the story of a man struggling against fate to prove himself worthy of his family's name.

## THE SILVER FOUNTAIN
### by Michael Legat

Jean-Paul Fontaine came to London in 1870 with a burning ambition to be the proprietor of an exclusive restaurant.

## THE CRUEL SEA
### by Nicholas Monsarrat

A classic record of the heroic struggle to keep the Atlantic sea lanes open against the German U-boat menace.

## BETWEEN TWO WORLDS
### by Maisie Mosco

Alison Plantaine was born to the theatre. As a child she knew only the backstage world of provincial theatres. Then as a young girl she discovers with the shock of the unexpected, her Jewish heritage.

## ANIMAL FARM
### by George Orwell

The world famous satire upon dictatorship. The history of a revolution that went wrong.

## THE FAMILY OF WOMEN
### by Richard Peck

A panoramic story of women whose indomitable spirit brings them through the turbulent, events of the 1850's Gold Rush to the Europe of 1939.

## SNAP SHOT
### by A.J. Quinnell

On Sunday, 7th June 1981 an Israeli F.16 jet aircraft bombed and destroyed the Iraqi nuclear installation at Tammuz. This is the subject of this thriller.

## THE BETSY
### by Harold Robbins

Loren Hardeman rose to become the driving force behind Bethlehem Motors. At 91, still dynamic but confined to a wheelchair, he makes a last desperate gamble to head the entire industry.

## SPELLBINDER
### by Harold Robbins

Takes the reader into the world of the newest and most disturbing phenomenon in contemporary American life—the rise of religious leaders.

## THE SEA CAVE
### by Alan Scholefield

The naked body of a woman is found washed up on a wild stretch of African coastline. A young immigrant is drawn inexorably into the resulting murder enquiry.